Multilevel and Longitudinal Modeling with IBM SPSS

Quantitative Methodology Series

George A. Marcoulides, Series Editor

This series presents methodological techniques to investigators and students. The goal is to provide an understanding and working knowledge of each method with a minimum of mathematical derivations. Each volume focuses on a specific method (e.g., Factor Analysis, Multilevel Analysis, Structural Equation Modeling).

Proposals are invited from interested authors. Each proposal should consist of: a brief description of the volume's focus and intended market; a table of contents with an outline of each chapter; and a curriculum vita. Materials may be sent to Dr. George A. Marcoulides, University of California–Riverside, george.marcoulides@ucr.edu.

Marcoulides • Modern Methods for Business Research

Marcoulides/Moustaki • Latent Variable and Latent Structure Models

Heck • Studying Educational and Social Policy: Theoretical Concepts and Research Methods

Van der Ark/Croon/Sijtsma • New Developments in Categorical Data Analysis for the Social and Behavioral Sciences

Duncan/Duncan/Strycker • An Introduction to Latent Variable Growth Curve Modeling: Concepts, Issues, and Applications, Second Edition

Heck/Thomas • An Introduction to Multilevel Modeling Techniques, Second Edition

Cardinet/Johnson/Pini • Applying Generalizability Theory Using EduG

Heck/Thomas/Tabata • Multilevel and Longitudinal Modeling with IBM SPSS

Hox • Multilevel Analysis: Techniques and Applications, Second Edition

Multilevel and Longitudinal Modeling with IBM SPSS

Ronald H. Heck
University of Hawai'i, Mānoa

Scott L. Thomas
Claremont Graduate University

Lynn N. Tabata
University of Hawai'i, Mānoa

Routledge
Taylor & Francis Group
New York   London

Routledge
Taylor & Francis Group
270 Madison Avenue
New York, NY 10016

Routledge
Taylor & Francis Group
27 Church Road
Hove, East Sussex BN3 2FA

© 2010 by Taylor and Francis Group, LLC
Routledge is an imprint of Taylor & Francis Group, an Informa business

Printed in the United States of America on acid-free paper
10 9 8 7 6 5 4 3 2

International Standard Book Number: 978-1-84872-862-2 (Hardback) 978-1-84872-863-9 (Paperback)

Library of Congress Cataloging-in-Publication Data

Heck, Ronald H.
  Multilevel and longitudinal modeling with IBM SPSS/ Ronald H. Heck, Scott L. Thomas, Lynn N. Tabata.
      p. cm. -- (Quantitative methodology series)
  Includes bibliographical references and index.
   ISBN 978-1-84872-862-2 (hbk. : alk. paper) -- ISBN 978-1-84872-863-9 (pbk. : alk. paper)
   1. Social sciences--Longitudinal studies. 2. Social sciences--Statistical methods. 3. PASW (Computer file) 4. SPSS (Computer file)
 I. Thomas, Scott Loring. II. Tabata, Lynn Naomi. III. Title.

HA32.H39 2010
005.5'5--dc22   2009053643

Visit the Taylor & Francis Web site at
http://www.taylorandfrancis.com

and the Psychology Press Web site at
http://www.psypress.com

Contents

Preface

Multilevel modeling has become a mainstream data analysis tool over the past decade, emerging from a somewhat niche technique in the late 1980s to a technique now figuring prominently in a range of social and behavioral science disciplines. As the approach gained popularity over the 1990s specialty software programs began to appear addressing the needs of an ever-widening group of users. Eventually, mainstream statistics packages such as SPSS, SAS, and Stata began to include routines for multilevel modeling in their programs.

While some devotees of the various mainstream packages began making use of this new multilevel modeling functionality, progress toward carefully documenting these routines was slow, thereby hindering meaningful access to the average user. In the meantime, the specialty software packages were becoming increasingly refined and accessible, offering the user a growing number of generalizations of the traditional multilevel model. In some ways the software proved to be both driving and limiting the development of the field.

The various approaches to multilevel modeling represented in these packages have in some ways made it difficult for a clear lingua franca to emerge and have long challenged those interested in teaching these techniques. In addition to the considerable expense of purchasing the better-documented specialty programs, there is also the additional challenge of mastering the new programming logic, syntax, and file structure unique to each program. This is the first book to demonstrate how to use the multilevel and longitudinal modeling techniques available in SPSS (version 18). We have devoted our energy in this book to addressing this problem and to providing both the budding or seasoned multilevel analyst with a set of concepts and programming skills within the SPSS environment. We have designed this book to enable the development, specification, and testing of a range of multilevel models using a statistical program, SPSS, that is standard in many graduate programs and organizations around the world.

Drawing on years of our own teaching and our work explicating the multilevel approach (Heck & Thomas 2009), we have chosen to adopt a workbook format here. Our intent is to help readers set up, run, and interpret a variety of different types of introductory multilevel and longitudinal models using the linear mixed-effects model (Mixed) procedure in SPSS. The routine enables users to fit linear-mixed effects models with continuous outcomes. We provide a concise conceptual treatment of the multilevel approach and then walk readers in a step-by-step fashion through data management, model conceptualization, and model specification issues related to the multilevel model. We offer multiple examples of several different types of multilevel models, carefully showing how to set up each model and how to interpret the output. Most chapters feature an extended example illustrating the logic of model development. These examples show readers the context and rationale of the research questions and the steps around which the analyses are structured. Annotated screen shots from SPSS are provided to help guide users through the program. We also provide an introduction to diagnostic tools, data management, and relevant graphics. Readers can work with the various examples developed in each chapter by using the corresponding data files on the book-specific web site at www.psypress.com/multilevel-modeling-techniques/. The screen shots provided and the supporting syntax statements in the workbook's appendix (also available online) should facilitate learning the various techniques developed sequentially in each chapter.

The workbook begins with an introductory chapter highlighting several relevant conceptual and methodological issues associated with defining and investigating multilevel and longitudinal models, followed by a discussion of SPSS data management techniques which we have found facilitate working with multilevel, longitudinal, and/or cross-classified data sets. In the next two chapters, we detail the basics of multilevel modeling, how to develop a multilevel model, and trouble-shooting techniques for common programming and modeling problems. We develop several models for investigating individual and organizational change in Chapters 5 and 6, followed by an introduction to multilevel models with multivariate outcomes in Chapter 7. Chapter 8 illustrates SPSS's facility for examining models with cross-classified data structures, a type of hierarchical structure that greatly expands the possibilities for following subjects through multiple organizational units or subunits over time. We conclude with thoughts about ways to expand on the various multilevel and longitudinal modeling techniques introduced and issues to keep in mind in conducting multilevel analyses. We hope the workbook becomes a useful guide to readers' efforts to learn more about the basics of multilevel and longitudinal modeling and the expanded range of research problems that can be addressed through their application.

Ideal as a supplementary text for graduate level courses on multilevel, longitudinal, latent variable modeling, multivariate statistics, and/or advanced quantitative techniques taught in departments of psychology, business, education, health, and sociology, we hope the workbook's practical approach will also appeal to researchers in these fields. We believe the workbook provides an excellent supplement to our other multilevel book, *An Introduction to Multilevel Modeling Techniques, 2nd edition*; however, it can also be used with any multilevel and/or longitudinal modeling book or as a stand-alone text.

Several people have played an important role in the development of this workbook. In particular, we wish to thank our reviewers: Karen A. Barrett of Colorado State University, Jason T. Newsom of Portland State University, Debbie L. Hahs-Vaughn of the University of Central Florida, and Dick Carpenter of the University of Colorado, Colorado Springs. Our series editor, George Marcoulides of the University of California, Riverside; Debra Riegert, our Senior Editor; Erin Flaherty, our Senior Editorial Assistant; and the Project Editor at Taylor & Francis, Michael Davidson, have all been incredibly supportive throughout the process. While we remain responsible for any errors remaining in the text, the book is much stronger as a result of their support and encouragement.

Ronald H. Heck
Scott L. Thomas
Lynn N. Tabata

CHAPTER 1

Introduction to Multilevel and Longitudinal Modeling With IBM SPSS

Social science research presents an opportunity to study phenomena that are multilevel or hierarchical in nature. Examples might be college students nested in institutions within states or elementary-aged students nested in classrooms within schools. Attempting to understand individual-level behavior or attitude in the absence of group contexts known to influence those behaviors or attitudes can severely handicap one's ability to explicate the underlying processes of interest. People within particular organizations may share certain properties including socialization patterns, traditions, attitudes, and goals. The interactions between individuals and their social groups within various settings therefore lend themselves to numerous investigations (Heck & Thomas, 2009).

Consider, as a different example, the examination of individual-level change within specific social or organizational settings. This becomes a problem of understanding change over time where a series of repeated measurements (Level 1) are nested within individuals (Level 2) who may be associated with particular groups (Level 3) that are also undergoing change over time. We could extend the analysis of such change trajectories to include situations where individual change processes accelerate or decelerate after the introduction of group-level treatments or where there are parallel change processes occurring (e.g., where people are changing in two or more domains simultaneously).

For studying the relationships between individuals and their social groupings, multilevel modeling is an attractive approach because it allows the incorporation of substantive theory about individual and group processes into the clustered sampling schemes of many research studies (e.g., repeated measures designs or multistage stratified samples) or into the hierarchical data structures found in many existing data sets. Multilevel modeling is fast becoming the standard analytic approach for examining data in many fields (e.g., sociology, education, psychology, management) due to its applicability to a broad range of research designs and data structures (e.g., nested, cross-classified, cross-sectional, and longitudinal data). Multilevel models are referred to by a variety of different names including random coefficient models, mixed-effect models, multilevel regression models, hierarchical linear models, and multilevel covariance structure (or structural equation) models. This diversity of names is an artifact of the statistical theory underlying multilevel models, theory that has developed out of methodological work in several different fields, and this has led to differences in the manner in which the methods (and software) are used in various fields. At the core of these types of procedures, however, is an interest in the decomposition of variance in outcomes across several hierarchical levels and the explanation of this variance with variables specified at corresponding levels.

Despite a growing recognition of the promise and importance of this approach, multilevel modeling procedures have not yet been fully integrated into research and statistics texts used in typical first- or second-year graduate courses. Two major obstacles are responsible for this reality. First, no standard language has emerged from this work. Second, until recently, the specification of multilevel models in many fields generally required special software programs such as HLM, Mplus, or MLwiN. In response to the first obstacle, as we have already stated, despite the varied ways in which these models are conceptualized, notated, and specified, at their core they focus on the decomposition of variance across multiple levels of hierarchy. While in no way claiming it as an emergent standard, Heck and Thomas (2009) have made an effort to frame the conceptualization of the multilevel model in these general terms.

The second obstacle, available software, has been a largely artificial barrier resulting from the evolution of the popularization of multilevel modeling in many areas of the social sciences. Simply put, our interpretation is that there have been several camps of scholars who have popularized these methods through the development of their own software and approach. Three of the best known of these packages are HLM (Raudenbush, Bryk, Cheong, & Congdon, 2004), MLwiN (Goldstein, 2003), and Mplus (Muthén & Muthén, 1998–2006). Although the mainstream emergence and acceptance of these methods is in large part due to the work and activity of these scholars, other much more widely used statistical packages have implemented routines over the years that enable the development and specification of a wide variety of multilevel models. SPSS (occasionally referred to as PASW, or Predictive Analytic Software), SAS, and Stata all have such routines (see Albright, 2007, for an overview of each package's offering). Despite the widespread availability of these packages, there is little available to help the researcher align the concepts and methods popularized through the specialty programs with the terminology and conceptualization used within these mainstream statistical packages. Important exceptions to this can be found with Rabe-Hesketh and Skrondal's (2008) *Multilevel and Longitudinal Modeling Using Stata* (2nd ed.) and in the efforts of authors such as Singer and Willett (2003) to provide detailed setups for examples from their book using the procedures in these widely available statistical packages. Also noteworthy are the resources available through the University of California at Los Angeles's Academic Technology Services Statistical Computing website (http://www.ats.ucla.edu/stat/) that have used a wide variety of statistical packages and developed annotated output for a number of multilevel texts. Few resources however provide a start to finish overview of how to actually carry out a multilevel analysis. This is the relative void that we hope to address.

Our Intent

The intent of this workbook is to help you set up, run, and interpret a variety of different types of introductory multilevel and longitudinal models using the linear mixed-effects model (Mixed) procedure in SPSS. The procedures enable users to fit linear mixed-effects models sampled from normally distributed data (SPSS, 2002). SPSS Mixed is differentiated from more familiar linear models (e.g., analysis of variance [ANOVA], multiple regression) through its capability of examining correlated data and unequal variances. Such data are commonly encountered as repeated measures on subjects or where subjects are nested in a data hierarchy. Where designs are unbalanced (i.e., different numbers of participants within groups) estimation procedures available in SPSS Mixed yield asymptotically efficient estimates of a model's structural parameters and covariance components. We run the models in this text using SPSS 18.0 and Windows Vista. Users running the models with other versions of SPSS/PASW for Mac or Windows (e.g., XP, Windows 7) may notice slight differences between their screens and our text screenshots.

We assume readers have had at least an introductory statistics course (e.g., descriptive statistics, analysis of variance, multiple regression) prior to using this text. The workbook is intended for use in a second course (e.g., multivariate statistics) or a third course (e.g., introduction to multilevel and longitudinal models). In our own series of courses, we have used the materials we develop here in multivariate statistics courses (i.e., after presenting multivariate analysis of variance [MANOVA], repeated measures analyses, and exploratory factor analysis) and in beginning multilevel modeling courses.

In this introductory chapter, we provide a number of conceptual and methodological issues associated with multilevel modeling, which foreshadows our further development of these issues in subsequent chapters. In Chapter 2, we present several issues to deal with in structuring and working with various types of multilevel, longitudinal, and cross-classified data sets. Chapter 3 develops the basics of two-level multilevel regression models. Chapter 4 extends this general two-level model to three-level, cross-sectional models. Chapter 5 presents the basic repeated measures design, beginning with repeated measures ANOVA and contrasting this approach with the SPSS Mixed (i.e., two-level) approach to examining individual change. Chapter 6 extends the individual-change model to a multilevel (three-level) growth model. Chapter 7 introduces the multilevel multivariate approach in SPSS. Chapter 8 presents examples of two-level and a three-level cross-classified data structures. Finally, Chapter 9 provides a short synthesis of our presentation.

Analysis of Multilevel Data Structures

We begin with the principle that quantitative analysis really deals with the translation (or operationalization) of abstract theories into concrete models and that theoretical frameworks are essential guides to empirical investigation. Our statistical models represent a set of proposed theoretical relations that are thought to exist in a population—a set of theoretical relationships that account for relationships actually observed in the sample data from that population (Singer & Willett, 2003). Decisions about analysis, therefore, are located within the researcher's methodological framework that begins with research questions, designs, data structures, and methods of analysis (Raudenbush, 1988). These decisions about how to conceptualize and conduct a study are critical to the credibility of one's results and the study's overall contribution to the relevant knowledge base.

Clearly also there is a place for less theoretically bound exploratory work and we believe that these models can provide a powerful platform for this purpose. The multilevel framework opens up a range of new possibilities for exploratory analyses. With opportunities to examine relationships at multiple levels of analysis, cross-level interactions, and to incorporate a time dimension, the potential for exploratory work is great. That opportunity also presents a risk, however. With multiple levels within which one could test for specific relationships and a wide range of potential interactions there is much to explore, and the models can easily bog down, yielding questionable and perhaps even nonsensical results. Multilevel models are very data demanding. Adequate sample sizes are needed at each level to ensure sufficient power to detect effects and, as a result, the models can very quickly become quite complicated, difficult to estimate, and even more difficult to interpret. Even in a simple two-level model, one might allow the intercept and multiple slopes to vary across groups, while sets of variables from the higher level are used to model the variances in this set of intercepts and slopes. Correct model specification in a single-level framework is one thing; correct specification with multilevel context is quite another (Goldstein, 1995). It is for this reason that we place an emphasis on the importance of sound conceptual frameworks to guide multilevel model development, even if it is largely exploratory in nature.

One's choice of analytic strategy and model specification is therefore critical to whether the research questions can be appropriately answered. More complete modeling formulations may suggest inferences based on relationships in the sample data that are not revealed in more simplistic models. At the same time, however, better modeling formulations may lead to fewer findings of substance than have often been claimed in studies that employ more simplistic analytical methods (Pedhazur & Schmelkin, 1991). We feel it important to draw a clear distinction between concerns over model specification limited to the exclusion or inclusion of theoretically relevant variables and model specification related to the mathematical explication of the relationships among these variables. Although theory should guide both considerations, the former concern deals with the availability of the relevant variables in the data set, whereas the latter deals with the structure of the data itself and the choice of modeling approach used to exploit theoretically important relationships presumed to exist in the population (Heck & Thomas, 2009). This is important to keep in mind because compromise is often necessary, since the complexity of proposed theoretical models (e.g., multiple levels, multiple random intercepts and slopes) can at times overwhelm the capability of the data and the statistical software. To illustrate, we provide one example in Chapter 7 where simply changing the structure of the covariance matrix of random effects in a three-level model from a more simplified (compromise) structure to one that might be considered as optimal resulted in lengthening the time it took to run the model by approximately two hours. At the end of all that, the model estimation procedures failed to achieve a viable solution. In short, this is a case where our data and model specification failed to meet the demands of the propositions we wished to test.

Besides the choices we make about methods of analysis, our inferences are also affected in practice by potential biases in our sample (e.g., size, sampling variation, missing data). Another of our guiding principles is that when making decisions about analytic methods, the responsible researcher should consider approaches that are likely to take full advantage of the features of particular data structures and the goals of the overall research.

Multilevel data sets are distinguished from single-level data sets by the nesting of individual observations within higher level groups. In single-level data sets, participants are typically selected through simple random sampling. Each individual is assumed to have an equal chance of selection, and (at least in theory) the participants do not belong to any groups that might influence their responses. For example, individuals can be differentiated by variables such as gender, religious affiliation, participation in a treatment or control group, but, in practice, in single-level analyses individual variation within and between these types of subgroups cannot be considered across a large number of groups simultaneously (e.g., cell means consisting of gender, religious affiliation, their interactions, and perhaps a large number of workplaces). The number of subgroups created quickly overwhelms the capacity of the analytic technique. In contrast, in multilevel (or nested) data sets, the groupings of participants which result from the overall sampling scheme used to select participants in a large study (e.g., neighborhoods are selected first, and individuals are selected second), or the social grouping of participants (i.e., their degree of common experiences due to closeness in space or time) is the focus of the theory and conceptual model proposed in the study (Kreft & de Leeuw, 1998). For example, we might be interested in whether organizations' productivity can be explained by their value and decision-making structures.

We refer to the lowest level of a data hierarchy (Level 1) as the *micro level,* with all successive levels in the data structure referred to as *macro levels.* The relationships among variables observed for the micro level often refer to individuals within a number of macro-level groups or contexts (Kreft & deLeeuw, 1998). Within a contextual model, therefore, one could envision successive levels extending well beyond an organization (e.g., region, state, nation, etc.). Each of these successive groupings might exert effects on organizational productivity. Organizational outcomes may be influenced by combinations of variables related to the backgrounds and attitudes of individuals (demographics, experience, education, work-related skills, attitudes, etc.), the processes of organizational work (e.g., leadership, decision making, professional development, organizational values, resource allocation, etc.), the context of the organization, or the cross-level interactions of these variables within the structure of the organization (e.g., size, management arrangements within its clustered groupings, etc.). We summarize some of these possible relationships within and between levels in Figure 1.1.

In the past, analytic strategies for dealing with the complexity of the multilevel, or contextual, features of organizations were somewhat limited. Researchers did not always consider the

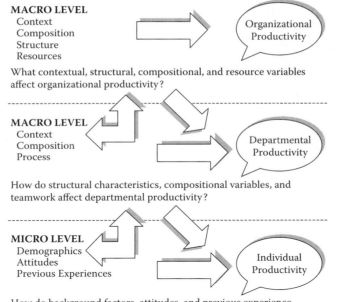

MACRO LEVEL
Context
Composition
Structure
Resources

Organizational Productivity

What contextual, structural, compositional, and resource variables affect organizational productivity?

MACRO LEVEL
Context
Composition
Process

Departmental Productivity

How do structural characteristics, compositional variables, and teamwork affect departmental productivity?

MICRO LEVEL
Demographics
Attitudes
Previous Experiences

Individual Productivity

How do background factors, attitudes, and previous experience affect an employee's productivity?

FIGURE 1.1   Defining variables in a multilevel model.

implications of the assumptions they make about measuring variables at their natural levels, or about moving them from one level to another level through aggregation or disaggregation. These possible choices are summarized in Figure 1.1 with two-headed arrows. *Aggregation*, for example, meant that the productivity level of individuals within departments or organizations would be combined at a higher level of the data hierarchy (e.g., the organizational unit). The comparison is then made between organizations' mean productivity outcomes. Failing to acknowledge the potential variability present among individuals within groups, however, can bias estimates of parameters between such units, a situation Robinson (1950) called the ecological fallacy. Averaging estimates over groups also drastically reduces the statistical power to detect proposed relationships by ignoring the number of individuals in a study (Tabachnick, 2008).

In contrast, *disaggregation* refers to moving a variable conceptualized at a higher level to a lower level of the data hierarchy. For example, in a different analysis we might have productivity measured at the organizational level but also have information about employee job satisfaction, motivation, and intention to leave the workplace. In this type of analysis, we might intend to analyze the data at the individual-employee level to see whether employees' perceptions influence their productivity. If we assign all employees the same value on the productivity outcome (and possibly other organizational variables), we attribute properties of the organization to individuals. This can also bias the estimation of model parameters, since we are basing analyses of some of the variables on the number of individuals in the study instead of the number of groups.

Examples such as these suggest that analyses conducted at the micro or macro levels may produce different results. Treating individuals as if they were independent of their organizational groupings ignores the complexity inherent in the data and introduces a potentially important source of bias into the analysis. This is because individuals in a group or context tend to be more similar on many important variables (e.g., attitudes, socialization processes, perceptions about the workplace, etc.) compared with individuals in other contexts. With hierarchical data, therefore, a more complex error structure must be added to the model to account for the dependence among observations within groups. Such dependencies violate key assumptions of single-level multiple regression models (e.g., simple random sampling that provides independent errors) and will lead to underestimated variances and standard errors that in turn may lead to erroneous conclusions (Thomas & Heck, 2001). As we have noted, eliminating within-group variability also biases relationships observed between groups. One important contribution of multilevel modeling is that it allows the researcher to avoid the aggregation or disaggregation problem.

Developing a multilevel conceptual framework of relationships to guide the analysis also helps the researcher avoid another potential source of bias in the analysis—that of ignoring the different levels of the explanatory (independent) variables. As the reader may surmise, it is important to develop a conceptual scheme to place the explanatory variables hypothesized to affect individuals and other types of processes in their proper hierarchical locations (Hox, 2002). In a single-level model we are faced with the problem of whether the outcome variable (or other predictors) should be defined as aggregate, or collective, measures or as individual (or disaggregated) measures. In a multilevel formulation, analysts must consider the implications of how they define variables within the proposed model before actually testing the model. This preliminary process of building a model helps clarify the organizational, or contextual, level to which they rightly belong. Examining variability in an outcome present at each level of the data hierarchy implies different types of research questions that can be asked, as summarized in Figure 1.1. These potential relationships are represented by horizontal arrows in the figure. A second contribution of multilevel modeling, therefore, is that through investigating the variation in outcomes that exists at different levels of the data hierarchy we can develop more refined conceptual models about how explanatory variables at each level contribute to variation in outcomes.

Finally, multilevel procedures also facilitate the investigation of variability in regression coefficients (slopes) across higher order units in the study. Cross-level interaction involves the effects of explanatory variables at a higher level of the data hierarchy on a relationship (e.g., employee motivation and productivity) at a lower level. Cross-level interactions are shown in Figure 1.1 with arrows that extend from the macro level toward the micro level. To illustrate, we might ask whether the relative degree of departmental teamwork moderates the relationship between employee motivation and productivity. In the past, mapping these sorts of relations has often been problematic, frequently focusing on single, discrete elements while ignoring the multidimensional and interrelated aspects of broader sets of organizational processes that influence subgroups or individuals within organizations.

Partitioning Variation in an Outcome

Generally, the first step in a multilevel analysis is partitioning the variance (referred to as σ^2) in an outcome variable into its within- and between-group components. If it turns out that there is little or no variation (perhaps less than 5%) in outcomes between groups, there would be no compelling need for conducting a multilevel analysis. In this case, a simple ordinary least squares (OLS) regression analysis conducted at the micro (individual) level would be adequate. The proportion of variance that exists between groups compared to the total variation is described by an intraclass correlation (ρ), or the proportion of variance explained by the grouping structure in the population (Hox, 2002). It is defined as

$$\rho = \sigma^2_b/(\sigma^2_b + \sigma^2_w), \tag{1.1}$$

where σ^2_b is the between-group variance and σ^2_w is the within-group variance. The intraclass correlation can also be interpreted as the expected correlation between any two randomly chosen individuals in the same group (Hox, 2002). If it is substantial, therefore, it suggests that the groups are relatively homogeneous and likely quite different from each other.

There are at least two ways to think about the relative homogeneity of groups. The first is in terms of the potential remedies required for conducting a conventional single-level analysis of data that are hierarchically differentiated. A common example is the multistage type of sampling strategy used in large-scale surveys (where higher units may first be sampled and then individuals within these units). The focus in this type of analysis to remedy possible bias due to multistage sampling is on statistical adjustments to yield unbiased estimates of variances and standard errors. Acknowledging the intraclass correlation (also referred to as the ICC) is important because it changes the error variance in single-level regression analyses. When clusters and nontrivial ICCs are present, the OLS regression assumption of independent errors resulting from simple random sampling will likely be violated. This problem results in a downward bias in the estimation of standard errors (i.e., the errors calculated will be too small).

To illustrate this important point: Because statistical tests of model parameters are based on the ratio of an estimate to its standard error, the underestimation of standard errors will often lead to more findings of significance than would be observed if clustering were considered. Suppose in a single-level analysis, we observe that the estimate of the effect of gender on achievement is 4.0 points, and the standard error is estimated as 2.0. This would result in a t-ratio of 2.0 (i.e., the ratio of the estimate to its standard error). At a commonly adopted significance level of $p = .05$ and a sample size of 500 individuals, the required t-ratio would be 2.0. Suppose the same analysis conducted as a two-level analysis (e.g., individuals clustered in schools) results in an estimated standard error of 2.5. Now when we calculate the t-ratio (4.0/2.5), the result would be 1.6, which would not be significant at $p = .05$. Single-level analytic approaches such as multiple regression ignore the clustered nature of individuals within higher-level groupings; therefore, in the presence of similarities among individuals within groups, estimated parameters may be biased. Although there are various ways to adjust the estimates produced by these analytic techniques, these remedies do not facilitate the investigation of models that specify presumed effects at different levels of the data hierarchy (Thomas & Heck, 2001).

To address this shortcoming, the second way to think about group-level homogeneity in hierarchical data is in terms of the opportunities it presents to specify conceptual models designed to operationalize organizational processes at more than a single level. After determining that an outcome varies across units, the analyst can investigate how various within-group and between-group variables explain variance in the outcome at each successive level. As readers may notice in Figure 1.1, with horizontal arrows we can model variability in intercepts; that is, the predictors at each level will account for variability in the outcome at that level. Moreover, the concept of investigating random slope coefficients across groups is also central to multilevel modeling. The cross-level arrows in Figure 1.1, which extend from the macro levels toward the micro level, suggest how higher level explanatory variables might explain random variability in slopes at that specific level.

Multilevel modeling, then, also contributes to our understanding of hierarchical data structures by allowing the analyst to estimate structural and variance/covariance parameters (e.g., residual variance in intercepts or slopes at Level 2, covariance between intercepts and slopes at Level 2) more efficiently and accurately. In a multilevel model, we typically focus on output concerning two types of model parameters. Structural parameters are referred to as the model's *fixed effects*. These include intercept coefficients (e.g., a group mean) or slope coefficients (e.g., the relationship between gender and achievement). The complete set of variances and covariances in model parameters is referred to as its *covariance components* (Singer & Willett, 2003). Specific parameters can be designated as *randomly varying*, which means that the sizes of the estimates are allowed to vary across groups. Investigating these randomly varying intercepts and slopes is at the center of our general multilevel modeling strategy presented in subsequent chapters.

What SPSS Can and Cannot Do

SPSS Mixed (which is a component of the SPSS Advanced add-on module for the PC and the Mac) is a very flexible routine that can be used to estimate a wide variety of multilevel, multilevel cross-classified, and multilevel repeated measures designs. It is important to note, however, that SPSS Mixed is currently limited to models with continuous outcomes (i.e., similar to multiple regression). This means several types of multilevel models of interest cannot be investigated with the current (version 18.0) software. In particular, these are multilevel models with dichotomous and ordinal outcome variables. This will be a considerable limitation for some fields of study (Leyland, 2004). Although individual-level repeated measures designs with dichotomous/ordinal indicators can be estimated using the SPSS generalized estimating equations (GEE) procedure, we do not present that procedure in this volume since it is currently aimed at single-level models.

A second limitation is the ability to deal with missing data. For examining multilevel models, there are several different approaches that can be used to estimate model parameters in the presence of missing data. Some of these include listwise (i.e., eliminating any case with at least one missing value) and pairwise (e.g., eliminating pairs of cases when missing data are present, as in calculating a correlation) deletion, mean substitution, maximum likelihood (ML) estimation with missing data included, and multiple imputation (see Raykov & Marcoulides, 2008, for further discussion). Generally, listwise, pairwise, mean substitution, and various regression-based approaches are not considered acceptable solutions because they lead to biased parameter estimation. Two approaches that are considered acceptable in the literature are multiple imputation (MI) and full information maximum likelihood (FIML) estimation in the presence of missing data (Peugh & Enders, 2004).

The default in SPSS is listwise deletion of cases when there is any missing data. For data sets that are horizontally organized (i.e., typically one row for each individual), this will result in eliminating the participant if data are missing on *any* variable in the analysis. Listwise deletion is only valid when the data are missing completely at random (e.g., as when selecting a random sample from a population), which is seldom the case using real data. This implies that ML estimation with missing data is not presently available in SPSS for this common type of multilevel analysis. For vertically arranged data (e.g., where a single individual may have several observations or rows representing time intervals), the data will only be dropped for that occasion. So if there are four observations per individual and one observation is missing for a particular individual, the other three observations would be used in calculating the individual's growth curve. This will typically yield unbiased estimates if data are missing at random (Raykov & Marcoulides, 2008). Although user missing values can be specified in SPSS, this approach is typically used for categorical responses, where some possible responses are coded as missing (e.g., "not applicable" in survey questions). If these user-defined missing values are included in the analysis, however, they will bias parameter estimates. It is incumbent upon the analyst to be aware of how missing data will affect the analysis.

We suggest, therefore, that users ideally should have close to complete data (e.g., 5% or less missing) when using SPSS Mixed, or they should first use some type of multiple imputation software to generate a "complete" data set, which can then be used to estimate models with SPSS Mixed. SPSS has a missing data module that can accomplish the multiple imputation for missing data, but it must be purchased as an add-on program. Students using the SPSS Graduate Pack may have to upgrade to a regular version of the SPSS Base and Advanced software to add on the missing data module to use prior to SPSS Mixed.

On the other hand, one attractive feature of SPSS Mixed is that it is not limited in terms of the number of levels in a nested or cross-classified data structure that can be analyzed simultaneously. The ability to specify multiple RANDOM (i.e., randomly varying intercept and slopes) commands at successive levels of a data hierarchy facilitates investigating a variety of multilevel models that are difficult, or not currently possible, to estimate optimally in other software packages. As with most current software programs, however, adding levels to examine in a data hierarchy, randomly varying parameters, and cross-level interactions can greatly increase the amount of time it takes to produce a solution (i.e., from seconds to several hours) and will require increasingly large amounts of memory and disk space as models become more complex.

We see another advantage in the easy manner in which various types of covariance structures can be specified at different levels of the data hierarchy. Our comparison of SPSS Mixed with other multilevel software suggests the program produces results substantively consistent with other programs, given similar model specification. Given our assessment of these limitations and several advantages, we feel using SPSS to investigate multilevel and longitudinal models is a useful way in which to introduce researchers to the uses and benefits of multilevel modeling, since it takes immediate advantage of a software program they are likely to have encountered already in their quantitative preparation.

Developing a General Multilevel Modeling Strategy

In this workbook, we apply a general strategy for examining multilevel models (e.g., Bryk & Raudenbush, 1992; Heck & Thomas, 2009; Hox, 2002). Multilevel models are useful and necessary only to the extent that the data being analyzed provide sufficient variation at each level. "Sufficiency" of variation is relative and depends as much on theoretical concerns as it does on the structure and quality of data. Multilevel modeling can be used to specify a hierarchical system of regression equations that takes advantage of the clustered data structure (Heck & Thomas, 2009). Multilevel models can be formulated in two ways: (1) by presenting separate equations for each of the levels in a data hierarchy (e.g., employees, workgroups, departments, divisions, corporations, etc.) or (2) by laying out the separate equations and then combining all equations through substitution into a single-model equation.

For readers familiar with HLM (Raudenbush et al., 2004), the software uses separate equations at each level to build the multilevel model. This approach results in the need to generate separate data sets at each level first (e.g., individuals, classrooms, schools, etc.) which are then "combined" within the software program to make the final data file (called a multivariate data matrix or .mdm file). The user can neither see nor edit the case-specific contents of this final data set. Most other software packages, such as SPSS Mixed, use single-equation representation, so all analyses can be conducted from within one data set. As we will show in Chapter 2, however, we sometimes need to reorganize the single data set for particular types of analyses (e.g., longitudinal and multivariate analyses).

As Hox (2002) describes, both ways of specifying multilevel models have advantages and disadvantages. The separate-equation approach such as that used in HLM has the advantage of being clear about how the proposed model is built up from Level 1 through successive levels. The disadvantage of this approach is that it hides from view the fact that modeling a cross-level interaction on a Level 1 regression slope results in adding an interaction to the overall model (Hox, 2002). The single-equation approach makes the existence of interactions obvious, but it conceals the role of the complicated error components that are created by modeling randomly varying slopes. We will walk readers through this process for one example in the following section. In successive chapters, however, we primarily adopt the approach of laying out separate equations by level for clarity in building models, leaving to users to recognize that the sets of equations are reduced to single-model equations in SPSS when substitution is applied.

Illustrating the Steps in Investigating a Proposed Model

We have found that in many instances multilevel investigations unfold as a series of analytic steps. Of course, there may be times when the analyst might change the specific steps, but, in general, we have found this overall model development strategy works pretty well. In Figure 1.2, we provide an illustration of what a simple two-level model to explore a random intercept describing productivity and a random slope describing the effect of employee attitudes on their productivity might look like. We use this model to provide a conceptual overview of the modeling strategy we adopt in successive chapters.

In a single-level model we could focus on the overall relationship between employee attitudes and their productivity. In the traditional OLS model we would get a slope expressing the relationship between the two variables and an intercept representing some adjusted value of the

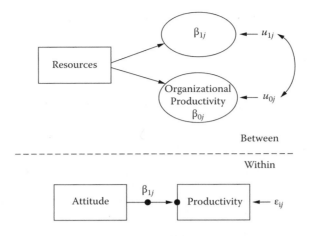
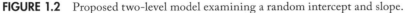

FIGURE 1.2 Proposed two-level model examining a random intercept and slope.

outcome. This would be fine if our interests were limited to an overall relationship. But if we were interested in understanding how employee groupings (e.g., workgroups or departments) might moderate that relationship (or even controlling for such a possibility), we would need to incorporate information about the organization or grouping of employees in our sample. Once we shift into thinking about such multilevel relationships, where employees are now nested within groups of some kind, a range of new analytical possibilities emerges.

Within groups we might define a randomly varying intercept (productivity) and randomly varying slope (i.e., the effect of employee attitudes on productivity). The random slope is shown in Figure 1.2 with a filled dot on the line representing the relationship between attitudes and productivity. The Greek symbol beta (β), which is often used to describe a slope or regression parameter at Level 1, is above the line. Between groups, we might propose that differences in resource allocation affect levels of organizational productivity. Additionally, we might propose these variables also moderate the size of the effect of employee attitudes on productivity. This type of effect, which is referred to as a cross-level interaction, implies that the magnitude of a relationship observed within groups is dependent on contextual or organizational features defined by higher level units. We therefore formulate a Level 2 model to explain variability in intercepts and variability in slopes (shown as ovals representing *unknowns*, or latent variables, in Figure 1.2) across organizations.

One-Way ANOVA (No Predictors) Model

A good first step is to examine the extent to which variation in a Level 1 outcome exists *within* Level 2 units relative to its variation *between* Level 2 units. In our example we want to know if there exists significant variance in productivity across groups—something that would be invisible to us in a single-level model. Little variability within the Level 2 units suggests greater homogeneity among all Level 1 observations than exists among Level 1 observations from different Level 2 groups—that is, such evidence suggests the nesting of Level 1 observations is not systematically associated with levels of an outcome. The partitioning of outcome variance into Level 1 and Level 2 components without other predictors in the model allows the researcher to test the validity of this assumption and provides important information about the sources of variation in the outcome variable; productivity in our example here.

Notice that in Equation 1.2, we add a subscript for individuals (i) and for organizations (j). The null model for individual i in organization j can be represented as

$$Y_{ij} = \beta_{0j} + \varepsilon_{ij}, \tag{1.2}$$

where β_{0j} is the mean of productivity (intercept) for the jth group, and the Greek lowercase letter epsilon (ε_{ij}) represents the errors in estimating individual productivity within groups. In a

TABLE 1.1   Model Dimension[a]

		Number of Levels	Covariance Structure	Number of Parameters	Subject Variables
Fixed effects	Intercept	1		1	
Random effects	Intercept	1	Identity	1	orgid
Residual				1	
Total		2		3	

[a] Dependent Variable: productivity.

two-level model, Level 1 fixed effects are typically expressed as unstandardized β coefficients. *Unstandardized* means the coefficients are in their original metrics. The subscript *j* indicates that the intercept varies across groups. Individual-level error (referred to as Residual in the SPSS Mixed output) is also considered a random effect.

Between groups, variation in intercepts (β_{0j}) can be represented as

$$\beta_{0j} = \gamma_{00} + u_{0j}. \tag{1.3}$$

Level 2 fixed-effect coefficients (which are also unstandardized) are generally expressed as the Greek lowercase letter gamma (γ). Variation in estimating organization intercepts is represented as u_{0j}. Through substituting Equation 1.3 into Equation 1.2, the single-equation model can be written as

$$Y_{ij} = \gamma_{00} + u_{0j} + \varepsilon_{ij}. \tag{1.4}$$

The null model therefore provides an estimated mean productivity score for all schools. It also provides a partitioning of the variance between Level 1 (ε_{ij}) and Level 2 (u_{0j}). Altogether, Equation 1.4 suggests there are three parameters to estimate: the intercept; the between-organization error, or deviation, from the average intercept (u_{0j}); and the individual-level residual, or variation in individual scores within organizations (ε_{ij}). We can confirm this by examining the output from the intercept-only model in SPSS (Table 1.1). The average intercept is considered a fixed component, while the between-group variation in average intercepts and the individual-level error (Residual), or variation in individual scores, are often referred to as the random, or stochastic, component. Information about the model's parameters is also useful in examining the baseline (no predictors) model with three estimated parameters against subsequent models with more estimated parameters.

Analyze a Level 1 Model With Fixed Predictors

Assuming that sufficient levels of variance in Y exist at each level, we can investigate a model with only fixed predictors at Level 1. Level 1 predictors are often referred to as X. For each individual *i* in organization *j* a proposed model similar to Equation 1.1 (summarizing the effect of employee attitudes on productivity) can be expressed as

$$Y_{ij} = \beta_{0j} + \beta_1 X_{ij} + \varepsilon_{ij}. \tag{1.5}$$

Equation 1.5 suggests that, within-groups, X_{ij} (employee attitude) is related to productivity levels. Often, the unstandardized within-group predictors ($\beta_1 X_{ij}$) are either grand-mean or group-mean centered to facilitate interpretation of the coefficients. Grand-mean centering indicates that the variable is compared against the mean for the sample. For example, if the sample mean for employee attitude were 3.4 (on a 5 point scale), an individual on the grand mean would have her or his score rescaled to 0. In contrast, group-mean centering implies that the individual's

TABLE 1.2 Model Dimension[a]

		Number of Levels	Covariance Structure	Number of Parameters	Subject Variables
Fixed effects	Intercept	1		1	
	attitude	1		1	
Random effects	Intercept	1	Identity	1	orgid
Residual				1	
Total		3		4	

[a] Dependent Variable: productivity.

attitude score is rescaled against the mean for her or his group, with the group mean now equal to 0. We describe in Chapter 2 how grand-mean and group-mean centered variables can be developed in SPSS.

At Level 2, Equation 1.6 implies that variation in intercepts can be described by an organization-level intercept (γ_{00}), or grand mean, and a random parameter capturing variation in individual organization means (u_{0j}) from the grand mean:

$$\beta_{0j} = \gamma_{00} + u_{0j}. \tag{1.6}$$

In the case where we wish to treat the within-group slope as fixed (i.e., it does not vary across organizations), Equation 1.7 would be written as

$$\beta_{1j} = \gamma_{10}. \tag{1.7}$$

This suggests the variance component of the slope is fixed at zero. As Equation 1.7 indicates, there is no random component (u_{1j}), so the slope coefficient is fixed to one value for the sample. Through substitution of β_{0j} and β_{1j} into Equation 1.5, the single-equation model can be summarized as

$$Y_{ij} = \gamma_{00} + u_{0j} + \gamma_{10}X_{ij} + \varepsilon_{ij} \tag{1.8}$$

and then reorganized with fixed parameters (γ s) and random parameters ($u_{0j} + \varepsilon_{ij}$) as

$$Y_{ij} = \gamma_{00} + \gamma_{10}(\text{attitude})_{ij} + u_{0j} + \varepsilon_{ij}, \tag{1.9}$$

where we have replaced X with the individual-level variable name. The following output from SPSS suggests (consistent with Equation 1.9) that there are four parameters to estimate (Table 1.2). The fixed effects are the intercept and Level 1 predictor *attitude*. The random parameters are the variation in intercepts across groups (referred to as a *random effect* in Table 1.2) and the Level 1 residual.

Add the Level 2 Explanatory Variables

At the third step, it is often useful to add the between-group predictors of variability in intercepts. Group variables are often referred to as W (or Z). From Figure 1.2, the Level 2 model with resources added will look like the following:

$$\beta_{0j} = \gamma_{00} + \gamma_{01}W_j + u_{0j}, \tag{1.10}$$

TABLE 1.3 Model Dimension[a]

		Number of Levels	Covariance Structure	Number of Parameters	Subject Variables
Fixed effects	Intercept	1		1	
	resources	1		1	
	attitude	1		1	
Random effects	Intercept	1	Identity	1	orgid
Residual				1	
Total		4		5	

[a] Dependent Variable: productivity.

where W_j refers to the level of resources in the organization. The combined model is therefore

$$Y_{ij} = \gamma_{00} + \gamma_{01}(\text{resources})_j + \gamma_{10}(\text{attitude})_{ij} + u_{0j} + \varepsilon_{ij}, \tag{1.11}$$

where we have included the names of the individual- and group-level predictors for W and X, respectively. We find that it is sometimes useful to write in the variable names to provide easy recognition of the predictors in the model. Readers will notice that in a two-level model, after substitution, all estimates of group-level and individual-level predictors are expressed as γ coefficients. We provide the SPSS output (Table 1.3) summarizing the five fixed and random parameters to be estimated in this model.

Examine Whether a Particular Slope Coefficient Varies Between Groups

We may next assess whether key slopes of interest have a significant variance component between the groups. Our theoretical model (Figure 1.2) proposes that the relationship between employee attitudes and productivity may vary across organizations. Testing random slopes is best accomplished systematically, one variable at a time, since if we test several slopes simultaneously, we are unlikely to achieve a solution that converges (Hox, 2002). As we suggested, if the within-unit slope (e.g., attitude–productivity) is defined to be randomly varying across units, the Level 2 slope model can be written as

$$\beta_{1j} = \gamma_{10} + u_{1j}. \tag{1.12}$$

Equation 1.12 suggests variability in slopes can be described by a group-level average intercept coefficient (γ_{10}), or grand mean, and a random parameter capturing variation in individual organization coefficients (u_{1j}) from the grand mean.

Through substitution, the combined model will be

$$Y_{ij} = \gamma_{00} + \gamma_{01}(\text{resources})_j + \gamma_{10}(\text{attitude})_{ij} + u_{1j}(\text{attitude})_{ij} + u_{0j} + \varepsilon_{ij}. \tag{1.13}$$

As we suggested previously, notice the substitution of β_{1j} in the within-group (Level 1) model (Equation 1.5) results in the addition of the interaction $u_{1j}X_{1ij}$ (i.e., where X_{1ij} is employee attitude) to the single-equation model. This interaction is considered as a random effect, which is defined as the deviation in slope for cases in group j multiplied by the Level 1 predictor score (X_1) for the ith case in group j (Tabachnick, 2008). We can confirm that there are six parameters to estimate from the following SPSS printout (Table 1.4). The three fixed effects are the productivity intercept, the Level 2 predictor (resources), and the Level 1 predictor (attitudes).

TABLE 1.4 Model Dimension[a]

		Number of Levels	Covariance Structure	Number of Parameters	Subject Variables
Fixed effects	Intercept	1		1	
	Resources	1		1	
	Attitude	1		1	
Random effects	Intercept + attitude	2	Diagonal	2	orgid
Residual				1	
Total		5		6	

[a] Dependent Variable: productivity.

The two random effects are the variability in intercepts and the variability in the attitude–productivity slope ($u_{1j}X_{1ij}$). The Level 1 residual variance is the final estimated parameter.

Adding Cross-Level Interactions to Explain Variation in the Slope

Finally, we would build a Level 2 model to explain variation in the Level 1 randomly varying slope of interest (i.e., assuming the slope has significant variance across groups). Our simplified model in Figure 1.2 suggests that organizational resource levels may moderate the within-unit (e.g., attitude–productivity) slope:

$$\beta_{1j} = \gamma_{10} + \gamma_{11}(\text{resources}*\text{attitude})_j + u_{1j}. \tag{1.14}$$

This cross-level interaction term is built during the model specification phase in SPSS. Substitution of the β_{1j} coefficient results in the following single-equation model to be estimated:

$$Y_{ij} = \gamma_{00} + \gamma_{01}(\text{resources})_j + \gamma_{10}(\text{attitude})_{ij} + \gamma_{11}(\text{resources}*\text{attitude})_j + u_{1j}(\text{attitude})_{ij} + u_{0j} + \varepsilon_{ij}. \tag{1.15}$$

This model represented in Equation 1.15 results in seven parameters to estimate. The four fixed effects are the intercept, resources, employee attitudes, and the cross-level interaction (attitude * resources). The three random variance parameters are the intercept (u_{0j}), the attitude–productivity slope (u_{1j}), which are the random effects, and the individual-level residual (ε_{ij}). We can confirm this with the output statement from SPSS (Table 1.5).

Significance tests can be used (along with changes in the model deviance, changes in variance components, etc.) in determining suitability of models. We discuss these issues in more detail in subsequent chapters. Three-level models are more complicated to estimate than two-level models

TABLE 1.5 Model Dimension[a]

		Number of Levels	Covariance Structure	Number of Parameters	Subject Variables
Fixed effects	Intercept	1		1	
	Resources	1		1	
	Attitude	1		1	
	attitude * resources	1		1	
Random effects	Intercept + attitude	2	Diagonal	2	orgid
Residual				1	
Total		6		7	

[a] Dependent Variable: productivity.

(e.g., more cross-level interactions, changing sample sizes, etc.), but the strategy is basically the same. It is best to keep models simplified, for example, by including only random effects that are of strong theoretical or empirical interest. Although it is desirable to include covariances between intercepts and slopes, it is not always possible to achieve model convergence. We will address this issue more completely in subsequent chapters.

When investigating covariance structures associated with random effects, we adopt a similar strategy. One of the advantages of SPSS Mixed is the ease in which users can specify alternative covariance structures for random effects. Changing the covariance structure of the random effects can also change the estimates and tests of fixed effects. We can then use various objective tests (e.g., likelihood ratio test) to determine which structure best describes the data. This procedure allows the analyst to compare several models before arriving at a model that provides the closest fit to the observed data.

With one random effect, the default covariance matrix is an identity (ID) covariance matrix. This is because there is only one Level 2 variance in the model (i.e., the variance related to the randomly varying intercept). Using "Variance Components" (VC) also results in the same output. With a random slope and intercept, we typically use a diagonal (DIAG) covariance matrix at Level 2 first (VC will also provide this same specification). A diagonal covariance matrix provides an estimate of the variance for each random effect, but the covariance between the two random effects is restricted to be 0. In the earlier case, readers will note the diagonal covariance matrix specified for the covariance structure results in seven total parameters being estimated.

If this model converges, or reaches a solution without any warnings in the output, we can also try using a completely unstructured (UN) covariance matrix of random effects. Specifying an unstructured covariance matrix at Level 2 provides an additional interaction term in the estimated model, which represents the covariance between the random intercept and random slope (i.e., there are three parameters to be estimated in the unstructured covariance matrix in Table 1.6). This additional term in the covariance structure of the model will result in eight total parameters estimated (instead of the seven specified in Equation 1.15). We note, however, that this type of covariance matrix for random effects results in more models that fail to converge. We will provide tips along the way with what are possible challenges that come up in using this type of general approach and how certain frequently encountered problems can be remedied.

For models that have repeated measures, there are also several types of covariance matrices that can be used to account for possible temporal dependencies in the data. When there are repeated measures on individuals, it is likely that the error terms within each individual are correlated (SPSS, 2002). Autoregressive error structures, for example, allow the analyst to investigate the extent to which the measurements are correlated. The model assumes the errors within each subject are correlated but are independent across subjects.

TABLE 1.6 Model Dimension[a]

		Number of Levels	Covariance Structure	Number of Parameters	Subject Variables
Fixed effects	Intercept	1		1	
	Resources	1		1	
	Attitude	1		1	
	attitude * resources	1		1	
Random effects	Intercept + attitude	2	Unstructured	3	orgid
Residual				1	
Total		6		8	

[a] Dependent Variable: productivity.

Syntax Versus SPSS Menu Command Formulation

In SPSS Mixed, we can formulate models using either syntax statements or menu commands. We suspect most users are more familiar with the menu framework, since they have likely used that to examine single-level models (e.g., analysis of variance, multiple regression, factor analysis). We have chosen the menu command approach, but we also provide examples of syntax in Appendix A. Readers should keep in mind that with more complex models, it is often a benefit to use the syntax to formulate and run models for a couple of reasons. First, the syntax statements provide a nice record of a progression of models (if you save the syntax files and label them according to the general modeling steps we have laid out). This is helpful if you close the SPSS program. You can return later and easily start up from where you left off.

Second, we have found that it is easier to reorganize the syntax statements than to rebuild the whole model from the menu commands if you wish to change the order of the variables in your output tables. Generally, we like to organize the output such that the predictors explaining intercepts are organized by levels of the data hierarchy and predictors that explain variation in slopes (i.e., cross-level interactions) can be similarly organized. In the SPSS Windows format, one can always use the PASTE function (within the SPSS Mixed dialog box) to generate the underlying syntax before actually running the model. The syntax is sent to its own window within SPSS and can be saved for future use. We find this is a good way to check whether the model you are running actually corresponds with the model that you had in mind. Often, we find doing this helps us see where we have forgotten or incorrectly specified something. This gets more important when the multilevel models one is investigating take a considerable amount of time to produce a solution.

For readers unaccustomed to the syntax approach, following is an example of the syntax generated by SPSS Mixed when we built the model within the menu system to produce the model in Equation 1.15.

```
MIXED
 productivity WITH attitude resources
 /CRITERIA = CIN(95) MXITER(100) MXSTEP(5) SCORING(1)
 SINGULAR(0.000000000001) HCONVERGE(0, ABSOLUTE) LCONVERGE(0, ABSOLUTE)
 PCONVERGE(0.000001, ABSOLUTE)
 /FIXED = resources attitude resources*attitude | SSTYPE(3)
 /RANDOM INTERCEPT attitude | SUBJECT(orgid) COVTYPE(DIAG)
 /METHOD = REML
 /PRINT = SOLUTION TESTCOV.
```

The initial syntax lines provide the dependent variable (productivity) identifies covariates in the analysis (signified by the key word "With"). Categorical variables (variables with two or more categories) can be specified with the key word "By," with the last category serving as the reference group. Note that dichotomous variables (0, 1) can be defined as continuous (covariate) variables as in multiple regression. The criteria command (/CRITERIA) provides information concerning SPSS default values (e.g., confidence intervals for estimates, iteration information, convergence criteria) for the estimation algorithm. The statements can be excluded if the analyst chooses to maintain the default criteria. We recommend that the analyst exercise caution in reflexively adopting the SPSS defaults as these will sometimes introduce problematic conditions on the models being estimated. Regardless of the type of model being developed, it is always good practice to review the default setting to ensure that they are appropriate for your purposes. Following, the fixed effects (/FIXED = resources, attitudes, resources*attitudes) in the model are defined, with the intercept also included as a default, and the random effects (/RANDOM = intercept, attitude). The Level 1 residual is also estimated as a default. The syntax also identifies the Level 2 cluster (SUBJECT) variable (orgid) and the type of covariance matrix used for the random effects (DIAG). Finally, the syntax includes the default estimation procedure used (/METHOD = REML), which is restricted maximum likelihood, default model convergence criteria, and user-specified output (/PRINT = G SOLUTION TESTCOV). SOLUTION provides the tests of fixed effects and TESTCOV the tests of random variances and covariances. Predicted values and residuals can be saved using the /SAVE command.

One can easily change the method of estimation (/METHOD), for example, from restricted maximum likelihood (REML) to maximum likelihood (ML) by typing ML to replace REML in the appropriate syntax line. The order of the fixed effects (FIXED = resources attitude resources*attitude) in the output can easily be changed by switching the order of the variables in that command line. Keep in mind that you can also add information to the SPSS output tables (through using the Chart Editor) to help readers understand your presentation of output. We will explore many of these options in subsequent chapters.

Model Estimation and Other Typical Multilevel Modeling Issues

We now turn our attention to several important issues related to model estimation (see Raudenbush & Bryk, 2002; Heck & Thomas, 2009; Hox, 2002; or Marcoulides & Hershberger, 1997, for further discussion). Model estimation attempts to determine the extent to which the sample covariance matrix representing our model specification is a good approximation of the true population covariance matrix. This determination is made through a formal test of a null hypothesis that the data are consistent with the model we have proposed. Note that, in general, confirmation of a proposed model relies on a failure to reject the null hypothesis. In contrast to the common use of the null hypothesis that readers may be more familiar with (e.g., rejecting the null hypothesis that two means are the same), here one wishes to accept the null hypothesis that the model cannot be rejected on statistical grounds alone. This implies that the model is a plausible representation of the data (although it is important to emphasize that it may not be the only plausible representation).

Unlike traditional single-level approaches using OLS, SPSS Mixed (and other multilevel modeling programs) employs ML estimation. ML determines the optimal population values for parameters in a model that maximize the probability or likelihood function; that is, the function that gives the probability of finding the observed sample data given the current parameter estimates (Hox, 2002). This involves an iterative process that determines a set of weights for random parameters in the model that minimizes the negative of the natural logarithm multiplied by the likelihood of the data. Because the likelihood, or probability, can vary from 0 to 1, minimizing this discrepancy function amounts to maximizing the likelihood of the observed data.

If we consider the sample covariance matrix (S) to represent the population covariance matrix (Σ), then the difference between the observed sample matrix S and the model-implied covariance matrix ($\hat{S}$) should be small if the proposed model fits the data. The evaluation of the difference between these two matrices depends on the estimation method used to solve for the model's parameters (Marcoulides & Hershberger, 1997). The mathematical relationships implied by the model are solved iteratively until the estimates are optimized. As suggested, the difference between S and $\hat{S}$ is described as a discrepancy function, that is, the actual difference in the two estimates based on a likelihood. The greater the difference between these two covariance matrices, the larger the discrepancy in the function becomes (Marcoulides & Hershberger, 1997). ML estimation produces a model deviance statistic, defined as $-2*LN(Likelihood)$, where Likelihood is the value of the Likelihood function at convergence and LN is the natural logarithm (Hox, 2002). The deviance is an indicator of how well the model fits the data. Models with lower deviance (i.e., a smaller discrepancy function) fit better than models with higher deviance. Nested models (i.e., where a more specific model is formed from a more general one) can be compared by examining differences in these deviance coefficients under specified conditions (e.g., changes deviance between models per differences in degrees of freedom).

SPSS Mixed offers two estimation choices: ML estimation and REML estimation, which is the default setting. In ML estimation, both regression coefficients and variance components are included in the likelihood function, whereas in REML only the variance components are included in the likelihood function (Hox, 2002). REML, therefore, is a *restricted* solution. The difference suggests that REML considers the regression coefficients to be unknowns, which can lead to better estimates when there are small numbers of groups in the study (Raudenbush & Bryk, 2002). In other words, REML takes into account the loss in degrees of freedom due to the estimation of the $P + 1$ regression coefficients in the model in order to obtain unbiased estimation of the variance components (Snijders & Bosker, 1999). To illustrate this concept, in a simple model for estimating the variance in a sample mean, the REML approach amounts to dividing the sum of the squared deviations about the mean by the total sample size minus 1 ($N - 1$) instead of N (Hox, 2002). As previously described, when a series of nested models is to be compared in terms of fixed effects (e.g., regression coefficients), ML should be used, because the approach takes into consideration the regression coefficients in solving the likelihood function (Hox, 2002). In later chapters we show that SPSS also provides other fit indices that can be used to compare various models.

Sample Size

Under various sampling conditions (size of sample, normality of data) there has been considerable debate among methodologists about the efficiency of maximum likelihood estimation, given nonnormal features of the data (Goldstein, 1995; Longford, 1993; Morris, 1995). An important conceptual difference between single-level and multilevel approaches is that sample size considerations are quite different. The multilevel approach requires a sufficient sample size at each level of analysis. In smaller group samples, the difference in estimation between ML and REML results in a downward bias in variance components estimated with ML compared to REML. With small group samples, therefore, we generally prefer REML estimation. With large sample sizes, there should be no difference in the estimates produced by either method. It is important to keep in mind that under less-than-ideal sampling conditions (e.g., small numbers of groups, convenience samples) it may be difficult to determine whether model results might be replicated in other samples. SPSS applies the Satterthwaite correction to standard errors, which provides more conservative estimates of standard errors, especially in small groups (e.g., Loh, 1987).

Power

Power refers to the ability to detect an effect, should one exist. In the single-level analysis, most researchers know that the significance level (α), the effect size (i.e., with larger effects easier to detect), and the sample size are determinants of power. Multilevel models raise a number of additional issues involving power. Issues about power typically concern the appropriate (or minimum) sample size needed for various types of multilevel analyses (e.g., determining whether an intercept or slope varies across groups). As we suggested previously, one issue refers to the sample size required to ensure that estimates of fixed effects (e.g., at Level 1 and Level 2) and variances are unbiased (i.e., sampling bias). In most multilevel studies, the estimation of Level 2 effects is generally of greater concern as the number of groups available may be limited. As Snijders (2005) shows, when fixed effects are the focus, characteristics of the groups themselves have little bearing on the precision of Level 1 estimates. In general, we prefer adding groups (as opposed to individuals) to reduce parameter bias.

Another issue refers to the minimum sample size required to ensure that an effect would be detected if, in fact, one exists (i.e., power). In addition to these two determinants of power, in multilevel analyses there are at least two other considerations that inform estimates of power: sample size at each level (i.e., the number of individuals i within each group j, and the number of j groups) and the intraclass correlation (see Muthén & Satorra, 1995, for further discussion).

With higher intraclass correlations, the power to detect Level 1 effects will be lower (since the groups are more homogeneous), holding sample size constant at all levels. This suggests that the power to detect Level 2 effects is much more sensitive to the number of groups in the sample, as opposed to the number of observations within groups.

As designs become more complex, the need for larger samples at both levels increases. For example, in a given sample of individuals within groups, slopes in some units may be less reliably estimated than intercepts because, while intercepts depend only on the average level (mean) of a variable within each group, slope estimates depend both on the levels of an outcome and a particular covariate, as well as the variability of their covariance among individuals within each group (Mehta & Neale, 2005). This means that estimating variability in random slopes across units generally requires larger sample sizes for more stable estimates than simply estimating random intercepts. Complications can also arise due to correlations between random effects and the investigation of cross-level interactions (Raudenbush & Bryk, 2002). As this limited discussion of power suggests, a number of considerations must take place to assess potential bias in parameter estimates and power in various types of multilevel designs (see Heck & Thomas, 2009; Scherbaum & Ferreter, 2009; or Snijders, 2005, for further discussion of issues related to power).

Differences Between Multilevel Software Programs

In preparing this handbook, we compared models estimated in SPSS with models estimated with other multilevel software with which we are familiar (e.g., HLM, Mplus). Different software programs use slightly different algorithms to estimate models, for example, in calculating standard errors, especially in small groups. There are also differences in the means of testing the variance components. For example, SPSS uses a Wald Z test, and HLM uses a chi-square test. In general, however, we have found that the differences in software are generally small—that is, output will carry the same substantive interpretation. We provide a couple of examples in Appendix B.

A Note About Standardized and Unstandardized Coefficients

We present analyses in subsequent chapters using unstandardized regression coefficients. Unstandardized coefficients provide estimates of changes in the dependent variable associated with a unit change in the explanatory variable (e.g., male versus female; a standard deviation increase in motivation). Standardizing variables is useful in comparing the size of effects due to several variables measured on different scales within a sample. If the goal is to compare estimates across samples, one should use unstandardized estimates (Hox, 2002). Standardizing estimates is more complicated in multilevel modeling, however, due to the presence of variance components for outcomes at different levels of the data hierarchy. Because standardizing variables depends on their standard deviations, in multilevel modeling the analyst faces the issue of using Level 1 standard deviations and Level 2 standard deviations to compute standardized effects (Bloom, Hill, Black, & Lipsey, 2008).

There are a number of different ways to approach standardizing variables in multilevel modeling. Some software programs (e.g., Mplus, LISREL) provide a variety of different standardizations. For example, standardizing estimates to the within-group variance implies a focus on within-group relations without concern for how large or small the portion is of the within-group variance to the total variance. Mplus standardizes estimates within each level (which requires the between-group and within-group covariance matrices to construct accurate estimates). Other programs (e.g., HLM, SPSS Mixed) currently do not provide standardized solutions.

One could standardize all the indicators in the model first (e.g., by saving standardized estimates of each variable which can be obtained using the Descriptives command in SPSS). Essentially, this amounts to modeling with all z-scores. This approach succeeds in putting the variables in the same metric, but does not completely resolve the issue about the "proper" size of the coefficients in relation to an assumption about decomposing variance in the model. As Hox (2002) notes, this type of linear transformation of the fixed coefficients in a model also has the effect of changing estimates of the random part of the model (i.e., the model's variance components). Interactions are more challenging to standardize, since standardizing before the analysis can change the size of the interaction, the model's variance components, and also significance levels of variables (Hox, 2002; Preacher, 2003). We note in passing that various assumptions about standardizing variables (i.e., standardizing with respect to within-group variance only, the between-group variance only, within each level of the data hierarchy, or with respect to total variance) can lead to very different sets of coefficients and interpretations of the results, such that it can be difficult to determine what each standardization means (Heck & Thomas, 2000).

Summary

In this chapter, we have developed a context and rationale for the use of multilevel models in the social and behavioral sciences. The use of multilevel analysis can add substantive information about how processes unfold at various levels of a data hierarchy. We suggested that multilevel techniques support the specification of more complex theoretical relationships than is possible using traditional single-level regression analyses. Analytical approaches that can be used to model complex relationships have greatly expanded over the past couple of decades and these analytical alternatives allow us to investigate social processes in more theoretically and methodologically appropriate ways. Substantive progress in a field is often achieved when headway occurs simultaneously on conceptual and methodological fronts.

In the next chapter we take care of a bit of housekeeping by providing an overview of some important data management techniques. Arranging the data for analysis in SPSS is fairly straightforward. We provide the reader with a few essential steps necessary to put their data sets in proper order for analysis using SPSS Mixed.

CHAPTER 2

Preparing and Examining the Data for Multilevel Analyses

Essential to any type of analysis is the organization and vetting of the data that will be analyzed. In this chapter we identify a number of practical and substantive issues associated with preparing data for analysis in SPSS Mixed and assessing the adequacy of those data for a variety of multilevel analyses.

Data Requirements

In this workbook we deal exclusively with multilevel models using continuous level outcomes. Whereas other multilevel statistical programs can accommodate binary or ordinal outcomes, SPSS Mixed is restricted to outcomes measured on a continuous scale. Although we deal only with continuously measured outcomes, predictors can be continuous, ordinal, or dichotomous.

The sample sizes we employ throughout our examples are large at each level of the analysis. The variables used may come from a variety of sources, many of which are specific to a particular level of analysis. One might, for example, draw on student-level attitudinal, behavioral, or performance data from national surveys such as the National Educational Longitudinal Study of 1988 (Curtin, Ingels, Wu, & Heuer, 2002). If an objective were to understand the effects of school settings on these individual characteristics, we might assemble school-level data drawing on information from the Common Core of Data (Sable & Noel, 2008). School-level data might include school size, demographic composition, financial characteristics such as state dollars per enrolled student, on-time progression or graduation rates, teacher and administrative numbers, and the like. To carry this to a third level, we could draw on U.S. Census data to define characteristics of the school districts in which the schools at Level 2 were located (e.g., household income, number of people in the household, their levels of education, etc.).

We will show that there are many variants on this modeling framework. We might, for example, want to understand change in some outcome over time. In such an instance, we might conceptualize time points across which we presume change to occur within students who could, in turn, be nested within schools, and so on. However the nesting is conceptualized, each level of analysis will have its own set of variables defining features of the units being measured at that level. Although conceptualizing data at discrete levels of the hierarchy may be relatively straightforward, organizing the data set requires an understanding of how the data need to be arranged to represent that hierarchical conceptualization correctly. In the next section, we outline the main organizational features of data sets that can be used in a multilevel analysis. We return to data requirements in more detail in a subsequent section.

File Layout

We described in the previous chapter an important difference between the single-equation and multiple-equation approach to estimating multilevel models. The multiple-equation approach (e.g., used in HLM) requires a separate data set for each level of data being analyzed. This can make conceptualization of the different levels clear. If Level 1 consisted of 6,871 students, for example, the Level 1 file would contain student data, including information about higher order group membership (e.g., the classroom or school membership for each of the 6,871 students in the file).

Figure 2.1 shows what such a Level 1 file might look like, based on the data set used in Chapter 3. In this particular example (*ch2level-1data.sav*) we have included a student ID variable (*id*); a school ID variable (*schcode*); and three variables describing student characteristics: gender (*female*), socioeconomic status on a normalized scale (*ses*), and a raw math score (*math*).

If Level 2 in the analysis consisted of schools of which students were members, the Level 2 data set would contain all information about those 419 schools, including a unique school identifier and perhaps aggregated data from the Level 1 student file.

The Level 2 file (*ch2level-2data.sav*) shown in Figure 2.2 contains a unique school identifier (*schcode*), two variables describing the characteristics of the school, average socioeconomic status (*ses_mean*), and the proportion of students planning to attend a 4-year college (*per4yr*). The data sets are linked through a group-level identifier (in this case, *schcode*) during the multilevel analysis.

In contrast, the single-level approach makes use of one file that combines data from each level (Figure 2.3). In the univariate multilevel model, the file will consist of one record for each Level 1 unit. Values for variables from higher levels will be constant within groups. For

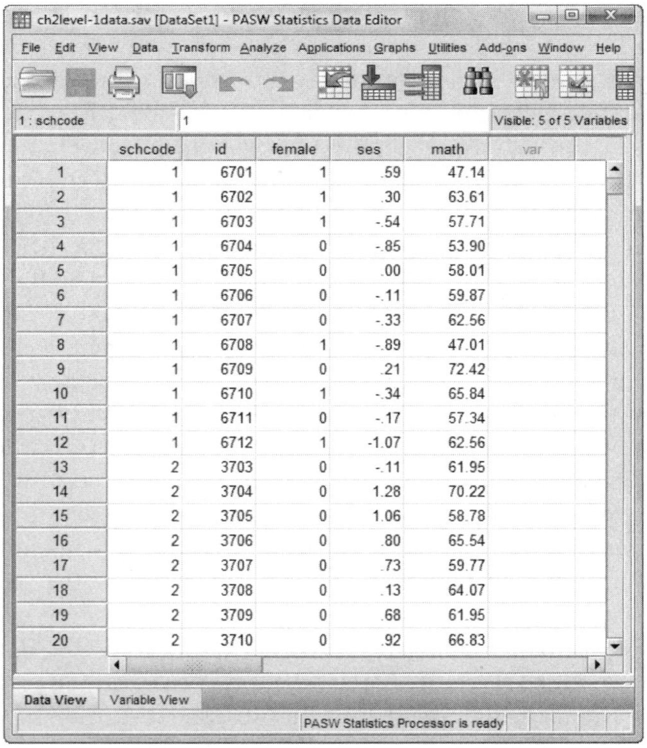

	schcode	id	female	ses	math	var
1	1	6701	1	.59	47.14	
2	1	6702	1	.30	63.61	
3	1	6703	1	-.54	57.71	
4	1	6704	0	-.85	53.90	
5	1	6705	0	.00	58.01	
6	1	6706	0	-.11	59.87	
7	1	6707	0	-.33	62.56	
8	1	6708	1	-.89	47.01	
9	1	6709	0	.21	72.42	
10	1	6710	1	-.34	65.84	
11	1	6711	0	-.17	57.34	
12	1	6712	1	-1.07	62.56	
13	2	3703	0	-.11	61.95	
14	2	3704	0	1.28	70.22	
15	2	3705	0	1.06	58.78	
16	2	3706	0	.80	65.54	
17	2	3707	0	.73	59.77	
18	2	3708	0	.13	64.07	
19	2	3709	0	.68	61.95	
20	2	3710	0	.92	66.83	

FIGURE 2.1 A Level 1 data file (multiple-equation approach, $N = 6{,}871$).

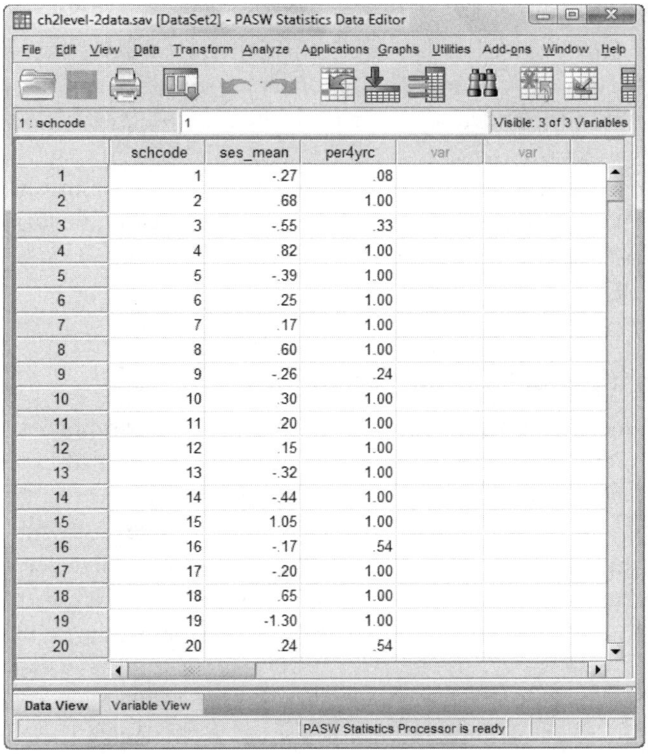

	schcode	ses_mean	per4yrc
1	1	-.27	.08
2	2	.68	1.00
3	3	-.55	.33
4	4	.82	1.00
5	5	-.39	1.00
6	6	.25	1.00
7	7	.17	1.00
8	8	.60	1.00
9	9	-.26	.24
10	10	.30	1.00
11	11	.20	1.00
12	12	.15	1.00
13	13	-.32	1.00
14	14	-.44	1.00
15	15	1.05	1.00
16	16	-.17	.54
17	17	-.20	1.00
18	18	.65	1.00
19	19	-1.30	1.00
20	20	.24	.54

FIGURE 2.2 A Level 2 data file (multiple-equation approach, $n = 419$).

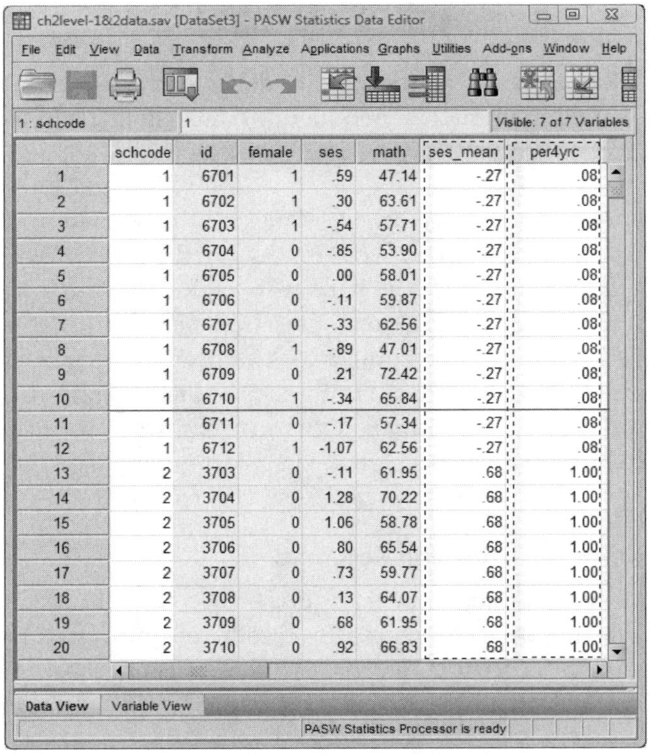

	schcode	id	female	ses	math	ses_mean	per4yrc
1	1	6701	1	.59	47.14	-.27	.08
2	1	6702	1	.30	63.61	-.27	.08
3	1	6703	1	-.54	57.71	-.27	.08
4	1	6704	0	-.85	53.90	-.27	.08
5	1	6705	0	.00	58.01	-.27	.08
6	1	6706	0	-.11	59.87	-.27	.08
7	1	6707	0	-.33	62.56	-.27	.08
8	1	6708	1	-.89	47.01	-.27	.08
9	1	6709	0	.21	72.42	-.27	.08
10	1	6710	1	-.34	65.84	-.27	.08
11	1	6711	0	-.17	57.34	-.27	.08
12	1	6712	1	-1.07	62.56	-.27	.08
13	2	3703	0	-.11	61.95	.68	1.00
14	2	3704	0	1.28	70.22	.68	1.00
15	2	3705	0	1.06	58.78	.68	1.00
16	2	3706	0	.80	65.54	.68	1.00
17	2	3707	0	.73	59.77	.68	1.00
18	2	3708	0	.13	64.07	.68	1.00
19	2	3709	0	.68	61.95	.68	1.00
20	2	3710	0	.92	66.83	.68	1.00

FIGURE 2.3 Combined multilevel data file (single-equation approach, $N = 6{,}871$).

example, in a data set (*ch2level-1&2data.sav*) with 6,871 students from 419 schools there would be a single file of 6,871 records. The values for the student-level variables would vary across all 6,871 students. However, values on the school-level variables would be constant within each of the 419 schools—that is, students within each school would all have the same value on each of the school-level variables.

SPSS Mixed uses the single-equation approach and one omnibus file containing data on each level of the analysis. In the sections that follow, we provide an overview of some of the data management steps within SPSS that will help you organize and prepare your data and files for use within the SPSS Mixed routine.

Getting Familiar With Basic SPSS Data Commands

Organizing and managing the data at various levels is accomplished through five basic SPSS procedures. There are, of course, many other procedures that can be used to modify a data set, but we feel these are primary to the data management tasks associated with organizing files for multilevel analyses within SPSS. We will have much more to say about the SPSS commands and the menu system itself in the chapters that follow. Here, however, we wish only to introduce these commands and a few principles of data management that we think will prove helpful for getting the most out of the workbook. The five primary procedures are (in order of importance)

1. RECODE: Changes, rearranges, or consolidates the values of an existing variable.
2. COMPUTE: Creates new numeric variables or modifies the values of existing string or numeric variables.
3. MATCH FILES: Combines variables from SPSS-format data files.
4. AGGREGATE: Aggregates groups of cases in the active data set into single cases and creates a new aggregated file or creates new variables in the active data set that contain aggregated data. The values of one or more variables in the active data set define the case groups.
5. VARSTOCASES: Restructures complex data structures (i.e., in which information about a variable is stored in more than one column) into a data file in which those measurements are organized into separate rows of a single column.

In this section we will build a multilevel data set using each of the five primary commands. The data set we use here (*ch2multivarML1.sav*) is based on the example used in Chapter 5 but modified to exclude missing data. The data set contains three raw test scores taken over time (*test1*, *test2*, *test3*), dichotomous indicators of teacher effectiveness (*effective*) and gender (*female*), a continuous variable capturing the number of Advanced Placement courses a student has taken (*courses*), and a continuous measure of family socioeconomic status (*ses*). There is also an identifier for students (*id*) and for the schools in which they are enrolled (*nschcode*). The descriptive statistics in Table 2.1 show that there are 8,335 records in the data set. Each record represents a single student. Figure 2.4 displays a partial view of the data structure.

Recode: Creating a New Variable Through Recoding

Our first task will be to create a new categorical SES variable by recoding *ses* into a variable called *ses4cat* (suggesting that we are going to recode this into a four-category variable). We will use three somewhat arbitrary cut points to create four categories for our recoded variable: −.5180, .0250, and .6130 (these actually represent the 25th, 50th, and 75th percentiles, respectively).

TABLE 2.1 Descriptive Statistics

	N	Minimum	Maximum	Mean	Std. Deviation
Id	8335	1	8670	4308.35	2510.578
nschcode	8335	1	525	261.98	152.817
test1	8335	24.35	69.25	47.6438	6.32465
test2	8335	27.48	74.78	52.3792	7.78136
test3	8335	26.96	79.72	57.1085	9.44951
effective	8335	.00	1.00	.5622	.49614
courses	8335	.00	4.00	.7481	.79013
female	8335	0	1	.51	.500
ses	8335	−2.41	1.87	.0333	.78389
Valid *N* (listwise)	8335				

	id	nschcode	test1	test2	test3	effective	cours...	female	ses
1	1	1	49.66	50.09	54.72	.00	.00	1	.59
2	2	1	47.92	58.26	64.33	.00	.00	1	.30
3	3	1	49.12	50.63	55.74	.00	.00	1	-.54
4	4	1	38.77	50.93	46.12	.00	.00	0	-.85
5	5	1	47.54	51.53	60.90	1.00	1.00	0	.00
6	6	1	41.74	48.82	54.55	1.00	2.00	0	-.11
7	7	1	32.83	42.43	48.73	.00	.00	0	-.33
8	8	1	55.91	56.36	60.91	.00	.00	1	-.89
9	9	1	52.93	63.75	68.37	.00	.00	0	.21
10	10	1	39.47	42.30	44.15	.00	.00	1	-.34
11	11	1	42.69	52.43	56.36	.00	.00	0	-.17
12	12	1	48.64	58.98	62.17	.00	.00	1	-1.07
13	13	2	47.54	51.53	59.26	1.00	1.00	0	-.10
14	14	2	46.83	53.70	52.09	.00	.00	0	1.28
15	15	2	45.89	52.95	56.16	.00	.00	0	1.06
16	16	2	47.54	51.53	58.06	1.00	1.00	0	.80
17	17	2	34.11	51.72	43.65	.00	.00	0	.73
18	18	2	47.54	51.53	60.87	1.00	1.00	0	.13
19	19	2	40.04	35.03	34.99	.00	.00	0	.68
20	20	2	36.94	43.72	48.66	.00	.00	0	.92

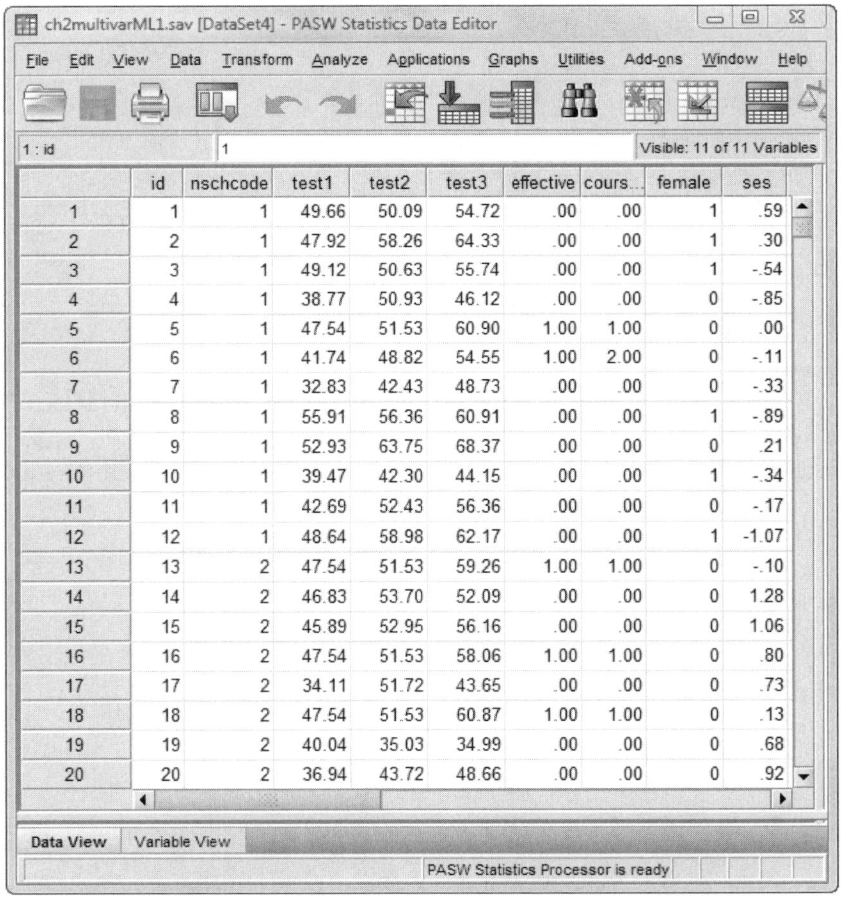

FIGURE 2.4 Horizontal data matrix.

Launch the SPSS* application program and select the data file *ch2multivarML1.sav*.

1. Go to the toolbar and select TRANSFORM, RECODE INTO DIFFERENT VARIABLES.

This command will open the *Recode into Different Variables* dialog box.

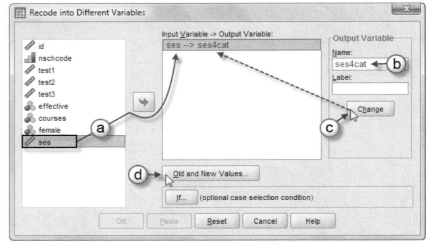

2a. The *Recode into Different Variables* enables creating a new variable using a variable from the current data set. First, click to select *ses* from the left column, then click the right-arrow button to move the variable into the *Input Variable -->Output Variable* box.

b. Now enter the new variable name by typing *ses4cat* into the *Output Variable Name* box.

c. Then click the CHANGE button, which will add *ses4cat* and complete the RECODE command for *ses -->ses4cat*.

d. Click the OLD AND NEW VALUES button, which will then display the *Recode into Different Variables: Old and New Values* screen.

---

* At the time the artwork was submitted SPSS was called PASW, so all SPSS screenshots refer to the program as PASW.

3a. The *Recode into Different Variables: Old and New Values* screen displays multiple options. To define the first cut point (-.5180), click to select the option *Range, LOWEST through value*.

b. Now enter the value -.5180.

c. Next, enter 1 as the *New Value*.

d. Then click the ADD button which will place the first range command *Lowest thru -.5180 -->1* into the *Old -->New* box.

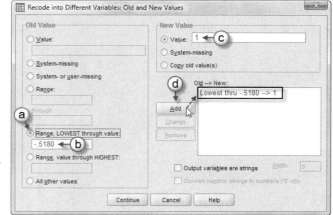

e. To enter the second range of values first click the *Range* option.

f. Now enter the low value of -.5181 then the upper value limit of .0250.

g. Next, enter 2 as the *New Value*.

h. Then click the ADD button which will place the first range command *-.5180 thru .0250 -->2* into the *Old -->New* box.

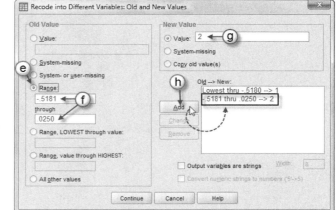

i. The third value also uses a range of values but since the *Range* option was selected previously, only the values need to be entered. First, enter .0251 then .6130.

j. Next, enter 3 as the *New Value*.

k. Then click the ADD button which will place the range command *-.5180 thru .0250 -->2* in the *Old -->New* box.

1. To define the final cutpoint value click to select the *Range, value through HIGHEST* option.
m. Now enter the value .6131.
n. Next, enter 4 as the *New Value*.
o. Then click the ADD button which will place the range command *.6131 thru Highest -->4* into the *Old-->New* box.

Click the CONTINUE button to return to the *Recode into Different Variables* main dialog box.

4. Click the OK button to generate the recoded variable *ses4cat* and corresponding values.

5. The new variable *ses4cat* with its recoded categorical scores will be found in the last column of the data window.

You may also verify the raw *ses* scores conform to the categories defined through the RECODE process.

	id	nschcode	test1	test2	test3	effective	cours...	female	ses	ses4cat
1	1	1	49.66	50.09	54.72	.00	.00	1	.59	3.00
2	2	1	47.92	58.26	64.33	.00	.00	1	.30	3.00
3	3	1	49.12	50.63	55.74	.00	.00	1	-.54	1.00
4	4	1	38.77	50.93	46.12	.00	.00	0	-.85	1.00
5	5	1	47.54	51.53	60.90	1.00	1.00	0	.00	2.00
6	6	1	41.74	48.82	54.55	1.00	2.00	0	-.11	2.00
7	7	1	32.83	42.43	48.73	.00	.00	0	-.33	2.00
8	8	1	55.91	56.36	60.91	.00	.00	1	-.89	1.00
9	9	1	52.93	63.75	68.37	.00	.00	0	.21	3.00
10	10	1	39.47	42.30	44.15	.00	.00	1	-.34	2.00
11	11	1	42.69	52.43	56.36	.00	.00	0	-.17	2.00

Note: The asterisk displayed next to the filename at the top of the display window is a reminder that the original file has been changed. If you wish to save the modifications made here and the following examples, go to the toolbar and select FILE, SAVE at the conclusion of each tutorial section.

Compute: Creating a New Variable That is a Function of Some Other Variable

Suppose that we wanted to create a variable that was a summary of the three existing test scores. Using the TRANSFORM > COMPUTE VARIABLE menu command, we call up the *Compute Variable* dialog box.

Continue using the *ch2multivarML1.sav* data file.

1. Go to the toolbar and select TRANSFORM, COMPUTE VARIABLE.

This command will open the *Compute Variable* dialog box.

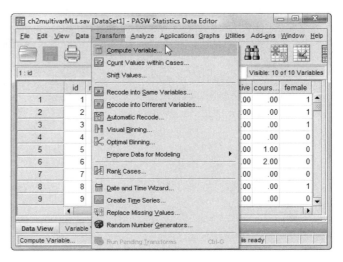

2a. Enter *testmean* as the *Target Variable*.
 b. Scroll down the *Function group* list to locate then click to select the *Statistical* group, which displays assorted statistical *Functions and Special Variables*.
 c. Click to select the *Mean* function then click the up-arrow button, which will place it in the *Numeric Expression* box formatted as: MEAN(?,?). The question marks indicate the placement for a variable.
 d. The mean will be computed from three variables: *test1*, *test2*, and *test3*. To build the corresponding numeric expression, click *test1* then click the right arrow button to place the variable in the box. Note that a comma must appear following the variable: MEAN(test1,?).

e. Continue to build the numeric expression by next clicking *test2* then the right arrow button to move the variable into the box: MEAN(test1,test2,?).

f. Complete the numeric expression by clicking *test3* then the right arrow button to move the variable into the box: MEAN(test1,test2,test3).

Click the OK button to perform the function.

3. Scroll across the columns and the new variable *testmean* with its computed mean from the three test scores is found in the last column of the data window.

You may also verify the raw *testmean* values represent the average of the three test scores for each individual in the data set.

Although we have created two new variables using the RECODE and COMPUTE commands, our data file is still strictly an individual-level (Level 1) file. More specifically, aside from the school id (*nschcode*), we do not have any variables that are school specific and therefore do not have anything to analyze at Level 2. Typically, data from other sources would be brought in and merged with our Level 1 file. If we had information about the schools these students attend (e.g., public or private control, etc.), we could very easily merge those data with the individual-level file with which we have been working.

Match Files: Combining Data From Separate SPSS Files

The MATCH FILES command allows us to combine data from different sources. To demonstrate one use of this command we will use the existing Level 1 file we have been working with. MATCH FILES can combine data in two general ways: by adding variables to the existing data set or by adding cases to the data set. We will limit our interest here to the addition of variables that are found in a separate data set. For our example, we are going to show how to merge a file containing school-level information with our existing file containing student level data. We want to add information about the frequency of Advanced Placement testing at each school. The file containing this information (*apexams.sav*) has two variables in it. The first is a school identifier that is the same as the school identifier used in our Level 1 data file (*nschcode*). The second variable is named apexams. It is a ratio of the number of Advanced Placement exams taken by students at the school to the total number of students in the 12th grade at the school. While our student-level (Level 1) file contains 8,335 observations (i.e., the number of students), the school-level (Level 2) file contains 525 observations representing the schools that the 8,335 students attend. Consider the contents of Table 2.2 and Table 2.3. The Level 1 file will be the target for the data contained in the Level 2 (*apexams.sav*) file; that is, we are going to merge the data from the Level 2 file onto the records in the Level 1 file.

TABLE 2.2   Descriptive Statistics

	N	Minimum	Maximum	Mean	Std. Deviation
id	8335	1	8670	4308.35	2510.578
nschcode	8335	1	525	261.98	152.817
test1	8335	24.35	69.25	47.6438	6.32465
test2	8335	27.48	74.78	52.3792	7.78136
test3	8335	26.96	79.72	57.1085	9.44951
effective	8335	.00	1.00	.5622	.49614
courses	8335	.00	4.00	.7481	.79013
female	8335	0	1	.51	.500
ses	8335	−2.41	1.87	.0333	.78389
Valid N (listwise)	8335				

TABLE 2.3   Descriptive Statistics

	N	Minimum	Maximum	Mean	Std. Deviation
nschcode	525	1	525	263.00	151.699
apexams	525	.00	.80	.1636	.13311
Valid N (listwise)	525				

Because this is not a one-to-one match (i.e., there are not the same number of records in each file), we will have to identify a "key" to be used to match the data from the schools to the data from the students. Notice that matching student data to the schools would require aggregating student-level variables because there are fewer schools than students in this case. We will use the single common identifier variable, *nschcode*, which represents the schools in both files. Both data sets will need to be sorted on the key variable. This can be accomplished by opening each data set and choosing the DATA > SORT CASES menu and dialog box. For each file, the sort should be on the variable *nschcode*, and each file needs to be saved after sorting.

This example will combine data from two files: *ch2multivarML1.sav* (primary file) and *apexams.sav* (secondary file). When combining data from separate files we recommend that the cases are sorted before you begin this procedure to prevent interruption of the workflow.

If you are continuing from the prior section concerning the COMPUTE function, the *ch2multivarML1.sav* file is already open. If not, locate and open the data file.

1. Go to the toolbar and select DATA, SORT CASES.

This command will open the *Sort Cases* dialog box.

2a. Within the *Sort Cases* dialog box, select *nschcode* from the left column, then click the right-arrow button to transfer the variable into the *Sort by* box.
  b. The default *Sort Order setting* is *Ascending* (low to high), which we will retain.

Click the OK button to begin sorting the cases. The next step is to sort the cases for the secondary file, *apexams.sav*.

3. Begin by opening the secondary file (*apexams.sav*) while keeping the *ch2multivarML1.sav* file open.

Go to the toolbar and select FILE, OPEN, DATA.

This command will then display the *Open Data* screen.

4a. Locate and click to select the data file (*apexams.sav*).
  b. Then click the OPEN button.

5. With the data file *apexams.sav* opened, go to the toolbar and select DATA, SORT CASES.

This command will open the *Sort Cases* dialog box.

6a. Within the *Sort Cases* dialog box, select *nschcode* from the left column, then click the right-arrow button to transfer the variable into the *Sort by* box.
   b. The default setting for sorting is the *Ascending* order, which we will retain.

Click the OK button to begin sorting the cases.

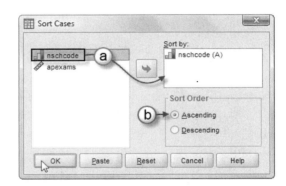

7. Once the files are sorted then merging may begin.

Return to the primary data file (*ch2multivarML1.sav*). Then go to the toolbar and select DATA, MERGE FILES, ADD VARIABLES. This command will open the *Add Variables* dialog box.

8. Since the data file *apexams.sav* is an opened file, the option *An open dataset* is preselected and displays the file name in the box below. If *apexams.sav* had not been opened, the option *An external SPSS Statistics data file* would have been preselected instead, requiring you to locate and identify the file using the *Browse* button.

Now click to select *apexams.sav(DataSet2)* then click the CONTINUE button to access the *Add Variables from* screen.

9a. Within the *Add Variables from* display screen, click to select *nschcode(+)* from the *Excluded Variables* box. This action will activate the *Match cases on key variables in sorted titles* option below, enabling the box to be checked.

  b. Click to select the *Non-active dataset is keyed table* option.

Note: A "keyed" table or table lookup file is a file that contains data for each case that can be applied to numerous cases in another data file.

  c. Now click the right-arrow button to move *nschcode* into the *Key Variables* box.

Click the OK button to process this function.

10. A warning to presort the data appears but may be disregarded since the data from both files had been sorted using the *nschcode* variable at the outset.

Click the OK button.

11. Scroll across the columns and the merged variable *apexams* taken from the *apexams.sav* data file is found in the last column of the *ch2multivarML1.sav* data window.

	test3	effective	courses	female	ses	ses4cat	testmean	apexams
1	54.72	.00	.00	1	.59	3.00	51.49	.08
2	64.33	.00	.00	1	.30	3.00	56.84	.08
3	55.74	.00	.00	1	-.54	1.00	51.83	.08
4	46.12	.00	.00	0	-.85	1.00	45.27	.08
5	60.90	1.00	1.00	0	.00	2.00	53.32	.08
6	54.55	1.00	2.00	0	-.11	2.00	48.37	.08
7	48.73	.00	.00	0	-.33	2.00	41.33	.08
8	60.91	.00	.00	1	-.89	1.00	57.73	.08
9	68.37	.00	.00	0	.21	3.00	61.68	.08
10	44.15	.00	.00	1	-.34	2.00	41.97	.08
11	56.36	.00	.00	0	-.17	2.00	50.49	.08

Once the merge is complete the new variable, *apexams*, will appear in the active data set window as shown in Figure 2.5. Notice that while the individual-level variables vary across all cases within the window, the new school-level variable, *aprexams*, is constant within each school (compare *nschcode* 4 with *nschcode* 5 in Figure 2.5).

Descriptive statistics on the data set will now show a value for *apexams* for each of the 8,335 Level 1 observations (Table 2.4). Notice that the descriptive statistics provide no hint of the lack of variance within each *nschcode* for the *apexams* variable. It now looks like an individual-level variable.

	id	nschcode	test1	test2	test3	effective	courses	female	ses	ses4cat	testmean	apexams
51	51	4	48.07	52.33	40.29	.00	.00	1	.90	4.00	46.90	.18
52	52	4	63.14	59.53	59.92	.00	.00	1	1.24	4.00	60.86	.18
53	53	4	48.14	54.19	60.15	.00	.00	1	.27	3.00	54.16	.18
54	54	4	48.16	55.26	58.39	.00	.00	1	.87	4.00	53.94	.18
55	55	4	63.12	67.70	74.36	1.00	2.00	1	.72	4.00	68.39	.18
56	56	4	48.23	50.12	48.41	.00	.00	1	.56	3.00	48.92	.18
57	57	4	55.85	52.96	52.41	.00	.00	1	.45	3.00	53.74	.18
58	58	4	49.45	54.17	52.31	.00	.00	1	1.12	4.00	51.98	.18
59	59	4	39.52	42.13	49.77	1.00	2.00	1	1.46	4.00	43.81	.18
60	60	4	48.24	56.77	59.24	.00	.00	1	.74	4.00	54.75	.18
61	61	5	47.63	51.70	56.88	1.00	1.00	1	-1.50	1.00	52.07	.41
62	62	5	42.50	49.41	51.18	.00	.00	0	.58	3.00	47.70	.41
63	63	5	47.63	51.70	69.95	1.00	1.00	1	-.32	2.00	56.43	.41
64	64	5	62.91	61.95	59.46	1.00	2.00	1	-.17	2.00	61.44	.41
65	65	5	59.77	70.32	62.56	1.00	2.00	1	-.12	2.00	64.22	.41

FIGURE 2.5 Data matrix after performing the MATCH FILES function.

TABLE 2.4   Descriptive Statistics

	N	Minimum	Maximum	Mean	Std. Deviation
id	8335	1	8670	4308.35	2510.578
nschcode	8335	1	525	261.98	152.817
test1	8335	24.35	69.25	47.6438	6.32465
test2	8335	27.48	74.78	52.3792	7.78136
test3	8335	26.96	79.72	57.1085	9.44951
effective	8335	.00	1.00	.5622	.49614
courses	8335	.00	4.00	.7481	.79013
female	8335	0	1	.51	.500
ses	8335	−2.41	1.87	.0333	.78389
apexams	8335	.00	.80	.1659	.12952
Valid N (listwise)	8335				

Aggregate: Collapsing Data Within Level 2 Units

Many times the analyst will be interested in creating group-level measures by aggregating the characteristics of individuals within each group. One candidate variable might be student socioeconomic status (*ses*). Another might be gender (*female*; aggregating this to the mean will yield the proportion of students at Level 1 who are female). In this section we will use the AGGREGATE command to create both of these variables.

The objective in this instance is to take the within school means of the variables *female* and *ses*. This will yield the proportion of females in the sample for each school and the average socioeconomic status of students in the sample for each school.

If you are continuing from the prior section concerning the *Merge Files* function, the *ch2multivarML1.sav* file is already open. If not, locate and open the data file.

1. Go to the toolbar and select DATA, AGGREGATE.

This command will open the *Aggregate Data* dialog box.

2a. Click to select *nschcode* from the left column of the *Aggregate Data* dialog box then click the right arrow button to move the variable into the *Break Variable(s)* box.

b. Now click to select *female* and *ses* from the left column, then click the right-arrow button to move the variables into the *Summaries of Variable(s)* box.

Note: SPSS uses MEAN as the default function, which will be used for this example. Other functions besides MEAN are also available to generate a variety of aggregated data.

c. Click the option *Add aggregated variables to active dataset*, which will add the two variables *female_mean* and *ses_mean* directly into the active Level 1 data set.

Note: Besides the *Add aggregated variables to the active dataset* option we could also choose two other options: *Create a new dataset containing only the aggregated variables* or *Write a new data file containing only the aggregated variables*. The latter choices would require us to use the MATCH FILES routine to merge the new aggregated variables back onto the individual-level data set. Choosing to have the variables written straight to the active dataset is much more efficient and reduces the risk of errors.

Click the OK button to run the aggregation and merge the new variables to the student-level data set (shown in the active data window).

3. Scroll across the columns and the new aggregated variables *female_mean* and *ses_mean* appear in the last two columns of the *ch2multivarML1.sav* data window.

Notice that school 4 (*nschcode* = 4) has an all female sample (*female_mean* = 1.00) while less than one-half of the school 5 sample was female (*female_mean* = .47). The SES average for school 4 was also higher than the average for school 5 (.82 vs. -.39, respectively).

The RECODE, COMPUTE, MATCH FILES, and AGGREGATE commands provide all the tools necessary for structuring our SPSS files for a multilevel analysis within SPSS Mixed. We will expand on some of the commands in subsequent sections to create variables that can be very useful in multilevel analyses. Before turning our attention to those additional examples, however, we introduce a different data structure that enables multivariate analyses and analyses of change over time using the multilevel model through SPSS Mixed.

Varstocases: Vertical Versus Horizontal Data Structures

The data sets we created in the previous sections are arranged horizontally; that is, each observation is contained on a single row with variables arrayed across the columns. In the horizontal data sets we have the variables arranged in such a way the lower-level units can be seen as nested within high-level units (e.g., students within schools where student values vary within and between schools, while school-level values vary only between schools).

In multivariate and time-varying models we reconceptualize the nesting and deal with vertical rather than horizontal data structures. Instead of students being our Level 1 unit of analysis, we might nest time periods or indicator variables within students who could, in turn, be nested within schools. So our time periods or indicator variables become Level 1, students become Level 2, and schools become Level 3. In terms of the data structure, what this means is that each individual (i.e., students to continue our example) will have multiple records. If there are three occasions of interest, each student will have three records, one for each occasion. Similarly, if we are interested in defining a latent variable with five indicators, each student would have five records. So if we have a data set with 1,000 students and we are interested in looking at change, say in test scores, over 3 occasions, our data set will have 3 occasions × 1,000 students = 3000 records. Using the latent variable example, if we had 1,000 students and 5 indicators, we would have 5,000 records in the data set. This is quite in contrast to the univariate outcome models in which individuals are nested in successively higher organizational levels. In those models, the individual defines Level 1 of the analysis, and there are as many records as there are individuals.

Rearranging the data to accommodate the change and multivariate models is quite straightforward. Let's refresh our memory of the data set we have been using. Note that in the data view in Figure 2.6 there is a single record for each student, and we have three test scores across successive time periods.

Our objective is to create three records for each student, each representing a distinct time point for each individual in the sample. In other words, we are going to nest these three testing occasions within each student (students will still be nested within their schools). To accomplish this we will use the VARSTOCASES routine that is contained in the SPSS *Restructure Data Wizard*.

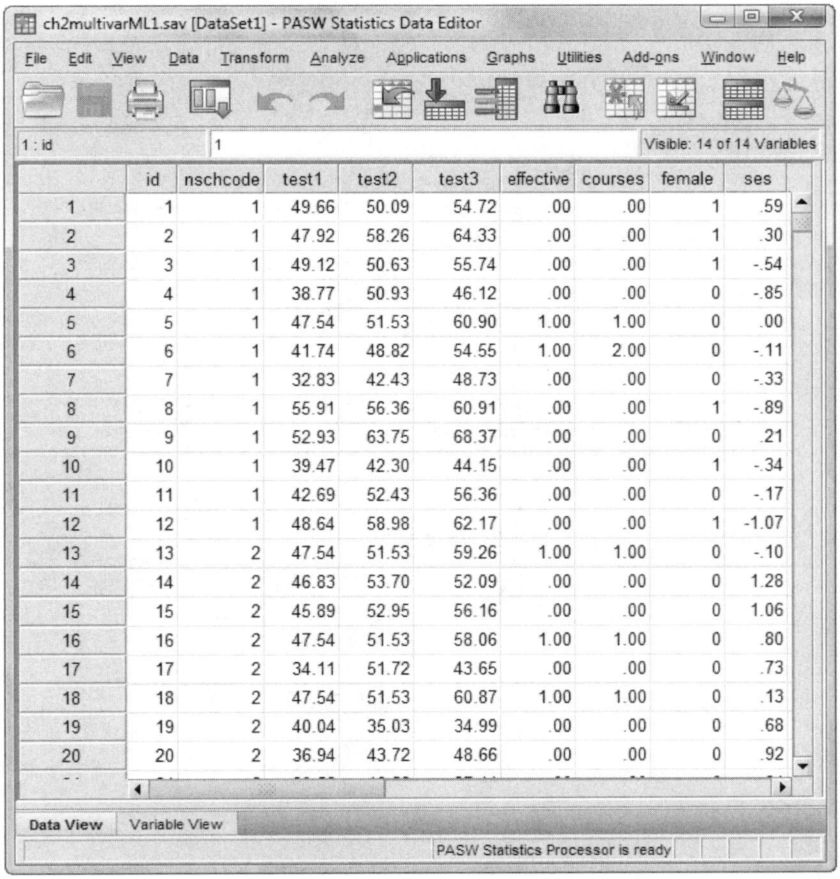

FIGURE 2.6 Horizontal data matrix.

If you are continuing from the prior section concerning the MERGE FILES function, the *ch2multivarML1.sav* file is already open. If not, locate and open the data file.

1. Go to the toolbar and select DATA, RESTRUCTURE.

Note: If you're prompted to save the file before proceeding, you may save it or elect not to do so.

This command will open the *Welcome to the Restructure Data Wizard* dialog box.

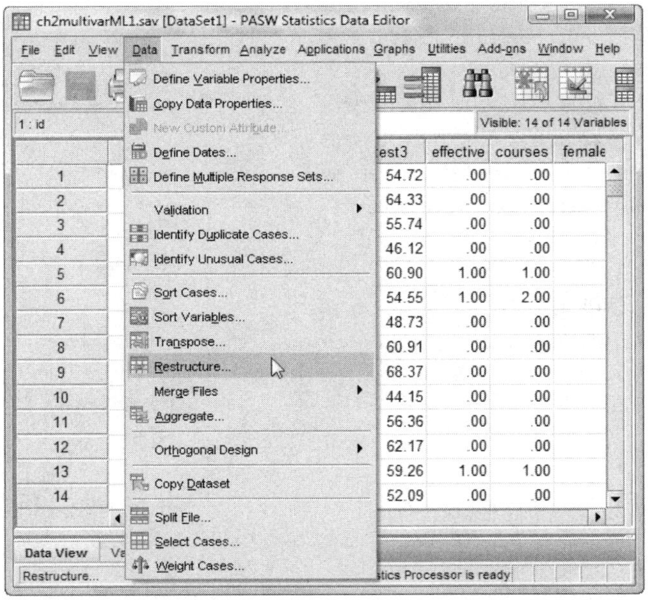

2. The *Restructure Data Wizard* presents three options: *Restructure selected variables into cases*, *restructure selected cases into variables*, and *transpose all data*.

For this situation we want to treat the three test variables (*test1, test2, test3*) as a single grouped variable so we will use the default setting: *Restructure selected variables into cases*.

Click the NEXT button to go to the *Variables to Cases* screen.

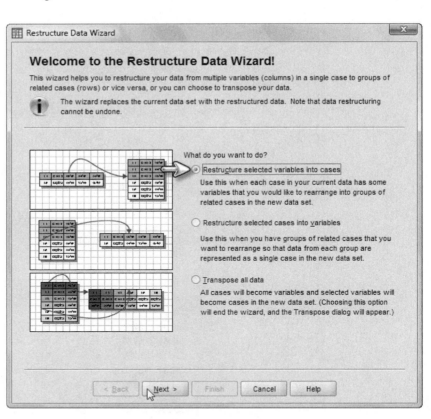

3. The *Variables to Cases: Number of Variable Groups* display screen allows defining the number of variable groups to create in the new data file.

In this case, the three tests (*test1, test2, test3*) are to be treated as a single group so the default setting of *One* will be used.

Click the NEXT button to continue to the next screen.

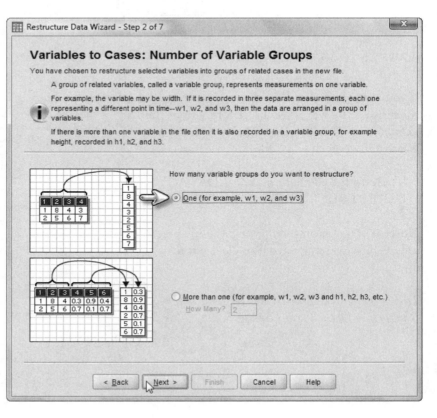

4. The *Variables to Cases: Select Variables* allows defining the variables for the new data. This includes specifying a new group ID (Case Group Identification), the variables to define the transposition (Variables to be Transposed), and the variables to include with each new record (Fixed Variables).

a. Begin by entering *Rid* (recoded ID) as the *Case Group Identifier Name.*

b. Enter *test* as the *Target Variable.*

c. Click to select *test1, test2,* and *test3* from the left column, then click the right-arrow button to move the variables into

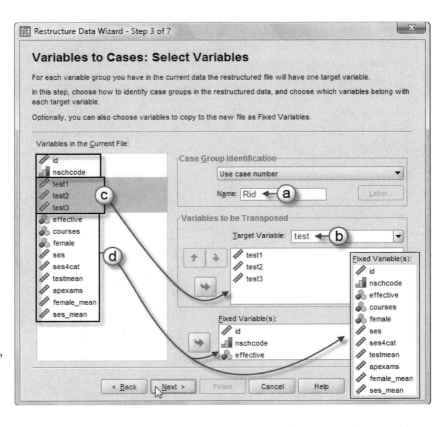

the *Variables to be Transposed* box. The three variables will be combined to form a single variable (*test*) that is related to each record (row).

d. Click to select all the remaining variables (excluding *test1, test2,* and *test3*) from the left column, then click the right-arrow button to move them into the *Fixed Variable(s)* box. (Refer to the *Fixed Variables* boxed insert.) These variables will then be appended to each of the new rows in the data set.

Click the NEXT button to continue to the *Variables to Cases: Create Index Variables* screen.

5. *The Variables to Cases: Create Index Variables* allows for creating one or more index variables.

In this case we want to create one indexed variable encompassing the "timing" of each test. Since *One* is the default option, click the NEXT button to continue to the *Variables to Cases: Create One Index Variable* screen.

Restructure Data Wizard - Step 4 of 7

Variables to Cases: Create Index Variables

In the current data, values for a variable group appear in a single case in multiple variables. For example, a single case contains the values for w1, w2, and w3.

In the new data, values for a variable group will appear in multiple cases in a single variable. For example, there will be three cases, one each for w1, w2, and w3.

An index is a new variable that identifies the group of new cases that was created from the original case. For example, an index named "w" would have the values 1, 2, and 3.

How many index variables do you want to create?

⊙ One
Use this when a variable group records the effects of a single factor, treatment or condition.

○ More than one   How many? 2
Use this when a variable group records the effects of more than one factor, treatment or condition.

○ None
Use this if index information is stored in one of the sets of variables to be transposed.

[< Back] [Next >] [Finish] [Cancel] [Help]

6. Further information may be specified for the one indexed variable.
   a. *Sequential numbers* is the default setting, which will be retained for this example.
   b. The variable name may be changed by clicking on *Index1* then changing it to *time*.

Click the FINISH button to indicate no further changes will be made.

Restructure Data Wizard - Step 5 of 7

Variables to Cases: Create One Index Variable

You have chosen to create one index variable. The variable's values can be sequential numbers or the names of variables in a group.

In the table you can specify the name and label for the index variable.

What kind of index values?

(a) ⊙ Sequential numbers
     Index Values: 1, 2, 3

○ Variable names
     Index Values: test1, test2, test3

Edit the Index Variable Name and Label:

	Name	Label	Levels	Index Values
1	index1 (b)		3	1, 2, 3

Edit the Index Variable Name and Label:

	Name	Label
1	time	

[< Back] [Next >] [Finish] [Cancel] [Help]

7. After clicking the *Finish* button a message immediately appears warning that some of the original data will remain in use and that care should be administered to ensure use of the appropriate data set for subsequent analyses.

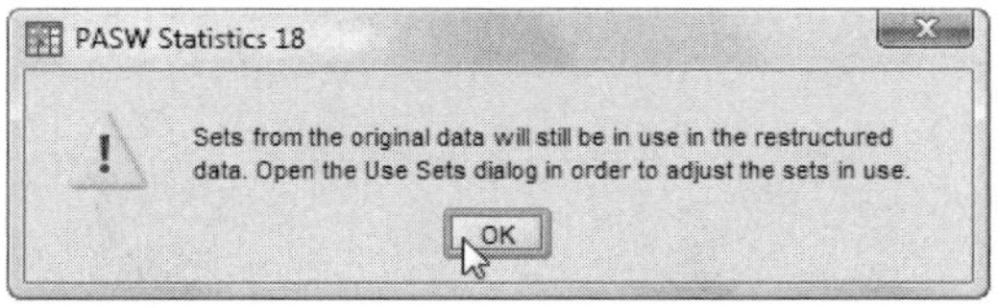

Click the OK button to proceed with generating the new data set.

8. The new data set appears, and scrolling across the columns, the *time* and *test* variables are found in the last two columns. A truncated view of the data set shows each student (as identified by *Rid* and *id*) now has three lines of data, one line for each of the three tests and time periods. A more complete picture is presented in Figure 2.7.

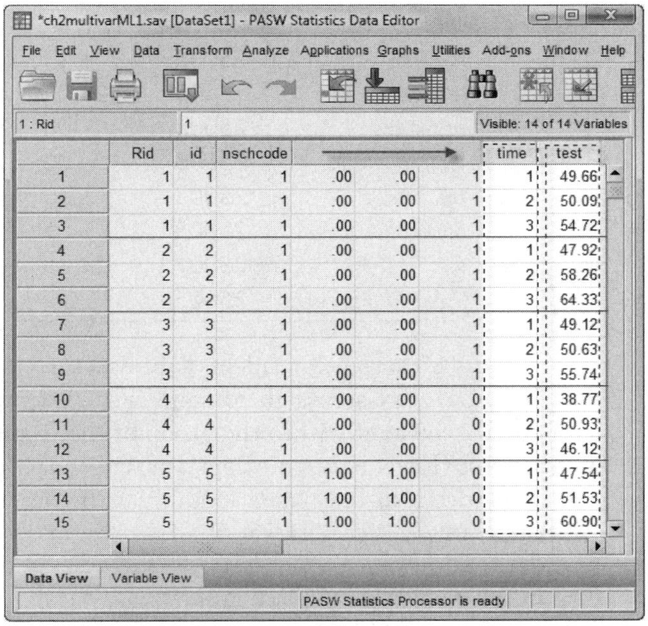

Note: Save the new data set under a different name (*ch2multivarMLvertical.sav*) to avoid overwriting the original *ch2multivarML1.sav* data file.

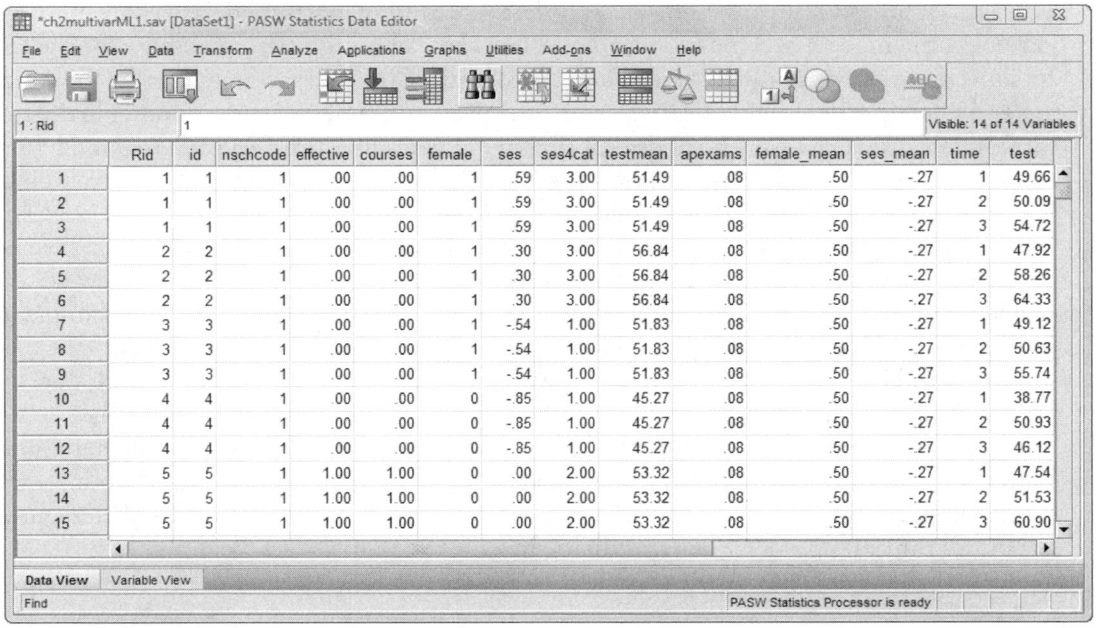

	Rid	id	nschcode	effective	courses	female	ses	ses4cat	testmean	apexams	female_mean	ses_mean	time	test
1	1	1	1	.00	.00	1	.59	3.00	51.49	.08	.50	-.27	1	49.66
2	1	1	1	.00	.00	1	.59	3.00	51.49	.08	.50	-.27	2	50.09
3	1	1	1	.00	.00	1	.59	3.00	51.49	.08	.50	-.27	3	54.72
4	2	2	1	.00	.00	1	.30	3.00	56.84	.08	.50	-.27	1	47.92
5	2	2	1	.00	.00	1	.30	3.00	56.84	.08	.50	-.27	2	58.26
6	2	2	1	.00	.00	1	.30	3.00	56.84	.08	.50	-.27	3	64.33
7	3	3	1	.00	.00	1	-.54	1.00	51.83	.08	.50	-.27	1	49.12
8	3	3	1	.00	.00	1	-.54	1.00	51.83	.08	.50	-.27	2	50.63
9	3	3	1	.00	.00	1	-.54	1.00	51.83	.08	.50	-.27	3	55.74
10	4	4	1	.00	.00	0	-.85	1.00	45.27	.08	.50	-.27	1	38.77
11	4	4	1	.00	.00	0	-.85	1.00	45.27	.08	.50	-.27	2	50.93
12	4	4	1	.00	.00	0	-.85	1.00	45.27	.08	.50	-.27	3	46.12
13	5	5	1	1.00	1.00	0	.00	2.00	53.32	.08	.50	-.27	1	47.54
14	5	5	1	1.00	1.00	0	.00	2.00	53.32	.08	.50	-.27	2	51.53
15	5	5	1	1.00	1.00	0	.00	2.00	53.32	.08	.50	-.27	3	60.90

FIGURE 2.7 Data matrix after performing the VARSTOCASES function.

TABLE 2.5 Descriptive Statistics

	N	Minimum	Maximum	Mean	Std. Deviation
Rid	25005	1	8335	4168.00	2406.155
id	25005	1	8670	4308.35	2510.477
nschcode	25005	1	525	261.98	152.811
effective	25005	.00	1.00	.5622	.49613
courses	25005	.00	4.00	.7481	.79009
female	25005	0	1	.51	.500
ses	25005	−2.41	1.87	.0333	.78386
ses4cat	25005	1.00	4.00	2.4973	1.11714
testmean	25005	28.03	74.58	52.3772	6.96450
apexams	25005	.00	.80	.1659	.12951
female_mean	25005	.00	1.00	.5052	.15325
ses_mean	25005	−1.30	1.42	.0333	.50002
time	25005	1	3	2.00	.817
test	25005	24.35	79.72	52.3772	8.84348
Valid N (listwise)	25005				

Notice that each student now has three lines of data—one for each test. The test scores (Level 1) vary across all respondents, student characteristics vary across all students (Level 2) but are constant within the group of three test scores, and school characteristics vary across all schools (Level 3) but are constant within the group of students attending each school.

Notice also that when looking at the descriptive statistics for the new data set (Table 2.5), there are 25,005 observations. The original data set had 8,335 observations. From our earlier description we can see that 8,335 (students) multiplied by 3 (test scores) equals 25,005 records in the new data set.

Using "Rank" to Recode the Level 1 or Level 2 Data for Nested Models

From this it becomes apparent how quickly data sets can expand as models become more complicated. As the models become more complicated, the computing time necessary for the solution to converge within each level can become substantial. This is especially true in the multivariate and change models where variables or time periods are nested within individuals. Leyland (2004) notes one can save a great deal of the time it takes to estimate a proposed model by reindexing the Level 1 (and, in some cases, the Level 2) identifiers within each school. Reindexing the individual-level data in these models can yield significant savings in run time, and, in some cases, may make a difference in whether the model can even be estimated within the confines of the computer's available memory. The objective of reindexing is to create a new set of individual identifiers that are numbered only with reference to each group. So, for example, the 10 individuals in Group 1 would be numbered from 1 to 10 (assuming there were only 10 in the group), and the 14 individuals in Group 2 would be numbered from 1 through 14, and so forth (1, 2, … , n).

Situations in which this may prove beneficial will be identified in later chapters. For now, however, we want to introduce the steps involved. This reindexing can be easily accomplished using the SPSS RANK command. From the TRANSFORM > RANK CASES menu within SPSS, we can call up the *Rank Cases* dialog box.

Creating an Identifier Variable

Creating identification variables is straightforward in SPSS. We will first show how to generate an ID variable for each case. This can be useful in those instances when an identifier is not found in the file being used. For this first example we will use the *ch2level–1data.sav* we introduced at the beginning of this chapter (see Figure 2.1). You may recall that this data set is single level and cross-sectional with 6,871 observations. We have removed the id variable that appeared in the version of the data set we used earlier. Our first task will be to recreate an individual-level identifier using the COMPUTE command.

Creating an Individual-Level Identifier Using Compute

Continue using the *ch2multivarMLvertical.sav* data set, which was created in the prior section (VARSTOCASES).

1. Begin by deleting the current *id* variable from the data set.
   a. Click on the *Variable View* tab, which displays the variables in the data set.
   b. To delete *id*, first locate and click to select the row (2). Right-click your mouse to display the submenu and select *Clear*, which will delete the variable. An alternative method to deleting the variable is to go to the toolbar and select EDIT, CLEAR.

2. After removing *id* from the data set, go to the SPSS toolbar and select TRANSFORM, COMPUTE VARIABLE.

This command will open the *Compute Variable* dialog box.

3a. Enter *id* as the *Target Variable*.

b. Within the *Function group* list, click to select *All*, which will display assorted functions in the *Functions and Special Variables* box.

c. Click to select the *$Casenum* function then click the up-arrow button, which will place the term into the *Numeric Expression* box.

Click the OK button to perform the function.

4. Scroll across the columns and the new variable *id* is found in the last column of the data window and corresponds to the case number (or row number) for each case.

Note: The decimal place-setting may be adjusted by clicking on the *Variable View* tab and changing the number to the desired setting (i.e., 0).

Once a Level 1 identifier exists it is quite easy to create a variety of different within-group identifiers. These within-group identifiers will become very important in later chapters where we use more complex models. Using the TRANSFORM > RANK CASES commands from the SPSS menu we will now create another identifier assigning a sequential id variable *Rid* within each group. The *Rid* variable will range from 1 through *n* within each Level 2 unit.

Creating a Group-Level Identifier Using Rank Cases

1. Begin by deleting the current *Rid* variable from the data set. Click on the *Variable View* tab, which displays the variables in the data set. To delete *Rid*, first locate the variable's row, then click to select the corresponding row (1). You may then delete *Rid* by one of two methods:

a. Right-click your mouse to display the submenu then select *Clear*, which will delete the variable, or

b. Go to the toolbar and select EDIT, then CLEAR.

2. After removing *Rid* from the data set, go to the SPSS toolbar and select TRANSFORM, RANK CASES.

This command will open the *Rank Cases* dialog box.

3a. Click to select the Level 1 identifier (*id*) from the left column, then click the right-arrow button to move it into the *Variable(s)* box.

b. Next click to select group identifier (*nschcode*) from the left column, then click the right-arrow button to move the variable into the *By* box.

c. In the *Assign Rank 1 to* section, confirm that *Smallest value* (default setting) is selected.

d. Click the RANK TYPES button, which will open the *Rank Cases: Type* dialog box.

e. *Rank* is the default setting, so click the CONTINUE button to close the dialog box.

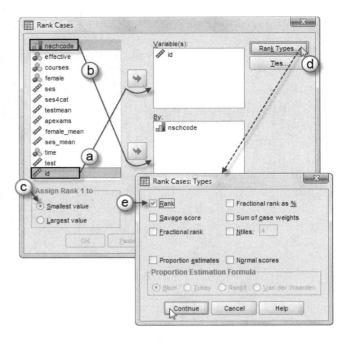

4a. Now click the TIES button, which will open the *Rank Cases: Ties* dialog box.

b. Among the options listed for *Rank Assigned to ties*, click to select *Sequential ranks to unique values*. The option must be selected to ensure that each person is assigned an identifier within each unit. Then click the CONTINUE button to close the box.

Now click the OK button to create the *Rid* Level 1 group identifier.

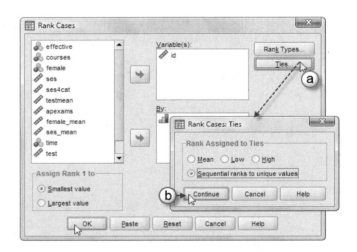

5. Scroll across the columns and the *Rid*
Level 1 group identifier variable is located
in the last column of the data window.

Note that each Level 2 unit (*nschcode*) will have
its own sequence of *Rid* beginning with 1.

Finally, we will take this one step further by creating a new within-group id (*Rid*) variable for
the multivariate data set shown in *ch2multivarML2.sav* (see Figure 2.7).

Creating a Within-Group-Level Identifier Using Rank Cases

1. Begin by deleting the current *Rid* variable
from the data set. Click on the *Variable
View* tab, which displays the variables in
the data set. To delete *Rid*, first locate
the variable's row then click to select the
corresponding row (1). You may then
delete *Rid* by one of two methods:
   a. Right-click your mouse to display the
      submenu, then select *Clear*, which will
      delete the variable, or
   b. Go to the toolbar and select EDIT
      then CLEAR.

2. After removing *Rid* from the data set, go to the SPSS toolbar and select TRANSFORM, RANK CASES.

This command will open the *Rank Cases* dialog box.

3. The default settings from the prior example display *id* within the *Variable(s)* box and *nschcode* in the *By* box.

In the previous example we selected only one group identifier, *schcode*. Since the data in the multivariate example are vertically arranged (that is, there are multiple records for each individual), we need to generate sequential, within-group identifiers for each person, constant across the three time points (recall that we had three time points nested within each person).

We will now add the other grouping variable *time* to the *By* box. This will generate a sequential identifier for each person across the three time periods within each group.

The settings for *Rank Types* and *Ties* remain the same as the prior example so skip over these buttons and click OK.

4. Scroll across the columns and the *Rid* variable is shown in the last column of the data viewer.

Notice that the *Rid* variable reflects the number of observations in the data set but not the number of individuals.

	nschcode	effective	courses				Rid
1	1	.00	.00	1	.59	3.00	1.000
2	1	.00	.00	1	.59	3.00	1.000
3	1	.00	.00	1	.59	3.00	1.000
4	1	.00	.00	1	.30	3.00	2.000
5	1	.00	.00	1	.30	3.00	2.000
6	1	.00	.00	1	.30	3.00	2.000
7	1	.00	.00	1	-.54	1.00	3.000
8	1	.00	.00	1	-.54	1.00	3.000
9	1	.00	.00	1	-.54	1.00	3.000
10	1	.00	.00	0	-.85	1.00	4.000
11	1	.00	.00	0	-.85	1.00	4.000
12	1	.00	.00	0	-.85	1.00	4.000

ch2multivarMLvertical.sav [DataSet1] - PASW Statistics Data Editor. File Edit View Data Transform Analyze Applications Graphs Utilities Add-ons Window Help. 1: nschcode — 1. Visible: 14 of 14 Variables. Data View. Variable View. PASW Statistics Processor is ready.

In this section we have shown the primary commands necessary to create new variables, recode existing variables, merge new data onto the existing data set, create group-level aggregates from individual-level variables, and how to restructure the data set for multivariate analyses using SPSS Mixed. In the sections that follow, we use these data management procedures to offer instruction on the creation of new variables that will be needed for the analyses presented in subsequent chapters.

Centering

The basic multilevel model (i.e., a random intercept model) treats the Level 1 intercept as an outcome with variance that can be explained using variables from a higher level. While we develop this model in some detail in the following chapter, we want to convey the importance of the intercept here. Consider as a starting point the traditional fixed-effect ordinary least squares (OLS) regression model using test1 as a predictor for some outcome:

$$Y_i = \beta_0 + \beta_1(test1)_i + \varepsilon_i \qquad (2.1)$$

From the earlier descriptive statistics table (Table 2.3), we know that values on *test1* range from 24.35 to 69.25 with a mean of 47.64. Recall that the intercept in a model, such as that in Equation 2.1, is the value of the outcome (Y) when the predictor (*test1* in this example) is equal to zero. When additional terms are added to the model, the interpretation generalizes to the value of the outcome (Y) when each of the predictors in the model is equal to zero. So instances where the predictor cannot be zero (such as this example with the test score), the intercept is of little substantive use. This is fine when the emphasis is on the interpretation of slopes that are constant across groups that may exist in the sample.

But imagine a scenario in which, for some reason, we did have an interest in an interpretable slope. One way to ensure a meaningful and interpretable intercept is to alter the predictor in a way that makes zero a meaningful value. This is often accomplished by "centering" the predictor on zero (or some other value). First consider the results of the OLS model specified earlier. We will use scores on *test1* to predict scores on *test3* (which has a mean of 57.11).

TABLE 2.6 Coefficients[a]

Model		Unstandardized Coefficients		Standardized Coefficients		
		B	Std. Error	Beta	t	Sig.
1	(Constant)	13.272	.620		21.414	.000
	test1	.920	.013	.616	71.351	.000

[a] Dependent Variable: test3.

TABLE 2.7 Coefficients[a]

Model		Unstandardized Coefficients		Standardized Coefficients		
		B	Std. Error	Beta	t	Sig.
1	(Constant)	57.108	.082		700.254	.000
	gmtest1	.920	.013	.616	71.351	.000

[a] Dependent Variable: test3.

From these results (Table 2.6), we can see that a 1 point increase in performance on *test1* is associated with a 0.92 point increase on *test3*. The intercept value is 13.272. With these two values one could calculate a predicted value for *test3* given knowledge of performance on *test1*. The intercept is used only to generate that predicted value for *test3* and has no real interpretative use because zero is not a valid option for *test1* performance.

By centering the *test1* variable on zero we can make the intercept more interpretable. To do this we simply subtract the mean of *test1* from the *test1* score for each student in the data set. That is

$$\left(X_{ij} - \bar{X}_{..} \right). \tag{2.2}$$

We will show how to do this in a moment. For now let us just consider the change in the OLS results (Table 2.7). Notice that the *test1* slope coefficient (and standard error) remains the same as in the previous model but that the intercept is now 57.11 or the raw mean for *test3*. So when *test1* is equal to 0 (and 0 is now the overall mean for *test1*) *test3* is equal to its overall mean. The intercept now has a useful interpretation.

Because the multilevel model treats the intercept as an outcome, as we will show in the next chapter, it is very important that the Level 1 model yield an interpretable value for β_0. Centering makes this possible and therefore is an important feature of the multilevel model. There are two types of centering that we will be concerned with throughout the workbook: grand-mean centering, such as that used in the previous example; and group-mean centering, which centers the variable on the mean of each higher level group. In the sections that follow, we demonstrate how to create these within SPSS Mixed. We further develop the rationale of each of these methods at length in subsequent chapters. Here, however, we focus on how to compute the variables that will be needed.

Grand-Mean Centering

As in our previous example, variables in a multilevel model are most frequently grand-mean centered. For example, the grand mean for *test1* is 47.64. Using COMPUTE in SPSS, one can name the new variable *gmtest1* and then compute the new variable by subtracting the grand mean of *test1* from students' scores on that variable (i.e., test1 – 47.64). This will transform the scores in terms of the grand mean of the sample. So, if a student has a *test1* score of 50.64, her new score will be 3 (50.64 – 47.64 = 3), which carries the meaning that its relative position is 3 points above the grand mean with respect to other students in the sample. Grand-mean centering results in unit-level means that have been adjusted for differences among individuals within the units. Notice that the distribution remains exactly the same when we center. The only thing that shifts is the scale itself.

Use the *ch2multivarML1.sav* data file for this section. (You may use the original data set containing 9 variables or the 14-variable data set resulting from following the previous instructional sections. For this example we will use the original 9-variable data set.)

1. Go to the toolbar and select TRANSFORM, COMPUTE VARIABLE.

This command will open the *Compute Variable* dialog box.

2a. In the *Compute Variable* display enter *gmtest1* as the *Target Variable*.
  b. Now select *test1* and click the right-arrow button to move the variable into the *Numeric Expression* box.
  c. Use the numeric keypad (or enter from your keyboard) to complete the equation: *test1 – 47.643788*.

Click the OK button to create the computed variable *gmtest1*.

3. Scroll across the columns and the computed variable *gmtest1* is found in the last column of the *ch2multivarML1.sav* data window.

A quick look at the descriptive statistics (Table 2.8) of the original *test1* variable and its grand-mean centered counterpart show that while the standard deviation remains the same, the means and ranges stay the same while the minimum and maximum values have changed. Again, this simply demonstrates that only the scale has changed and that the distribution (or variability around the mean) itself remains the same. Note that we have not standardized the variable but rather we have simply readjusted it so its mean is equal to zero.

TABLE 2.8   Descriptive Statistics

	N	Minimum	Maximum	Mean	Std. Deviation
test1	8335	24.35	69.25	47.6439	6.32466
gmtest1	8335	–23.29	21.61	.0001	6.32466
Valid N (listwise)	8335				

Group-Mean Centering

Group-mean centering of variables yields values that represent the unadjusted mean for group *j*. So rather than using the overall mean as the reference, the group mean is used instead:

$$X_{ij} - \bar{X}_{.j}. \tag{2.3}$$

Group-mean centering variables is a two-step process that first involves the aggregation of the focal variable to the group level and then follows a logic similar to that used for grand-mean centering. We will use the AGGREGATE and COMPUTE commands to accomplish this.

Continue using the *ch2multivarML1.sav* data file.

1. Go to the toolbar and select DATA, AGGREGATE.

This command opens the *Aggregate Data* dialog box.

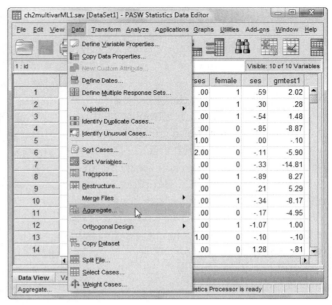

2a. Within the *Aggregate Data* dialog box, click to select *nschcode* from the left column then click the right-arrow button to move the variable into the *Break Variable(s)* box.

b. Next click to select *test1* from the left column, then click the right-arrow button to move the variable into the *Summaries of Variable(s)* box. (SPSS uses MEAN as the default function, which will be used for this example.)

c. Change the output variable name by clicking on the NAME & LABEL button, which will open the *Aggregate Data: Variable name and Label* box. Then replace the initial variable name from *test1_mean* to the current *test1gpm*. Click the CONTINUE button to close the box when completed to return to the *Aggregate Data* main dialog box.

Click the OK button to perform the aggregation and create the new *test1gpm*.

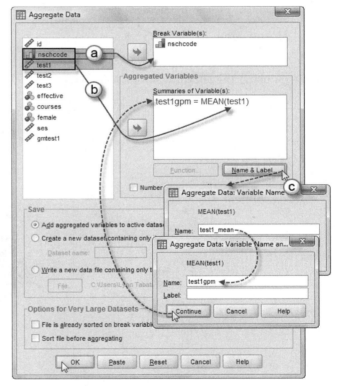

3. Scroll across the columns and the new aggregated variable *test1gpm* appears in the last column of the *ch2multivarML1.sav* data window.

Notice that this new variable is constant within each Level 2 unit (schools). That is, the value represents the mean *test1* score within each school. These values provide the reference value for the group centering of *test1* (just as the overall mean provided the reference value for grand-mean centering). With the group mean value known, it is easy to calculate the group-centered *test1* variable, which we will call *grouptest1*.

We will specify the target variable we wish to create (*grouptest1*) and create the Numeric Expression *test1 – test1gpm*.

Continue using the *ch2multivarML1.sav* data file.

1. Go to the SPSS toolbar and select TRANSFORM, COMPUTE VARIABLE.

The command opens the *Compute Variable* dialog box.

Note: The formula *test1 – 47.643788* used in the preceding exercise may appear in the *Numeric Expression* box. To remove the formula, click the RESET button at the bottom of the screen.

2a. Enter *grouptest1* as the *Target Variable*.

b. Click to select *test1* from the left column, then click the right-arrow button to move the variable into the *Numeric Expression* box. Insert a minus sign (-) by clicking on the key.

c. To complete the numeric expression click *test1gpm* from the left column, then click the right-arrow button to move the variable into the box. This completes the *Numeric Expression* of subtracting *grouptest1* from *test1*.

Click the OK button to perform the function.

3. Scroll across the columns and the new *grouptest1* variable appears in the last column of the data window.

We can now compare the three variables: *test1*, *gmtest1*, and *grouptest1* (Table 2.9). Notice that while the uncentered *test1* and the grand-mean centered test1 variables share the same distribution (but different means), the group-mean centered *test1* variable has a mean of 0 (like the grand-mean version) but a different standard deviation. This results from the variance in *test1* means across the schools in the sample—an artifact that will become very important in subsequent analyses.

TABLE 2.9 Descriptive Statistics

	N	Minimum	Maximum	Mean	Std. Deviation
test1	8335	24.35	69.25	47.6439	6.32466
gmtest1	8335	−23.29	21.61	.0001	6.32466
grouptest1	8335	−22.90	22.90	.0000	5.87943
Valid N (listwise)	8335				

For reasons we will discuss in Chapter 4, researchers often enter dummy variables in the model as uncentered (although there are occasions when analysts may also wish to grand-mean center them), and they grand-mean center the continuous variables at Level 1 and at Level 2. We will also show how this logic generalizes to situations in which there are more than two levels of analysis.

Checking the Data

The diligent analyst always takes great care to examine the data thoroughly. As data sets for multilevel analyses can become quite complex, in terms of structure and content, great attention to detail should be given when reviewing the contents of the data set. SPSS has a rich set of tools for the exploratory analysis of the data. The SPSS EXPLORE routine, for example, can provide rich detail on data coding, distributions, missing data, and the like (this can be accessed through the ANALYZE > DESCRIPTIVE STATISTICS > EXPLORE menu). From Chapter 1 it should be clear that missing data can prove to be a real headache when using SPSS Mixed or any other multilevel modeling routine. We highly recommend that missing data be carefully assessed to determine any patterns that may exist and to find remedies where at all possible.

Beyond a careful examination of the data, thought should be given to model specification and the distribution of residuals. Raudenbush and Bryk (2002, p. 253) point out that model specification assumptions apply at each level and that misspecification at one level can impact the results at other levels. Moreover, as with OLS regression at a single level, there are assumptions about the distribution of the residuals that apply at each level in the multilevel model. Although we do not spend a great amount of time addressing these important issues in this workbook, we do recommend that the reader familiarize himself or herself with the possibilities that exist for model checking in the multilevel framework.

A Note About Model Building

As will become clear in the chapters that follow, developing and testing multilevel models requires a great deal of thought as well as trial and error. Even with a basic two-level model there are many intermediate steps over which the model evolves. Keeping track of this evolution is essential for understanding the way the model is behaving and for replicating the models in subsequent steps.

We have over the years developed a fairly simple naming scheme for our models and take care to document each model as fully as possible. Moreover, while we may use the SPSS graphical user interface to develop the model, we always have SPSS export the syntax so we can save it for future reference. Our naming scheme is applied to the syntax files themselves. At a glance we can determine the type of model specified through the syntax (e.g., from a simple ANOVA model to a fully specified three-level, random-slopes and intercept model). With the syntax for each model saved and annotated we can always document the evolution of model specification and easily modify models at any point in the future. We will have more to say about this throughout the workbook.

Summary

This chapter has provided an overview of the data management tools necessary for understanding and working with the hierarchical data files used in multilevel modeling. We have introduced five primary commands for manipulating data files to suit the needs of univariate and multivariate analyses using SPSS Mixed. There is, of course, a great deal more than could be presented. Our main purpose in this workbook is, however, the modeling techniques themselves rather than treating the more universal data management skills used to structure data within SPSS. The treatment provided in this chapter is designed to highlight the elementary skills associated with data management relating to the specification of the multilevel model within SPSS.

CHAPTER 3

Defining a Basic Two-Level Multilevel Regression Model

This chapter introduces the basic approach to two-level, multilevel modeling. The material is challenging because the models are more complex than the general linear model, with which most readers will be familiar with from their basic statistics courses. Like everything else, however, one has to start somewhere. The general concepts we present in this chapter become more familiar as one reads more research that makes use of multilevel techniques. After first reviewing some basic concepts of the single-level multiple regression model, we develop the basic steps of conducting a multilevel regression analysis using an extended example. Our intent is to develop the rationale behind the specification of this general class of models in a relatively nontechnical manner and to illustrate its use in an applied research situation. The methods presented in this chapter should provide a basis for the application of these techniques to a wider set of research problems in the chapters that follow.

From Single-Level to Multilevel Analysis

Linear models (e.g., analysis of variance [ANOVA], analysis of covariance, multiple regression, multivariate analysis of variance [MANOVA]) have long been used in the social sciences to analyze data from experimental, quasi-experimental, and nonexperimental designs. Univariate analysis such as multiple regression is concerned with examining the variability in a single outcome (or dependent) variable from information provided by one or more predictor (or independent) variables. Multivariate analysis (e.g., MANOVA, factor analysis) is the more general case of univariate analysis; that is, it facilitates the examination of multiple independent and dependent variables in one simultaneous model. A commonality between these univariate and multivariate approaches, however, is that they are confined to single-level analyses; that is, either individuals are the unit of analysis or groups (aggregates) are the unit of analysis.

Multiple linear regression requires a continuous dependent variable (i.e., measured on an interval or ratio scale) and can handle both continuous and dichotomous (e.g., gender) independent variables. It cannot handle categorical variables (i.e., referred to as factors in analysis of variance terminology) without recoding them in some way. There are two broad conceptual approaches to the regression model, predictive and explanatory. Through the predictive approach, the analyst uses the multiple regression model to optimize predictions about an outcome based on values of a set of independent variables. The linear regression model assumes that a unit increase in the independent variable is related to an expected constant change in the dependent variable. For example, we might wish to predict someone's likely starting salary in a new job if she or he has a certain level of education and experience. For the linear model to hold, it is assumed that an increase in education (or experience) will bring an expected similar change in starting salary, regardless of where someone starts in terms of education. In this type of single-level regression model, the coefficients that describe the prediction equation (i.e., the intercept and slope coefficients for each predictor in the model) are generally considered as fixed values in the population estimated from the sample data. For this type of research purpose, the focus of the analysis is primarily on the efficiency of the prediction and the parsimony of variables included in the prediction equation (in other words, the analyst hopes to make the best predictions using the smallest number of variables).

The second broad approach is explanatory rather than predictive. Through the explanatory approach, the analyst sets out to determine how a set of independent variables affects a dependent variable and to estimate the magnitude of the effects for each independent variable. For example, existing research may suggest that a particular model (for example, consisting of identified market processes, individual background, and perhaps organizational factors) interact in a way that influences beginning salary. The focus in this type of study rests on the correct specification and testing of a theoretical model that is under consideration. In this case, it is important to include in the model a set of variables identified as important by theory and previous research. More specifically, the researcher formulates a model from theory, tests the model against the data, and determines how well the empirical test of the model conforms to theoretical expectations.

Of course, these goals are not mutually exclusive. We distinguish between these two goals, however, because in predictive studies variables might be retained in a model only because they are statistically significant and dropped simply because they are not (Heck & Thomas, 2009). In other words, theory would not enter into decisions about model efficiency. In contrast, in the explanatory approach, the specification of the theoretical model should be carefully considered, and subsequent changes (i.e., whether to add or remove a variable from a model) should be made sparingly with careful attention to theory. Otherwise, it may be difficult to attach any substantive meaning to the final model. This latter point has particular relevance to the investigation of multilevel data (i.e., data on individuals and the groups they define) that tend to go with more complex theories about how processes operate across multiple social groupings.

Although researchers were aware of problems due to the nesting of individuals within higher level units of the data hierarchy in the past, the presence of similarities among individuals in the same groups did not enter directly into single-level analyses. For example, in analyses of large-scale survey data, the analyst typically applied sample weights to address the oversampling of some subgroups in the data set (e.g., by socioeconomic status, by ethnicity). Failure to account for similarities among individuals (due to grouping) within the study, however, can lead to biased estimates of model parameters and therefore erroneous conclusions about the effects of some predictors in the model (Thomas & Heck, 2001).

Multilevel modeling represents a compromise between modeling each unit separately and modeling all unit contexts simultaneously within the same model (Kreft & de Leeuw, 1998). These models obviate the forced choice of conducting either an individual-level analysis or a group-level analysis. We use the term *multilevel model* with respect to two separate statistical objectives described within one model. The first objective concerns inferences made about a model's structural parameters (Morris, 1995), often referred to as the model's fixed effects. The second objective concerns inferences about the unknown variance parameters in the model, referred to as the random parameters (Morris, 1995). Although researchers are generally most interested in the model's structural parameters, the distribution of a model's random parameters (e.g., variances, covariances) is also of interest.

There are several advantages of multilevel analysis over traditional single-level univariate and multivariate approaches (Heck & Thomas, 2009). First, as we have stated, multilevel analysis helps researchers avoid the choice of individuals or groups as the unit of analysis. Second, it allows researchers to deal with more complicated sampling strategies. Single-level analyses are based on the assumption of simple random samples. In many data collection strategies, however, individuals may be sampled within the same neighborhoods or schools, or subgroups of individuals (e.g., by ethnicity or SES) may be oversampled compared with their representation in the population. Such complex sampling strategies create clustering effects that violate the assumptions of simple random sampling (i.e., that every individual has an equal chance of being selected in the sample). Third, where similarities among individuals are present (e.g., clustering effects due to sharing similar circumstances), multilevel models are acknowledged to provide more accurate estimates of model parameters than single-level analyses (Hox, 2002). This is primarily due to their greater accuracy in calculating standard errors associated with parameter estimates. Because hypothesis tests are based on the ratio of the unstandardized estimate to its standard error, ignoring the presence of nested data structures can lead to underestimating standard errors and, therefore, false inferences about the significance of model parameters (Thomas & Heck, 2001). Fourth, multilevel analysis allows the researcher to define variables at their correct theoretical level of the data hierarchy. So, for example, in a two-level hierarchy, a variable such as school size can be determined with respect to the number of schools in the sample, while a variable like gender can be evaluated with respect to the number of individuals in the sample. Finally, multilevel modeling allows researchers to ask more complex questions about the data. One is about the distribution of outcomes (e.g., means or regression slopes) across a sample of groups (such as schools). We may attempt to determine what types of school variables might account for variability in school outcomes, net of the individuals within the school. Examples might be the quality of a school's teachers, its leadership, and its classroom processes.

Building a Two-Level Model

The basics of multilevel modeling involve the investigation of randomly varying outcome parameters. These typically include variation in the levels of the outcome (intercepts) and the strength of within-group relationships indicated by regression coefficients (slopes) across groups. Once we identify that variation exists in the parameters of interest, we can build models to explain this variation. As we suggested in Chapter 1, in some cases, we may have a specific theoretical model in mind that we wish to test; in others, however, we might be trying to explore possible new mechanisms that explain this variation.

Consider an analysis where the researcher wishes to determine whether there is an association between a predictor, *X*, such as student socioeconomic status (SES) and an outcome, *Y*, such as a math test score. Because the current educational policy context in the United States demands increasing accountability for student outcomes, schools are accountable for reducing gaps in achievement due to students' social backgrounds. Such concerns are related to the social distribution of learning within schools (e.g., see Lee & Bryk, 1989). Ideally, we may wish to identify school settings where achievement is generally high for all the students in the school and where there is little or no relationship between student SES and outcomes. Such schools would be considered both effective (i.e., producing high achievement outcomes) and equitable (i.e., having little or no social distribution of learning due to students' social backgrounds). In contrast, we may also wish to identify schools where achievement is consistently low for students and where student SES background is consequential for their outcome levels. We might be able to intervene effectively (e.g., increase teacher quality, reallocate resources) if we could identify such settings that are ineffective and inequitable for students.

Research Questions

Our first research question focuses on whether student achievement in math varies across schools. We can ask simply: Does student math achievement vary across schools? We might then investigate the relationship between students' socioeconomic status and their math achievement. Second, we might ask whether the effects of individual SES tend to compound at the school level to influence student math achievement; that is, do both individual-level SES and school-level aggregate (or average) student SES influence math achievement? Third, we investigate whether features of schools' contexts (i.e., student composition, type of school) and their academic environments (i.e., the number of students planning to attend 4-year universities after they graduate from high school) affect the relationship between individual student SES and math achievement. More specifically, we ask: Do features of schools' contexts and academic environments moderate the relationship between individual student SES and math achievement? Our research questions, therefore, provide an illustration of building a two-level model to investigate (1) a randomly varying intercept (math achievement level) and, subsequently, (2) a randomly varying slope (i.e., the individual SES–math achievement relationship).

The Data

The data set used in this example consists of 6,871 secondary students in 419 schools. We will begin with a single-level analysis (i.e., considering only the students and not their nesting within schools) as a starting point. One typical research question for a single-level analysis might be: Is there a relationship between students' SES background and their achievement levels in math? We might hypothesize that socioeconomic status is positively related to the subject's score on the math test. The single-level multiple regression model to explain an individual's (i) math achievement outcome would be

$$Y_i = \beta_0 + \beta_1 (\text{SES})_i + \varepsilon_i, \tag{3.1}$$

where β_0 is the intercept, β_1 is a slope parameter, and ε_i represents error in predicting individual outcomes from the equation. The intercept represents the expected math achievement score for a student whose SES is 0. It is often useful to consider the scaling of the independent variable or variables in a model. In this simple case, because SES (which is a continuous variable) was standardized (i.e., rescaled into a standardized score, or z-score), the mean is 0 and the standard deviation (SD) is 1.0. This is often a convenient scale for continuous variables in multilevel modeling, since a score of 0 on SES, therefore, represents score for a person whose SES background is equal to the SES grand mean for the sample. We discuss these types of "centering" decisions in further detail in the next chapter. The slope coefficient (β_1) represents the expected change in math achievement for a one-unit (in this case 1 SD) change in SES.

The key point about a single-level model is that the estimates of the intercept and slope are each fixed to one value that describes the average for the sample. For example, the slope expressing the relationship between SES and math scores will be the same across all cases. This also means that the errors (ε) in estimating the intercept and slope parameters are assumed to be independent, normally distributed, have constant variance, and a mean of zero.

To examine her research question preliminarily, the researcher might first develop a scatterplot of the relationship between student SES and math achievement. To illustrate this in relation to single and multilevel designs, we will develop a scatterplot for the first 80 students in the data set. The resulting graph is summarized in Figure 3.1. The figure suggests that as student SES increases, so do math scores. The goal of the overall analysis is to determine what the best fitting line that describes the relationship between student SES and test scores in this sample. This is accomplished by estimating values for the intercept and slope. Of course, once we estimate the predicted values for each subject on the two variables, there will be a discrepancy between the predicted values (which would lie on the line) and subjects' actual values on the SES and math test score measures. The difference between observed and predicted values is represented as error. The intercept coefficient represents the average level of student scores when SES is zero (which represents a mean adjusted for SES) and the slope represents the average effect of SES on the math score across the sample of students. These values become "fixed" for the entire sample; that is, because individuals are randomly sampled, it is assumed that the value represents population averages.

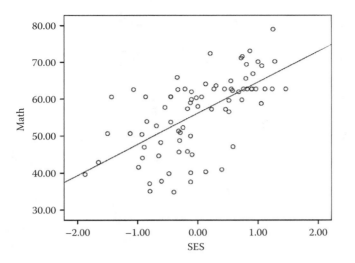

FIGURE 3.1 Regression line describing the fixed intercept and slope for student SES and math achievement.

Fixing the values of the intercept and slope results in the regression line in Figure 3.1 that summarizes the relationship between SES and math test scores. The principle of least squares states that the correct regression line is the one that best fits the data points. Model fit is assessed by summing the squared distances of each observed value from the predicted value that rests on the regression line. The line that minimizes the sum of these squared distances (they are squared to cancel out positive and negative errors above or below the line) is said to fit the data best; hence, the term least squares regression (Neter, Kutner, Nachtsheim, & Wasserman, 1996). In the linear regression model, the error term is a random source of variation, which we assume is zero on average and normally distributed, varies independently of *X*, and has constant variance across all levels of *X*. Interested readers can reproduce the scatterplot in Figure 3.1 in SPSS menu commands.

Graphing the Relationship Between SES and Math Test Scores With SPSS Menu Commands

Launch the SPSS application and select the data file *ch3multilevel.sav*.

1. Go to the toolbar and select DATA, SELECT CASES.

This command will open the *Select Cases* dialog box.

2a. Within the *Select Cases* dialog box, select the option *Based on time or case range,* and click the RANGE button.

b. Within the *Select Series: Range box*, enter 1 as the *First Case* and enter 80 as the *Last Case.* This setting will select the first 80 individuals in the study. Then click the CONTINUE button, which will close the *Select Cases: Range* box.

Click the OK button to close the main *Select Cases* dialog box and return to the SPSS main screen.

3. In the SPSS toolbar, select GRAPHS, LEGACY DIALOGS, SCATTER/DOT.

This command will open the *Scatter/Dot* box.

4. Click the SIMPLE SCATTER option in the *Scatter/Dot* box. Then click the DEFINE button to open the *Simple Scatterplot* box.

5a. Within the *Simple Scatterplot* box, click to select the *math* variable from the left column. Then click the right-arrow button to move *math* into the *Y Axis* box.

b. Next click *ses* to select the variable from the left column, then click the right-arrow button to move the variable into the *X Axis* box.

Click OK to generate the scatterplot.

6. The SPSS output will display the scatterplot.

Place your cursor on the image and double-click to open the *Chart Editor.*

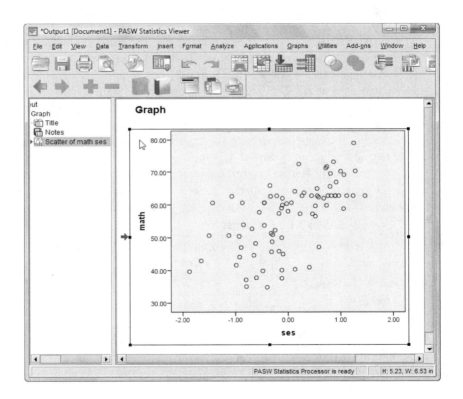

7. On the *Chart Editor* shortcut icon bar, click the ADD FIT LINE AT TOTAL icon that has the X and Y axes. This will generate the fit line and the linear R^2 of 0.387 for this subset of the sample.

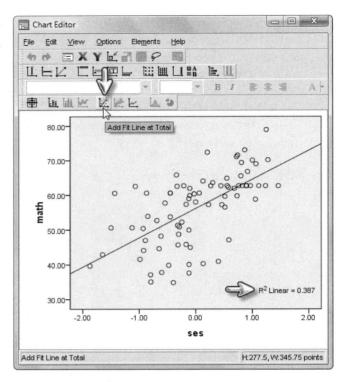

As Figure 3.1 emphasizes, in a single-level linear model, the coefficients describing the intercept and slope are generally considered as fixed values in the population estimated from the sample data. As shown in Table 3.1 (based on an analysis of the full sample), the intercept is estimated as 57.598. This can be interpreted as the sample mean adjusted for individual SES (note that, while not shown, the sample mean unadjusted for SES is 57.734). The unstandardized regression coefficient describing the effect of individual SES (β_1) on math achievement is 4.255. The slope coefficient suggests that, on average, as student SES goes up by 1 unit, student test scores go up by about 4.3 points.

The analysis also provides a table describing the variability in math achievement accounted for by the predictors in the model (Table 3.2). This can be used to calculate and estimate of

TABLE 3.1 Coefficients[a]

Model		Unstandardized Coefficients		Standardized Coefficients		
		B	Std. Error	Beta	t	Sig.
1	(Constant)	57.598	.098		586.608	.000
	ses	4.255	.126	.378	33.858	.000

[a] Dependent Variable: math.

TABLE 3.2 ANOVA[b]

Model		Sum of Squares	df	Mean Square	F	Sig.
1	Regression	75813.316	1	75813.316	1146.382	.000[a]
	Residual	454265.500	6869	66.133		
	Total	530078.816	6870			

[a] Predictors: (Constant), ses.
[b] Dependent Variable: math.

the variance accounted for in achievement by mean student composition and individual SES. From the table we can calculate R^2 as the ratio of the regression variance to the total variance (75813.316/530078.8 = .143).

As we have noted, however, there would likely be problems in the accuracy of this analysis. The assumptions necessary for multiple regression models to yield the best, unbiased estimates are most realistic when the data have been collected through simple random sampling. Random sampling assumes that subjects in a study are independent of each other. As groups are added as a feature of a study, however, this assumption becomes more tenuous. In large-scale educational research, for example, simple random sampling would rarely be used. Instead, various types of complex sampling strategies are employed to select schools, classrooms, and students. These can include multistage sampling strategies where individuals may be sampled within various groups and the likely oversampling of some groups. Clustered data, therefore, result from the strategies used in large-scale databases, as well as the natural groupings of students in classrooms and schools.

The single-level regression model cannot take into consideration that the students may be clustered within a number of schools with other students having similar backgrounds and math scores. In our example, the analysis does not take into consideration that students are nested within the 419 schools in the sample (or that the estimated slope might be different between these schools). Multilevel models imply that individuals are "clustered" in higher order social groupings (a department, a school, or some other type of organization). In these types of studies, simple random sampling does not hold because people clustered in groups will tend to be "similar" in some ways. In this example, the size of the student samples within their schools ranges from 12 to 37 (mean = 17.4, SD = 4.74). If the clustering of students is ignored, it is likely that bias will be introduced in estimating the coefficients and their standard errors.

We can again develop a scatterplot of the relationship between student SES and math achievement from Figure 3.1, this time taking into consideration their schools (i.e., in this case the 80 students are in 6 schools). We can therefore estimate a separate regression equation for each school. Each school would have its own intercept (describing the level of its students' outcomes adjusted for SES) and a slope (describing the relationship between SES and math achievement within that school). Where data hierarchies exist, the school intercepts (i.e., average math scores adjusted for student SES) would likely vary across the sample of schools in the study. Moreover, there might be some schools where the effect of student SES on math achievement (represented by the slope of regression line) is greater than or less than the average (or fixed) effect. There might also be some schools where there is no relationship at all. In other words, where there are clustered data, it is likely that there is a distribution of both intercepts and slopes around their respective average fixed effects. In this situation, we might wish to investigate the "random" variability in intercepts and slopes across the sample of higher level units in the study (e.g., classrooms, schools).

Figure 3.2 presents the relationship between SES and math achievement for the previous subset of 80 individuals nested in 6 schools. The figure suggests that the slope relationship account for differing amounts of variance (i.e., with R^2 coefficients ranging from 0.02 to 0.205). This suggests considerable social distribution of math learning within these 6 schools.

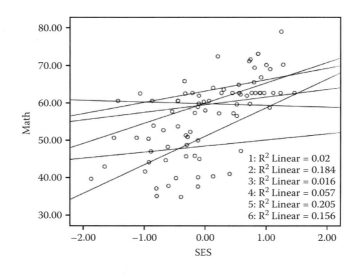

FIGURE 3.2   Randomly varying SES–achievement slopes in six schools.

Graphing the Subgroup Relationships Between SES and Math Test Scores With SPSS Menu Commands

(Settings will default to the prior scatterplot.)

1. In the SPSS toolbar, select GRAPHS, LEGACY DIALOGS, SCATTER/DOT.

This command will open the *Scatter/Dot* box.

2. The default selection from the prior scatterplot is set to *Simple Scatter*.

Click the DEFINE button to open the *Simple Scatterplot* box.

3. The *Simple Scatterplot* box displays the variables *math* (*Y Axis*) and *ses* (*X Axis*).

Click to select *schcode* from the left column. Then click the right-arrow button to move *schode* into the *Set Markers by* box.

Click OK to generate the scatterplot.

Multilevel modeling can be used to specify a hierarchical system of regression equations that take advantage of the clustered data structure (Heck & Thomas, 2009). Multilevel regression modeling involves first estimating a Level 1 model within each higher level unit (e.g., schools) and then estimating a series of between-unit models using the within-unit estimates (i.e., intercepts or slopes) as dependent variables. In contrast to a single-level regression model, where the impact of a variable like SES is assumed to be fixed across all individuals in the sample, within multilevel regression modeling one can specify a single-level regression equation that can be estimated within each school (as shown in Figure 3.2). In this way, the researcher can determine whether the effect of SES on math achievement is stronger or weaker in some schools.

In this case, the researcher might be interested in estimating the average intercept and SES effect on math achievement across the set of schools as well as how particular schools deviate from the overall average intercept and SES–achievement slope. Although the researcher's primary concern is usually with a model's structural parameters, in some cases examining the appropriateness and distribution of these residual variance parameters (e.g., residual variance associated with intercepts, slopes, and covariances between intercepts and slopes) may be of equal interest to the researcher. In a multilevel model, the math achievement intercept and the SES–achievement slope can be defined to vary as probability distributions across the set of schools. The variability of intercepts (i.e., where each unit's regression line crosses the *Y* axis) and slopes (the steepness of each institution's regression line) gives rise to different types of questions that can be asked of the data. In addition to our initial research question (Is there a relationship between student SES and math achievement?), we can now ask other questions of the data.

Visually, it looks like the levels of the intercepts might vary in Figure 3.2. In one school, a student somewhat below 2 *SD* in SES would have a math score of about 34.0. In contrast, in another school, a similar student (somewhat below 2 *SD* in SES) would score approximately 61.0 in math. This observed variability in intercepts gives rise to a second question: Do the average math scores students receive vary across schools in the sample? Answering this question would provide information about each school's effectiveness, given the SES background of its students. The figure also suggests the possibility of randomly varying slopes in the data set. Five of the six schools in our illustrative subsample (Figure 3.2) have positive slope relationships, and one school has a negative slope relationship. One can also notice that the R^2 coefficients (which summarize the strength of the relationship between student SES and math) also vary considerably in the first six schools (i.e., from 0.02 to 0.21). This suggests that there might be schools where there is little gap in math achievement due to students' SES background. These schools could be viewed as more equitable in terms of the social distribution of learning due to students' social backgrounds (e.g., SES or perhaps gender and race/ethnicity if we were to include those variables).

In other schools, students' social background might be very consequential in determining their achievement. A second question that could be posed: Do the slopes (i.e., the strength of relationship between student SES and math achievement) vary across schools? Answering this question would provide information about schools' equity in producing outcomes, given the social backgrounds of their students. We might examine whether the relationship between individual SES and math achievement is stronger or weaker in schools of differing average social composition. Moreover we can investigate whether there is a difference in the strength of association between individual SES and achievement in public and private schools or in schools having a stronger academic focus, after controlling for the mean SES level at the school.

Parameters that are proposed to vary randomly across units are referred to as random effects or random coefficients from various statistical perspectives. In experimental research, for example, a *random effect* describes a situation where the treatment (or levels of a treatment) is assumed to represent a sample drawn from a universe of treatments or treatment levels. Because the effect is considered as randomly varying across a universe of treatments, the intent is to make inferences beyond the specific treatment levels included in the study. The effects, therefore, are not assumed to be constant. In contrast, a *fixed effect* describes the situation where all possible treatments are present in the experiment (Kreft & de Leeuw, 1998). In this latter case, inferences can only be made about the specific treatments used. The effects are considered to be constant and measured without error because all possible cases are included.

Unlike single-level (ordinary least squares [OLS]) regression, where random errors are assumed to be independent, normally distributed, and have constant variance, in multilevel models, error structures are more complex. The individual-level errors are dependent within each unit because they are common to every individual within that unit (Heck & Thomas, 2009). Errors do not have constant variance because the residual components describing intercepts and slopes may also vary across units. The estimation of these unknown random parameters associated with intercepts or slopes may also depend on characteristics of the data (e.g., sample size, degree of imbalance in sample sizes of higher level units, degree of similarity among individuals within groups), the type of analysis conducted, and the measurement scale of the dependent variables (Muthén & Muthén, 1998–2006; Raudenbush & Bryk, 2002). Because the model's random parameters must be estimated with group samples containing differing numbers of individuals, iterative estimation procedures must be used to obtain efficient estimates (Muthén & Muthén, 1998–2006).

Building a Multilevel Model With SPSS Mixed

We can use SPSS Mixed to run a variety of different multilevel cross-sectional and longitudinal (e.g., growth) models. The program is flexible and can be used to estimate a number of different types of models with random intercepts (i.e., means that vary across groups) and random slopes (i.e., within-group regression coefficients that vary across groups). It is also useful in looking at individual change over repeated measurements or in studies of changes of individuals within organizations over time. In addition, it can also be applied to situations where individuals may be cross-classified by higher level groupings (e.g., in several different classrooms within schools or within various high schools and subsequent universities). In the chapters that follow we develop each of these possibilities in more detail. In the remainder of this chapter, we focus on the univariate cross-sectional multilevel model.

There are several ways to develop models using SPSS Mixed. Some users prefer the SPSS graphical user interface (GUI), while others favor using syntax statements to define the model. We will build models in the chapters that follow using the GUI, but also provide some of the key syntax in Appendix A. As we mentioned in Chapter 2, syntax can be very useful on occasions, since one does not have to return to the specific window to make successive changes in a model that is being investigated. Syntax also provides a record of what has been done previously. This record can be saved and used on subsequent occasions without having to set the model up again through the SPSS menu system (i.e., GUI). We have found small differences may result depending on whether models are developed with syntax commands or the GUI (e.g., owing to some default commands that users may not specify with the syntax commands). Also we note that if users have different versions of SPSS (e.g., version 15, 16, 17, or 18), estimates may be slightly different (owing to different default rounding procedures). In this chapter, we take the reader through the steps in the SPSS GUI to develop the basic two-level regression model. An alternative to writing your own syntax is to develop models using the SPSS GUI and then tell SPSS to generate the syntax (which is then pasted into a syntax window). Although we use the GUI interface, we will also demonstrate how to generate syntax through the menu system. We follow this convention throughout the remainder of the book. Note that all screen shots from the SPSS GUI provided here are based on SPSS for Windows version 18.0.

Step 1: Examining Variance Components Using the Null Model

There are three distinct steps in developing the multilevel model. We develop these in this chapter in the following order: (1) specification of the null, or no predictors model; (2) specification of the Level 1 model; and (3) specification of the Level 2 model. This latter step can include the model to explain intercepts and the model or models to explain randomly varying slopes. The first step in a multilevel analysis usually is to develop a null (or no predictors) model to partition the variance in the outcome into its within- and between-groups components. This will help the researcher determine how much of the variance in math achievement lies between the schools in the sample. Notice that in Equation 3.2, we add a subscript for schools (j). The null model for individual i in school j can be represented as

$$Y_{ij} = \beta_{0j} + \varepsilon_{ij}, \tag{3.2}$$

where β_{0j} is the intercept and ε_{ij} represents variation in estimating individual achievement within groups. Between groups, variation in intercepts can be represented as

$$\beta_{0j} = \gamma_{00} + u_{0j}. \tag{3.3}$$

Through substitution, the null model can be written as

$$Y_{ij} = \gamma_{00} + u_{0j} + \varepsilon_{ij}. \tag{3.4}$$

The null model therefore provides an estimated mean achievement score for all schools. It also provides a partitioning of the variance between Level 1 (ε_{ij}) and Level 2 (u_{0j}). Altogether there are three effects to estimate: the intercept, the between-school variation in intercepts (u_{0j}), and the variation in individual scores within schools (ε_{ij}).

This model also provides a measure of dependence within each Level 2 unit by way of the intraclass correlation (ρ). The intraclass correlation (or ICC) describes the proportion of variance that is common to each unit, as opposed to variation that is associated with individuals within their units. It can be thought of as the population estimate of the amount of variance in the outcome explained by the grouping structure (Hox, 2002). The proportion of variance found between groups can be calculated in SPSS by using either the Variance Components or Mixed procedures. Both will give the same estimation of within-groups and between-groups variance components. The ICC can be represented as

$$\rho = \sigma_B^2 \big/ \left(\sigma_B^2 + \sigma_W^2 \right),\tag{3.5}$$

where σ^2 represents the variance and B and W stand for between groups and within groups, respectively. Stated differently, the ICC is the ratio of between-groups variance to the total variance. The higher the ICC, the more homogeneous are the units (i.e., there exists substantial variability between schools). In contrast, if the ICC is quite small (i.e., researchers often use 0.05 as a rough "cutoff" point), then there would be little advantage to conducting a multilevel analysis. Simply put, the higher level grouping does not affect the estimates in any meaningful way. In these cases, a single-level analysis conducted at the individual level would suffice.

Defining the Null Model With SPSS Menu Commands

Note: If continuing after creating Figures 3.1 and 3.2, remove the *Select Cases* conditional setting before proceeding. This is achieved by going to the SPSS toolbar, and selecting DATA, SELECT CASES, RESET, OK.

1. Go to the SPSS toolbar and select ANALYZE, MIXED MODELS, LINEAR.

This command opens the *Linear Mixed Models: Specify Subjects and Repeated* dialog box.

2. From the *Linear Mixed Models: Specify Subjects and Repeated* dialog box, click to select the *schcode* variable from the left column. Then click the right-arrow button to transfer *schcode* into the *Subjects* box.

Click the CONTINUE button to display the *Linear Mixed Models* dialog box.

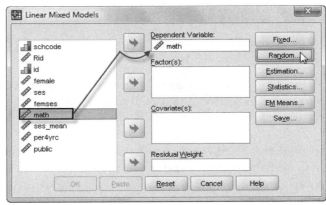

3. The *Linear Mixed Models* dialog box is used to define the dependent variable as well as any factors (categorical variables) or covariates (interval variables) in the analysis. Click to select the *math* variable from the left column. Then click the right-arrow button to transfer *math* into the *Dependent Variable* box.

In this case, there are no predictors in the "null" model. Since there are no fixed effects in the model, skip over the FIXED button and click the RANDOM button to access the *Linear Mixed Models: Random Effects* dialog box.

4. The RANDOM command is used to specify the random effects; that is, which variables are to be treated as randomly varying across groups.

a. At the top of the *Linear Mixed Models: Random Effect 1 of 1* display screen, *Covariance Type* refers to several different types of covariance matrices that can be used for multilevel analyses. The default is VARIANCE COMPONENTS (VC), which we will use for the first model.

VC is the default covariance structure for random effects. This specifies a diagonal covariance matrix for the random effects; that is, it provides a separate variance estimate for each random effect, but not covariances between random effects.

In this case, there is only one random effect (the intercept), so we can use the default VC. For models with random intercepts and slopes, a common choice is an "unstructured" (UN), or a completely general, covariance matrix, which fits all variances and covariances between random effects.

b. In the *Random Effect 1 of 1* display screen you can build other random effects for the predictors. In this case, however, only the intercept is going to be randomly varying so click to select the *Include intercept* option.

c. Click to select the *Subject Groupings* variable *nschcode*. Then click the right-arrow button to transfer the variable into the *Combinations* box.

Click the CONTINUE button to return to the *Linear Mixed Models* dialog box.

5. In the *Linear Mixed Models* dialog box, click the ESTIMATION button to access the *Linear Mixed Models: Estimation* dialog box. The estimation method choices are maximum likelihood (ML) or restricted maximum likelihood (REML). In ML, both regression coefficients and variance components are included in maximizing the likelihood function; that is, the process of minimizing the difference between the sample covariance matrix and the model-implied covariance matrix. In REML, only the variance components are included in estimating the likelihood function; thus, REML is a restricted solution.

Because in REML the regression coefficients are considered to be unknowns, taking the loss in degrees of freedom due to estimating $P + 1$ regression coefficients in the model results in unbiased estimates of variance components when there are small numbers of groups (Snijders & Bosker, 1999). With sufficient numbers of groups, the differences in estimation methods are negligible. Restricted maximum likelihood (REML), the default estimation method for both SPSS techniques, which also is the better choice with small data sets, will be used to develop the variance component estimates.

We will use the REML default setting.

Click the CONTINUE button to return to the *Linear Mixed Models* dialog box.

6. In the *Linear Mixed Models* dialog box, click the STATISTICS button to access the *Linear Mixed Models: Statistics* dialog box.

Click and select the following three statistics: Parameter estimates, tests for covariance parameters, and covariances of random effects.

Then click the CONTINUE button to return to the *Linear Mixed Models* dialog box.

7. Finally, in the *Linear Mixed Models* dialog box, click the OK button to run the model.

Interpreting the Output From the Null Model

The first table (Table 3.3) in the resulting output summarizes the total number of parameters being estimated (3). This is the same as we noted in Equation 3.4. The total parameters estimated include the fixed effect value for the intercept, random Level 2 variance, and the Level 1 variance (referred to as "Residual" in the SPSS output).

The column referred to as "Number of Levels" describes the fixed effects (1) and the number of random effects (1). There is one fixed effect to be estimated (the intercept) and one random effect (the randomly varying intercept). The column referred to as "Subject Variables" indicates the number of levels in the analysis (i.e., in this case, schcode [the school identifier] implies a two-level analysis). The covariance structure describes the way the covariance matrix of random effects is dimensionalized at the group level. In this case, we use the default (VC, or variance components), which provides an estimate of the intercept variance (σ_I^2). However, in this first example, at Level 2 there is no random slope variance (σ_S^2) or covariance between the intercept and slope. In this case, the VC covariance matrix will be the same as an identity matrix.

The next piece of SPSS output describes model-fitting criteria (Table 3.4). This can be useful in examining the improvement of model fit when comparing two successive (or nested) models (e.g., using the change in log likelihood). Note that comparing nested models should only be done when using ML estimation (and not REML, unless only the random parameters are compared, see Heck & Thomas, 2009 for a complete treatment of these estimators). This output also includes other type of information about overall model fit. We will discuss model fit in further detail in Chapter 4.

Table 3.5 reports the estimates of fixed effects in the model. The intercept (or grand mean for school outcomes) is estimated as 57.67.

The variance component output (Table 3.6) indicates the proportion of variance in achievement that lies between schools is .138. This can calculated be from Equation 3.5

TABLE 3.3 Model Dimension[b]

		Number of Levels	Covariance Structure	Number of Parameters	Subject Variables
Fixed Effects	Intercept	1		1	
Random Effects	Intercept[a]	1	Variance Components	1	schcode
Residual				1	
Total		2		3	

[a] As of version 11.5, the syntax rules for the RANDOM subcommand have changed. Your command syntax may yield results that differ from those produced by prior versions. If you are using version 11 syntax, please consult the current syntax reference guide for more information.

[b] Dependent Variable: math.

TABLE 3.4   Information Criteria[a]

−2 Restricted Log Likelihood	48877.256
Akaike's Information Criterion (AIC)	48881.256
Hurvich and Tsai's Criterion (AICC)	48881.257
Bozdogan's Criterion (CAIC)	48896.925
Schwarz's Bayesian Criterion (BIC)	48894.925

Note: The information criteria are displayed in smaller-is-better forms.

[a] Dependent Variable: math.

TABLE 3.5   Estimate of Fixed Effects[a]

Parameter	Estimate	Std. Error	df	t	Sig.
Intercept	57.674234	.188266	416.066	306.344	.000

[a] Dependent Variable: math.

TABLE 3.6   Estimates of Covariance Parameters[a]

Parameter		Estimate	Std. Error	Wald Z	Sig.
Residual		66.550655	1.171618	56.802	.000
Intercept [subject = nschcode]	Variance	10.642209	1.028666	10.346	.000

[a] Dependent Variable: math.

[10.642/(10.642 + 66.551) = 10.642/77.193], or 13.8%. The intraclass correlation provides a sense of the degree to which differences in the outcome *Y* exist between Level 2 units; that is, it helps answer the question of the existence or nonexistence of meaningful differences in outcomes between the Level 2 units. The results of the null or no-predictors model (basically a one-way ANOVA analysis) suggest that the development of a multilevel model is warranted. Because intercepts vary significantly across schools (Wald $Z = 10.346$, $p < .001$), and the ICC suggests that about 13.8% of the total variability in math scores lies between schools, we can develop a multilevel model first to explain this variability in intercepts within and between schools.

The reliability of the sample mean for any unit as an estimate for its population mean can also be assessed with information drawn from the variance components. This can provide the analyst with a means by which the assumption of differences in outcomes across units can be checked. Because sample sizes are likely to differ within each unit *j*, this reliability will vary across the Level 2 units. Reliability within any particular unit can be estimated as

$$\lambda = \frac{\sigma_B^2}{\left[\sigma_B^2 + \left(\sigma_W^2/n_j\right)\right]}. \tag{3.6}$$

In this example, the within-group sample sizes range from 12 to 37. Using the within-group sample sizes we can estimate the reliability for the smallest unit as 10.64/[10.64 + (66.55/12)] = 0.657. This is contrasted with the school that has 37 students tested: 10.64/[10.64 + (66.55/37)] = 0.855.

Our first type of multilevel question was: Do the average math scores students receive vary across schools in the sample? We can answer that question from Table 3.6. The Residual parameter describes the variance due to individuals within groups. As the table suggests, there is significant variance to be explained within groups (Wald $Z = 56.802$, $p < .001$). Similarly, the intercept parameter indicates that the intercepts vary significantly across the sample of schools

(Wald $Z = 10.346$, $p < .001$). The Wald Z test provides a Z statistic summarizing the ratio of the estimate to its standard error.

Researchers have noted several problems with this statistic, however, that analysts may want to keep in mind. First, the Wald Z test is a two-tailed test. Because variances cannot be smaller than 0 (i.e., the null hypothesis is that the parameter = 0), the test should be conducted as a one-tailed test (Hox, 2002). This means that when testing variances (as in Table 3.6), the significance level should be divided by 2 to reflect a one-tailed probability level. Of course, in this instance this will not make a difference, since the two-tailed p value is very small. Note that for testing covariances between random effects (which can be positive or negative) the two-tailed significance test can be maintained. Second, for a large estimated variance coefficient, the standard error can be inflated, which lowers the Wald statistic value and, therefore, can make it overly conservative. Third, the Wald Z test can also perform poorly under conditions of extreme multicollinearity and in situations with small sample sizes. For small samples, the likelihood-ratio test (which is also provided as SPSS output) tends to be more reliable than the Wald test.

Step 2: Building the Individual-Level (or Level 1) Random Intercept Model

In a multilevel analysis, we work primarily with three equations: a within-group (or individual-level) equation, a between-groups intercept equation, and a between-groups slope equation. For each individual i in school j a proposed model similar to Equation 3.1 (summarizing the effect of student SES on math achievement) can be expressed as

$$Y_{ij} = \beta_{0j} + \beta_1(\text{SES})_{ij} + \varepsilon_{ij}. \tag{3.7}$$

Equation 3.7 suggests that at the individual level, within-groups student SES is related to achievement levels.

Equation 3.8 (which is the same as Equation 3.4) implies that variation in intercepts can be described by a school-level intercept (γ_{00}), or grand mean, and a random parameter capturing variation in individual school means (u_{0j}) from the grand mean:

$$\beta_{0j} = \gamma_{00} + u_{0j}. \tag{3.8}$$

Equation 3.9 implies that a within-unit slope (e.g., SES–achievement) can also be examined as randomly varying across units in the sample:

$$\beta_{1j} = \gamma_{10} + u_{1j}. \tag{3.9}$$

Equation 3.9 suggests variability in slopes can be described by a school-level average slope coefficient (γ_{10}), or grand mean, and a random parameter capturing variation in individual school coefficients (u_{1j}) from the grand mean. Because the slope is considered to be randomly varying across schools, the corresponding test of significance of the parameter will be based on the number of schools in the sample. Often, in building models, we may treat the within-group slopes as fixed in preliminary analyses (i.e., in situations where we are not testing a particular hypothesized relationship). In the case where we wish to treat the within-group slope as fixed (i.e., it does not vary across schools), Equation 3.9 would be rewritten as

$$\beta_{1j} = \gamma_{10}. \tag{3.10}$$

As Equation 3.10 indicates, there is no random component (u_{1j}), so the slope coefficient is fixed to one value for the sample. In the case where the Level 1 slope coefficient is fixed, the significance test for the slope will be based on the number of individuals in the sample. If it turns out that both intercepts and slopes vary randomly across schools, Equations 3.8 and 3.9 suggest that group-level models can subsequently be built to explain variation in the random intercept and slope across groups.

Model 1: Defining the Level 1 Random Intercept Model With SPSS Menu Commands

(SPSS settings will default to those used for the preceding Null Model.)

1. Go to the SPSS toolbar and select ANALYZE, MIXED MODELS, LINEAR.

This command opens the *Linear Mixed Models: Specify Subjects and Repeated* dialog box.

2. The *Linear Mixed Models: Specify Subjects and Repeated* dialog box, displays *schcode* in the *Subjects* box.

Click the CONTINUE button to display the *Linear Mixed Models* dialog box.

3. The *Linear Mixed Models* dialog box displays *math* in the *Dependent Variable* box.

Locate and click the *ses* variable from the left column. Then click the right-arrow button to transfer *ses* into the *Covariate(s)* box.

Click the FIXED button to access the *Linear Mixed Models: Fixed Effects* dialog box.

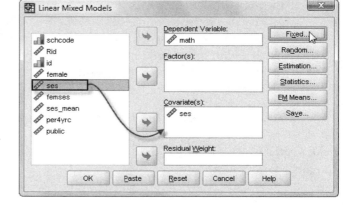

4a. Within the *Linear Mixed Models: Fixed Effects* dialog box, click the pull-down menu to change the factorial setting to *Main Effects*.
  b. Click to select *ses* from the *Factors and Covariates* box, then click the ADD button to move the variable into the *Model* box.
  c. Note on the lower left of the screen the intercept is selected and the sum of squares is the default setting.

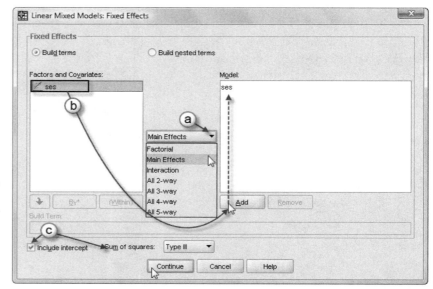

Click the CONTINUE button to return to the *Linear Mixed Models* dialog box. In the *Linear Mixed Models* dialog box, click the RANDOM button to access the *Linear Mixed Models: Random Effects* dialog box.

5a. The *Random Effect 1 of 1* screen displays the default settings of the prior model. We will stay with variance components (VC) for the covariance structure, since only the intercept will be randomly varying in this within-school model.

b. Confirm *Include Intercept* is selected.

c. Confirm *schcode* appears in the *Combinations* box.

Click the CONTINUE button to return to the *Linear Mixed Models* dialog box.

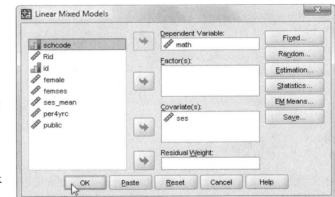

6. In the *Linear Mixed Models* dialog box, the estimation and statistics settings remain the same as those used for the Null Model so skip over these buttons and click OK to run the model.

Note: It is possible to save predicted estimates and residuals for random and fixed effects using the SAVE button. This would allow us to examine their normality and linearity.

Since no further changes are to be made, click OK to run the model.

We will first build a model to examine variability in intercepts across schools (as in Equations 3.3 and 3.4). The individual-level model is represented as Equation 3.7, which suggests that students' SES background affects math achievement. The school-level model is represented as Equation 3.8, suggesting only that the school-level intercepts vary randomly across schools. We discuss the school-level model in a subsequent section.

Interpreting the Output From Model 1

Following is the SPSS output generated from the Level 1 model. Table 3.7 summarizes the total number of parameters being estimated (4). This fits with Equations 3.8 and 3.9 (suggesting one within-school predictor SES, the intercept, the Level 2 variance, and the residual [or Level 1] variance). The column referred to as "Number of Levels" describes the fixed effects (2) and the number of random effects (1). There are two fixed effects to be estimated (the intercept and SES) and one random effect (the Level 2 variance component describing variability in the intercept across schools in the sample). The covariance structure describes the way the covariance matrix

TABLE 3.7 Model Dimension[b]

		Number of Levels	Covariance Structure	Number of Parameters	Subject Variables
Fixed Effects	Intercept	1		1	
	ses	1		1	
Random Effects	Intercept[a]	1	Variance Components	1	schcode
Residual				1	
Total		3		4	

[a] As of version 11.5, the syntax rules for the RANDOM subcommand have changed. Your command syntax may yield results that differ from those produced by prior versions. If you are using version 11 syntax, please consult the current syntax reference guide for more information.

[b] Dependent Variable: math.

TABLE 3.8 Type III Tests of Fixed Effects[a]

Source	Numerator *df*	Denominator *df*	F	Sig.
Intercept	1	375.699	187802.817	.000
ses	1	3914.638	803.954	.000

[a] Dependent Variable: math.

of random effects is dimensionalized at the group level. In this case, we use the default (VC), which provides an estimate of the intercept variance but again no slope variance because we have opted to fix the slope (nor will there be covariance between intercept and slope). This is the same as specifying an identity covariance matrix.

Table 3.8 presents the typical ANOVA table for examining the significance of the fixed-effect parameters in the model. The large *F*-ratio associated with SES in the table suggests that student SES is significantly related to student math scores. The test of the significance of the intercept is generally not of interest (unless perhaps the mean for math has been standardized to 0), as it is merely a test of whether the intercept is 0 in the model. As the table shows, we can reject the null hypothesis that it is 0 (and we already know from the null model and descriptive analysis that it is approximately 57.6).

Table 3.9 provides the estimates of the fixed effect coefficients. First, we can see that the intercept (adjusted for student SES) is 57.596. This represents the average school mean adjusted for student SES. The standard error is 0.133. The degrees of freedom reported for each fixed effect, which reflect the Satterthwaite correction for approximating the denominator degrees of freedom for significance tests of fixed effects in models where there are unequal variances and group sizes, are useful in determining at what level each variable is measured in the model. For example, we know there are 419 schools in the sample. This is consistent with the 375.7 degrees of freedom reported in Table 3.9. In contrast, we know that SES is an individual-level variable. There are 6,871 individuals in the sample, so the degrees of freedom of 3914.6 are consistent with a variable measured at Level 1. Once again, the *t*-test of the significance of the parameter is not really interesting, since it is a test of whether the intercept is equal to 0.

TABLE 3.9 Estimates of Fixed Effects[a]

Parameter	Estimate	Std. Error	*df*	*t*	Sig.
Intercept	57.595965	.132905	375.699	433.362	.000
ses	3.873861	.136624	3914.638	28.354	.000

[a] Dependent Variable: math.

When we compare the intercepts between this model and the single-level linear regression analysis at the beginning of the chapter, we find they are very similar (57.598 for the OLS model vs. 57.596 for the multilevel model). The difference in standard errors between these two estimates is larger, as we would expect given the clustering and associated intraclass correlation. More specifically, the estimated standard error (*SE*) from the OLS model was 0.098, and the standard error from the Level 1 multilevel model is 0.133, which is 36% larger. In that original single-level OLS analysis, the intercept described the average student achievement in the sample, without regard for students' school settings.

Second, in this case, we are more interested in the slope for SES (β = 3.874) and the standard error (0.137). When we compare these against the single-level model, we find they are considerably different (i.e., for the single-level analysis the slope was 4.255 and the standard error was 0.126). When we test hypotheses about model estimates (e.g., whether an unstandardized regression coefficient is significantly related to the dependent variable), the hypothesis test (often a *t*-test) is based on the ratio of the unstandardized estimate to its standard error (e.g., for SES this in the single-level model this is 4.255/.126 = 33.858). If the *t*-ratio is significantly large, given the sample under consideration, the parameter is considered statistically significant. In the multilevel analysis, the ratio of the unstandardized estimate of SES to its standard error is smaller (*t*-ratio = 28.344, but still is significant as we might expect).

These different results in our example illustrate the general point that parameter estimates and standard errors can be different in single-level versus multilevel analyses. As this simple multilevel analysis suggests, standard errors are often underestimated in single-level analyses, which can lead to a greater number of significant *t*-values and, hence, support for a proposed model than would be observed if a proposed model were tested with multilevel techniques. Directly as a result, in a multilevel analysis, adjusting for clustering generally results in a reduction of Type I errors (false rejection of the null hypothesis).

The output also provides information about the model's random parameters. The output suggests that the addition of the within-group predictor, SES, reduces the residual (within-group) variability (i.e., from 66.551 in the null model to 62.807 in the Level 1 model). This reduction in variance between the one-way ANOVA (or null) model and the current model can be used to calculate a reduction in variance estimate (or R^2) estimate for the within-school and between-school portions of the model. For each level, it is calculated as follows:

$$\left(\sigma^2_{M1} - \sigma^2_{M2}\right)\big/\sigma^2_{M1}, \tag{3.11}$$

where $M1$ refers to the one-way ANOVA (no predictors) Level 1 or Level 2 variance components and $M2$ refers to the current model's variance components. For the within-groups portion, this is calculated as 0.056 (66.551 − 62.807 = 3.744/66.551 = 0.056). This suggests that student SES background accounts for about 6% of the within-school variability in student scores. Notice also that the within-school predictor also affects that residual variability in intercepts at the school level. In particular, the initial variance component for schools, from the null model, was 10.642. After SES is added, however, the between-school variance in math achievement shrinks to 3.469 (see Table 3.10). For the reduction in variance between schools, this would be calculated as 0.674 [(10.642 − 3.469)/10.642]. This suggests that within-group SES accounts for almost

TABLE 3.10   Estimates of Covariance Parameters[a]

Parameter		Estimate	Std. Error	Wald *Z*	Sig.
Residual		62.807187	1.108877	56.640	.000
Intercept [subject = schcode]	Variance	3.469256	.538821	6.439	.000

[a] Dependent Variable: math.

TABLE 3.11 Random Effect Covariance Structure (G)[a]

	Intercept	nschcode
Intercept	schcode	3.469256

Variance Components
[a] Dependent Variable: math.

two-thirds (67.4%) of the between-groups variability in achievement. In other words, a full two-thirds of the variation in means across schools can be attributed to differences in the socio-economic status of students in those schools. Another way of looking at this is that the initial variability in math achievement observed between schools (i.e., the ICC) is reduced considerably after controlling for student SES. From Equation 3.2, we find that ICC is now a little over 5% [3.469/(3.469 + 62.807) = 0.052].

We note, however, this reduction-in-variance type of R^2 statistic should be interpreted cautiously, because it is sometimes possible to obtain negative values for R^2. This is because the variance components may be less accurately estimated when there are no predictors in the model. For example, when an individual variable is sampled through a multilevel sampling process, it may show some between-group variability even if there is no between-group variability present in the population (Hox, 2002). In these cases, Hox (2002) notes that the reduction-in-variance procedures described previously may work as described in our example (i.e., where the within-group variable reduces between-group variability). In other situations, however, there may be variables that have almost no variation at one of the levels in the model. For example, this might occur if we had exactly the same percentage of males and females (50%) in each school. If there were no school-level variation in average gender composition, this would be less variance than expected by simple random sampling and could produce negative explained variance (see Hox, 2002, or Snijders & Bosker, 1999, for further discussion). Hox notes that another problem that can occur is that if random slopes are present, the estimated residual variances are related to the scale of measurement chosen for the explanatory variables (i.e., how they are centered, whether they might be standardized). When the interest is in the size of the variance components produced, it is therefore desirable to center the explanatory variables with random slopes on their grand means, since this will provide estimates for an "average" sampling unit (Hox, 2002). We discuss centering decisions further in subsequent chapters.

The covariance parameters table (Table 3.10) also suggests that after the introduction of SES into the model, there is still significant variability to be explained both within schools (Wald Z = 56.640, $p < .001$) and between schools (Wald Z = 6.439, $p < .001$). The Wald Z test suggests that, even after controlling for student SES within schools, a statistically significant amount of variation in outcomes still remains both within and between schools. This suggests that we could add other predictors (e.g., gender, ethnicity, motivation) within schools and between schools (e.g., student composition, school process indicators) that might explain this residual variability in intercepts.

The final piece of output (Table 3.11) provides the random effect covariance structure for Level 2. In this case there is only one random effect. Because we specified the SES–achievement slope to be fixed within schools, there is no variance component describing variability in slopes.

Step 3: Building the Group-Level (or Level 2) Random Intercept Model

Next, we will add school-level variables to explain the variability in intercepts across schools. In this case, our thesis is that school context variables (i.e., aggregated student SES composition, type of school [public coded 1, other = 0]) and the focus of the school's academic program (i.e., the aggregate percentage of students who intend to study at 4-year universities after high school) will impact the remaining variability in achievement between schools. It is important to note that when Level 2 predictors are added to the model, care should be taken that every individual in each unit has the same value on that variable. This will ensure that the estimates are calculated based on the number of Level 2 units rather than the number of Level 1 units in the model. If there are different values or missing values for some individuals, they should be changed for consistency.

At the school level, we must modify Equation 3.4 to indicate the three predictors that we are adding to the model:

$$\beta_{0j} = \gamma_{00} + \gamma_{01}(ses\_mean)_j + \gamma_{02}(per4yrc)_j + \gamma_{03}(public)_j + u_{0j}. \tag{3.12}$$

Public school is a dummy coded variable (1 = public, 0 = private). Because it is dichotomous, we can add it either as a categorical variable or as a covariate. Variables with three or more categories should be added as factors. When categorical variables are entered as factors, the reference group is the last category. If the user wishes to select a different category as the reference group, she or he could recode the variable.

We will first demonstrate how to add a public school indicator to the model as a factor. The other two variables are continuous, so they are added as covariates. In all, we are adding three fixed effects, but the other parameters remain the same, so we are estimating a total of seven parameters in this model (five fixed effects, one random between-school residual variance, and one within-group residual variance).

Model 2: Defining the Group-Level Random Intercept Model With SPSS Menu Commands

(SPSS settings will default to those used for Model 1.)

1. Go to the SPSS toolbar and select ANALYZE, MIXED MODELS, LINEAR.

This command opens the *Linear Mixed Models: Specify Subjects and Repeated* dialog box.

2. The *Linear Mixed Models: Specify Subjects and Repeated* dialog box, displays *schcode* in the *Subjects* box.

Click the CONTINUE button to display the *Linear Mixed Models* dialog box.

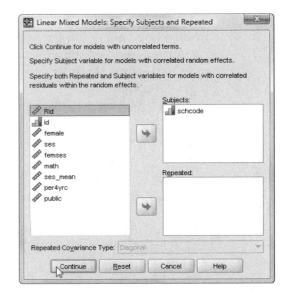

3. The *Linear Mixed Models* dialog box displays *math* in the *Dependent Variable* box.

If there is a categorical indicator, it should be added as a factor. Each level of a factor can have a different linear effect on the value of the dependent variable. If a variable is dichotomous it may be added as either a factor or a covariate. We will demonstrate by adding *public* as a factor first.

The variable *ses* appears in the *Covariate(s)* box. The variables *ses_mean*, and *per4yrc* may be added to the *Covariate(s)* box by selecting them and clicking the right-arrow button. However, it is recommended to change the sequence of the entered variables so the output tables will be easier to interpret.

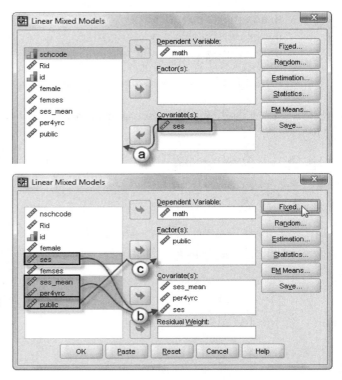

a. This may be achieved by selecting *ses* then clicking the left-arrow button to first clear contents of the *Covariate(s)* box.

b. Now add the variables in the recommended sequence: *ses_mean*, *per4yr*, and *ses*.

Note: An alternate method is to add the additional variables then rearrange them within the *Covariate(s)* box by selecting *ses* then dragging it below *per4yrc*.

c. Click to select *public* then click the right-arrow button to move the variable into the *Factor(s)* box.

Click the FIXED button to access the *Linear Mixed Models: Fixed Effects* dialog box.

4a. Within the *Linear Mixed Models: Fixed Effects* dialog box, confirm that *Main Effects* is selected.

b. Click to select the variables *public, ses_mean, per4yrc,* and *ses* from the *Factors and Covariates* box. Then click the ADD button to move the variables into the *Model* box.

c. Confirm that the *Include Intercept* option is selected.

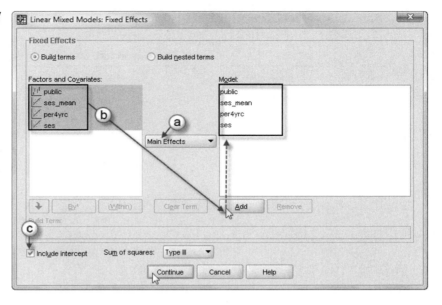

Click the CONTINUE button to return to the *Linear Mixed Models* dialog box.

5. The random effects, estimation, and statistics settings remain the same as those used for Model 1, so skip over these buttons and click the OK button to run the model.

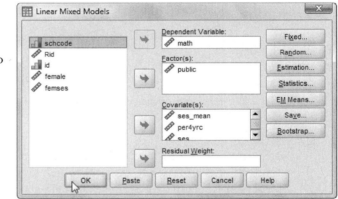

Interpreting the Output From Model 2

The first SPSS output table (Table 3.12) confirms that we are estimating seven total parameters in this model. Table 3.13 describes the fixed effect estimates. Regarding the school-level predictors, controlling for the other predictors in the model, we first note that school type does not affect achievement ($\gamma_{03} = 0.16$, $p > .05$). Since there is an intercept term in the model, the second category of public (private = 0; public = 1) is redundant. In contrast, the type of academic environment (i.e., as defined by students' perceptions of their plans about attending 4-year institutions after high school) affects achievement ($\gamma_{02} = 1.42$). Turning to SES, aggregate student SES composition affects math achievement ($\gamma_{01} = 2.47$), even after controlling for individual SES within schools. The addition of aggregate student SES background somewhat reduces the size of the SES effect on achievement within schools (β_1 slope for SES has a school-level intercept, $\gamma_{10} = 3.19$ vs. 3.87 in the previous model). The model, therefore, indicates that the effects of student SES background are significant both within schools and between schools (i.e., this latter parameter was not estimated in the previous model). This is an example of a composition effect, or an effect that tends to compound across levels of the organization—that is, compositional effects occur when the aggregate of a person-level characteristic is related to the outcome, even

TABLE 3.12   Model Dimension[b]

		Number of Levels	Covariance Structure	Number of Parameters	Subject Variables
Fixed Effects	Intercept	1		1	
	public	2		1	
	ses_mean	1		1	
	per4yrc	1		1	
	ses	1		1	
Random Effects	Intercept[a]	1	Variance Components	1	schcode
Residual				1	
Total		7		7	

[a] As of version 11.5, the syntax rules for the RANDOM subcommand have changed. Your command syntax may yield results that differ from those produced by prior versions. If you are using version 11 syntax, please consult the current syntax reference guide for more information.

[b] Dependent Variable: math.

TABLE 3.13   Estimates of Fixed Effects[b]

Parameter	Estimate	Std. Error	df	t	Sig.
Intercept	56.277288	.429669	411.160	130.978	.000
[public=0]	.164264	.275903	409.345	.595	.552
[public=1]	0[a]	0			
ses_mean	2.473244	.306897	709.247	8.059	.000
per4yrc	1.419812	.471391	413.879	3.012	.003
ses	3.190801	.157803	6448.937	20.220	.000

[a] This parameter is set to zero because it is redundant.

[b] Dependent Variable: math.

after controlling for the effect of the individual-level variable (Raudenbush & Bryk, 2002). The compositional effect is the extent to which the size of the organizational relationship differs from the person-level effect. Compositional effects often represent proxies for other types of organizational processes that occur (e.g., curricular organization, expectations for students, etc.).

Readers may also notice that the addition of the school-level variables changes the intercept (γ_{00} = 56.28 here vs. 57.60 in the previous model). This reflects that the intercept in this model represents the mean for public schools (i.e., with private schools [coded 0] being 0.16 of a point higher). Note that if we add the public school intercept and private school estimate (56.28 + .16) we obtain 56.44, which is intercept in Table 3.14 when public school is entered in the model as a covariate. (SPSS menu commands for treating public school as a covariate are provided at the end of this section.) In this case, public schools are 0.16 of a point lower than this intercept. This suggests the two model formulations are the same (as we would expect). Since the estimates are the same, we will continue to define school type as a covariate for the rest of the analysis (similar to Table 3.14).

The estimates of the variance components in Table 3.15 suggest that student SES at Level 1 and the three Level 2 predictors (public, ses_mean, and per4yrc) reduce the variance component at the school level substantially (i.e., from 10.64 in the one-way ANOVA to 2.40 in Table 3.15).

TABLE 3.14   Estimates of Fixed Effects[a]

Parameter	Estimate	Std. Error	df	t	Sig.
Intercept	56.441552	.474433	421.055	118.966	.000
public	−.164264	.275903	409.345	−.595	.552
ses_mean	2.473244	.306897	709.247	8.059	.000
per4yrc	1.419812	.471391	413.879	3.012	.003
ses	3.190801	.157803	6448.937	20.220	.000

[a] Dependent Variable: math.

TABLE 3.15   Estimates of Covariance Parameters[a]

Parameter		Estimate	Std. Error	Wald Z	Sig.
Residual		62.630370	1.102966	56.784	.000
Intercept [subject = schcode]	Variance	2.395178	.443654	5.399	.000

[a] Dependent Variable: math.

From Equation 3.11, the reduction in variance observed at Level 2 between Models 1 and 2 can be used to calculate the amount of variance accounted for (R^2) at Level 2, which is 0.774 [(10.64 − 2.40)/10.64]. We could also calculate an R^2 coefficient for Level 1 using the Level 1 one-way ANOVA and current Level 1 variance components in the same manner [(66.55 − 62.63)/66.55 = .059]. Student SES therefore accounts for about 6% of the Level 1 variance in individual math achievement (about the same as the estimate in Table 3.10).

Defining the Public School Variable as a Covariate Using SPSS Menu Commands

1. To generate results shown in Table 3.14 go to the SPSS toolbar and select ANALYZE, MIXED MODELS, LINEAR.

This command opens the *Linear Mixed Models: Specify Subjects and Repeated* dialog box.

2. The *Linear Mixed Models: Specify Subjects and Repeated dialog* box, displays *schcode* in the *Subjects* box.

Click the CONTINUE button to display the *Linear Mixed Models* dialog box.

3. In the *Linear Mixed Models* dialog box, the default setting from the prior model shows *math* (*Dependent Variable*), *public* (*Factors*), and *ses_mean, per4yrc,* and *ses* (*Covariates*).
   a. Click to select *public*, then click the left-arrow button to remove the variable from the *Factor(s)* box.
   b. Click to select *ses_mean, per4yrc,* and *ses*, then click the left-arrow button to remove the variables from the *Covariate(s)* box.
   c. Click to select the variables from the left column and enter them into the *Covariate(s)* box in the following sequence to facilitate reading of the output tables: *public, ses_mean, per4yrc,* and *ses*.

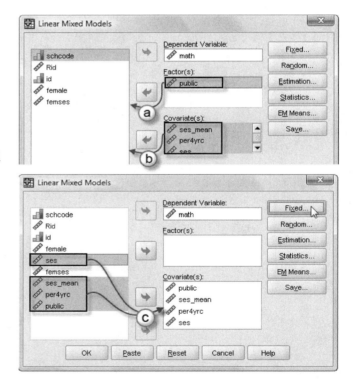

Note: An alternative method to Steps a and b is to remove *public* from the *Factor(s)* box and add it into the *Covariate(s)* box. Then arrange the variables into the recommended sequence by selecting and dragging them. (Click to select a variable, hold down the left button on the mouse, then drag the variable into position.)

4a. The *Linear Mixed Models: Fixed Effects* dialog box displays part of the *Main Effects* setting used for Model 2. Select the variables and click the REMOVE button to clear the *Model* box.

b. Click to select all the variables from the *Factors and Covariates* box, then click the ADD button to move them into the *Model* box.

Click the CONTINUE button to return to the *Linear Mixed Models* dialog box.

5. The random effects, estimation, and statistics settings remain the same as the prior model. Skip over these buttons and click OK to run the model.

Step 4: Adding a Randomly Varying Slope (the Random Slope and Intercept Model)

Since individual SES is significantly related to achievement, we might want to see if the slope varies across schools. This could help us identify schools that are more (or less) equitable in producing outcomes for students of varying SES backgrounds. It may be that school composition, school type, or school academic environment interact with the size of the within-school slope. We would like to find settings where the effect of individual SES on achievement is reduced. In this case, we might ask: Do the slopes vary randomly across schools, and if they do, is there a relationship between features of schools' environments and the strength of the slope relationship?

The important equation in this step is Equation 3.9. In this model, we will examine whether the slope varies, so we need to make a couple of changes to the model. First, we need to add the SES–achievement slope as a randomly varying parameter in the model. Second, we need to change the covariance matrix of random effects to accommodate the randomly varying slope. The other parameters in the model will remain the same. Adding the randomly varying slope will change the number of random effects in the model from one (i.e., the intercept) to two

Warnings

Iteration was terminated but convergence has not been achieved. The MIXED procedure continues despite this warning. Subsequent results produced are based on the last iteration. Validity of the model fit is uncertain.

FIGURE 3.3 Warning message.

(i.e., the intercept and the SES–achievement slope). If we only add the randomly varying slope, we will have a diagonal covariance structure. We can estimate this structure using the default Variance Components (VC) matrix or by specifying a diagonal covariance matrix (DIAG) in SPSS. As Equation 3.13 suggests, this provides estimates of the intercept and slope variances:

$$\begin{bmatrix} \sigma_I^2 & 0 \\ 0 & \sigma_S^2 \end{bmatrix}. \tag{3.13}$$

In contrast, an unstructured (UN) covariance matrix implies the intercept and slope variances are estimated, as well as the covariance between the intercept and slope. If we also estimate the covariance (σ_{IS}) between the intercept and slope, an additional parameter is added to the model:

$$\begin{bmatrix} \sigma_I^2 & \sigma_{IS} \\ \sigma_{IS} & \sigma_S^2 \end{bmatrix}. \tag{3.14}$$

Notice that because the covariance matrix is a square matrix, the covariance appears both above and below the diagonal. We can also specify an unstructured covariance–correlation matrix (abbreviated as UNR in SPSS). This would provide a correlation between the intercept and slope, which is often easier to interpret. Where we estimated seven parameters before (five fixed effects, one random Level 2 variance, one within-group residual variance), we will be estimating nine parameters now (five fixed effects, three random Level 2 effects, one within-group residual variance).

Although is usually desirable to obtain an estimate of the covariance between the intercept and slope, we note that sometimes a warning is issued when an unstructured covariance structure is used. For example, if the covariance or slope component is small, the computer may not be able to estimate the parameter. In this case, when we ran the model with an unstructured matrix (i.e., Equation 3.14), we received an error message (Figure 3.3).

In such cases, the user can try specifying a diagonal covariance structure for the random parameters. The Variance Components (VC) specification used in previous models will accomplish needed change. This means we will estimate a total of eight parameters, since we are eliminating the covariance between the intercept and slope at Level 2.

Model 3: Defining the Random Slope and Intercept Model With SPSS Menu Commands

(SPSS settings will default to those used for Model 2.)

1. Go to the SPSS toolbar and select ANALYZE, MIXED MODELS, LINEAR.

This command opens the *Linear Mixed Models: Specify Subjects and Repeated* dialog box.

2. The *Linear Mixed Models: Specify Subjects and Repeated* dialog box displays *schcode* in the *Subjects* box.

Click the CONTINUE button to display the *Linear Mixed Models* dialog box.

3. The *Linear Mixed Models* dialog box displays *math* in the *Dependent Variable* box.

The variables *public, ses_mean, per4yr,* and *ses* appear in the *Covariate(s)* box.

The *Fixed* effects settings remain the same so click the RANDOM button to access the *Linear Mixed Models: Random Effects* dialog box.

4. The *Random Effect 1 of 1* screen displays *Variance Components* as the covariance matrix.

   a. Confirm *Variance Components* is selected covariance structure.
   b. Confirm the *Include Intercept* option is selected.
   c. Click the pull-down menu to change the factorial setting to *Main Effects.*
   d. Click to select the variable *ses* from the *Factors and Covariates* box, then click the ADD button to move the variable into the *Model* box.
   e. Confirm *schcode* appears in the *Combinations* box.

Click CONTINUE to return to the *Linear Mixed Models* dialog box.

5. The estimation and statistics settings remain the same as Model 2, so skip over these buttons and click OK to run the model.

Interpreting the Output From Model 3

We can first confirm that we are estimating the eight parameters we anticipated (see Table 3.16).

Similar to the last model, the fixed effects table (Table 3.17) indicates that school aggregate SES, percentage of students attending 4-year universities, and individual SES all impact math achievement. We can observe that defining individual SES as randomly varying changes the estimates slightly from the previous model with a fixed SES–achievement slope. For example, the intercept changes slightly from 56.44 in Table 3.14 to 56.47, and the coefficient for percent 4-year university changes from 1.42 to 1.36.

TABLE 3.16 Model Dimension[b]

		Number of Levels	Covariance Structure	Number of Parameters	Subject Variables
Fixed Effects	Intercept	1		1	
	public	1		1	
	ses_mean	1		1	
	per4yrc	1		1	
	ses	1		1	
Random Effects	Intercept + ses[a]	2	Variance Components	2	schcode
Residual				1	
Total		7		8	

[a] As of version 11.5, the syntax rules for the RANDOM subcommand have changed. Your command syntax may yield results that differ from those produced by prior versions. If you are using version 11 syntax, please consult the current syntax reference guide for more information.
[b] Dependent Variable: math.

TABLE 3.17 Estimates of Fixed Effects[a]

Parameter	Estimate	Std. Error	df	t	Sig.
Intercept	56.469785	.471568	419.501	119.749	.000
public	–.119986	.274402	407.915	–.437	.662
ses_mean	2.659588	.313631	698.064	8.480	.000
per4yrc	1.360179	.467933	410.212	2.907	.004
ses	3.163898	.168888	635.541	18.734	.000

[a] Dependent Variable: math.

TABLE 3.18 Estimates of Covariance Parameters[a]

Parameter		Estimate	Std. Error	Wald Z	Sig.
Residual		62.114614	1.111312	55.893	.000
Intercept [subject = schcode]	Variance	2.112261	.445499	4.741	.000
ses [subject = schcode]	Variance	1.314246	.566455	2.320	.020

[a] Dependent Variable: math.

For this model, our primary interest is with the estimates of the variance components (see Table 3.18). Defining the SES–math slope as randomly varying slightly changes the variance remaining at Level 1 (i.e., from 62.63 to 62.11). The intercept variance is slightly different also (i.e., from 2.40 to 2.11). The remaining intercept variance is still significant (Wald Z = 4.74, p = .000), which indicates that even after adding the three predictors to the model, there is still variance in intercepts that could be explained across schools by adding additional school-level variables. Most important for our purposes, the slope variance (1.31) is significant (Wald Z = 2.320, one-tailed p = .02/2 = .01). This suggests that the slopes vary across schools in the sample.

Because we could not fit the model with a proposed covariance between the intercept and slope, we cannot examine their relationship with information from this model. It turns out in this case, the "public" school variable is the problem. If we remove that variable from the model, we can estimate the covariance as –1.59 (p < .01).

Step 5: Explaining Variability in the Random Slope (More Complex Random Slopes and Intercept Models)

The results in the variance components table (Table 3.18) suggest that a model could be developed to explain the variability in the SES–achievement slope across schools. Building such a model requires the introduction of cross-level interactions, or school-level variables that moderate (i.e., enhance or diminish) the size of the within-school SES–math achievement slopes. In simple models, the effects of predictors on the outcome do not depend on the values of other predictors in the model. Interactions indicate that the relationship between a predictor and the outcome depends on the value of a third variable. SPSS Mixed allows the analyst to build a variety of different interactions within the fixed effects syntax statements or within the model-building menu statements.

Interactions are built as product terms from two predictors in the model ($A*B$), so there are three relevant parameters in the model (A, B, and $A*B$). More specifically, interactions estimate the linear impact of A on Y when A increases by one unit and the slope of B remains constant. This implies that the slope coefficient of A added to the slope coefficient of $A*B$ should be the complete coefficient for A (Hamilton, 1992). The same would apply for predicting the complete impact of B on Y with the interaction.

Cross-level interactions indicate similar types of interactions but across levels of the data hierarchy. For example, assume we wish to estimate the cross-level interaction of student SES composition (ses_mean) on the individual SES–achievement slope within schools in our data set. This is an example of a covariate–covariate interaction. Table 3.19 suggests that if the impact of individual SES (A) on math achievement (Y) is 3.18 and the cross-level interaction term ses*ses_mean is –0.25, then the impact of individual SES on math achievement is 2.93 [3.18 + (–.25) = 2.93] when the slope of ses_mean is held constant (2.78).

A factor–covariate cross-level interaction (public*ses) implies that the linear relationship between SES (A) and math achievement (Y) changes for different levels of factor (B); that is, types of schools. The output will provide an estimate for each level of the factor except

TABLE 3.19 Estimates of Fixed Effects[a]

Parameter	Estimate	Std. Error	df	t	Sig.
Intercept	57.605578	.137615	495.962	418.600	.000
ses_mean	2.781962	.309212	794.877	8.997	.000
ses	3.178977	.158253	6483.723	20.088	.000
ses_mean * ses	−.251206	.257415	1607.930	−.976	.329

[a] Dependent Variable: math.

the last category (which is the reference group). A factor–factor cross-level interaction (e.g., public*female) implies that each combination of factor levels may have a different linear effect on the outcome. For this interaction, the output will provide coefficients for each nonredundant combination using the last category of each factor as the reference group. We will discuss how to build these types of models in further detail in the next chapter.

For our purposes here, we will simply note that we add the three school-level predictors to the slope model to determine whether they might account for variability in the size of the SES–math achievement relationships across schools. The model can be written as

$$\beta_{1j} = \gamma_{10} + \gamma_{11}(ses\_mean * ses)_j + \gamma_{12}(per4yrc * ses)_j + \gamma_{13}(public * ses)_j + u_{1j}. \quad (3.15)$$

The cross-level effects appear in the output interactions between aggregate school SES composition and the within-school SES–math achievement slope (i.e., ses_mean*ses), between aggregate percentage students planning to attend 4-year colleges and the within-school SES–math achievement slope (i.e., per4yrc*ses), and between school type and ses (public*ses). This will add three extra parameters to be estimated in the model, making a total of eleven parameters to estimate.

Model 4: Defining More Complex Random Slope and Intercept Models With SPSS Menu Commands

(SPSS settings will default to those used for the preceding Model 3.)

1. Go to the SPSS toolbar and select ANALYZE, MIXED MODELS, LINEAR.

This command opens the *Linear Mixed Models: Specify Subjects and Repeated* dialog box.

2. The *Linear Mixed Models: Specify Subjects and Repeated* dialog box displays *schcode* in the *Subjects* box.

Click the CONTINUE button to display the *Linear Mixed Models* dialog box.

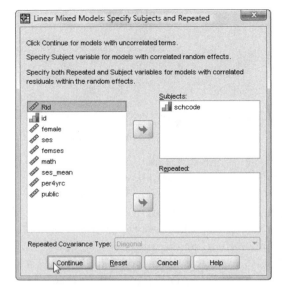

3. The *Linear Mixed Models* dialog box displays *math* in *the Dependent Variable* box.

The variables *public, ses_mean, per4yr,* and *ses* appear in the *Covariate(s)* box.

Click the FIXED button to access the *Linear Mixed Models: Fixed Effects* dialog box.

4. Three cross-interactions will be created from the *Linear Mixed Models: Fixed Effects* dialog box: *ses_mean*ses per4yrc*ses,* and *public*ses.*

a. Begin by clicking to select the *Build nested terms* option.

b. Click to select the variable *ses_mean* from the *Factors and Covariates* box.

c. Then click the down-arrow button, which will insert *ses_mean* into the *Build Term* construction section.

d. Next, click the BY* button, which will insert the computational symbol (*) to the term so it appears as *ses_mean*.*

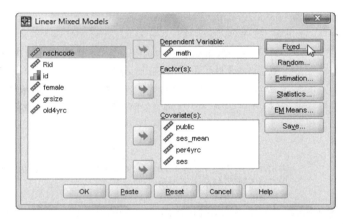

e. Now click to select *ses* from the *Factors and Covariates* box.

f. Then click the down-arrow button which will insert *ses* after the * (BY) term in the *Build Term* section. This completes the interaction command: *ses_mean*ses*.

g. Click the ADD button to move the interaction *ses_mean*ses* into the *Model* box.

5. The second cross-level interaction to create is *per4yrc*ses*.

a. Click to select the variable *per4yrc* from the *Factors and Covariates* box.

b. Then click the down-arrow button, which will insert *per4yrc* into the *Build Term* construction area.

c. Click the BY* button to insert the computation command symbol (*) to the term so it appears as *per4yrc**.

d. Next, click to select *ses* from the *Factors and Covariates* box.

e. Then click the down-arrow button to insert *ses* into the *Build Term* construction area. This completes the interaction *per4yrc*ses*.

f. Click the ADD button to move the interaction *ses_mean*ses* into the *Model* box.

Click the CONTINUE button to return to the *Linear Mixed Models* dialog box. Next click the RANDOM button to access *Linear Mixed Models: Random Effects*.

6. The third cross-level interaction to create is *public*ses*.

a. Click to select the variable *public* from the *Factors and Covariates* box.

b. Then click the down-arrow button, which will insert *public* into the *Build Term* construction area.

c. Click the BY* button to insert the computational command symbol (*) to the term so it appears as *public**.

d. Next, click to select *ses* from the *Factors and Covariates* box.

e. Then click the down arrow button to insert *ses* into the *Build Term* construction area. This completes the interaction *public*ses*.

f. Click the ADD button to move the interaction *public*ses* into the *Model* box.

Click the CONTINUE button to return to the *Linear Mixed Models* dialog box. Next click the RANDOM button to access *Linear Mixed Models: Random Effects*.

7. The *Random Effect 1 of 1* screen displays the prior model's settings.

a. Confirm the covariance structure is *Variance Components*.

b. Confirm *Include intercept* is selected.

c. Confirm *Main Effects* is selected.

d. Confirm *ses* appears in the *Model* box.

e. Confirm *schcode* appears in the *Combinations* box.

Click the CONTINUE button to return to the *Linear Mixed Models* dialog box.

8. The estimation and statistics settings remain the same as those used for Model 3, so skip over these buttons and click OK to run the model.

Interpreting the Output From Model 4

We can confirm in the model dimension table (Table 3.20) that we estimated 11 parameters. Notice also the Level 2 variance components table is designated as Variance Components (i.e., a diagonal matrix of random effects). The table confirms the three cross-level interactions (ses_mean*ses, public*ses, and per4yrc*ses) that were added to the fixed-effect portion of the model.

The fixed effects table (Table 3.21) suggests aggregate SES and aggregate percentage of students planning on attending 4-year postsecondary institutions affect achievement in math. School type (i.e., private or public) is not related to math achievement. Within schools, individual SES remains significantly related to math achievement.

Regarding the cross-level interactions, the results suggest that the within-school SES–achievement slope is different for different types of schools. More specifically, public schools have weaker SES–achievement slopes than private schools ($\gamma = -0.67$, $p < .05$). In public schools, the combined effect of individual SES on math achievement would be 3.09 [3.76 + (−0.67) = 3.09]. In private schools, the SES–achievement slope would be 3.76. This result suggests that the social distribution effects due to individual SES on math learning are less consequential for students in public schools than for students in private schools. Table 3.21 also suggests that aggregate school SES composition does not moderate the within-school SES–math achievement

TABLE 3.20 Model Dimension[b]

		Number of Levels	Covariance Structure	Number of Parameters	Subject Variables
Fixed Effects	Intercept	1		1	
	public	1		1	
	ses_mean	1		1	
	per4yrc	1		1	
	ses	1		1	
	ses_mean * ses	1		1	
	per4yrc * ses	1		1	
	public * ses	1		1	
Random Effects	Intercept + ses[a]	2	Variance Components	2	schcode
Residual				1	
Total		10		11	

[a] As of version 11.5, the syntax rules for the RANDOM subcommand have changed. Your command syntax may yield results that differ from those produced by prior versions. If you are using version 11 syntax, please consult the current syntax reference guide for more information.

[b] Dependent Variable: math.

TABLE 3.21   Estimates of Fixed Effects[a]

Parameter	Estimate	Std. Error	df	t	Sig.
Intercept	56.505254	.485329	450.229	116.427	.000
public	–.119925	.274238	405.467	–.437	.662
ses_mean	2.706473	.324107	759.554	8.351	.000
per4yrc	1.361887	.479336	439.899	2.841	.005
ses	3.757343	.605681	518.400	6.203	.000
ses_mean * ses	–.136539	.298571	303.798	–.457	.648
per4yrc * ses	–.130132	.592163	479.307	–.220	.826
public * ses	–.668237	.331145	404.838	–2.018	.044

[a] Dependent Variable: math.

slope ($\gamma = -0.14$, $p > .05$). Similarly, the proportion of students indicating they plan to attend a 4-year college also does not moderate the within-school SES–achievement slope ($\gamma = -0.13$, $p > .05$). These findings provide partial support for our initial research goal of identifying school settings where the within-school relationship between SES and math achievement (our measure of the social distribution of learning) is diminished.

The variance components table (Table 3.22) suggests that there is still significant variance in intercepts and slopes to be explained across schools, even after adding this set of school variables to the model. For example, the SES–achievement slope still varies across schools (Wald $Z = 2.375$, one-tailed $p = .018/2 = .009$).

We should remove the interaction terms that are not statistically significant to maintain a more parsimonious model (Table 3.23). The variables that comprise the interaction term, however, should be retained in the model even if they are not significant (e.g., public). In a subsequent chapter, we describe procedures for examining the fit of a comparison model against a more restricted model. We exclude the presentation of the variance components for this reduced model, as they are similar to the previous model.

We provide a simple graph to illustrate what the effect of a cross-level interaction looks like (Figure 3.4). (SPSS menu commands for creating the graph are provided at the end of this section.) For a factor*covariate interaction, the relationship implies the group regression

TABLE 3.22   Estimates of Covariance Parameters[a]

Parameter		Estimate	Std. Error	Wald Z	Sig.
Residual		62.101323	1.111295	55.882	.000
Intercept [subject = schcode]	Variance	2.087257	.445340	4.687	.000
ses [subject = schcode]	Variance	1.345094	.566327	2.375	.018

[a] Dependent Variable: math.

TABLE 3.23   Estimates of Fixed Effects[a]

Parameter	Estimate	Std. Error	df	t	Sig.
Intercept	56.440337	.470907	418.862	119.855	.000
public	–.123093	.273888	406.624	–.449	.653
ses_mean	2.659142	.313166	697.326	8.491	.000
per4yrc	1.404177	.467536	410.165	3.003	.003
ses	3.659485	.292123	461.438	12.527	.000
public * ses	–.682460	.328354	395.850	–2.078	.038

[a] Dependent Variable: math.

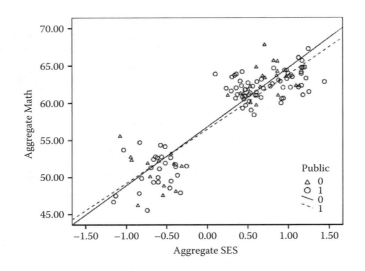

FIGURE 3.4 SES–achievement relationships in high- and low-achieving public and private schools.

lines are not parallel. A cross-level interaction represents the effect of a unit-level variable on a within-unit relationship. To illustrate this relationship in a rough way, we first aggregated individual math achievement and SES to the school level. We then created a subset of schools roughly 1 standard deviation above and below the grand mean of achievement. This illustrates the approximate 0.7 point steeper SES–achievement slope associated with private schools. Because we focused on groups of schools some distance from the grand mean, the graph also provides a sense of where the regression lines for public and private school SES–achievement slopes cross.

Graphing SES–Achievement Relationships in High- and Low-Achieving Schools With SPSS Menu Commands

To create Figure 3.4, select the data file *ch3schoolgraph.sav*.

1. Go to the toolbar and select DATA, SELECT CASES.

This command will open the *Select Cases* dialog box.

2a. Within the *Select Cases* dialog box, click to select IF CONDITION IS SATISFIED.

b. Then click the IF button which will activate the *Select Cases: If* box.

c. Click the variable *graph* from the left column listing, then click the right-arrow button to move it into the box. Use the keypad to enter the equal sign followed by the number 1. The resulting command (graph = 1) instructs SPSS to select cases where *graph* is coded as 1.

Click the CONTINUE button to return to the *Select Cases* dialog box.

3. Notice that the IF condition statement *graph = 1* is listed.

Click the OK button to return to the SPSS main menu.

4. To graph the selected cases, go to the SPSS toolbar and select GRAPHS, LEGACY DIALOGS, SCATTER/DOT.

5. Click the SIMPLE SCATTER option in the *Scatter/Dot* box. Then click the DEFINE button to open the *Simple Scatterplot* box.

6a. Within the *Simple Scatterplot* dialog box, click to select the variable *math_mean* from the left column listing. Then click the right-arrow button to move the variable into the *Y Axis* box.

b. Click to select *ses_mean* from the left column listing, then click the right-arrow button to move the variable into the *X Axis* box.

c. Click to select *public* from the left column listing, then click the right-arrow button to move the variable into the *Set Markers by* box.

Then click the OK button to generate the scatterplot.

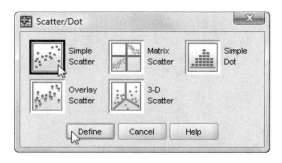

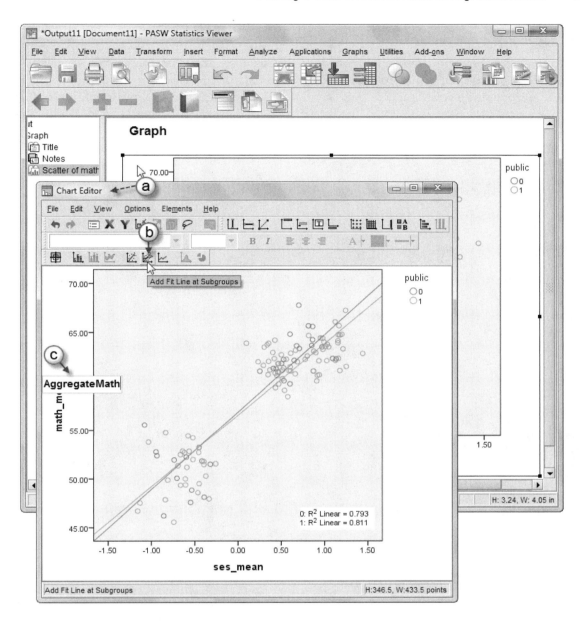

7. The graph appears in the *Viewer* screen.
   a. Click near the graph to activate the *Chart Editor*.
   b. On the *Chart Editor* shortcut icon bar, click the ADD FIT LINE AT SUBGROUPS. This will generate the fit lines and linear R-squares of 0.793 and 0.811 for this subset of the sample.
   c. Labels may be changed by modifying the contents. Other elements including chart lines, markers, and colors may also be modified through the Chart Editor's *Properties* box.

Summary

We have shown in this chapter how multilevel analyses allow the analyst to investigate a wider range of research questions than can be addressed in single-level analyses. In Chapter 4 we continue to illustrate the flexibility of multilevel techniques in the investigation of multilevel research problems. In that chapter, we address issues of variable centering and the building of a variety of within-level and cross-level interactions.

CHAPTER 4

Three-Level Univariate Regression Models

The examples presented in the previous chapter demonstrated the basic multilevel regression model for examining hierarchical data structures. The basic two-level model can be readily extended to cross-sectional models involving several levels in a data hierarchy, regression discontinuity designs, and to multilevel longitudinal models involving individuals and groups. In this chapter, we provide an overview of three-level, cross-sectional modeling. We also introduce a strategy for centering predictors in multilevel models to facilitate the interpretation of effects and a strategy for comparing the fit of successive proposed models to the data.

Three-Level Univariate Model

As a first example, consider a three-level model with a univariate outcome, *math achievement*. In this example, we primarily wish to examine whether classroom teaching effectiveness (i.e., a characteristic of teachers at Level 2) and aggregate teaching effectiveness (i.e., a characteristic of schools at Level 3) affect student outcomes. At the classroom level, we also focus on whether teacher effectiveness may be related to student composition. Finally, at the school level, we wish to examine whether the size of individual teacher effects varies across schools.

Research Questions

We investigate three research questions in this example. The first question concerns whether a key organizational process, in this case the effectiveness of students' teachers, has an individual and an organizational effect on their academic outcomes, after relevant background and organizational context indicators have been controlled. This involves examining whether effects at lower levels (i.e., the classroom) of the data hierarchy tend to compound at a higher level (i.e., the school). This type of relationship is sometimes referred to as a compositional effect and is often of interest to organizational researchers. More specifically, we might ask: Does having an effective teacher confer an academic advantage to those students at the classroom level, compared to their peers in the same school? Moreover, does being in a school with more effective teachers on average confer any additional advantage compared to students in schools with less effective teachers?

The second research question concerns whether the teacher effectiveness slope varies across schools. We can address this question by examining the variance components for the slope at Level 3 of the model. If the slope does vary across schools, we can focus on building a model that explains variability in the random slope at the school level. This type of model concerns the presence of cross-level interactions; that is, the potential effect a variable at a higher level of the data hierarchy may have on a relationship at a lower level.

The third question focuses on whether teacher effectiveness at the classroom level is contingent on the student composition at the classroom level. Addressing this question allows us to demonstrate how to investigate an interaction between two variables at the same level of the data hierarchy. This is also a common type of specification in a multilevel model. Interactions can be interpreted as the amount of change in the slope of *y* (achievement) with respect to *x* (teacher effectiveness) when *z* (student classroom SES composition) changes by one unit. More specifically, we ask: Does the dependence of a student's achievement score on the effectiveness of her teacher also depend on differing levels of socioeconomic status in the classroom? Keep in mind that interactions are not simply "additive," as are the main effects of variables in a model (i.e., the additional effect of teacher effectiveness in explaining achievement while holding SES composition constant), but, rather, depend on the specific levels of the two variables from which they are produced (effectiveness and classroom SES). We can then test whether the interaction term added to the model produces a better fit than the main-effects-only model.

The Data

For this example, we will use a random sample of 9,196 students nested in 516 classrooms in 160 schools. The outcome is student scaled scores on a standardized math test. The sample data are found in the file *ch4threelevelURM.sav*. The data have an identification code for the school (*schcode*) and teacher (*teachid*), as well as a recoded teacher id (*Rteachid*). The recoded Level 2 identification code (i.e., individual teachers within schools) substantially reduces the amount of time it takes to run the model. Next is a math score, a measure of individual student socioeconomic status (coded 1 = low SES, 0 = else), a standardized (*M* = 0, *SD* = 1) assessment of each teacher's classroom teaching effectiveness (*teacheffect*), a classroom SES composition variable (*classlowses_mean*), and an aggregate (school-level) measure of student SES composition (*schlowses_mean*). These latter two variables were created from the individual-level SES variable (*lowses*) by using the "aggregate" command within SPSS (DATA > AGGREGATE) and *teachid* and *schcode* as the "break" variables, respectively.

Defining the Three-Level Multilevel Model

Our notation follows that used by Raudenbush and Bryk (2002). For three-level models, coefficients at Level 1 are defined as π, so that Level 2 coefficients can be defined as β and Level 3 as γ. For individual *i* in class *j* in school *k*, the general Level 1 model can be defined as

$$Y_{ijk} = \pi_{0jk} + \sum_{p=1}^{P} \pi_{Pjk} a_{Pijk} + \varepsilon_{ijk}, \tag{4.1}$$

where π_{0jk} is an intercept, a_{pjk} represent Level 1 predictors (*p* = 1, ... , *P*), such as socioeconomic status, for individual *i* in Level 2 unit *j* and Level 3 unit *k*, and π_{pjk} are corresponding Level 1 coefficients, and ε_{ijk} is the Level 1 random effect. The Level 1 variance of ε_{ijk} is assumed to be normally distributed with the mean equal to 0 and variance σ^2.

At Level 2, the general classroom model may be described as

$$\pi_{pjk} = \beta_{p0k} + \sum_{q=1}^{Q_p} \beta_{pqk} X_{qjk} + r_{pjk}, \tag{4.2}$$

where β_{p0k} is the intercept for school *k* in modeling the teacher effect, X_{qjk} are Level 2 predictors (*q* = 1, ... , Q_p), such as teaching effectiveness, β_{pqk} are corresponding Level 2 coefficients, and r_{pjk} represent Level 2 random effects. Level 1 coefficients can be modeled at Level 2 as randomly varying as indicated in Equation 4.2, as fixed at the same value for all Level 2 units ($\pi_{pjk} = \beta_{p0k}$), or as varying nonrandomly among Level 2 units (i.e., Equation 4.2 without the random, r_{pjk}, component; see Raudenbush, Bryk, Cheong, & Congdon, 2004, for further discussion). The

Level 2 random effects are collected in a covariance matrix whose dimensions depend on the number of random effects specified in the Level 2 model.

Between schools (Level 3), a general model can be defined as

$$\beta_{pqk} = \gamma_{pq0} + \sum_{s=1}^{S_{pq}} \gamma_{pqs} W_{sk} + u_{pqk}, \tag{4.3}$$

where γ_{pq0} is an intercept, W_{sk} are Level 3 predictors ($s = 1, \ldots, S_{pq}$) for example, student composition), γ_{pqs} are corresponding Level 3 coefficients, and u_{pqk} represent Level 3 random effects (the dimensions of the Level 3 covariance matrix of random effects depend on the number of randomly varying effects in the model). As Raudenbush et al. (2004) suggest, Level 2 coefficients can be modeled at Level 3 as randomly varying as in Equation 4.3, as fixed ($\beta_{pqk} = \gamma_{pq0}$), or as nonrandomly varying (i.e., Equation 4.3 without the random component, u_{pqk}).

Centering Predictors and Interactions

In multilevel models, it is important that the fixed effect can be readily interpreted in relation to the proposed goals of the research. Centering decisions concern how to rescale the explanatory variables so that the intercept can be defined most advantageously. Alternative centering strategies can change the values of some parameters in a model (Bryk & Raudenbush, 1992). Mean centering is most commonly used in multilevel studies (e.g., grand mean, group mean), but there are other options (e.g., the median, the within-group standard deviation of the within-group coefficient of variation) for centering variables (Plewis, 1989). Centering provides the expected value of an outcome *y* when the covariate is equal to some designated value of theoretical interest (e.g., the unit mean, the overall sample mean). For models with fixed slopes, changing the scale of measurement for an explanatory variable merely shifts the level of the intercept (i.e., where the regression line crosses the *Y* axis) but does not change the intercept's variability, since the slope coefficient itself is fixed. With random slopes, however, the variance of the intercept changes when the scale of the explanatory variable changes, since the regression slopes are no longer fixed parallel lines. Centering decisions can also be important in models where there are anticipated cross-level interactions; that is, where the analyst wishes to explain variability in slopes across groups. Although there is no one correct decision in every instance, centering decisions should be made on the basis of the conceptual questions under investigation (Hofmann & Gavin, 1998).

We will illustrate two primary centering strategies used in multilevel modeling in this example: grand-mean and group-mean centering. Grand-mean centering (i.e., where the grand mean is subtracted from all values of the variable) results in a situation where the sample mean of the predictor variable is redefined to be zero (0.0). For example, if the mean level of student motivation in a sample were 5.6, it would be rescaled to 0.0. This is useful in the interpretation of results in a multilevel model, since it results in an intercept that can be interpreted as the expected value of *Y* when all the predictors are at their mean values (0). This has the effect of creating a metric for determining how a 1 standard deviation (SD) increase in a predictor changes the dependent variable. Standardizing a continuous predictor (mean = 0, *SD* = 1) has the same effect on the intercept as grand-mean centering the predictor, except that the predictor's metric will likely be different in either transformation. For example, when it is standardized (i.e., a *Z*-score), it is in standard deviation units.

Uncentered estimates (i.e., in their natural metrics as the example in Chapter 3) and grand-mean centered estimates will produce equivalent models (except for the location of their intercepts). In many cases, the uncentered or natural metric may be a logical choice since for the natural metric the intercept is defined as the level of *y* when *x* is zero (0.0). Some uncentered solutions, however, may have little practical importance in organizational studies (Kreft, de Leeuw, & Aiken, 1995). For example, if an analyst is using family income as a predictor, it might make little sense to interpret the math achievement intercept as the level where family income is zero.

Dummy-coded variables (0, 1) also present different options for centering. For dummy-coded variables such as low SES status (i.e., 1 = participated in federal free/reduced lunch program, 0 = else), if we present the result in the natural metric, the intercept for achievement will correspond to the expected scores for students who did not participate (coded 0) in school k, and the variance associated with the intercept will be interpreted as the variance in outcomes for that group of students across schools (Raudenbush & Bryk, 2002). In contrast, grand-mean centering the variable results in an intercept that may be defined as the mean outcome in school k, adjusted for differences among schools in the proportion of students participating in the federal free/reduced lunch program. This is an important difference, for example, if we are concerned with making comparisons between schools after adjusting the outcomes for differences due to the various backgrounds of students within each school. The latter choice may be viewed as a more equitable comparison. Centering the dummy variable on the grand mean or leaving it uncentered will result in similar coefficients but different estimated intercepts. The analyst should keep in mind the desired interpretation of the intercept, especially when there are a number of continuous and dummy-coded variables in the analysis. For categorical variables in SPSS Mixed, it is also important to note that the default reference group is the last category instead of the first (0) in a dummy-coded variable.

Regarding interactions, it is important to think about the meaning of the coding of each variable. Interactions suggest the relationship between a predictor (A) and the outcome (Y) are contingent on levels of another predictor (B). Because interactions are product terms ($A*B$) they depend on the levels of the predictors from which they are produced. For a factor*factor interaction (e.g., *female*lowSES*), with each variable coded 0 and 1, there are four possible cells (0, 0; 0, 1; 1, 0; and 1, 1). Multiplication in the first three cells will equal 0, leaving only the last cell (1, 1) as defining the added advantage or disadvantage for outcomes due to the interaction effect. The interpretation of the interaction will be the advantage or disadvantage associated with being female and low SES against the other three cells combined. This choice might be the one the analyst desires in interpreting the interaction. Centering the factors (A, B) in the interaction will carry a slightly different interpretation of the intercept from leaving them in their natural metrics.

When continuous variables that are part of an interaction are left in natural metrics, it may make it more difficult to interpret the meaning of the interaction (e.g., a family income score of 0). Because no one has a score of 0, it is often useful to recenter the scores in a way that they can be more meaningfully interpreted. Grand-mean centering each continuous A and B covariate facilitates this type of meaningful interpretation, since if we grand-mean center each, then the interpretation of the interaction slope is that it is the expected value of the slope when the other variable has the value of zero (i.e., the average effect). For a factor*covariate interaction (family income*ethnicity), the interaction can be interpreted as a test of parallel lines regarding the relationship between the continuous variable (family income) and Y. Here, grand-mean centering family income can facilitate interpreting the difference in "average effect" across levels of the factor.

One related advantage of grand-mean centering is that it helps analysts interpret the variances for the intercept and slopes as the expected variance when all explanatory variables are equal to zero; that is, the expected variances for the "average" individual (Hox, 2002). We also note in passing that where there is a random slope, different centering strategies can lead to different estimates and variance components.

In contrast, group-mean centering results in unit intercepts that are unadjusted for differences within groups (which we describe in more detail later in the chapter). Group-mean centering produces an intercept equal to the expected value of *y* for an individual when *x* is equal to the group's mean. Unlike grand-mean centering, in group-mean centered solutions, the unit means are *unadjusted* for differences among their members. Group-mean centering puts the attention more on relational advantages that some individuals may enjoy within their particular social group. It is important to emphasize that group-mean centered solutions are not the same as grand-mean or raw metric solutions.

At the top of the data hierarchy (e.g., schools), the centering choices are not as critical as for predictors at lower levels (Raudenbush & Bryk, 2002). Usually it is convenient to center continuous variables around their grand means. Dummy variables can be left in their natural metric, depending on the analyst's choice for the meaning of the reference group (coded 0) in the unit-level model. In SPSS, grand-mean or group-mean centered variables must be created using Compute and saved in the data set. In our examples, we designate variables that we have grand-mean centered by placing "gm" in front of the variable (e.g., *SES* becomes *gmSES*). We designate group-mean centered variables as "group" (e.g., *SES* becomes *groupSES*). Analysts, of course, can devise their own naming schemes.

The Null Model (No Predictors)

For this first no predictors or null model, we can examine the decomposition of variance in math achievement associated with students, classrooms, and schools. For a three-level model, the proportion of variability (intraclass correlation) in outcomes at Level 3 is defined as

$$\rho = \sigma^2_{\text{Level 3}} \Big/ \left(\sigma^2_{\text{Level 1}} + \sigma^2_{\text{Level 2}} + \sigma^2_{\text{Level 3}} \right). \tag{4.4}$$

For Level 2 the intraclass correlation (ICC) would be

$$\rho = \sigma^2_{\text{Level 2}} \Big/ \left(\sigma^2_{\text{Level 1}} + \sigma^2_{\text{Level 2}} + \sigma^2_{\text{Level 3}} \right), \tag{4.5}$$

and for Level 1 the ICC would be

$$\rho = \sigma^2_{\text{Level 1}} \Big/ \left(\sigma^2_{\text{Level 1}} + \sigma^2_{\text{Level 2}} + \sigma^2_{\text{Level 3}} \right). \tag{4.6}$$

Defining the Null Model (No Predictors) With SPSS Menu Commands

The appropriate baseline model from which to compare subsequent models is the intercept-only, or no predictors, model.

Launch the SPSS program application and select the *ch4threelevelURM.sav* data file.

1. Go to the SPSS toolbar and select ANALYZE, MIXED MODELS, LINEAR.

This command enables access to the *Linear Mixed Models: Specify Subjects and Repeated* dialog box.

2. Within the *Linear Mixed Models: Specify Subjects and Repeated* dialog box, click to select *schcode* and *Rteachid* (Rank of teach id) variable from the left column, then click the arrow button to transfer the variables into the *Subjects* dialog box.

Click the CONTINUE button to display the *Linear Mixed Models* dialog box.

3. In the *Linear Mixed Models* dialog box, click to select the *math* variable from the left column, then click the right-arrow button to move it into the *Dependent Variable* box.

Since there are no fixed effects in the model, skip over the *Fixed* button and click the RANDOM button to access the *Linear Mixed Models: Random Effects* dialog box.

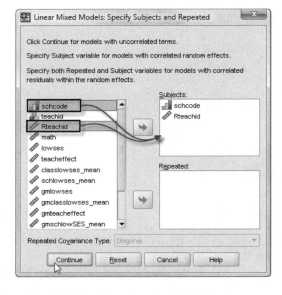

4. The *Linear Mixed Models: Random Effects* displays the *Random Effect 1 of 1* screen.

a. Change the covariance type by clicking on the pull-down menu and selecting *Scaled Identity*.

b. Click to select *Include Intercept*.

c. In the *Subject Groupings* box, click to select *schcode*, then click the right-arrow button to transfer the variable into the *Combinations* box.

d. At the top-right section of the window, click the NEXT button to access the *Random Effect 2 of 2* screen.

Note: The NEXT button may not work when creating multilevel models with random intercepts. This is a problem acknowledged by SPSS for assorted software versions including 18.0 and is resolved by adding then removing a covariate from the model, which is described in Steps e through i and Step 6.

Workaround to Activate the Random Effects "Next" Button

e. Click the CONTINUE button to return to the *Linear Mixed Models* dialog box.

f. Within the *Linear Mixed Models* dialog box click to select a variable (e.g., *lowses*) from the left column, then click the right-arrow button to transfer the variable into the *Covariate(s)* box.

Then click the RANDOM button to return to the *Linear Mixed Models: Random Effects* dialog box.

The *Linear Mixed Models: Random Effects* shows the *Random Effect 1 of 1* screen with the default settings established in Step 4.

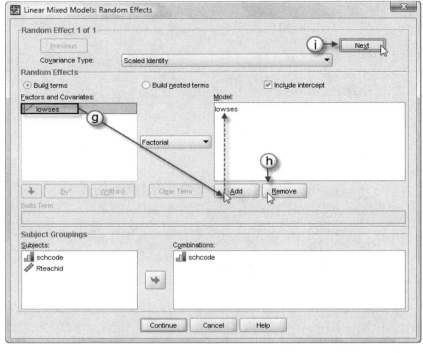

  g. Click to select the variable *lowses* from the *Factors and Covariates* box. Then click the ADD button to transfer the variable into the *Model* box, which activates the NEXT button (i).
  h. Click the REMOVE button to remove *lowses* from the model.
  i. Click the NEXT button to access the *Random Effect 2 of 2* screen.

  5. The *Random Effect 2 of 2* screen display is similar to the first screen and requires the following changes.
  a. Change the covariance type by clicking on the pull-down menu and selecting *Scaled Identity.*
  b. Click to select *Include Intercept.*
  c. In the *Subject Groupings* box, click to select *schcode* and *Rteachid*, then click the right-arrow button to transfer the variables into the *Combinations* box.

Click the CONTINUE button to return to the *Linear Mixed Models* dialog box.

6. From the *Linear Mixed Models* dialog box, remove *lowses* from the *Covariate(s)* box. Click to select the variable, then click the left-arrow button.

Now click the ESTIMATION button to access the *Linear Mixed Models: Estimation* dialog box.

7. The *Linear Mixed Models: Estimation* dialog box displays two estimation method choices: maximum likelihood (ML) or restricted maximum likelihood (REML). In this chapter, we will use maximum likelihood to estimate the models, which facilitates making comparisons between successive models having regression coefficients using model fit criteria (Hox, 2002).

Click to select ML, then click the CONTINUE button to return to the *Linear Mixed Models* dialog box.

8. In the *Linear Mixed Models* dialog box, click the STATISTICS button to access the *Linear Mixed Models: Statistics* dialog box.

Click and select the following three summary statistics, which will appear in the output: *parameter estimates*, *tests for covariance parameters*, and *covariances of random effects*.

Click the CONTINUE button to return to the *Linear Mixed Models* dialog box.

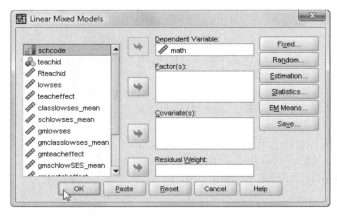

9. Finally, in the *Linear Mixed Models* dialog box, click the OK button to run the Null Model.

Interpreting the Output From the Null Model

Table 4.1 presents the variance decomposition for the no predictors model. The variance component associated with schools is 189.89; with classrooms it is 131.42; and within individuals it is 1333.79. From Equation 4.4, we can calculate the proportion of variance between schools as 0.115 [189.8867/(1333.7850 + 131.4211 + 189.8867)] or 11.5%. Following Equation 4.5 the variance is 0.079 (7.9%) between classrooms, and from Equation 4.6 the student-level variance is 0.806 (80.6%). This suggests there is adequate variability at each level to conduct a multilevel analysis.

We reiterate here that in multilevel modeling, explaining variance is more complex than in single-level regression models (Hox, 2002). First, there is the issue of dealing with unexplained

TABLE 4.1   Estimates of Covariance Parameters[a]

Parameter		Estimate	Std. Error	Wald Z	Sig.
Residual		1333.784938	20.836413	64.012	.000
Intercept [subject = schcode]	Variance	189.886674	27.933185	6.798	.000
Intercept [subject = schcode * Rteachid]	Variance	131.422051	15.962729	8.233	.000

[a] Dependent Variable: math.

variance at several levels. Second, if there are random slopes, the model becomes more complex, and explained variance (at each level) has no unique definition. As we noted in Chapter 3, one approach often used is to examine the change in residual variance that occurs by adding predictors within a sequence of models. The analyst begins with the intercept-only model as we have just presented. This serves as a baseline against which to evaluate subsequent reduction in the variance at each level as other variables are subsequently added to the model. The analyst should keep in mind, however, that when variables are added at Level 1, they can explain (i.e., reduce) variance at both Level 1 and at Level 2 (and perhaps even at Level 3). In contrast, variables added at higher levels of the model do not affect the variance present at lower levels. In other situations, a variable added at a lower level may appear to explain negative variance, so we remind analysts to be cautious about placing too much emphasis on variance reduction approaches in accounting for outcome variance. Adding random slopes can also complicate accounting for variance at each level (Hox, 2002). For these reasons, it can be more challenging to account for variance in multilevel models.

Model 1: Defining Predictors at Each Level

We will next illustrate the three-level model by building a basic explanatory model with a single predictor at each level. This results in combining a couple of general steps in our overall modeling strategy we laid out previously (i.e., no predictors model, within-group model, group-level model, random slope, cross-level interactions). In our first model, all predictors have been grand-mean centered by first creating the grand-mean centered predictors using Compute and saving the new variables in the data set. This will result in school intercepts that have been adjusted for the individual SES in the Level 1 portion and student SES composition in the Level 2 portion of the model.

At Level 1, we will propose that for individual i in class j in school k, student SES background (*gmlowses*) affects math achievement:

$$Y_{ijk} = \pi_{0jk} + \pi_{1jk}(gmlowses)_{ijk} + \varepsilon_{ijk}. \tag{4.7}$$

At Level 2 (classrooms), we will add a measure of teacher effectiveness (with higher standardized scores indicating greater effectiveness) in producing student learning in the classroom and an aggregate measure of classroom SES composition:

$$\pi_{0jk} = \beta_{00k} + \beta_{01k}(gmteacheffect)_{jk} + \beta_{02k}(gmclasslowses\_mean)_{jk} + r_{0jk},$$

$$\pi_{1jk} = \beta_{10k}. \tag{4.8}$$

For this model, we will assume that student SES (*gmses*) is fixed at the same value for all Level 2 units.

At Level 3 (schools), we will add aggregated measures of school SES and teacher effectiveness to explain variation in between-school math achievement:

$$\beta_{00k} = \gamma_{000} + \gamma_{001}(gmschlowSES\_mean)_k + \gamma_{002}(gmaggtcheffect)_k + u_{00k},$$

$$\beta_{10k} = \gamma_{010},$$

$$\beta_{02k} = \gamma_{020}. \tag{4.9}$$

In this model, we therefore assume all Level 2 slopes are fixed, but the adjusted math intercept varies across schools.

Defining Model 1 (Predictors at Each Level) With SPSS Menu Commands

Note: SPSS settings will default to those used for the Null Model.

1. Go to the SPSS toolbar and select ANALYZE, MIXED MODELS, LINEAR.

This command enables access to the *Linear Mixed Models: Specify Subjects and Repeated* dialog box.

2. Within the *Linear Mixed Models: Specify Subjects and Repeated* dialog box, the variables *schcode* and *Rteachid* (Rank of teach id) appear in the *Subjects* dialog box.

Click the CONTINUE button to display the *Linear Mixed Models* dialog box.

3. In the *Linear Mixed Models* dialog box, the *math* variable appears in the *Dependent Variable* box.

Click to select the following variables, then click the right-arrow button to transfer them into the *Covariates* box.

While the variables could be transferred in the order they appear, to facilitate reading of the output tables, the recommended sequence for entering the variables into the *Covariates* box is *gmlowses, gmteacheffect, gmclasslowses_mean, gmschlowSES_mean, gmaggtcheffect.*

Note: The sequence for entering the variables may be achieved through one of two methods: (1) adding each variable one by one, or (2) adding all the variables as a group, then dragging them to achieve the recommended order.

Click the FIXED button to access the *Linear Mixed Models: Fixed Effects* dialog box.

4a. Within the *Linear Mixed Models: Fixed Effects* box, locate the *Factorial* effects setting and click on the pull-down menu to change the selection to *Main Effects*.

b. Next, click to select the variables from the *Factors and Covariates* box, then click the right-arrow button to move the variables into the *Model* box. One may wish to change the sequence of the variables so the output tables will be easier to interpret.

The recommended sequence for entering the variables is *gmschlowSES_mean, gmaggtcheffect, gmteacheffect, gmclasslowses_mean, gmlowses.*

c. Confirm *Include Intercept* is selected.

Finally, click the CONTINUE button to return to the *Linear Mixed Models* dialog box.

5. The random effects, estimation, and statistics elements remain the same as those used for the Null Model, so skip over these buttons and click OK to run the model.

Interpreting the Output From Model 1

The output for Model 1 is presented in Table 4.2. The Table 4.2 fixed effects output suggests a composition effect associated with student SES; that is, there is an effect at the individual level (gmlowses = –14.53, p < .01), which compounds significantly at the classroom level (gmclasslowses_mean = –11.07, p < .01) and the school level (gmschlowSES_mean = –31.14, p < .01). As developed in Chapter 3, compositional effects refer to the extent to which the size of the organizational-level effect differs from the size of the individual-level effect. With grand-mean centering, the compositional effect for schools is estimated directly as the between-group fixed effect for SES (γ = –31.14). At school level, the effect for SES can be interpreted as the expected difference in math outcomes between two students who have the same individual SES background (and are in classes with the same SES composition) but attend schools differing by one unit (i.e., in this case, 1 SD in mean SES). Similarly, the composition effect at the classroom level (γ = –11.07) is the difference in size between the individual SES and class-level SES effects. At the classroom level, the compositional effect for SES can be interpreted as the expected difference in math outcomes between two students who have the same individual SES but who are in classes differing by one unit in classroom mean SES.

The output also provides support for our initial contention that there is an academic advantage for students that compounds due to teacher effectiveness. First, the table suggests the classroom-level effect is significant (γ = 7.57, p < .01). This suggests students in a classroom with a teacher whose effectiveness is 1 SD above the grand mean would score about 7.6 points higher than their peers in classrooms with teachers at the grand mean of effectiveness. Moreover, the effect of teachers on outcomes compounds at the school level (γ = 7.45, p < .01). The interpretation of this

TABLE 4.2 Estimates of Fixed Effects[a]

Parameter	Estimate	Std. Error	df	t	Sig.
Intercept	596.742372	.741423	148.020	804.861	.000
gmschlowSES_mean	–31.137671	4.564877	436.869	–6.821	.000
gmaggtcheffect	7.448295	1.963428	208.719	3.794	.000
gmteacheffect	7.571058	.619427	656.308	12.223	.000
gmclasslowses_mean	–11.072598	3.471651	1759.121	–3.189	.001
gmlowses	–14.533519	.861592	8841.429	–16.868	.000

[a] Dependent Variable: math.

school-level coefficient is straightforward: For two students having teachers of average effectiveness, attending a school differing by 1 *SD* in collective teacher effectiveness is associated with a 7.45 point increase on the standardized math test. This output, therefore, provides evidence to answer our first research question regarding potential academic advantages associated with teacher effectiveness.

Model 2: Group-Mean Centering

We contrast these results in Model 1 with a second model where we group-mean centered the within-school variables. It is important to keep in mind that cross-level interactions can be a source of instability in a model's estimates. If this may be a potential problem, group-mean centering is a good centering choice, since this approach removes correlations between variables across levels (Kreft & deLeeuw, 1998). Group-mean centering results in an intercept for each unit that is unadjusted for Level 1 or Level 2 predictors. In group-mean centered solutions, the effects of between-group predictors will also be unadjusted for within-group predictors.

Because grand-mean centering results in adjusted group means, given the predictors, in some modeling situations the adjustments for some units may not be very reliable. This can occur where there are small within-group sample sizes and considerable variability in slopes for particular covariates. For units with small sample sizes, the random slope may be estimated with little precision, which weakens the likelihood of detecting relationships between groups (Raudenbush & Bryk, 2002). In this situation, it can be difficult to disentangle parameter variance and error variance. In cases where the slope varies considerably across units for a predictor, and there is also variability across units in the levels of the predictors, resulting grand-mean centered estimates may be less credible than group-mean centered estimates (Raudenbush & Bryk, 2002). It is also important to note that compositional effects may change the size and significance of other parameters in the model. It is, therefore, important to give attention to decisions about model specification, especially when the focus is on the cross-level interactions.

Defining Model 2 With SPSS Menu Commands

Note: SPSS settings will default to those used for Model 1.

1. Go to the SPSS toolbar and select ANALYZE, MIXED MODELS, LINEAR.

This command enables access to the *Linear Mixed Models: Specify Subjects and Repeated* dialog box.

2. The variables *schcode* and *Rteachid* (Rank of teach id) appear in the *Subjects* box within the *Linear Mixed Models: Specify Subjects and Repeated* dialog box.

Click the CONTINUE button to display the *Linear Mixed Models* dialog box.

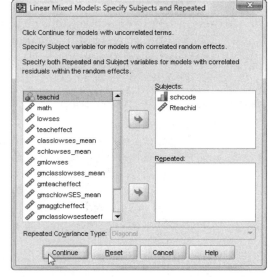

3. In the *Linear Mixed Models* dialog box, the *math* variable appears in the *Dependent Variable* box.
   a. Click to select and remove all of the variables from the *Covariate(s)* box.
   b. Then click to select the variables from the left column listing and enter them in the following sequence: *gmschlowSES_mean, gmaggtcheffect, groupteacheffect, groupclasslowses_mean, grouplowses.*

Click the FIXED button to access the *Linear Mixed Models: FIXED Effects* dialog box.

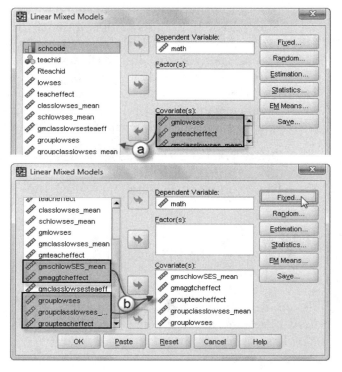

4a. Within the *Linear Mixed Models: Fixed Effects* box confirm the factorial setting is *Main Effects*.

b. Click to select the variables from the *Factors and Covariates* box.

The recommended sequence for entering the variables is *gmschlowSES_mean*, *gmaggtcheffect*, *groupteacheffect*, *groupclasslowses_mean*, *grouplowses*.

c. Confirm *Include Intercept* is selected.

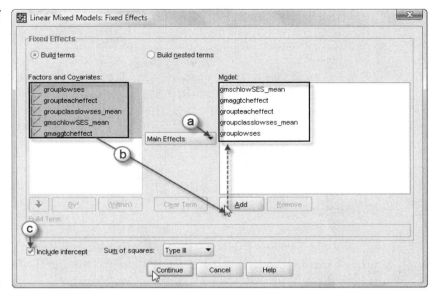

Finally, click the CONTINUE button to return to the *Linear Mixed Models* dialog box.

5. The random effects, estimation, and statistics settings remain the same as those used for Model 1, so skip over these buttons and click OK to run the model.

Interpreting the Output From Model 2

Given the previous grand-mean centered estimates in Model 1, if we instead used group-mean centering, we should expect a classroom-level SES group-centered effect of approximately –25.6 (i.e., –14.5 + –11.1 in Table 4.2) and a school level effect of approximately –56.7 (i.e., –25.6 + –31.1 in Table 4.2). For teacher effectiveness, we would expect an aggregated Level 3 teacher effectiveness coefficient of about 15.02 (i.e., 7.57 + 7.45 in the previous table).

The group-mean centered estimates are presented in Table 4.3 and are consistent with our expected output translated from the grand-mean estimates. Note that the Level 3 estimates are still grand-mean centered. This is because the estimates of the highest level in the data set cannot be centered on a group—that is, their group is the sample. Comparison of Tables 4.2 and 4.3 suggests it would be easy to misinterpret the meaning of the coefficients without a clear understanding between the two centering strategies.

TABLE 4.3   Estimates of Fixed Effects[a]

Parameter	Estimate	Std. Error	df	t	Sig.
Intercept	596.758782	.741456	148.049	804.847	.000
gmschlowSES_mean	−56.743788	3.697696	192.134	−15.346	.000
gmaggtcheffect	15.019353	1.882490	176.732	7.978	.000
groupteacheffect	7.571058	.619427	656.308	12.223	.000
groupclasslowses_mean	−25.606117	3.411002	1628.983	−7.507	.000
grouplowses	−14.533519	.861592	8841.429	−16.868	.000

[a] Dependent Variable: math.

Covariance Estimates

The covariance estimates in Table 4.4 (which are virtually the same for either group-mean or grand-mean centered fixed effects) suggest that the addition of predictors at each level reduces the proportion of variance associated with each level substantially (i.e., from 1333.79 to 1288.36 at the student level; from 131.42 to 73.31 at the classroom level; and from 189.89 to 43.37 at the school level). These reductions in variance can be used to calculate an estimate of R^2 at each level.

It is important to reiterate that Level 1 variables entered into the model can affect variance accounted for at Level 1, and they may also affect the variance accounted for at higher levels. For example, if grand-mean centering is used, adjustments for Level 1 predictors may change the level and variability in the intercept across higher groupings. If group-mean centering is used, however, the Level 1 predictors will not affect the level of the intercept or its variance across groups. In situations where accounting for variance is an important aim, the analyst may want to consider developing a Level 1 model first and then adding Level 2 and Level 3 predictors as separate sets of variables, so that the variance accounted for at each subsequent level is only affected by predictors added at that level.

Another point to keep in mind is that where there are multiple random effects (e.g., a random intercept and random slope), accounting for variance at successive levels may become more complicated if the slope and intercept are correlated. In this case, predictors entered into the slope equation, for example, may also affect variance estimates in the intercept equation (Raudenbush & Bryk, 2002). Centering on the group means tends to stabilize the model because it removes correlations (Paccagnella, 2006), so the resulting estimates may be more accurate. Group-mean centering may also be advantageous where the slope varies considerably for a particular predictor, and there is also considerable variability in the levels of the predictors across the units (Raudenbush & Bryk, 2002).

In our example (which contains only one Level 1 predictor and a random intercept), at the school level (Level 3) the reduction in variance would be calculated as (189.89 − 43.37)/189.89. This calculation takes into consideration the initial value for the school-level intercept (189.89) in the covariance parameter matrix for the no predictors model in Table 4.1, and results in an R^2 coefficient of 0.772.

TABLE 4.4   Estimates of Covariance Parameters[a]

Parameter		Estimate	Std. Error	Wald Z	Sig.
Residual		1288.362778	19.974173	64.501	.000
Intercept [subject = schcode]	Variance	43.369378	9.758659	4.444	.000
Intercept [subject = schcode * Rteachid]	Variance	73.310253	11.639777	6.298	.000

[a] Dependent Variable: math.

TABLE 4.5 Model Dimension[b]

		Number of Levels	Covariance Structure	Number of Parameters	Subject Variables
Fixed Effects	Intercept	1		1	
	gmschlowSES_mean	1		1	
	gmaggtcheffect	1		1	
	gmteacheffect	1		1	
	gmclasslowses_mean	1		1	
	gmlowses	1		1	
Random Effects	Intercept + gmteacheffect[a]	2	Unstructured	3	schcode
	Intercept[a]	1	Identity	1	schcode * Rteachid
Residual				1	
Total		9		11	

[a] As of version 11.5, the syntax rules for the RANDOM subcommand have changed. Your command syntax may yield results that differ from those produced by prior versions. If you are using version 11 syntax, please consult the current syntax reference guide for more information

[b] Dependent Variable: math.

Model 3: Does the Slope Vary Randomly Across Classrooms and Schools?

We next investigate whether the random teacher effect varies across schools. This will help us answer our second research question. The appropriate baseline slope model is the model with random slopes but no cross-level interactions (Hox, 2002). To indicate a random slope for the teacher effect, we make a change in Equation 4.9 as follows:

$$\beta_{01k} = \gamma_{010} + u_{01k}. \tag{4.10}$$

In this model (Model 3), we will need to change the covariance matrix from identity (ID) to unstructured (UN) at Level 3 in order to accommodate the two additional random parameters in the model (i.e., the randomly varying slope and the covariance between the intercept and slope). We will leave the Level 2 covariance matrix as an identity matrix since there is only one random effect (the intercept) at that level. Tables 4.3 and 4.4 imply nine parameters to estimate (six fixed effects and three random parameters). The addition of the two random parameters in Model 3 makes a total of eleven parameters to estimate. We can verify this from the model dimension output for Model 3 in Table 4.5. To look at this table in a little more detail, there are now two random effects at Level 3 (intercept and teacher effectiveness slope) and one random effect at Level 2 (intercept). In addition, there are two other random parameters (i.e., Level 1 residual, Level 3 slope-intercept covariance). The estimates for these five random parameters are summarized in Table 4.6.

Defining Model 3 With SPSS Menu Commands

Note: SPSS settings will default to those used for Model 2.

1. Go to the SPSS toolbar and select ANALYZE, MIXED MODELS, LINEAR.

This command enables access to the *Linear Mixed Models: Specify Subjects and Repeated* dialog box.

2. The variables *schcode* and *Rteachid* (Rank of teach id) appear in the *Subjects* box within the *Linear Mixed Models: Specify Subjects and Repeated* dialog box.

Click the CONTINUE button to display the *Linear Mixed Models* dialog box.

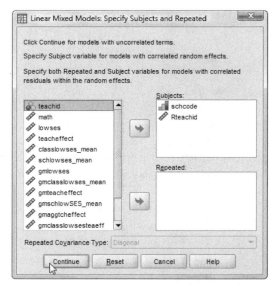

3. In the *Linear Mixed Models* dialog box, the *math* variable appears in the *Dependent Variable* box.

   a. Remove the variables from the *Covariate(s)* box by selecting them and clicking the left-arrow button.

   b. Click to select the variables from the left column listing and enter them in the following sequence: *gmlowses, gmteacheffect, gmclasslowses_mean, gmschlowSES,_mean gmaggtcheffect.*

Click the FIXED button to access the *Linear Mixed Models: Fixed Effects* dialog box.

Click the CONTINUE button to return to the *Linear Mixed Models* dialog box.

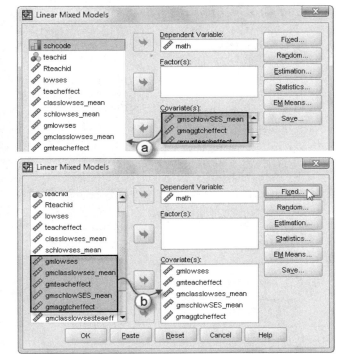

4a. From the *Linear Mixed Models: Fixed Effects* box confirm that *Main Effects* is selected.

   b. Next, click to select the variables from the *Factors and Covariates* box, then click the ADD button to move them into the *Model* box. The recommended sequence for adding the variables is *gmschlowSES_ mean, gmaggtcheffect, gmteacheffect, gmclasslowses_mean, gmlowses.*

   c. Confirm *Include Intercept* is selected.

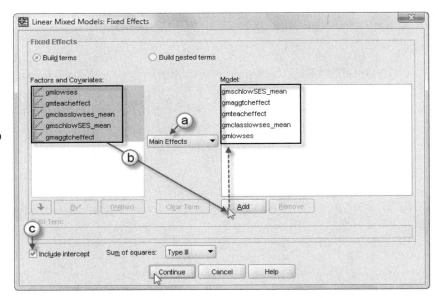

Click the CONTINUE button to return to the *Linear Mixed Models* dialog box. Then click the RANDOM button to access the *Random Effect 2 of 2* screen.

5a. The *Random Effect 2 of 2* screen displays the previous settings and will remain the same, so click the PREVIOUS button to access the *Random Effect 1 of 1*.

b. Click the pull-down menu to change the covariance type from *Scaled Identity* to *Unstructured*.

c. Confirm *Include Intercept* is selected.

d. Confirm *Main Effects* is selected.

e. Click to select *gmteacheffect* from the *Factors and Covariates* box, then click the ADD button to move the variable into the *Model* box.

f. Confirm *schcode* appears in the *Combinations* box.

Click the CONTINUE button to return to the *Linear Mixed Models* dialog box.

6. The estimation and statistics elements in the model remain the same settings as those used for Model 2, so skip over these buttons and click OK to run the model.

Interpreting the Output From Model 3

Table 4.6 provides the new variance components for Model 3. As Table 4.6 shows, however, the variance in teacher effectiveness slopes (UN 2, 2) is not significant between schools ($\sigma_{2,2}^2 = 5.759$, Wald $Z = .877$, one-tailed $p = .1905$). Therefore, in this sample data it would not be necessary to try to build a Level 3 model with cross-level interactions to explain variation in the size of teacher classroom effects across schools. We therefore can answer our second research question by noting that the size of individual teacher effects do not seem to vary between schools. This may suggest that differences in individual teacher effects are more apparent between classrooms but within schools, rather than between schools.

TABLE 4.6 Estimates of Covariance Parameters[a]

Parameter		Estimate	Std. Error	Wald Z	Sig.
Residual		1288.878287	19.989452	64.478	.000
Intercept + gmteacheffect [subject = schcode]	UN (1,1)	42.152969	9.656862	4.365	.000
	UN (2,1)	2.825679	4.886594	.578	.563
	UN (2,2)	5.758925	6.568496	.877	.381
Intercept [subject = schcode * Rteachid]	Variance	68.700692	12.359108	5.559	.000

[a] Dependent Variable: math.

Developing an Interaction Term

Because classroom teacher effectiveness did not vary across schools, we turn our attention to answering our third research question. This concerns whether the impact of teacher effectiveness on student learning is contingent on various types of classroom composition features. As we noted previously, interaction effects imply that the relationship between a predictor and outcome Y depend on levels of another predictor. We initially proposed that teacher effectiveness is a stronger predictor of achievement in classrooms with more challenging student composition. If this is true, then we would expect a positive interaction effect between teacher effectiveness and classroom composition. We mentioned previously the factor*covariate interaction (e.g., *lowSES* and motivation), which is basically a test of parallel lines; that is, is the relationship between motivation and achievement the sample for different levels of the factor? In this case, we will investigate a covariate*covariate interaction (class SES*teacher effectiveness).

We will next define an interaction term between teacher effectiveness and classroom SES composition (defined as the percentage of low SES students) and add it to the Level 2 model:

$$\pi_{0jk} = \beta_{00k} + \beta_{01k}(gmteacheffect)_{jk} + \beta_{02k}(gmclasslowses\_mean)_{jk} + \tag{4.11}$$

$$\beta_{03k}(gmclasslowses\_mean * gmteacheffect)_{jk} + r_{0jk}.$$

Preliminary Investigation of the Interaction

Before actually running the full model, we will pause for a moment to consider the proposed interaction in a little more detail. We can create this interaction variable implied in Equation 4.11 using the Menu commands by combining classroom composition and classroom teacher effectiveness. Interactions can also easily be computed using the syntax statements (or by using COMPUTE and saving the interaction in the data set). We focus on just the two main effects and the interaction to make a point about how centering the interactions differently can affect the interpretation of the coefficients.

In Table 4.7 are the estimates for the natural metric solution. The intercept is 611.33, which can be interpreted as the point where class SES is 0; that is, where there is no student participating in

TABLE 4.7 Estimates of Fixed Effects[a]

Parameter	Estimate	Std. Error	df	t	Sig.
Intercept	611.325531	1.512181	418.514	404.267	.000
classlowses_mean	−35.528897	2.919605	968.719	−12.169	.000
teacheffect	5.988375	1.427170	761.815	4.196	.000
teacheffect * classlowses_mean	4.511112	3.126802	817.176	1.443	.149

[a] Dependent Variable: math.

TABLE 4.8   Estimates of Fixed Effects[a]

Parameter	Estimate	Std. Error	df	t	Sig.
Intercept	596.638763	.900013	134.905	662.922	.000
gmclasslowses_mean	–35.597917	2.918045	968.849	–12.199	.000
gmteacheffect	7.837931	.606266	679.915	12.928	.000
gmclasslowses_mean * gmteacheffect	4.511112	3.126802	817.176	1.443	.149

[a] Dependent Variable: math.

the federal free/reduced lunch program. We might be able to find a better centering solution for this variable, however, since over 40% of the sample participated in the free/reduced lunch program. The intercept can also be interpreted as the achievement level where teacher effectiveness is 0. Since teacher effectiveness is a factor score (developed from a separate analysis with M = 0, SD = 1) this can be interpreted roughly as "average" teacher effectiveness, but it is uncentered within the current multilevel model. In the table, both the main effects (classroom SES and teacher effectiveness) are significant predictors of math scores. The interaction, however, is not significant, so we could consider removing it if desired. When an interaction term ($A*B$) is significant, however, we suggest leaving both the direct effects of A and B in the model whether they are significant or not.

Next we provide the grand-mean centered solution (Table 4.8). Notice that the intercept is different, which results from classlowses_mean and teacher effectiveness being centered around their grand means. The intercept can now be interpreted as the point where the proportion of students participating in free/reduced lunch is the average for the sample (0). This is a more meaningful centering because of the high proportion of students in the sample who participate in this program. We reiterate the point that grand-mean centering the interaction slope facilitates interpretation since it implies what the expected value of the slope is when the other variable has the value of zero (i.e., the average effect).

Model 4: Examining a Level 2 Interaction

This investigation of adding a Level 2 interaction term to the model also allows us to demonstrate how an analyst can compare successive models to see whether an added variable (or set of variables) makes a difference in the overall fit of the proposed model to the data. We will again use ML estimation to facilitate the comparison of the previous model without the regression coefficient for the Level 2 interaction against this current model with the interaction added. Using REML to compare successive models would only be optimal when the focus is on a difference in random parameters (Hox, 2002). The rest of the model remains as Model 3.

Defining Model 4 With SPSS Menu Commands

Note: SPSS settings will default to those used for Model 3.

1. Go to the SPSS toolbar and select ANALYZE, MIXED MODELS, LINEAR.

This command enables access to the *Linear Mixed Models: Specify Subjects and Repeated* dialog box.

2. The variables *schcode* and *Rteachid* (Rank of teach id) appear in the *Subjects* box within the *Linear Mixed Models: Specify Subjects and Repeated* dialog box.

Click the CONTINUE button to display the *Linear Mixed Models* dialog box.

3. In the *Linear Mixed Models* dialog box, the *math* variable appears in the *Dependent Variable* box.

The *Covariate(s)* box displays the variables from the prior model: *gmlowses*, *gmteacheffect*, *gmclasslowses_mean*, *gmschlowSES_mean*, *gmaggtcheffect*.

Click the FIXED button to access the *Linear Mixed Models: Fixed Effects* dialog box.

4. The *Linear Mixed Models: Fixed Effects* dialog box displays settings used for Model 3.

Adding a Cross-Level Interaction to Model 4
gmclasslowses_mean* gmteacheffect

5a. Click to select the *Build nested terms* option.
   b. Click to select the variable *gmclasslowses_ mean* from the *Factors and Covariates* column.
   c. Click the down-arrow button to move *gmclasslowses_mean* into the *Build Term* box.
   d. Click the BY* button to add the computational symbol (*) to the *Build Term* box.

e. Click to select the variable *gmteacheffect* from the *Factors and Covariates* column.

f. Click the down-arrow button to move *gmteacheffect* into the *Build Term* box.

g. Click the ADD button to move the term *gmclasslowses_mean*gmteacheffect* into the *Model* box.

Although the *Model* variables may remain in their current order we recommend placing *gmlowses* below the cross-level interaction to facilitate reading of the output tables.

h. Click to select *gmlowses*, then click the REMOVE button.

i. Select the *Build terms* option.

j. Now click to select *gmlowses* from the *Factors and Covariates* box, then click the ADD button.

Click the CONTINUE button to return to the *Linear Mixed Models* dialog box.

6. The random effects, estimation and statistics elements in the model remain the same settings as those used for Model 3, so skip over these buttons and click OK to run the model.

Interpreting the Output From Model 4

We present the results for Model 4 in Table 4.9. The first two variables below the intercept are the between-school predictors of math outcomes. Both school SES composition and aggregate teacher effectiveness are significant predictors of achievement. Next are the classroom variables (i.e., classroom composition, teacher effectiveness, and the interaction term). The results suggest that the interaction between teacher effectiveness and classroom SES composition (β_{03}) is significant at $p < .10$ ($\gamma_{030} = 5.38$). Because of coding, this result suggests that in a classroom 1 *SD* above the grand mean (0) in low SES composition, the combined teacher effect would be considerably larger (7.43 + 5.38 = 12.81) than the teacher effect (7.43) in a class at the grand mean (0) in SES composition. This provides supportive evidence for answering our third research question, which focused on whether teacher effectiveness might be contingent on classroom composition factors. Table 4.10 suggests that the variance at Level 2 was little affected by adding the interaction effect to the model.

TABLE 4.9 Estimates of Fixed Effects[a]

Parameter	Estimate	Std. Error	df	t	Sig.
Intercept	596.858608	.732578	147.494	814.737	.000
gmschlowSES_mean	−31.181036	4.516817	429.003	−6.903	.000
gmaggtcheffect	7.676212	1.949885	208.991	3.937	.000
gmteacheffect	7.432082	.677468	74.918	10.970	.000
gmclasslowses_mean	−10.932678	3.468614	1748.372	−3.152	.002
gmteacheffect * gmclasslowses_mean	5.384761	3.137823	373.263	1.716	.087
gmlowses	−14.543222	.861579	8837.068	−16.880	.000

[a] Dependent Variable: math.

TABLE 4.10 Estimates of Covariance Parameters[a]

Parameter		Estimate	Std. Error	Wald Z	Sig.
Residual		1288.767869	19.985440	64.485	.000
Intercept + gmteacheffect [subject = schcode]	UN (1,1)	41.227128	9.543882	4.320	.000
	UN (2,1)	3.041303	4.931827	.617	.537
	UN (2,2)	6.201300	6.535734	.949	.343
Intercept [subject = schcode * Rteachid]	Variance	68.320823	12.279244	5.564	.000

[a] Dependent Variable: math.

Comparing the Fit of Successive Models

We can compare model-fitting evidence from the previous model with no interaction at Level 2 (Model 3) and the current model (Model 4) to determine whether the addition of the interaction term enhanced the fit of the model. Tests of nested models should be conducted with ML when regression coefficients are being compared for their fit to the data. Model 3 without the interaction term included (11 estimated parameters) yields the model fit criteria shown in Table 4.11. Model 4 (estimated similarly with ID and UN matrices and the Level 2 interaction) yields the model fit criteria (for 12 estimated parameters) shown in Table 4.12.

With ML estimation, the probability of obtaining the observed results given the parameter estimates is referred to as the likelihood function. Since the likelihood is less than 1.0, it is common to use –2 times the log of the likelihood (–2LL) as a measure of model fit to the data. Good models result in a high likelihood of obtaining the observed results (which corresponds to a small value for –2LL). A perfect model would have a likelihood of 1, and the log of likelihood would be 0 (which when multiplied by –2 is also 0).

The analyst can test the difference between the log likelihoods of two models if the models are nested, which means a specific model can be derived from a more general model by removing parameters from the more general model. The difference in –2LL for two nested models has a chi-square distribution, with degrees of freedom (df) equal to the difference in the number of parameters estimated in the two models (SPSS, 1990).

In this case, we will assume that the model with the interaction is more general since it has 12 estimated parameters. We then compare it against the more restricted model, which has the interaction removed (i.e., 11 parameters are estimated). The difference in –2LL between the two models is 2.928. There is 1 degree of freedom in the model test, since one regression parameter is being removed. The required chi-square at $p = .05$ for 1 degree of freedom is 3.84. Therefore, we can conclude the model with 11 estimated parameters (i.e., without the interaction term) does not fit the data better than the model with the interaction term. Another way of looking at this would be that adding the interaction does not "significantly improve" the model's fit but does not cause it to "decay significantly" either. Therefore, in this case, we will accept that the model with the significant interaction term fits the data as well as the model without the interaction.

A second way of comparing models is to use the Akaike information criterion (AIC), which provides information about the number of parameters to include in a model. The model with the number of parameters that produces the smallest AIC is favored. In this example, that would be the interaction model with 12 parameters (AIC = 92346.389) compared with the restricted model with 11 parameters (AIC = 92347.317). Other criteria presented as part of the output represent similar ways of comparing alternative models (users can consult SPSS Mixed Help for further information).

TABLE 4.11   Information Criteria[a]

–2 Log Likelihood	92325.317
Akaike's Information Criterion (AIC)	92347.317
Hurvich and Tsai's Criterion (AICC)	92347.346
Bozdogan's Criterion (CAIC)	92436.693
Schwarz's Bayesian Criterion (BIC)	92425.693

Note: The information criteria are displayed in smaller-is-better forms.
[a] Dependent Variable: math.

TABLE 4.12   Information Criteria[a]

–2 Log Likelihood	92322.389
Akaike's Information Criterion (AIC)	92346.389
Hurvich and Tsai's Criterion (AICC)	92346.423
Bozdogan's Criterion (CAIC)	92443.891
Schwarz's Bayesian Criterion (BIC)	92431.891

Note: The information criteria are displayed in smaller-is-better forms.
[a] Dependent Variable: math.

Summary

The previous discussion suggests researchers should proceed with caution when building multilevel models. It is often the case that different sets of variables are hypothesized to explain variation in random intercepts and slopes. Raudenbush and Bryk (2002) suggest using a common set of variables when building the models between groups. We decided to add the intercept predictors first and then to consider variation in slopes.

CHAPTER 5

Examining Individual Change With Repeated Measures Data

In our previous chapters, the outcome and explanatory variables were only measured on one occasion. One of the limitations of such cross-sectional analyses is that they are not well suited to studying processes that are assumed to be developmental. Because data are collected only at one point in time, they are insufficient to examine possible temporal relationships in a theoretical model. Time is a key factor in understanding how processes unfold. When an outcome is measured several times for an individual, we have a repeated measures design (RMD). A simple example of an RMD is the pretest and posttest design. For examining developmental processes, adding measurement occasions between the pretest and posttest can provide a more thorough examination of developmental processes (e.g., by examining the shape of developmental processes for different groups of individuals) and often increase the power of the statistical test used to determine whether a change has taken place (Willett, 1989).

In the past, analyses of repeated observations on individuals were conducted as univariate analysis of variance (ANOVA) or multivariate analysis of variance (MANOVA), depending on the goals of the research (e.g., whether the focus is on examining a single outcome over time, or two or more outcomes that may change together over time) and the specific features of the data (e.g., sample size, correlations between the repeated observations, characteristics of the between-group covariance matrices). These types of analyses, however, are limited to change within- and between-individuals (i.e., single-level analyses). Increasingly, both the concepts and methods are becoming available that can provide a more rigorous and thorough examination of various types of longitudinal data. The RMD can also be approached as another type of hierarchical (or nested) data structure, with measurement occasions nested within individuals. In multilevel terminology, change involving individuals can be conceptualized as a two-level analysis with the repeated measures nested within individuals defined as Level 1 and differences between individuals (e.g., background, an experimental treatment) defined as Level 2.

Models of individual change encourage researchers to ask a number of different questions of the data: Is there a change in the level of the means over time? If so, what is the shape of the change trajectory? Is the change the same for different groups of individuals? Using a multilevel framework, analyses of individual growth can easily be extended to include differences in growth across successive groupings such as classrooms and schools. Such analyses could have three (or even four) hierarchical levels.

An Example Study

We first present an extended example of individual change using repeated measures ANOVA. This traditional approach for examining repeated measures over time provides a good beginning point for investigating change over time. We then use the same data to build a two-level model of individual change using SPSS Mixed and provide some comparisons and points of departure between these two approaches for examining individual change.

Research Questions

Consider a study to examine students' growth trajectories in achievement over time and to assess whether their SES background and teacher effectiveness are related to different achievement growth patterns. We may be interested first in asking whether a change takes place in student achievement over time. This type of question addresses whether the levels of the means for an outcome are the same or different over the occasions of measurement. The assumption is that if we can reject the null hypothesis of no difference in means across measurement occasions, it implies that a change in individuals has taken place.

A second question concerns what the shape of the developmental change might look like for individuals in the study. For example, we might ask whether the rate of individual change per occasion is linear. If the answer is yes, this would imply that individuals change at the same rate over time. The pattern of change might also be nonlinear; for example, adding a quadratic term to the model implies that the rate of individual development accelerates or decelerates over time. We might also assume other, more complex patterns of development exist.

Once we have determined that a change takes place over time and described the shape of the change, we might ask a third question: Are there differences in development across groups of individuals? These differences might be due to an experimental treatment or other types of factors (e.g., background). We might also wish to adjust our estimates for the presence of covariates that might affect individuals' development over time. In this case, we examine whether student growth is related to their individual perceptions about their teachers, using students' socioeconomic status as a covariate.

Data

The data used for this study consists of 8,670 secondary students. We will assume that they have been randomly sampled from a larger population of students.

Univariate or Multivariate Approach

In SPSS with a single outcome analyzed over time, it is possible to base the hypothesis tests on either multivariate (e.g., Wilks's lambda) or univariate F tests. SPSS MANOVA produces a variety of tables for investigating student growth from both perspectives. When both approaches lead to the same results, choosing between them does not matter much. When they lead to differences, however, the question of which approach is more appropriate arises (see Raykov & Marcoulides, 2008, for further discussion of differences in each approach). In this example, the subjects are measured on fixed occasions; that is, let us say at the beginning, middle, and end of the academic year. This can be contrasted with more complex designs where measurements might be taken for different individuals at different points in time (Hox, 2002). These latter types of designs can be effectively examined using different types of multilevel modeling techniques.

In this case, we will base the tests of our hypotheses on the univariate approach. The univariate approach requires certain assumptions about the sphericity of the measurements (i.e., the similarity between the variances and covariances of the repeated measures over time), but if the conditions are met, especially in small sample sizes, the results are more powerful than the multivariate approach (Raykov & Marcoulides, 2008). The primary assumption tested is that the variances of the repeated measures should be the same over time (referred to as being homogeneous), and the covariances between any two occasions should also be the same. This assumption can be tested with Mauchly's test of sphericity. If the observed significance level is small (e.g., < .001), a correction can be applied (e.g., Huynh–Feldt epsilon) to the degrees of freedom of the *F*-ratio. This correction is used in calculating the adjusted significance level associated with the *F*-ratio test.

If we use the univariate approach to examine our proposed research questions, following are some general analytic steps and corresponding tests in which we would be interested.

1. Mauchly's test of sphericity —The sphericity assumption implies that the variances for the repeated measures are the same and that the covariances between pairs of the repeated measures are the same. This assumption is not likely to hold in many univariate applications as the time period lengthens. If the test is not significant, then we can report the *F*-ratio for "sphericity assumed." If it is significant, it will tend to lead to making more Type I errors; for example, incorrectly rejecting the null hypothesis of no difference when it should be accepted. In this case, we can (a) report a different coefficient (using Box's lower bound, Greenhouse–Geisser's adjustment, or Huynh–Feldt's correction, which correct the degrees of freedom associated with significance tests); or (b) use the multivariate approach.

2. The effect for time—This is related to the proposition of whether the individuals are changing over time. Within-subjects factors represent repeated measurements comprising one or more achievement outcomes (which, in this example, we have named "test") collected on the same subjects over time. This part of the model represents the change we would anticipate that each individual would experience over the course of the study (Singer & Willett, 2003). The first hypothesis examined in an RMD is one related to the means of the observations over the repeated measurements; that is, one examines whether there is a difference in the levels of the means over time (Raykov & Marcoulides, 2008).

3. The shape of the within-subject growth trend—If we use a polynomial contrast (*contrast* = polynomial), selected from several available options for examining changes over time between individuals, the second hypothesis examined concerns the shape of the growth trend. The polynomial contrast addresses the shape of the individual change by providing a test for whether the within-subject trend is linear, quadratic (curved), or perhaps cubic (i.e., if we have four measurements). A linear trend can be interpreted as the rate of change over an interval of time (a). A quadratic trend is interpreted as a change in the rate of change (i.e., accelerating or decelerating) over an interval of time (a^2). The addition of higher degree polynomial terms to a proposed model depends on the number of occasions comprising the trend. For example, for three measurement occasions, the highest degree term is a^2 (quadratic), or one less than the number of measurement occasions.

4. Between-subjects factors —In repeated measures designs, it is important to distinguish between within-subjects factors and between-subjects factors. Between-subjects factors identify variables for which subjects may belong to only one category (e.g., treatment or control, male or female). The third hypothesis often tested in an RMD is a test of parallelism (Raykov & Marcoulides, 2008); that is, are the trajectories the same for different levels of a factor (e.g., different subgroups of subjects)?

5. Covariates—Covariates (interval variables) that might affect the rate of growth can also be added to the model. When covariates are added, the means for each occasion are adjusted for the presence of the covariates.

Examining the Shape of Students' Growth Trajectories

SPSS MANOVA produces a variety of tables for investigating individual change from either a univariate or multivariate perspective. Designs that combine both within-subjects factors and between-subjects factors are generally referred to as "mixed" designs (Raykov & Marcoulides, 2008), a terminology that was adopted in developing SPSS Mixed for a variety of more complex longitudinal and multilevel designs.

TABLE 5.1   Grand Mean

Measure:Test

Mean	Std. Error	95% Confidence Interval	
		Lower Bound	Upper Bound
52.945	.081	52.786	53.103

TABLE 5.2   Time

Measure:Test

Time	Mean	Std. Error	95% Confidence Interval	
			Lower Bound	Upper Bound
1	48.632	.104	48.428	48.837
2	53.107	.106	52.899	53.315
3	57.094	.106	56.886	57.303

In this example, we will begin with a model consisting only of the within-subject factor (Test) to get a sense of what the individual growth trajectories look like (see Table 5.1). For this example, the grand mean is 52.945. The grand mean is often not of much interest in examining growth, since it just represents the average achievement level across the three measurement occasions.

Of more interest are the means associated with each measurement occasion (Table 5.2). Examining the means more closely, one can see that the change between the first two test means is about 4.5 points, and between the second two means it is about 4.0. This suggests slightly less growth during the latter part of the trend compared with the initial part.

Visual inspection of the data can provide important preliminary clues about the shape of change that is taking place among individuals over time. Figure 5.1 provides a plot of the linear growth trajectories of the first 17 subjects in the data set. The plot of these individuals' scores over time suggests that individuals are increasing in their knowledge. Readers will note that the intercepts (i.e., individuals' status at Time 1) appear to vary considerably (i.e., from about 32 to 55) and the steepness of the growth over time also seems to vary within this subset of individuals. Many times, with a few waves of data, a linear model will be adequate to describe individuals' growth. Notice, however, that in the graph of these individuals' growth, the linear

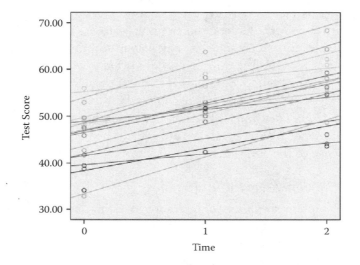

FIGURE 5.1   Individual linear growth trajectories.

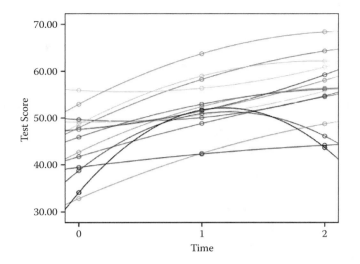

FIGURE 5.2   Individual nonlinear growth trajectories.

model does not seem to capture the change over time of all individuals equally well (i.e., not all of the individuals' scores fall on their growth lines).

For purposes of contrast, Figure 5.2 is a graph of the same 17 subjects, this time using a quadratic trajectory. With three time points, one can observe that the fit of the curved lines to the data points will be perfect. For some individuals, the following plot of their trajectories suggests that a linear shape might be adequate to describe the growth. For others, however, it appears their growth is better described by a curvilinear trajectory. These plots show visually our preliminary interest in determining whether a linear shape, or both linear and quadratic components, would be required to describe the shape of individuals' growth trajectories accurately.

Graphing the Linear Growth Trajectories With SPSS Menu Commands

We can use the SPSS menu commands to display the information for the subset of individuals in the study. The series of steps are provided in the next section.

Launch the SPSS application and select the *ch5vertest.sav* data file.

1. Go to the toolbar and select DATA, SELECT CASES.

This command will open the *Select Cases* dialog box.

2a. Within the *Select Cases* dialog box, click to select IF CONDITION IS SATISFIED.

b. Then click the IF button, which will activate the *Select Cases: If* dialog box.

c. Click the variable *id* from the left column listing, then click the right-arrow button to move *id* into the box.

Use the keypad to enter the less than sign (<) followed by the number 18. The resulting command (*id* < 18) instructs SPSS to select only the first 17 cases of the data set.

Click the CONTINUE button to return to the *Select Cases* dialog box.

3. Notice that the IF condition statement *id < 18* is listed.

Click the OK button to return to the SPSS main menu.

4. To graph the 17 cases, go to the SPSS toolbar and select GRAPHS, LEGACY DIALOGS, SCATTER/DOT.

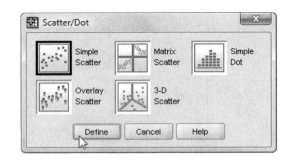

5. Click on the SIMPLE SCATTER icon to select this option among those shown.

Click DEFINE button to open the *Simple Scatterplot* dialog box.

6a. Within the *Simple Scatterplot* dialog box click to select the variable *test* from the left column listing. Then click the right arrow to move the variable into the *Y Axis* box.

b. Click to select *time* from the left column listing, then click the right-arrow button to move the variable into the *X Axis* box.

c. Click to select *id* from the left column listing, then click the right-arrow button to move the variable into the *Set Markers by* box.

Then click the OK button to generate the scatterplot.

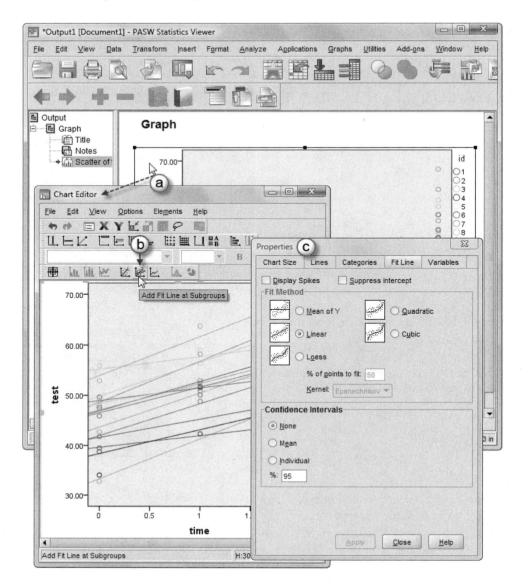

7a. Double-click on the graph in the SPSS output to select it and activate the *SPSS Chart Editor.*

b. In the *Chart Editor,* click on the icon ADD FIT LINE OF SUBGROUPS, which will insert lines on the graph.

c. Clicking the *Add Fit Line of Subgroups* icon also activates the *Properties* box, which provides assorted options.

8a. SPSS default settings insert 0.5 increments to the *X*-axis representing time. To change the increment, double-click the number to access the *Properties* dialog box.

b. In the *Properties* box the *Scale* tab displays the *Range* options for changing the increments.

c. Change the *Major Increment* by unchecking the box then replacing 0.5 with 1.

d. Click the APPLY button to make the change and activate the CLOSE button.

e. Click the CLOSE button to exit from the *Properties* box.

9a. To display the 17 subjects using a quadratic trajectory as shown in Figure 5.2, double-click the graph to select the graph's fit lines, which will also open the *Properties* box.

b. In the *Properties* box, click to select QUADRATIC.

c. Click the APPLY button to make the change and activate the CLOSE button.

d. Click the CLOSE button to exit from the *Properties* box.

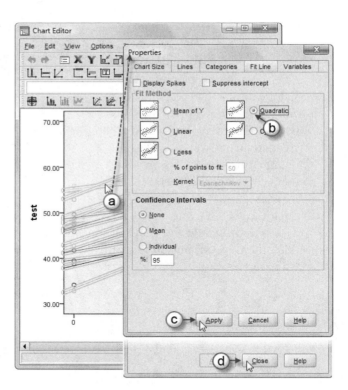

10. The *Chart Editor* displays the graph's quadratic trajectory.

Graph labels for the *Y* and *X* axes may be changed by clicking and typing the preferred name.

Close the *Chart Editor* box and return to the SPSS output document by either clicking the *x* located on the upper-right hand corner or by selecting FILE, CLOSE, or CTRL+F4.

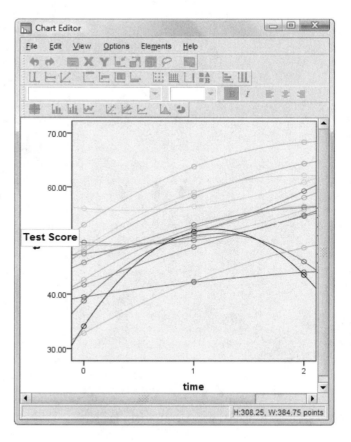

Examining Growth Trajectories Using Repeated Measures ANOVA

In repeated measures ANOVA, our first interest in examining the individual growth trajectories in some detail. We next provide the steps for examining our initial within-subjects model.

Conducting Repeated Measures ANOVA With SPSS Menu Commands

For this section use the data file *ch5hortest.sav*.

1. Go to the toolbar and select ANALYZE, GENERAL LINEAR MODEL, REPEATED MEASURES.

This command opens the *Repeated Measures Define Factor(s)* dialog box.

2a. Within the *Repeated Measures Define Factor(s)* dialog box, type in *time* as the *Within-Subject Factor Name*.
   b. Type in the number 3 in the *Number of Levels* box.
   c. Click the ADD button, which will place *time(3)* into the box.
   d. Type in *Test* into the *Measure Name* box.
   e. Click the ADD button, which will place *Test* into the box.

Click the DEFINE button, which will open the *Repeated Measures* dialog box.

3. Within the *Repeated Measures* dialog box, click to select *test1, test2,* and *test3* from the left column listing. Then click the right-arrow button to move the three variables into the *Within-Subjects Variables (time)* box.

Click the PLOTS button to access the *Repeated Measures: Profile Plots* dialog box.

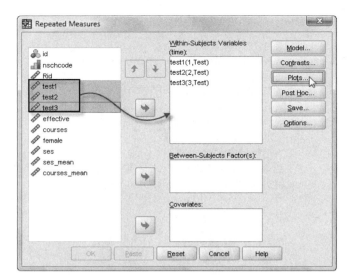

4. This option will create the curvilinear growth trend graph shown in Figure 5.3.
   a. Within the *Repeated Measures: Profile Plots* box, click to select *time* from the *Factors* box. Then click the right-arrow button to transfer *time* into the *Horizontal Axis* box.
   b. Click the ADD button to move *time* into the *Plots* box.

Click the CONTINUE button to return to the *Repeated Measures* dialog box.

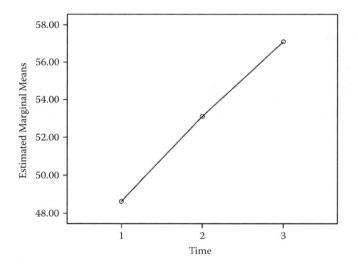

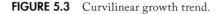

FIGURE 5.3   Curvilinear growth trend.

5. Click OPTIONS from the *Repeated Measures* dialog box.

6. Within the *Repeated Measures: Options* box, click to select *(OVERALL)* and *time*, then click the right-arrow button to move them into the *Display Means for* box.

Click the CONTINUE button to return to the *Repeated Measures* main window.

7. From the *Repeated Measures* main window, click the OK button to run the model and generate the plot graph (Figure 5.3).

Interpreting the Output From the Repeated Measures ANOVA

Mauchly's test of sphericity provides an examination of whether the variances and covariances between the repeated measures are the same (Table 5.3). As is often the case, the sphericity test is significant (p = .000), which implies that we should reject the null hypothesis that the variances and covariances of the measures are the same. This suggests corrections to degrees of freedom for conducting the F-tests should be used in determining tests of significance.

For a single outcome (Y) with repeated measures ($Y_1 - Y_3$), the univariate ANOVA within-subjects table (Table 5.4) can be used to determine the shape of the growth trend by using the default polynomial contrast (i.e., for three repeated measures, the tests for linear and quadratic components are relevant). Since Mauchly's test was significant, we can instead report the significance tests using either the Greenhouse–Geisser or the Huynh–Feldt correction for degrees of freedom in calculating the significance of the test of equality of means across time. The lower-bound correction will likely be too conservative (Raykov & Marcoulides, 2008). For the test of equal means (time), we can reject the null hypothesis that the scores are the same and conclude there are significant differences in means across the three assessment occasions (F = 2581.645, p < .001). Because the adjustment to the F-test is made in calculating the significance

TABLE 5.3   Mauchly's Test of Sphericity[b]

Measure: Test

Within-Subjects Effect	Mauchly's W	Approx. Chi-Square	df	Sig.	Epsilon[a]		
					Greenhouse–Geisser	Huynh–Feldt	Lower-bound
time	.977	206.113	2	.000	.977	.977	.500

Note: Tests the null hypothesis that the error covariance matrix of the orthonormalized transformed dependent variables is proportional to an identity matrix.

[a] May be used to adjust the degrees of freedom for the averaged tests of significance. Corrected tests are displayed in the Tests of Within-Subjects Effects table.

[b] Design: Intercept.

Within Subjects Design: time.

TABLE 5.4 Tests of Within-Subjects Effects

Measure:Test

Source		Type III Sum of Squares	df	Mean Square	F	Sig.
time	Sphericity Assumed	310760.337	2	155380.168	2581.645	.000
	Greenhouse–Geisser	310760.337	1.954	159031.307	2581.645	.000
	Huynh–Feldt	310760.337	1.955	158995.891	2581.645	.000
	Lower-bound	310760.337	1.000	310760.337	2581.645	.000
Error(time)	Sphericity Assumed	1043513.536	17338	60.186		
	Greenhouse–Geisser	1043513.536	16939.944	61.601		
	Huynh–Feldt	1043513.536	16943.717	61.587		
	Lower-bound	1043513.536	8669.000	120.373		

TABLE 5.5 Tests of Within-Subjects Contrasts

Measure:Test

Source	time	Type III Sum of Squares	df	Mean Square	F	Sig.
time	Linear	310416.221	1	310416.221	4801.239	.000
	Quadratic	344.115	1	344.115	6.176	.013
Error(time)	Linear	560479.947	8669	64.653		
	Quadratic	483033.589	8669	55.720		

level (rather than to the *F*-ratio), the analyst may not be able to directly observe the correction in every case.

The within-subject contrasts in Table 5.5 can provide us with information about the shape of the growth trend. For example, if the shape is linear, it suggests a constant rate of individual change (e.g., growth or decline) over time. If the quadratic estimate is significant, it suggests the rate of individual growth or decline changes over time. In this case, the linear and quadratic effects for time are significant. This suggests that the shape of the growth trend is curvilinear. We can see in Figure 5.3, the shape of the "average" trend is not quite linear. The shape suggests a slight slowing of the growth rate between the second and third intervals.

Adding Between-Subjects Predictors

Our next concern is whether between-subjects factors might alter the average growth pattern of individuals shown in the graph. This amounts to a test of parallelism across subgroups in the study (e.g., teacher effectiveness); that is, is the growth the same for different groups of individuals? In our example, we subdivided students according to the general effectiveness of their teachers. For purposes of demonstration, we add a dichotomized measure of teacher effectiveness (i.e., yes = 1, else = 0). We will also add a student SES covariate ($M = 0$, $SD = 1$) to the model.

Adding Between-Subjects Predictors With SPSS Menu Commands

(SPSS settings will default to those of the prior model.)

1. Go to the toolbar and select
ANALYZE, GENERAL LINEAR
MODEL, REPEATED MEASURES.

This command will open the *Repeated Measures Define Factor(s)* dialog box.

2a. Within the *Repeated Measures Define Factor(s)* dialog box, the default setting shows the factor name (time) and number of levels (3) as *time(3)* with *Test* as the *Measure Name*.

Click the DEFINE button, which will open the *Repeated Measures* dialog box.

3. Within the *Repeated Measures* dialog box, *test(1)*, *test2(2)*, and *test3(3)* appear as default settings in the *Within-Subjects Variables (time)* box.

a. Click to select *effective* from the left column listing, then click the right-arrow button to move the variable into the *Between-Subjects Factor(s)* box.

b. Click to select *ses* from the left column listing, then click the right-arrow button to move the variable into the *Covariate(s)* box.

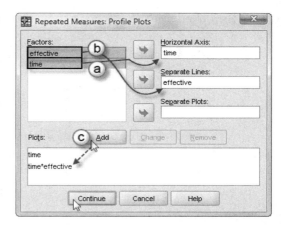

Click the PLOTS button to access the *Repeated Measures: Profile Plots* dialog box.

Note: The plots option enables comparing growth trends shown in Figure 5.4.

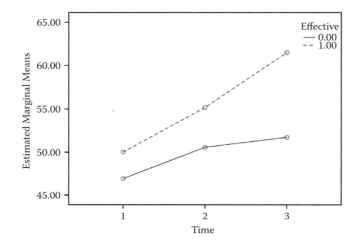

4a. Within the *Repeated Measures: Profile Plots* box, click to select *time* from the *Factors* box. Then click the right-arrow button to transfer *time* into the *Horizontal Axis* box.

b. Click to select *effective* from the *Factors* box. Then click the ADD button to move *effective* into the *Separate Lines* box.

c. Click the ADD button to move *time*effective* into the *Plots* box.

Click the CONTINUE button to return to the *Repeated Measures* dialog box.

FIGURE 5.4 Comparison of growth trends.

5. Click the OPTIONS button from the *Repeated Measures* main window.

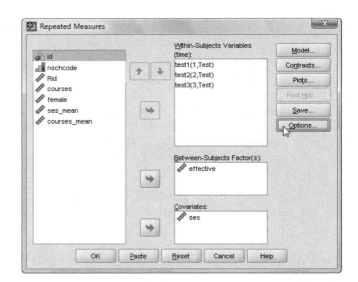

6. The default setting shown in the *Repeated Measures: Options* box displays *(OVERALL)* and *time*.

   a. Click to select *effective*time* from the left column listing in the *Factor(s) and Factor Interactions* box. Then click the right-arrow button to move the interaction into the *Display Means for:* box.

   b. Click to select the *Parameter estimates* option.

Then click the CONTINUE button to return to the *Repeated Measures* main window.

7. From the *Repeated Measures* main window, click the OK button to run the model and create the plot graph (Figure 5.4).

Interpreting the Output From Adding Between-Subjects Predictors

We can next examine the effects of the explanatory variables on student growth rates in Table 5.6. Once again, the effect for time is significant ($p < .001$). Readers may note that the variables enter the model as interactions with the within-subjects factor (time). The test of parallelism for teacher effectiveness is significant ($p < .001$), suggesting that student growth rates are affected by the overall effectiveness of their classroom teachers. We can also conclude that student SES does not affect growth rates ($p > .10$). Regarding this test, readers may notice that the various corrections for the significance levels associated with the lack of sphericity provide different results, with the lower-bound correction being the most conservative ($p = .143$).

TABLE 5.6 Tests of Within-Subjects Effects

Measure: Test

Source		Type III Sum of Squares	df	Mean Square	F	Sig.
time	Sphericity Assumed	284416.583	2	142208.292	2486.938	.000
	Greenhouse–Geisser	284416.583	1.941	146558.224	2486.938	.000
	Huynh–Feldt	284416.583	1.942	146492.120	2486.938	.000
	Lower-bound	284416.583	1.000	284416.583	2486.938	.000
time * ses	Sphericity Assumed	245.937	2	122.969	2.150	.116
	Greenhouse–Geisser	245.937	1.941	126.730	2.150	.118
	Huynh–Feldt	245.937	1.942	126.673	2.150	.118
	Lower-bound	245.937	1.000	245.937	2.150	.143
time * effective	Sphericity Assumed	52072.332	2	26036.166	455.320	.000
	Greenhouse–Geisser	52072.332	1.941	26832.572	455.320	.000
	Huynh–Feldt	52072.332	1.942	26820.470	455.320	.000
	Lower-bound	52072.332	1.000	52072.332	455.320	.000
Error(time)	Sphericity Assumed	991194.398	17334	57.182		
	Greenhouse–Geisser	991194.398	16819.517	58.931		
	Huynh–Feldt	991194.398	16827.107	58.905		
	Lower-bound	991194.398	8667.000	114.364		

TABLE 5.7 Parameter Estimates

Dependent Variable	Parameter	B	Std. Error	t	Sig.	95% Confidence Interval	
						Lower Bound	Upper Bound
test1	Intercept	50.020	.139	360.028	.000	49.748	50.293
	ses	.221	.132	1.681	.093	−.037	.479
	[effective=.00]	−3.103	.207	−14.990	.000	−3.509	−2.697
	[effective=1.00]	0ᵃ	—	—	—	—	—
test2	Intercept	55.178	.139	395.910	.000	54.905	55.451
	ses	.088	.132	.669	.504	−.171	.347
	[effective=.00]	−4.610	.208	−22.201	.000	−5.017	−4.203
	[effective=1.00]	0ᵃ	—	—	—	—	—
test3	Intercept	61.483	.125	491.978	.000	61.238	61.728
	ses	−.082	.118	−.696	.486	−.315	.150
	[effective = .00]	−9.747	.186	−52.348	.000	−10.112	−9.382
	[effective = 1.00]	0ᵃ	—	—	—	—	—

ᵃ This parameter is set to zero because it is redundant.

TABLE 5.8 Tests of Between-Subjects Effects

Measure: Test
Transformed Variable: Average

Source	Type III Sum of Squares	df	Mean Square	F	Sig.
Intercept	71220898.072	1	71220898.072	4.929E5	.000
ses	91.225	1	91.225	.631	.427
effective	218038.615	1	218038.615	1509.048	.000
Error	1252273.450	8667	144.488		

We can follow this with an examination of the parameter estimates associated with the explanatory variables. In Table 5.7, the effect of SES on achievement is not significant at any time point. There is an increasing difference in means at each occasion due to the type of teacher, however. More specifically, students with an ineffective teacher fall further behind their peers who have more effective teachers.

From this examination of the effect at each particular time, in Table 5.8 we can also examine the test of between-subjects effects, which addresses the presence of an overall SES effect and a teacher-effectiveness effect after pooling over the levels of the time variable across the repeated measures. In this case, teacher effectiveness is again significant ($p < .01$) but not student SES.

The table of means in Table 5.9 and the corresponding figure (Figure 5.4) summarize the growth for students with effective teachers versus ineffective teachers (controlling for student SES).

Using SPSS Mixed to Examine Individual Change

The previous analyses provided evidence to answer our research questions concerning individuals' developmental change in achievement over time. We can also examine student growth using SPSS Mixed to perform the longitudinal analyses. Using a random-coefficients approach to investigating individual change provides considerably more flexibility in examining situations where there may be missing data, varying occasions of measurement, and more complex error structures.

TABLE 5.9 effective * time

Measure:Test

effective	time	Mean	Std. Error	95% Confidence Interval	
				Lower Bound	Upper Bound
.00	1	46.926[a]	.154	46.625	47.226
	2	50.572[a]	.154	50.270	50.873
	3	51.733[a]	.138	51.462	52.004
1.00	1	50.028[a]	.139	49.756	50.301
	2	55.182[a]	.139	54.908	55.455
	3	61.480[a]	.125	61.235	61.725

[a] Covariates appearing in the model are evaluated at the following values: ses = .0370.

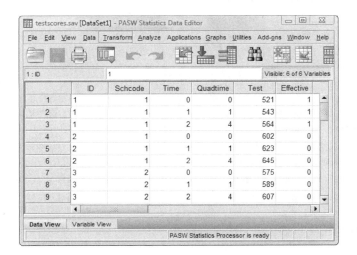

FIGURE 5.5 Vertical data matrix for repeated measures analysis in SPSS.

To examine growth within and between individuals using SPSS Mixed, the data must first be organized differently (see Chapter 2). In the previous ANOVA or MANOVA of change, the data on occasions were arranged horizontally in the data matrix, since they form a multivariate matrix of repeated observations of Y. In SPSS Mixed, however, the time-related observations must be organized vertically, which requires multiple lines for each subject. As explained in Chapter 2, we can use DATA and RESTRUCTURE menu commands to restructure the data vertically. Figure 5.5 presents data on three subjects in a hypothetical data set.

Closer inspection suggests there are three test observations per individual and that individual and school identifiers, as well as any predictors (i.e., SES, teacher effectiveness), are repeated in the data set for each time interval. The "Test" variable represents the repeated measurements of achievement. We can observe that the repeated observations of test are nested within individual identification (*id*) numbers, and student IDs are nested within school identifiers (*schcode*). The grouping variables (*id, schcode*) are used to identify each predictor as belonging to a particular level of the data hierarchy. The linear time variable (*time*) has been coded 0 for year 1, 1 for year 2, and 2 for year 3. This coding pattern identifies the intercept in the model as students' initial (*time 1*) achievement level. This is the most common type of coding for models examining individual change. A quadratic time variable (*quadtime*) is also defined to capture any changes (acceleration or deceleration) in the rate of change that might occur over the three measurement occasions. Quadtime has been correspondingly coded 0, 1, 4. If we instead coded the time variable 2, 1, 0 (and the quadratic variable 4, 1, 0), we would be identifying the intercept in the model as students' ending achievement level (at time 3). We could also code the time-related variables to indicate the second measurement (i.e., time 2) is to represent the intercept. After setting up the data set appropriately, we are then ready to build a series of models.

Developing a Two-Level Model of Individual Change

Many examinations of individual changes can be represented as a two-level growth model. At Level 1, each person's successive measurements over time are defined by an individual growth trajectory and random error. At Level 2, differences in trajectories between groups of individuals can be examined. We will use two subscripts to describe individuals (i) and occasions of measurement (t). We assume the observed status, Y_{ti}, at time t for individual i is a function of a systematic growth trajectory plus random error. As we saw earlier in the chapter, polynomial curves are often used for examining individual change because they can be estimated using standard linear modeling procedures (Hox, 2002).

At Level 1, the model to capture linear ($\pi_{1i}a_{ti}$) and quadratic ($\pi_{2i}a_{ti}^2$) components of individual change can be formulated as follows:

$$Y_{ti} = \pi_{0i} + \pi_{1i}a_{ti} + \pi_{2i}a_{ti}^2 + \varepsilon_{ti}, \tag{5.1}$$

where a_{ti} and a_{ti}^2 are time-varying variable of interest (e.g., which are coded to indicate the linear and quadratic components hypothesized to describe the shape of the growth trajectories), π_{0i} is an intercept, π_{1i} and π_{2i} describe the linear and quadratic growth rates respectively, and ε_{ti} represents variation in estimating growth within individuals. Because we have coded the first repeated measure as 0, the intercept parameter is interpreted as the child's true score at initial status (or the beginning) of the study, or the point where the growth trajectory crosses the Y axis.

The slope parameters (π_{1i} and π_{2i}) represent the change in individuals over each interval. The linear component describes the rate of change per unit of time. A quadratic component can be interpreted as a "change" in the rate of change (e.g., accelerating or decelerating). As we showed previously in Figure 5.5, the linear component of the time-related variable a is coded 0, 1, 2 in the data set (referred to as "*time*"), which ensures that the intercept is interpreted as students' *true* initial status (i.e., their corrected achievement level at time 1). We can also add a quadratic component to the model to test for a change in the rate of growth. This component is also coded as a variable (*quadtime*). The interval values for the variable can be generated using COMPUTE and multiplying the time variable by itself (*time*time*).

In this study, because of the coding, the linear component (π_{1i}) represents the semester growth rate for each child in the study. The quadratic component (π_{2i}) represents any increase or decrease in the rate of change for each time interval. Alternatively, the time-related variable might also be conceptualized as students' age in months at the time of each measurement. The intercept and slope coefficients represent the model's *structural*, or fixed, effects.

Level 1 Covariance Structure

The other part of the Level 1 model is the *stochastic* part, or the part that represents the variation in measuring each individual i on occasion t. This part of the model reflects there is some error (ε_{ti}) associated with measuring each individual's true change trajectory (i.e., the difference between the observed and true trajectory). Residual terms can be included for each measurement occasion. The errors are unobserved, which means that we must make some assumptions about their distribution at Level 1 (Singer & Willett, 2003). Most common, a simple residual structure is assumed from occasion to occasion and person to person, with each error independently and normally distributed, a mean of zero, and constant variance:

$$\varepsilon_{ti} \sim N(0, \sigma_\varepsilon^2), \tag{5.2}$$

where $\sim$ means "distributed as," N refers to normal distribution, 0 refers to the mean, and σ_ε^2 refers to the variance. This type of error structure can be represented as an identity matrix in SPSS, which provides a single residual variance associated with measurement occasions.

With longitudinal data, however, this type of simple Level 1 error structure may have less credibility (Singer & Willett, 2003). SPSS provides a considerable number of choices for the Level 1 residual covariance matrix in a repeated measures model. We will summarize a few commonly used structures. A complete list of covariance structures can be obtained from the Mixed Commands in the SPSS Help Menu. The Level 1 covariance matrix is accessed by using the "repeated" dialog box in the Commands menu or with a "repeated" syntax command. If the repeated dialog box (or repeated syntax statement) is not used, the default Level 1 matrix will be a scaled identity matrix (i.e., which assumes a constant variance for occasions), where σ^2 is a constant. This simplified within-subject error structure is often sufficient for repeated measures studies of short duration:

$$\sigma^2 \begin{bmatrix} 1 & 0 & 0 \\ 0 & 1 & 0 \\ 0 & 0 & 1 \end{bmatrix}. \tag{5.3}$$

As we mentioned in the previous example, if we used a univariate ANOVA, sphericity (i.e., equal variances and equal covariances across occasions) must be assumed (Hox, 2002). This type of covariance structure is referred to as compound symmetry (abbreviated CS in SPSS syntax). As Hox (2002) notes, for a multilevel model of repeated measures, the residual variance at any occasion can be defined as $\sigma^2 + \sigma_1^2$ (the sum of the occasion-level and person-level residual variances, respectively) in the diagonals of the matrix, and the covariance between any two occasions (i.e., the off-diagonal elements) is σ_1. Because the covariance matrix is a square matrix, the same element appears above and below the diagonals. The Level 1 matrix of variances and covariances among occasions would then be defined as

$$\begin{bmatrix} \sigma^2 + \sigma_1^2 & \sigma_1 & \sigma_1 \\ \sigma_1 & \sigma^2 + \sigma_1^2 & \sigma_1 \\ \sigma_1 & \sigma_1 & \sigma^2 + \sigma_1^2 \end{bmatrix}. \tag{5.4}$$

An alternative Level 1 structure assuming different variances across measurement occasions could also be summarized as a diagonal covariance matrix. This type of covariance matrix assumes heterogeneous variances for each measurement occasion in the diagonals of the matrix and 0s for the off-diagonal elements, which indicates no covariances between occasions:

$$\begin{bmatrix} \sigma_1^2 & 0 & 0 \\ 0 & \sigma_2^2 & 0 \\ 0 & 0 & \sigma_3^2 \end{bmatrix}. \tag{5.5}$$

The limitation of this type of covariance structure, however, is that it assumes no relationship between measurement occasions. In a repeated measures study, it is probably more likely that the residual covariances between measurement occasions within subjects are correlated.

The within-individual error structures for longitudinal data may often be more complex. For example, an autoregressive error covariance matrix indicates the residuals are correlated from occasion to occasion within individuals:

$$\sigma_\varepsilon^2 \begin{bmatrix} 1 & \rho & \rho^2 \\ \rho & 1 & \rho \\ \rho^2 & \rho & 1 \end{bmatrix}, \tag{5.6}$$

where the Level 1 variance σ_ε^2 is a constant and the autocorrelation coefficient rho (ρ) is the correlation between any two adjacent occasions (i.e., p^2 represents the correlation when there is a skip between occasions). The constraint $|\rho| \leq 1$ is imposed for stationarity. The assumption here is that the residual errors are correlated within each individual but are independent across individuals. In SPSS Mixed, it is also possible to assume heterogeneity among the variances (i.e., the diagonal elements can be replaced with separate variance estimates) in the autoregressive structure.

In contrast to an autoregressive error structure, a completely *unstructured* covariance matrix provides separate variance estimates in the diagonals with separate covariances estimated for the off-diagonal elements:

$$\begin{bmatrix} \sigma_1^2 & \sigma_{21} & \sigma_{31} \\ \sigma_{21} & \sigma_2^2 & \sigma_{32} \\ \sigma_{31} & \sigma_{32} & \sigma_3^2 \end{bmatrix}. \tag{5.7}$$

This type of error structure, however, can become overly complex when the number of measurement occasions increases beyond three or four. In this example, we will first assume an identity Level 1 covariance matrix within individuals.

It is important to note that under some circumstances different user choices regarding the error variance structure at Level 1 may affect the outcome of tests for random effects at higher levels. Often, it is necessary to exercise some type of compromise between the complexity of some covariance structures and the parsimony provided by others in arriving at a covariance structure that defines model covariance structures adequately. We illustrate some of these differences in Level 1 covariance matrices subsequently. As Hox (2002) notes, if the focus is primarily on the model's fixed effects, one can assume a more simplified variance and covariance structure across occasions, as some misspecification in the random part of the model does not generally affect the model's fixed effects (see also Verbeke & Lesaffre, 1997).

As Singer and Willet (2003) note, the Level 1 model assumes that all the individual change trajectories have the same algebraic form in Equation 5.1, but not every individual has the exact same trajectory. Because each person can have different intercept and slope coefficients, the Level 1 model represents another type of random-coefficients model. At Level 1, variables should be measured on repeated occasions (as they are nested within individuals). We could add other types of time-varying covariates to the Level 1 model (e.g., motivation). The key parameters in an analysis of individual change are the intercept (i.e., the level of the outcome at a particular point in time, such as initially) and the growth rate (i.e., the rate at which the outcome is changing).

For our example, we will first test whether the intercept and slope coefficients (i.e., describing linear and quadratic change vary across individuals) vary across individuals. Between individuals we can examine the three within-individual coefficients as randomly varying:

$$\pi_{0i} = \beta_{00} + r_{0i}, \tag{5.8}$$

$$\pi_{1i} = \beta_{10} + r_{1i}, \tag{5.9}$$

$$\pi_{2i} = \beta_{20} + r_{2i}, \tag{5.10}$$

where β coefficients represent the intercepts and r the respective residual components for each equation. It turns out that the quadratic component does not vary across individuals, so we can treat it as a fixed parameter by removing the random term (r_{2i}). With the quadratic component fixed, through the substitution of Equations 5.8 through 5.10 into Equation 5.1, we can arrive at the single-equation model for examining the fixed and random components without Level 2 predictors:

$$Y_{ti} = \beta_{00} + \beta_{10}(time)_{ti} + \beta_{20}(quadtime)_{ti} + r_{0i} + r_{1i} + \varepsilon_{ti}. \tag{5.11}$$

Level 2 Covariance Structure

It is also possible to define different residual covariance structures at different levels of the model. The dimensionality of the covariance matrix of residual variances and covariances depends on the number of Level 2 random effects in the model. In this case because we are treating the quadratic component as fixed across individuals due to our preliminary examination, we will assume a 2×2 *unstructured* covariance matrix of random effects for the intercept (I) and slope (S) at Level 2:

$$\begin{bmatrix} \sigma_I^2 & \sigma_{I,S} \\ \sigma_{I,S} & \sigma_S^2 \end{bmatrix}. \tag{5.12}$$

The variances for the intercept and slope are contained in the diagonals, and the covariance is represented by the off-diagonal element.

Model 1: Does the Slope Vary Randomly Across Individuals?

The first model focuses on defining the shape of students' growth trajectories and determining whether the initial intercept and random time slope vary across individuals.

Defining Model 1 With SPSS Menu Commands

Use the *ch5vertest.sav* data file.

Note: If continuing after creating Figures 5.1 and 5.2, remove the *Select Cases* conditional setting before proceeding. This is achieved by going to the SPSS toolbar, and selecting DATA, SELECT CASES, RESET, OK.

1. Go to the SPSS toolbar and select ANALYZE, MIXED MODELS, LINEAR.

This command enables access to the *Linear Mixed Models: Specify Subjects and Repeated* dialog box.

2. From the *Linear Mixed Models: Specify Subjects and Repeated* dialog box, click to select the *id* variable from the left column listing. Then click the right-arrow button to transfer *id* into the *Subjects* box.

Click the CONTINUE button to display the *Linear Mixed Models* dialog box.

3. The *Linear Mixed Models* dialog box is used to define the dependent variable as well as any factors (categorical variables) or covariates (interval variables) in the analysis.

   a. Click to select the *test* variable from the left column listing. Then click the right-arrow button to transfer *test* into the *Dependent Variable* box.

   b. Locate and click the variables *time* and *quadtime* from the left column listing, then click the right-arrow button to move the variables into the *Covariate(s)* box.

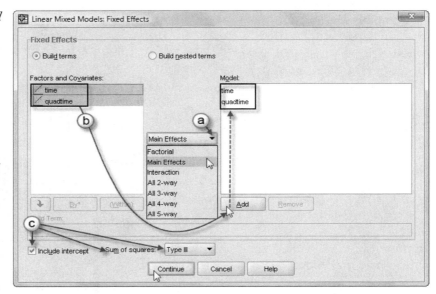

Click the FIXED button to access the *Linear Mixed Models: Fixed Effects* dialog box.

4a. Within the *Linear Mixed Models: Fixed Effects* dialog box, locate the *Factorial* setting and click on the pull-down menu to select *Main Effects*.

   b. The predictor variables *time* and *quadtime* appear in the *Factors and Covariates* box. Click to select *time* and *quadtime*, then click the ADD button to move the variables into the *Model* box.

   c. Note on lower left of the screen the *intercept* is included and the *sum of squares* is the default.

Click the CONTINUE button to return to the *Linear Mixed Models* dialog box. In the *Linear Mixed Models* dialog box, click the RANDOM button to access the *Linear Mixed Models: Random Effects* dialog box.

5a. Within the *Linear Mixed Models: Random Effects* box, change the covariance type by clicking on the pull-down menu and selecting *Unstructured*.

b. Confirm the *Include Intercept* option is selected.

c. Change *Factorial Effects* by clicking on the pull-down menu and selecting *Main Effects*.

d. Click to select *time* from the *Factors and Covariates* box, then click the ADD button to move the variable into the *Model* box.

e. Click the variable *id* from the *Subjects* box, then click the right-arrow button to move the variable into the *Combinations* box.

Click the CONTINUE button to return to the *Linear Mixed Models* dialog box.

6. From the *Linear Mixed Models* dialog box, Click the ESTIMATION button to access the *Linear Mixed Models: Estimation* dialog box.

In this chapter, we will use the default setting of restricted maximum likelihood (REML).

Click the CONTINUE button to return to the *Linear Mixed Models* dialog box.

7. In the *Linear Mixed Models* dialog box, click the STATISTICS button to access the *Linear Mixed Models: Statistics* dialog box.

Click and select the following three statistics: *parameter estimates*, *tests for covariance parameters*, and *covariances of random effects*.

Then click the CONTINUE button to return to the *Linear Mixed Models* dialog box.

8. Finally, in the *Linear Mixed Models* dialog box, click the OK button to run the model.

Interpreting the Output From Model 1

Results of this first model test are presented in the following tables. As in previous chapters, it is often useful to examine the total number of parameters being estimated and the number of random and fixed effects to make sure it corresponds with what the analyst might have in mind. The first output (Table 5.10) suggests there are seven total parameters being estimated including three fixed effects, three random parameters (intercept and time slope variances, covariance between the intercept and slope), and the residual (within individuals) variance. This

TABLE 5.10   Model Dimension[a]

		Number of Levels	Covariance Structure	Number of Parameters	Subject Variables
Fixed Effects	Intercept	1		1	
	time	1		1	
	quadtime	1		1	
Random Effects	Intercept + time[a]	2	Unstructured	3	id
Residual				1	
Total		5		7	

[a] Dependent Variable: test.

TABLE 5.11 Estimates of Fixed Effects[a]

Parameter	Estimate	Std. Error	df	t	Sig.
Intercept	48.632275	.102850	10597.930	472.847	.000
time	4.719043	.205643	10329.959	22.948	.000
quadtime	−.243999	.098184	8669.000	−2.485	.013

[a] Dependent Variable: test.

specification is consistent with Equation 5.11, with an additional parameter added for the covariance between the intercept and slope as shown in Equation 5.12.

The fixed effect results of the two-level model in Table 5.11 are summarized as β parameters from Equations 5.8 to 5.10. For the true intercept (π_{0i}), the estimate for initial status (β_{00} in Equation 5.8) is 48.632. This estimate is consistent with the repeated measures ANOVA estimate for Time 1 in Table 5.1 (i.e., 48.632). For the linear growth rate (π_{1i}), the estimate (β_{10} in Equation 5.9) is 4.72 points per year. For the quadratic growth rate (π_{2i}), the estimate (β_{20} in Equation 5.10) is −0.244. The significance of each fixed effect is tested with a *t*-test (i.e., defined as the ratio of the unstandardized estimate to its standard error). As in other chapters, we have eliminated the confidence intervals in the output to save space in reproducing the tables. The significant *t*-tests for the linear and quadratic growth terms suggest that both should be retained in the analysis and that, on average, individuals' growth rates slow slightly over time. This analysis is therefore consistent with the repeated measures ANOVA, suggesting that both linear and quadratic terms are useful in describing students' growth trajectories.

Next, we can examine the covariance parameters. The variance and covariance estimates can be more difficult to interpret than the fixed effects, since their coefficients have little absolute meaning and graphic aids are not helpful (Willett & Singer, 2003). The variance component table (Table 5.12) is used to determine how much variability in the outcomes is left at each level. At Level 1, the "residual" variance (σ_ε^2) summarizes the population variability in the average individual's achievement estimates around her or his own true change trajectory (Willett & Singer, 2003). The estimate is 55.72. Tests for evaluating variance components provide information about whether there is remaining residual outcome variation to be explained by other variables at either Level 1 or Level 2. The null hypothesis is that the population parameter for the variance is 0 (Singer & Willett, 2003). The Wald test calculates a *Z* statistic (the ratio of the estimate to its standard error). Keep in mind that the Wald *Z* statistic provides a two-tailed test and because the null hypothesis is that the population variance is 0, we must use a one-tailed test for variances. For the Level 1 residual variance (σ_ε^2), the Wald *Z* coefficient is 65.837 and the significance level is less than .001. This Level 1 covariance structure implies the residuals associated with individuals and occasions are independent and normally distributed.

The Level 2 variance components summarize the between-individual variability in change trajectories. In this example, we specified an unstructured covariance matrix at Level 2, which means there are variance estimates for the random intercept (UN 1,1), the random linear slope (UN 2,2), and an estimate of the covariance between them (UN 2,1). Table 5.12 suggests that there is significant variability in the random intercept to be explained between individuals

TABLE 5.12 Estimates of Covariance Parameters[a]

Parameter		Estimate	Std. Error	Wald Z	Sig.
Residual		55.719643	.846328	65.837	.000
Intercept + time [subject = id]	UN (1,1)	35.992459	1.436950	25.048	.000
	UN (2,1)	−1.246911	.764304	−1.631	.103
	UN (2,2)	4.466856	.648198	6.891	.000

[a] Dependent Variable: test.

(Wald $Z = 25.048$, $p < .001$). The linear time slope also varies significantly across individuals (Wald $Z = 6.891$, $p < .001$). The third parameter represents the covariance between the Level 2 residuals for initial status and linear growth (which tests whether true initial status and growth rate are positively or negatively correlated). In this model, however, the covariance between the initial status intercept and growth rate is uncorrelated ($p = .103$). Because the covariance can be positive or negative, the two-tailed test provided for the covariance therefore suggests that we could treat this parameter (UN 2,1) as fixed in subsequent models.

We note that researchers have cautioned about the use of these types of single parameter tests of the significance of the model's variance components (Hox, 2002; Raudenbush & Bryk, 2002). Regarding the Wald Z statistic, for example, for large estimated coefficients, the standard error can be inflated, which lowers the Wald statistic value. This can make the test overly conservative. The Wald Z test can also perform poorly under multicollinearity problems and in small sample sizes. For small samples, the likelihood-ratio test (which is also provided as SPSS output) tends to be more reliable than the Wald test. We discussed how this can be used to test the significance of model parameters in Chapter 4.

Investigating Other Level 1 Covariance Structures

As we suggested previously, we can consider other types of Level 1 covariance structures. We might examine whether the residual variance is heteroscedastic over occasions within individuals. For example, we might propose a diagonal covariance structure at Level 1, which implies difference variances for each occasion but not covariances between measurement occasions, as summarized in Table 5.13. Notice that the variability seems to be less on Occasion 3 within individuals. Between individuals, the intercept and slope still vary significantly across individuals. The absence of a significant covariance between the intercept and slope implies that we could fix that parameter to 0 between individuals. This suggests we could define a diagonal covariance matrix of random effects (i.e., with no covariance present) at Level 2.

Instead, we might also consider an unstructured covariance matrix at Level 1 and a diagonal covariance matrix at Level 2. When we do, however, we receive an error message regarding a lack of convergence for the proposed model (Figure 5.6). This type of covariance structure does not appear to fit the data at Level 1. More specifically, when we designate an unstructured covariance matrix at Level 1, the program cannot estimate the Level 2 variance components for the randomly varying intercept and slope.

TABLE 5.13 Estimates of Covariance Parameters[a]

Parameter		Estimate	Std. Error	Wald Z	Sig.
Repeated Measures	Var: [time = 0]	63.583481	2.025908	31.385	.000
	Var: [time = 1]	58.778811	1.158060	50.756	.000
	Var: [time = 2]	35.619135	1.980283	17.987	.000
Intercept + time [subject = id]	UN (1,1)	30.749900	1.841123	16.702	.000
	UN (2,1)	.354646	1.053148	.337	.736
	UN (2,2)	7.526024	.964305	7.805	.000

[a] Dependent Variable: test.

Warnings

Iteration was terminated but convergence has not been achieved. The MIXED procedure continues despite this warning. Subsequent results produced are based on the last iteration. Validity of the model fit is uncertain.

FIGURE 5.6 Warning message.

TABLE 5.14 Estimates of Covariance Parameters[a]

Parameter		Estimate	Std. Error	Wald Z	Sig.
Repeated Measures	AR1 diagonal	59.644473	1.349246	44.206	.000
	AR1 rho	.056248	.018970	2.965	.003
Intercept + time [subject = id]	Var: Intercept	32.142176	1.171808	27.430	.000
	Var: time	2.885435	.462885	6.234	.000

[a] Dependent Variable: test.

TABLE 5.15 Comparing Models, AIC Index, and Number of Parameters

Model Description	AIC	Parameters
Independent errors, level 1		
Unstructured matrix, level 2	189, 288.3	7
Diagonal covariance matrix, level 1		
Unstructured covariance matrix, level 2	189, 123.5	9
Autoregressive errors, homogeneous, level 1		
Diagonal covariance matrix, level 2	189, 282.7	7

After also investigating other combinations of Level 1 and Level 2 covariance structures, we note that with an autoregressive covariance structure at Level 1 and a diagonal covariance matrix at Level 2, we can obtain a model that converges (i.e., no warning statements in the output). With this structure, summarized in Table 5.14, we get 59.64 as the variance for occasions and rho correlation (ρ) of 0.056 (which represents the correlation between any two successive occasions). This implies there is little covariance between occasions. This Level 1 covariance structure can be compared against the diagonal Level 1 structure.

As we noted previously, in many occasions there will be little difference in terms of the fixed effects associated with different covariance structures. How can we then decide? We could conduct log likelihood tests (distributed as chi-square for nested models). Another easy way to compare the models is to examine the Akaike information criterion (AIC) index for each one. We prefer the smallest AIC, regardless of the number of parameters (Marcoulides & Hershberger, 1997). We summarized the three models and the number of parameters estimated in Table 5.15. Based on this comparison, we might select the model with diagonal covariance structure at Level 1 is a reasonable choice based on available model-fitting information as well as the finding of almost no covariance between measurement occasions in these data (see Table 5.13).

Investigating Other Level 1 Covariance Structures Using SPSS Menu Commands

(Settings will default to those used for the Model 1.)

Diagonal Covariance Matrix

1. Go to the SPSS toolbar and select ANALYZE, MIXED MODELS, LINEAR.

This command enables access to the *Linear Mixed Models: Specify Subjects and Repeated* dialog box.

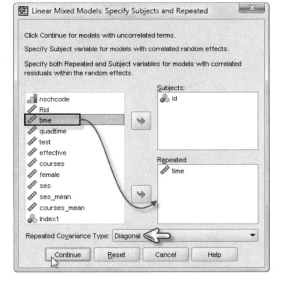

2. From the *Linear Mixed Models: Specify Subjects and Repeated* dialog box, click to select the *time* variable from the left column listing. Then click the right-arrow button to transfer *id* into the *Repeated* box. (Note the command will activate the *Repeated Covariance Type* function and default *Diagonal* setting.)

Click the CONTINUE button to display the *Linear Mixed Models* dialog box.

3. The *Linear Mixed Models* dialog box shows the prior settings: *test* (Dependent Variable), *time* and *quadtime* (Covariates).

The fixed and random effects as well as the estimation and statistics settings remain the same, so click the OK button to run the model.

Unstructured Covariance Matrix

1. Go to the SPSS toolbar and select ANALYZE, MIXED MODELS, LINEAR to access to the *Linear Mixed Models: Specify Subjects and Repeated* dialog box.

2. In the *Linear Mixed Models: Specify Subjects and Repeated* dialog box, click the pull-down menu to change the *Repeated Covariance Type* to *Unstructured*.

Click the CONTINUE button to display the *Linear Mixed Models* dialog box.

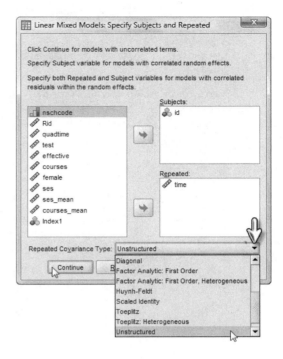

3. The *Linear Mixed Models* dialog box shows the prior settings: *test* (Dependent Variable), *time* and *quadtime* (Covariates).

The fixed and random effects as well as the estimation and statistics settings remain the same, so click the OK button to run the model.

Autoregressive Covariance Matrix

1. Go to the SPSS toolbar and select ANALYZE, MIXED MODELS, LINEAR to access to the *Linear Mixed Models: Specify Subjects and Repeated* dialog box.

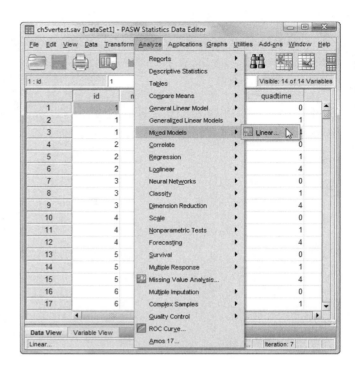

2. In the Linear *Mixed Models: Specify Subjects and Repeated* dialog box, click the pull-down menu to change the *Repeated Covariance Type* to *AR(1)*.

Click the CONTINUE button to display the *Linear Mixed Models* dialog box.

3. In the *Linear Mixed Models* dialog box, click the RANDOM button to access the *Linear Mixed Models: Random Effects* dialog box.

4a. Change the covariance type by clicking on the pull-down menu and selecting *Diagonal*.
   b. Confirm the *Include Intercept* option is selected.
   c. Confirm the *Main Effects* option is selected.
   d. Confirm the variable *time* appears in the *Model* box.
   e. Confirm the variable *id* appears in the *Combinations* box.

Click the CONTINUE button to return to the *Linear Mixed Models* dialog box.

5. The fixed and random effects, estimation, and statistic settings remain the same, so click the OK button to run the model.

Model 2: Adding the Between-Subjects Predictors

The initial results presented previously suggest that intercepts and growth rates vary across individuals. At Level 2, a set of predictors (e.g., socioeconomic status, gender, an instructional treatment) could be added to the model to explain the observed differences in students' initial achievement level and their growth trajectories. In this case, similar to the previous repeated measures ANOVA, we will propose that teacher effectiveness (effective) and students' socioeconomic status (SES) might explain differences in students' intercepts and linear growth rates. For examining the parallelism hypothesis regarding variability in growth rates for different student subgroups (i.e., that growth rates are the same for students having effective versus not effective teachers), or for considering the impact of an interval variable such as SES on student growth rates, we need to create cross-level interaction terms.

Cross-level interactions involve the effects of Level 2 (between-individuals) variables such as teacher effectiveness on a Level 1 slope coefficient; that is, students' yearly test growth rates. These interaction terms can be created within SPSS Mixed in the menu command format. We emphasize that for this exercise teacher effectiveness is defined as a between-student factor, that is, it is simply used as a means of identifying subsets of students (e.g., similar to gender) likely to have different growth trajectories. In this example, we do not link groups of students to their individual teachers, so we will not consider the more complicated nesting of students within teachers. We examine a model with students nested within classrooms and schools in the next chapter.

At Level 2, the following equations can be formulated:

$$\pi_{0i} = \beta_{00} + \beta_{01}(ses)_i + \beta_{02}(effective)_i + r_{0i}, \tag{5.13}$$

$$\pi_{1i} = \beta_{10} + \beta_{11}(time * ses)_i + \beta_{12}(time * effective)_i + r_{1i}, \tag{5.14}$$

where r_{0i} and r_{1i} represent variation associated with measuring the intercept and slope parameters between individuals.

If we wished to examine possible differences in the quadratic component (even though we will treat this component as fixed across individuals) we could also add time-related interactions to that portion of the model:

$$\pi_{2i} = \beta_{20} + \beta_{21}(quadtime * ses)_i + \beta_{22}(quadtime * effective)_i + r_{2i}. \tag{5.15}$$

Keep in mind that SPSS Mixed is a very flexible program and, therefore, there are several different ways the models can be specified. To have confidence that the model is correctly specified, one has to be fairly clear about what choices are being made. Some of those choices include how to handle the nesting of measurements within individuals; whether the nesting of individuals within groups (such as classrooms or schools) is to also be considered in the model; the structure of the covariance matrix for random effects; and whether only the intercept, or the intercept and growth slope, are to be defined as randomly varying parameters across particular levels of the data hierarchy. These choices will affect the fixed effects and variance estimates produced.

Defining Model 2 With SPSS Menu Commands

In this model, we proposed that students' initial status intercept (π_{0i}) will vary across individuals and this variation in intercepts will in part be explained by students' socioeconomic status and teacher effectiveness. We also proposed that variation in students' average linear growth rates (π_{1i}) will be explained by the same predictors.

(SPSS settings will default to those used for the preceding model.)

1. Go to the SPSS toolbar and select ANALYZE, MIXED MODELS, LINEAR.

This command enables access to the *Linear Mixed Models: Specify Subjects and Repeated* dialog box.

2. The *Linear Mixed Models: Specify Subjects and Repeated* dialog box, displays the variables *id* and *time* within the *Subjects* and *Repeated* boxes.

Click the *Repeated Covariance Type* pull-down menu and select *Diagonal*.

Click the CONTINUE button to display the *Linear Mixed Models* dialog box.

3. The *Linear Mixed Models* dialog box displays *test* in the *Dependent Variable* box.

   a. Entering variables in sequential order helps facilitate reading of the output tables. So first remove *time* and *quadtime* from the *Covariate(s)* box by clicking to select them. Next click the left-arrow button to return the variables to the left column list.

   b. Select the following variables and click on the right-arrow button to enter them into the *Covariate(s)* box in the following sequence: *ses, effective, time,* and *quadtime*.

Click the FIXED button to access the *Linear Mixed Models: Fixed Effects* dialog box.

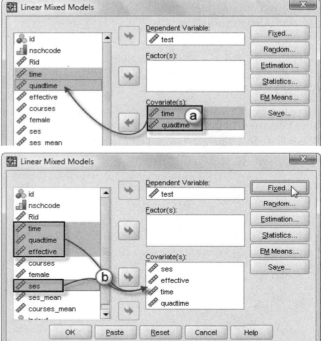

4a. Within the *Linear Mixed Models: Fixed Effects* dialog box confirm that *Main Effects* is selected.

   b. Confirm that *Include Intercept* is selected.

   c. Click to select the variables *ses, effective,* and *time* from the *Factors and Covariates* column. These variables are the "main effects" in the model and will modify the intercept. Then click the ADD button to move the variables into the *Model* box.

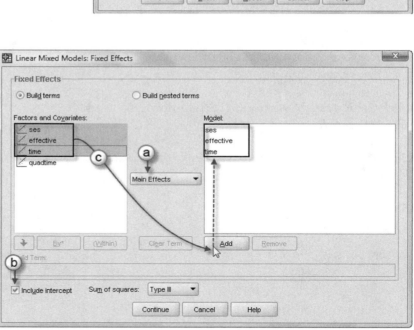

5. Two cross-level interactions (or nested terms) will be created and added to the model: *time*ses* and *time*effective*. These interactions will tell us if the growth trajectories are parallel for different groups of students.

a. Click to select *Build nested terms*.
b. Click to select the variable *time* from the *Factors and Covariates* box.
c. Then click the arrow button below the *Factors and Covariates* box. This moves *time* into the *Build Term* box to create a cross-level interaction by linking variables and terms.
d. Next, click the BY* button, which will insert the computational symbol: *time**.

e. Click to select *ses* from the *Factors and Covariates* box.
f. Then click the arrow button below the *Factors and Covariates* box. This will complete the interaction term: *time*ses*.
g. Click the ADD button to move *time*ses* into the *Model* box.

This completes the first cross-level interaction term.

6. The second interaction term to create is *time*effective*.

   a. Click to select the variable *time* from the *Factors and Covariates* box.

   b. Then click the arrow button located below the *Factors and Covariates* box to insert *time* in the *Build Term* box.

   c. Next, click the BY* button, which will insert the computational symbol *Build Term* to the term list so it appears as *time**.

   d. Click to select *effective* from the *Factors and Covariates* box.

   e. Then click the arrow button located below the *Factors and Covariates* box. This will complete the cross-level interaction term: *time*effective*.

   f. Click the ADD button to move the interaction *time*effective* into the *Model* box.

g. Click to select *Build terms*.

h. Click to select *quadtime* from the *Factors and Covariates* box. Then click the ADD button.

Click the CONTINUE button to return to the *Linear Mixed Model* dialog box.

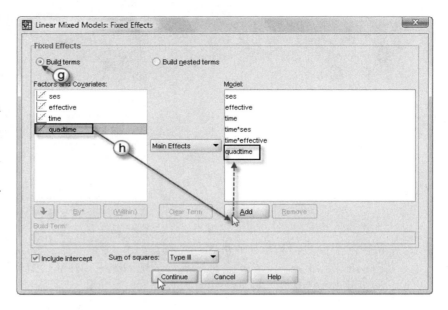

7a. Change the covariance type by clicking on the pull-down menu and selecting *Unstructured*.

b. Confirm the *Include Intercept* option is selected.

c. Confirm the *Main Effects* option is selected.

d. Confirm the variable *time* appears in the *Model* box.

e. Confirm the variable *id* appears in the *Combinations* box.

Click the CONTINUE button to return to the *Linear Mixed Model* dialog box.

8. The estimation and statistics settings remain the same as the prior model, so click the OK button to run the model.

Interpreting the Output From Model 2

Results of the second model test are presented next (Table 5.16). Once again, it is useful to examine the random effects and total parameters estimated. There are seven fixed effects estimated. In addition, there are six variance–covariance parameters to be estimated. At Level 1 (within individuals) there are three variance parameters (i.e., the variances for each occasion). These are listed in the diagonal covariance matrix at Level 1. In addition, there are two random effects (the intercept and slope) proposed to vary across individuals. These two parameters and the covariance between them are summarized in the Level 2 unstructured covariance matrix. Thirteen total parameters are therefore estimated in the proposed model (as noted in Table 5.16).

The fixed effect estimates are summarized next (Table 5.17). Students' initial achievement intercept (β_{00}) is 47.28. This can be described as students' true initial status adjusted for SES and teacher effectiveness. The intercept in this case can be interpreted as the initial test score for students who do not have an effective teacher (coded 0) and their SES status is 0.00 (which is near the grand mean for SES). For comparative purposes, in Table 5.9 the corresponding intercept for students with perceived ineffective teachers at Time 1 is 46.926 (controlling only for SES).

The first question we can ask is whether the predictors are related to differences in initial achievement. We can see that teacher effectiveness is related to students' initial achievement level ($p < .001$). The coefficient for effectiveness ($\beta_{02} = 2.44$) suggests that students with effective

TABLE 5.16 Model Dimension[b]

		Number of Levels	Covariance Structure	Number of Parameters	Subject Variables	Number of Subjects
Fixed Effects	Intercept	1		1		
	ses	1		1		
	effective	1		1		
	time	1		1		
	ses * time	1		1		
	effective * time	1		1		
	quadtime	1		1		
Random Effects	Intercept + time[a]	2	Unstructured	3	id	
Repeated Effects	time	3	Diagonal	3	id	8670
Total		12		13		

[a] As of version 11.5, the syntax rules for the RANDOM subcommand have changed. Your command syntax may yield results that differ from those produced by prior versions. If you are using version 11 syntax, please consult the current syntax reference guide for more information.

[b] Dependent Variable: test.

TABLE 5.17   Estimates of Fixed Effects[a]

Parameter	Estimate	Std. Error	df	t	Sig.
Intercept	47.283765	.148416	9227.021	318.590	.000
ses	.228228	.123403	8667.000	1.849	.064
effective	2.436212	.194017	8667.000	12.557	.000
time	2.795098	.223571	10048.373	12.502	.000
ses * time	–.153810	.073581	8667.000	–2.090	.037
effective * time	3.508072	.115686	8667.000	30.324	.000
quadtime	–.243999	.098184	8669.000	–2.485	.013

[a] Dependent Variable: test.

TABLE 5.18   Estimates of Covariance Parameters[a]

Parameter		Estimate	Std. Error	Wald Z	Sig.
Repeated Measures	Var: [time=0]	61.399873	2.003852	30.641	.000
	Var: [time=1]	61.448416	1.155968	53.158	.000
	Var: [time=2]	27.124323	1.726829	15.708	.000
Intercept + time [subject = id]	UN (1,1)	30.649177	1.828750	16.760	.000
	UN (2,1)	–3.305822	1.012774	–3.264	.001
	UN (2,2)	7.465096	.873415	8.547	.000

[a] Dependent Variable: test.

teachers would have an estimated starting achievement level of about 49.72 (47.28 + 2.44). For comparison, in Table 5.9 the observed Time 1 adjusted mean for students with effective teachers is slightly higher at 50.03 (controlling for SES). The reason for this initial difference across the two groups of teachers is unknown, but we could speculate that informal processes might lead to more effective teachers receiving academically more capable students. In this model, student SES is a significant predictor of initial achievement at $p < .10$.

The second question we can ask is whether there are differences in student growth rates related to the predictors. The average growth rate (which varies randomly across schools) is 2.80. This indicates that on average scores increase significantly over each measurement interval within individuals. Because the growth parameter is specified as a random effect in the model, we are primarily interested in whether it varies between individuals in the study. The variation in the size of the within-individual growth parameter across schools can be examined using the Wald Z test in Table 5.18 (Wald $Z = 8.547$, $p < .01$). The significant test suggests we can reject the null hypothesis that the population growth parameter is 0 and infer that growth varies significantly across the population of individuals. We note in passing that when the random effect varies significantly across individuals (i.e., Level 2), it is unnecessary to interpret the significance of the fixed effect (Tabachnick, 2008).

Regarding variables that might explain variability in growth rates between individuals, we can see that the *time*ses* interaction is significant at $p < .05$ ($\beta_{11} = -.15$, $p = .037$). This coefficient can be interpreted as students' at higher SES levels make slightly less growth per interval compared with students on the grand mean for SES. For example, at the grand mean of SES, students' growth rate would be 2.80 points per year. At 1 *SD* above the mean in SES, students' growth rate would be 2.65 points (i.e., calculated as 2.80 – 0.15 = 2.65). The test for students' perceptions of teacher effectiveness was also significant ($\beta_{12} = 3.51$, $p < .001$). This suggests that students with effective teachers would have a growth rate 3.51 points above the average growth rate (2.80), which is actually the growth rate for students with ineffective teachers (since they are coded 0). The table also suggests that student growth rates slow significantly over time

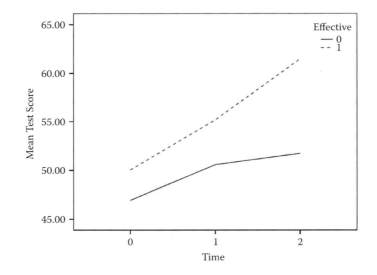

FIGURE 5.7 Growth rate trajectories by teacher effectiveness.

(β_{20} = −0.24, p < .001). In this model, we did not propose any cross-level interaction related to explaining the slowing of growth rates.

The SPSS Mixed model provides more parameter estimates than the repeated measures model (i.e., estimates of initial status and growth). For growth, the pattern of results is slightly different from the repeated measures model in the first part of the chapter. *Effective*time* was significant in both models. In the Mixed model, *ses* is significant for initial status at p < .10. For the *time*ses* interaction, the result was also significant (p < .05). However, in the repeated measures ANOVA model, the *ses*time* interaction was not significant.

After the addition of the predictors, the covariance table (Table 5.18) suggests there was still significant residual variance in initial intercepts to be explained (Wald Z = 16.76, p < .001). There was also significant residual variance in slopes left to be explained across individuals (Wald Z = 8.547, p < .001). The relationship between the intercept and slope was negative (−3.31) and also significant (p < .01). If desired, we could select an unstructured covariance matrix with a correlation for the slope parameter (UNR).

Finally, we can summarize the initial difference in growth trajectories with a graph of different growth rates by teacher effectiveness (Figure 5.7). The trajectories are best interpreted as not parallel over time; that is, the initial observed gap in test learning between students with effective and ineffective teachers widens over time. This graph will look slightly different from the one produced in *Repeated Measures* since there is no control for student SES in the latter graph. This graph can be produced using the following SPSS commands.

Graphing the Growth Rate Trajectories With SPSS Menu Commands

1. Go to the SPSS toolbar and select GRAPHS, LEGACY DIALOGS, LINE.

This command will open the *Line Charts* dialog box.

2. In the *Line Charts* dialog box, click to select *Multiple*. Confirm that *Summaries for groups of cases* is selected.

Click the DEFINE button to continue, which will open the *Define Multiple Line: Summaries for Groups of Cases* dialog box.

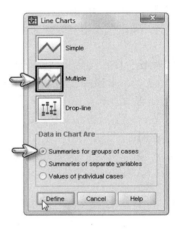

3a. Within the *Define Multiple Line: Summaries for Groups of Cases* dialog box, click to select *Other statistic (e.g., mean)*.

b. Click to select the variable *test* from the left column, then click the right-arrow button to move *test* into the *Variable* box.

c. Click to select *time* from the left column, then click the right-arrow button to move the variable into the *Category Axis* box.

d. Click to select *effective* from the left column, then click the right-arrow button to move the variable into the *Define Lines by* box.

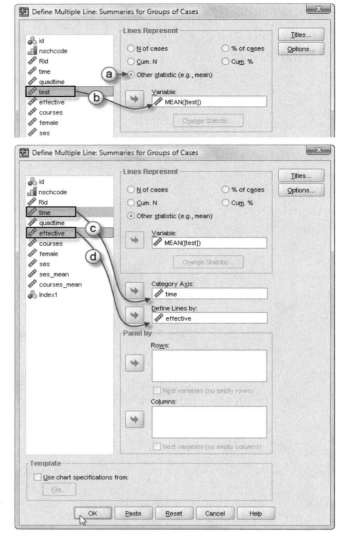

Click the OK button, which will generate the plot graph.

Note: The resulting plot graph's labels and lines may be edited or changed through the *SPSS Chart Editor*. To activate the *Chart Editor*, double-click on the plot graph in the output.

Summary

In this chapter we presented a basic two-level model for investigating individual change. Longitudinal analysis represents a rapidly growing application of basic multilevel modeling techniques. In comparison to ANOVA, we suggested that multilevel modeling of growth trajectories is a more flexible approach because of its ability to handle a wide range of data situations (incomplete data, varying occasions of measurement). The model provides considerably more information about students' initial status and growth rates. The individual growth model can easily be extended to include successive grouping structures above the individual level. We investigate models with individual and group components in the next chapter. Readers are also encouraged to consult a number of introductory sources that provide overviews of the assumptions, uses, and programming of longitudinal models (e.g., Duncan, Duncan, & Strycker, 2006; Raudenbush, Bryk, Cheong, & Congdon, 2004; Raykov & Marcoulides, 2008; Singer & Willett, 2003).

CHAPTER **6**

Methods for Examining Organizational-Level Change

I n this chapter we expand on our introduction to methods that can be used to examine changes in individuals presented in Chapter 5. As we noted in that chapter, time is often a key factor in understanding how developmental processes may unfold, as well as in observing their impact. Longitudinal data collection facilitates the investigation of proposed relationships whose effects become more apparent over time. Presently, there is a wider set of options available for including a temporal dimension in studies, depending on the specific goals of the research and the data structure used to investigate proposed theoretical models. We saw in the last chapter that the SPSS Mixed approach for examining individual growth is quite straightforward for repeated measures that are continuous. In this chapter, we consider group-level extensions of the two-level individual growth model provided in the last chapter. We build a three-level growth model to illustrate how a model is formed, tested against the data, and the results interpreted.

Examining Changes in Institutions' Graduation Rates

In the last chapter, we examined change in students' achievement scores related to differences in their backgrounds and the effectiveness of their teachers. In such cases, the unit of analysis is the individual student. The achievement measures were nested within individual students at Level 1, and differences in their backgrounds and overall effectiveness of their teachers were examined at Level 2. If we had linked individual students to their specific teachers or to their schools, perhaps that would have necessitated a third level of the model. In fact, if we included both teachers and schools, we would require a four-level model—repeated measures nested in individuals, between individuals, between teachers, and between schools. SPSS Mixed can actually facilitate this type of complex analysis, although it may take a considerable amount of time and some effort to reduce the computer space it takes to complete the analysis.

Consider a national study to investigate whether undergraduate degree completion levels are rising over time. In this example, we will consider an application of random-coefficients growth modeling to examine between-state differences in the proportion of undergraduates who graduate from public universities and changes in the proportion of graduates over an 11-year period. In our example study, the individual-level data (Level 1) consist of repeated measures on proportions of undergraduate students who graduate nested within institutions. The between-individual data (Level 2) consist of institutional characteristics that may explain differences in graduation levels between institutions, and the group-level data (Level 3) consist of state-level information such as resources allocated to support higher education.

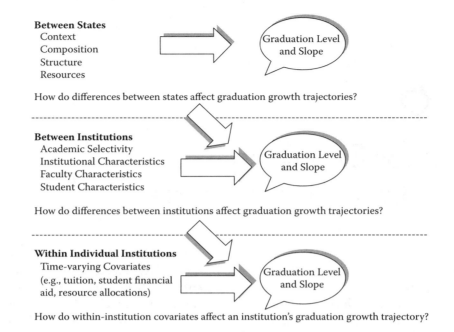

FIGURE 6.1   Proposed three-level graduation trajectory model.

Research Questions

The three-level growth formulation facilitates investigating a number of different types of multi-level relationships. As summarized in Figure 6.1, within institutions (Level 1) we can examine relationships involving various time-varying covariates that might influence institutional graduation levels. This means that the levels of the covariates change corresponding with the levels of the outcome over time. Time-varying covariates provide a way of accounting for temporal variation that may increase (or decrease) the value of an outcome predicted by the individual's growth trajectory (Raudenbush & Bryk, 2002). For example, we could focus on how fluctuation in various types of resource spending affects graduation rates, as well as whether tuition levels and financial aid levels are related to graduation rates. In contrast, we could also consider these as "static " variables (i.e., the average tuition level or the average financial aid level), which requires only one value for the covariate. In this case, we would then enter the covariate as a between-institution variable (i.e., Level 2). One of the advantages of the Level 1 (time varying) formulation, however, is that the slope of tuition levels on graduation levels can then be modeled as a random parameter at Levels 2 (between institutions) and 3 (between states). Possible cross-level interactions are shown in Figure 6.1 with arrows extending from a higher level in the conceptual model to a lower level in the model. For example, we might propose that differences in student selectivity moderate growth rates within institutions or that student composition might moderate tuition–graduation slopes within institutions.

Between institutions (Level 2), we can investigate how various institutional characteristics (e.g., mission, selectivity of admissions, student composition, faculty characteristics) are related to graduation proportions or changes in graduation proportions over time. As noted earlier, we could also investigate a random covariate–outcome slope that might be of theoretical interest (e.g., tuition–graduation rate or financial aid–graduation rate). Finally, at the state level (Level 3), we can examine how different patterns of state economic and political activity might affect graduation outcomes. For example, we might examine how family share or legislative support for higher education is related to graduation levels and changes in graduation levels over time. We could also examine whether a particular type of state higher education policy (such as merit-based tuition support) might influence graduation levels or growth rates.

The model in Figure 6.1 suggests several research questions including:

What is the average level and shape of institutions' graduation trajectories over time?
Which within- and between-institutional variables explain institutional graduation levels?
How do graduation trajectories vary according to features of states?

Data

In this example, we focus on subset of data from a larger study of growth in student graduation over time (Lam, 2008). The subset consists of undergraduate (6-year) graduation rates from 649 public, 4-year institutions within the 50 states. The graduation levels were compiled over an 11-year period.

Defining the Model

In growth, or change, models, we assume that a number of individuals, or in this case institutions, have been sampled and measured on one or more variables over several occasions. Because multilevel modeling does not require balanced data, it is not a problem if all measurements are not available on all participants (Hox, 2002). This can be beneficial if there are subjects who drop out during a longitudinal study. This model can be extended to include situations where the timing and spacing of the measurements differ across individuals. As we noted in the last chapter, in random-coefficients growth modeling, within- and between-individual changes are typically represented through a two-level univariate model (see also Hox, 2002; Raudenbush & Bryk, 2002; Singer & Willett, 2003). A third level (and successive levels) can be added to model changes between higher order units.

Level 1 Model

The Level 1 part of the model represents the change each member of the population is expected to experience during the time period under study (Singer & Willett, 2003). In this case, each institution's successive graduation measurements can be represented by an individual growth trajectory (or growth curve) and random error. We assume that the observed status at time t for institution i is a function of a systematic growth trajectory plus random error. This general Level 1 equation represents our hypotheses about the shape of each institution's true graduation trajectory over time (Singer & Willett, 2003). Polynomial curves are often used for describing individual growth because they can be estimated using standard linear modeling procedures, and they are very flexible (Hox, 2002). It is important to note that in the random-coefficients approach, the time-related variables describing the shape of the growth trajectory (e.g., linear, quadratic, or some other polynomial) are entered into the data set as variables. This is in contrast to the structural equation modeling approach (i.e., often referred to as *latent change* or *latent curve* analysis), where the shape of the growth trajectory is defined as factor loadings on a latent growth factor instead of as actual data points.

Following Raudenbush and Bryk's notation (2002), the systematic growth for each individual institution can be represented as a polynomial of degree P, with the Level 1 model for the proportion of undergraduates who graduate at time t for institution i in state j can be written as

$$y_{tij} = \pi_{0ij} + \pi_{1ij}\, a_{tij} + \pi_{2ij} a^2_{tij} + \ldots + \pi_{ijp} a^P_{tij} + \varepsilon_{tij}, \qquad (6.1)$$

where π_{0ij} is the intercept parameter (which is defined as the level of the institution's "true" status at some relevant point in the series of measurement occasions), a_{tij} is a time-varying variable of interest, with institution i in state j measured on T occasions, and π_{ijp} is the growth trajectory parameter p for institution i in state j associated with the polynomial of degree P (i.e., $p = 0$,

… , P). One or more time-varying covariates (X_t) can also be added to the Level 1 model as needed.

The growth trajectory (slope) parameter is the most important parameter because it represents the rate at which institution i within state j changes over time. The model facilitates the representation of several different trajectories including, for example, linear ($\pi_{1ij}a_{tij}$), quadratic ($\pi_{2ij}a^2_{tij}$), and cubic ($\pi_{3ij}a^3_{tij}$) growth. In terms of interpretation, however, if one considers that the linear trajectory model represents a *constant* rate of change over time and the quadratic trajectory models represent *change* (accelerating or decelerating) in the rate of change over time, it becomes increasingly more difficult to interpret models of higher polynomial degrees (Raykov & Marcoulides, 2008). The specification of the general Level 1 model implicitly assumes that all the change trajectories have a common algebraic form, but not every individual institution has the same trajectory (Singer & Willett, 2003). Each institution, therefore, draws its parameter values (i.e., intercept, slope) from an unknown (underlying) bivariate distribution of intercepts and slopes.

Most commonly, a simple error structure is assumed for ε_{tij}, represented as

$$\varepsilon_{tij} \sim N(0, \sigma^2_\varepsilon), \tag{6.2}$$

which suggests the errors are independent and normally distributed (N), with a mean of zero and constant variance across time (Raudenbush & Bryk, 2002). The residual variance parameter (σ^2_ε) represents the variation in residuals around each individual institution's true change trajectory (Singer & Willett, 2003). Restrictions about the residuals can be relaxed, however. As we noted in the last chapter, more complex error structures (e.g., autocorrelated, unstructured) can be considered where there are many measurements per subject.

Level 2 Model

At Level 2, a set of between-institution predictors (e.g., student selectivity, student composition) can be added to the model to explain variation in institutions' intercepts (often defined as initial status) and growth rates. Specifically, for each of the $P + 1$ individual growth parameters,

$$\pi_{pij} = \beta_{p0j} + \sum_{q=1}^{Qp} \beta_{pq}X_{qij} + r_{pij}, \tag{6.3}$$

where X_{qij} might include institutional characteristics; β_{pq} represents the effect of X_{qij} on the pth growth parameter; and r_{pij} is a matrix of random effects. The set of $P + 1$ random effects for institution i can be contained in one of several different types of covariance matrices at Level 2. Common choices are diagonal (i.e., with variances for random effects only and no covariances between intercepts and slopes) or a completely unstructured covariance matrix (with variances for each random effect and covariances between each pair of random effects). If the choice is an unstructured covariance matrix, it is dimensioned $(P + 1) \times (P + 1)$ and is assumed to be multivariate normally distributed, with means of 0, and some variances and covariances between Level 2 residuals.

Level 3 Model

At Level 3, we can model differences in growth between states using the general modeling framework to examine variation in the Level 2 random intercept (β_{p0}) and slope (β_{pq}) parameters. The model defining Level 3 relationships can be written as

$$\beta_{pqj} = \gamma_{pq0} \sum_{s=1}^{Spq} \gamma_{pqs}W_{sj} + u_{pqj}, \tag{6.4}$$

where γ_{pq0} is the intercept for the state-level model, W_{sj} are predictors such as level of state resources for public higher education, γ_{pqs} are structural parameters for the Level 3 predictors, and u_{pqj} represent the state-level random effects. There are also similar choices regarding the covariance matrix of residuals from the Level 3 equations (e.g., diagonal, unstructured). The exact dimensionality of the covariance matrix depends on the number of random Level 2 coefficients in the model.

Figure 6.2 summarizes the average of the institutional graduation rates over time, without regard to the nesting of institutions within states. One can see from the figure that public undergraduate graduation rates appear to increase over the decade by about roughly 3% to 4%.

We next provide a small sample of eight individual states' trajectories in Figure 6.3. Readers who wish to develop this graph can do so by using the SELECT IF command and then defining the subset (*stateid* > 15 & *stateid* < 24). There is one state trajectory considerably higher than the others in this subset. In general, however, it appears that most of the individual trajectories increase slightly over time.

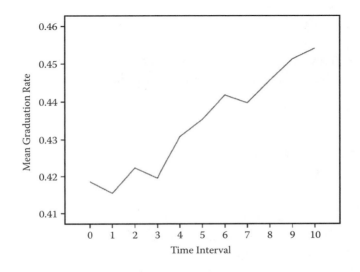

FIGURE 6.2 Institutional graduation levels.

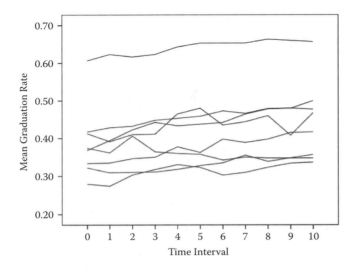

FIGURE 6.3 Graduation rates for selected states.

The first concern in the analysis is whether there is any significant change in graduation levels that took place over the period studied. For example, it might be that there was no increase in graduation rates over the series of measurements. Second, we might want to examine possible differences in institutions' and states' graduation rates over time due to their resources (e.g., tuition levels, percentages of students receiving financial aid), institutional characteristics (selectivity, faculty characteristics), and state characteristics (e.g., average student retention rates, family share of higher education).

Null Model: No Predictors

It is possible to examine only an *unconditional means* model; that is, a simple model consisting only of the repeated measurements of y_{tij} without the time-related parameter. This model can be used to partition the variance in the grand-mean estimate into its within-individual and between-individual components, regardless of time (see Singer & Willett, 2003, for further discussion). These components can be used to calculate an intraclass correlation (ICC). We begin with a simple unconditional model to examine the variance decomposition of graduation rates across levels of the data hierarchy:

$$y_{tij} = \pi_{0ij} + \varepsilon_{tij}, \tag{6.5}$$

where y_{tij} is the graduation proportion for institution i in state j measured at time point t. The intercept is π_{0ij} and ε_{tij} is the error term. At Level 2, the model is

$$\pi_{0ij} = \beta_{00j} + r_{0ij}, \tag{6.6}$$

where β_{00j} is the intercept and r_{0ij} is the error term for the between-individuals model. At Level 3, the model is

$$\beta_{00j} = \gamma_{000} + u_{00j}, \tag{6.7}$$

where γ_{000} is the intercept and u_{00j} is the errors in equations at Level 3.

For this first no predictors model, we can examine the decomposition of variance in graduation rates associated with differences within institutions, between institutions, and between states. The proportion of variability (ICC) in outcomes at Level 3 is defined as

$$\rho = \sigma^2_{\text{Level 3}} \Big/ \left(\sigma^2_{\text{Level 1}} + \sigma^2_{\text{Level 2}} + \sigma^2_{\text{Level 3}} \right). \tag{6.8}$$

For level 2, the ICC would be

$$\rho = \sigma^2_{\text{Level 2}} \Big/ \left(\sigma^2_{\text{Level 1}} + \sigma^2_{\text{Level 2}} + \sigma^2_{\text{Level 3}} \right), \tag{6.9}$$

and for Level 1, the ICC would be

$$\rho = \sigma^2_{\text{Level 1}} \Big/ \left(\sigma^2_{\text{Level 1}} + \sigma^2_{\text{Level 2}} + \sigma^2_{\text{Level 3}} \right). \tag{6.10}$$

Level 1 Error Structures

The Level 1 residuals (ε_{tij}) represent the variability in measuring individual-level outcomes at each occasion. They are typically assumed to be independent, normally distributed, with mean of zero and constant variance (σ_ε^2). For repeated measures models, SPSS has a variety of different error structures that can be considered. The default Level 1 structure is a diagonal covariance matrix with heterogeneous variances in the diagonals for each measurement occasion (and no off-diagonal covariances between occasions). Using just the first four occasions for ease of presentation, the diagonal Level 1 covariance matrix would look like the following (with variances σ_1^2 to σ_4^2 in the diagonals and 0s representing covariances):

$$\begin{bmatrix} \sigma_1^2 & 0 & 0 & 0 \\ 0 & \sigma_2^2 & 0 & 0 \\ 0 & 0 & \sigma_3^2 & 0 \\ 0 & 0 & 0 & \sigma_4^2 \end{bmatrix}. \tag{6.11}$$

Compound symmetry (CS) assumes one equal variance across all occasions and one equal covariance between pairs of covariances. At the other end of the spectrum, we could consider an unstructured (UN) covariance matrix, which assumes heterogeneous variances for each occasion and heterogeneous covariances for pairs of occasions. This may be overly complex, however, since it results in the calculation of many variances and covariances, which might not be of real substantive interest.

Another choice for repeated measures is an autoregressive covariance structure. Since we have reason to believe there are covariances between the off-diagonal elements in the matrix we might try either a heterogeneous first-order autoregressive structure (i.e., with separate variances in the diagonals and covariances in the off-diagonals) or the more simplified first-order autoregressive structure with constant diagonal variance and off-diagonal variance, as in the following (where the constant $|\rho| \le 1$ is imposed for stationarity):

$$\sigma^2 \begin{bmatrix} 1 & \rho & \rho^2 & \rho^3 \\ \rho & 1 & \rho & \rho^2 \\ \rho^2 & \rho & 1 & \rho \\ \rho^3 & \rho^2 & \rho & 1 \end{bmatrix}. \tag{6.12}$$

The covariance depends on the number of steps between occasions. For example, the covariance (σ) between two consecutive occasions will be equal to $\sigma^2\rho$ and if there is a step missing in between occasions, the covariance will be $\sigma^2\rho^2$ and so forth. To illustrate, since the error variance (σ^2) is constant, if the autocorrelation between adjacent occasions is $\rho = 0.4$, then with a lag of 2 occasions ρ^2 is 0.16, and with a lag of 3 occasions ρ^3 is 0.064. This covariance matrix therefore implies that correlations between repeated measures diminish over time.

We investigated several different covariance structures for the repeated measures estimates at Level 1. We can use REML estimation since we are only comparing differences in variance components (Hox, 2002). Because there are 11 years of measurements, it is quite likely that there are considerable correlations between occasions. Therefore, the default diagonal covariance (i.e., with variances only and no covariances) would not likely capture this complexity. The model with compound symmetry (five estimated parameters) did not converge. Similarly, the model with an unstructured covariance matrix was overly complex (i.e., taking over 2 hours to obtain a solution; defiance = –19,557.4, for 69 estimated parameters). It is likely we can find a more parsimonious structure. We also compared the autoregressive heterogeneous structure (deviance = –18,988.8) against the autoregressive homogeneous structure (deviance = –18,776.6). With the same degrees of freedom, the model with smaller deviance is preferred. The autoregressive homogeneous (AR1) structure should be a reasonable choice for this model.

Defining the Null Model (No Predictors) With SPSS Menu Commands

Launch the SPSS program application and select the *ch6multivarML.sav* data file.

1. Go to the SPSS toolbar and select ANALYZE, MIXED MODELS, LINEAR.

This command enables access to the *Linear Mixed Models: Specify Subjects and Repeated* dialog box.

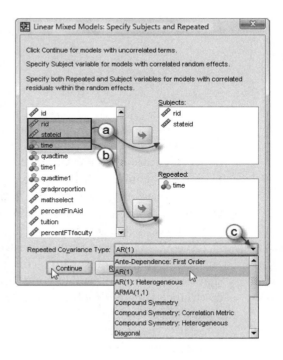

2a. Within the *Linear Mixed Models: Specify Subjects and Repeated* dialog box, click to select the *rid* and *stateid* variables from the left column, then click the arrow button to transfer the variables into the *Subjects* dialog box.

b. Click to select the *time* variable from the left column, then click the right-arrow button to transfer the variable into the *Repeated* box.

c. Click the pull-down menu to select the autoregressive covariance matrix, *AR(1)*, as the *Repeated Covariance Type*.

Click the CONTINUE button to display the *Linear Mixed Models* dialog box.

3. In the *Linear Mixed Models* dialog box, click to select the *gradproportion* variable from the left column listing, then click the right-arrow button to move it into the *Dependent Variable* box.

Since there are no fixed effects in the model, skip over the FIXED button and click the RANDOM button to access the *Linear Mixed Models: Random Effects* dialog box.

4. The *Linear Mixed Models: Random Effects* displays the *Random Effect 1 of 1* screen.
   a. Change the covariance type by clicking on the pull-down menu and selecting *Scaled Identity*.
   b. Check the *Include Intercept* option.
   c. In the *Subject Groupings* box, click to select *stateid*, then click the right-arrow button to transfer the variable into the *Combinations* box.
   d. At the top-right section of the window, click the NEXT button to access the *Random Effect 2 of 2* screen.

Note: The NEXT button may not work when creating multilevel models with random intercepts. This is a problem acknowledged by SPSS for assorted software versions including 18.0 and is resolved by adding then removing a covariate from the model, which is described in Steps e through i and Step 6.

Workaround to Activate the Random Effects "Next" Button

    e. Click the CONTINUE button to return to the *Linear Mixed Models* dialog box.

    f. Within the *Linear Mixed Models* dialog box click to select a variable (e.g., *lowses*) from the left column, then click the right-arrow button to transfer the variable into the *Covariate(s)* box.

    g. Then click the RANDOM button to return to the *Linear Mixed Models: Random Effects* dialog box.

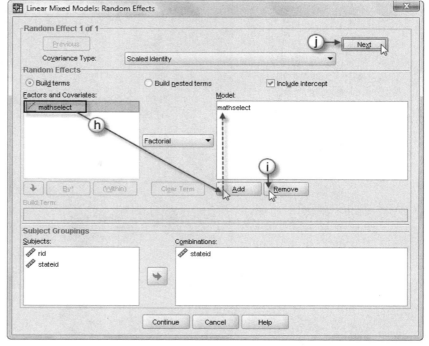

The *Linear Mixed Models: Random Effects* shows the *Random Effect 1 of 1* screen with the default settings established in Step 4.

    h. Click to select the variable *mathselect* from the *Factors and Covariates* box. Then click the ADD button to transfer the variable into the *Model* box, which activates the NEXT button (j).

    i. Click the REMOVE button to remove *mathselect* from the model.

5. The *Random Effect 2 of 2* screen display is similar to the first screen and requires the following changes.
   a. Change the covariance type by clicking on the pull-down menu and selecting *Scaled Identity*.
   b. Click to select the *Include Intercept* option.
   c. In the *Subject Groupings* box, click to select *rid* and *stateid*, then click the right arrow button to transfer the variables into the *Combinations* box.

Click the CONTINUE button to return to the *Linear Mixed Models* dialog box.

6. From the *Linear Mixed Models* dialog box, remove *mathselect* from the model by clicking to select the variable then clicking the left-arrow key.

Click the ESTIMATION button to access the *Linear Mixed Models: Estimation* dialog box.

7. In the *Linear Mixed Models* dialog box, click on the ESTIMATION button to access the *Linear Mixed Models: Estimation* dialog box.

The estimation method choices are maximum likelihood (ML) or restricted maximum likelihood (REML). In this chapter, we will use restricted maximum likelihood (REML) to estimate the models.

Since REML is the default setting, click the CONTINUE button to return to the *Linear Mixed Models* dialog box.

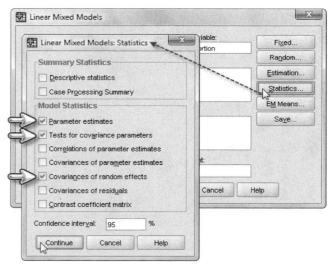

8. In the *Linear Mixed Models* dialog box, click the STATISTICS button to access the *Linear Mixed Models: Statistics* dialog box.

Click and select the following three statistics: *parameter estimates*, *tests for covariance parameters*, and *covariances of random effects*.

Then click the CONTINUE button to return to the *Linear Mixed Models* dialog box.

9. Finally, in the *Linear Mixed Models* dialog box, click the OK button to run the model.

Interpreting the Output From the Null Model

The output for the initial no predictors model is summarized in Table 6.1. Averaging across the period of time, the estimates suggest that about 13.7% [.003255/(.004104 + .016397) = .003255/.023756 = .137] of the variability in graduation rates is between states, about 69% (.016397/.023756 = .690) is between institutions, and about 17.3% (.004104/.023756 = .173) is within institutions over time. At Level 1, rho represents the correlation between any two consecutive occasions across the time series (i.e., 0.513).

In Table 6.2, the grand mean for graduation rates at the state level across the 11 observations (i.e., the average) is 0.431 or about 43%.

TABLE 6.1   Estimates of Covariance Parameters[a]

Parameter		Estimate	Std. Error	Wald Z	Sig.
Repeated Measures	AR1 diagonal	.004104	.000118	34.806	.000
	AR1 rho	.512654	.014174	36.169	.000
Intercept [subject = stateid]	Variance	.003255	.001000	3.254	.001
Intercept [subject = rid * stateid]	Variance	.016397	.001003	16.350	.000

[a] Dependent Variable: gradproportion.

TABLE 6.2   Estimates of Fixed Effects[a]

Parameter	Estimate	Std. Error	df	t	Sig.
Intercept	.431113	.010104	47.374	42.668	.000

[a] Dependent Variable: gradproportion.

Model 1: Adding Growth Rates

At the next step, we can add the growth rate indicators over time. In many situations where we examine change over time, it is convenient to propose that a linear growth trajectory will describe the data adequately. When the time periods are reasonably short and there are not too many observations per individual (i.e., an individual subject or, in this case, an individual institution), the linear growth model can often provide a good approximation for more complex models that cannot be fully modeled because of the sparse number of observations (Bryk & Raudenbush, 1992). In this case, we are not sure, so we may wish to check for the shape of the growth trajectory first. We can define a quadratic Level 1 model to take into consideration the idea that the growth rates may accelerate or decelerate over time.

Level 1 Model

For a quadratic model to describe the growth trajectories, the Level 1 equation can be written as

$$y_{tij} = \pi_{0ij} + \pi_{1ij} a_{tij} + \pi_{2ij} a_{tij}^2 + \varepsilon_{tij}, \tag{6.13}$$

where y_{tij} is the response variable for institution i in state j measured at time point t. The intercept is π_{0ij} and π_{1ij} is the linear growth rate for institution i in state j over the data collection period, representing the expected change during a fixed unit of time. The quadratic component π_{2ij} represents any change in the rate of change over a particular unit of time. Each institution, therefore, has its own growth trajectory (developed from the intercept and slope), with likely variability present in the random coefficients across the set of institutions.

Coding the Time Variable

It is important to note that the meaning of the intercept parameter (π_{0i}) depends on the scaling of the time variable. Figure 6.4 illustrates one coding scheme for time. We could code the time variable in yearly intervals (0, 1, 2, ... , $N = t$). Most often, researchers code the first measurement occasion as 0, so that the intercept parameter can be interpreted as the true initial status of graduation rates in institution i in state j at time point $a_{tij} = 0$. Defining the intercept as initial status serves as a baseline for interpreting the subsequent change that takes place over time for each individual institution in the sample. If there is a quadratic term (quadtime), the corresponding variable would be scaled in a similar manner (i.e., 0, 1, 4, 9, ... , $N = t$), as shown in the figure.

Readers should keep in mind that defining the time-related variable in different ways (i.e., initial status, end status, middle status) will affect the level of the intercept, the variance at higher levels (e.g., Level 2, Level 3), and the covariance between the intercept and slope (see Raudenbush & Bryk, 2002, for further discussion of centering options). For example, if we define the intercept as the initial status, the intercept is 0.41, and the correlation between the intercept and slope is negative. In contrast, if we define graduation rate as the end status, the intercept is 0.44 and the correlation between the intercept and slope is positive. Centering in the middle of the time series may also have desirable effects in some instances. In general, such decisions should be made with respect to the purposes of the study and characteristics of model and data.

Again, the time intervals are entered in the Level 1 data set in vertical format as a variable (time), and each time point corresponds to a specific graduation proportion for each institution, as shown in Figure 6.4. This necessitates 11 data lines per institution in the Level 1 data set. For example, for institution ID #1, the graduation percentage corresponding to time point 0 (the first year) is 17% and for time point 10 (the last year) it is 35%. The data are linked to successive levels with unique identifiers (e.g., institution, state).

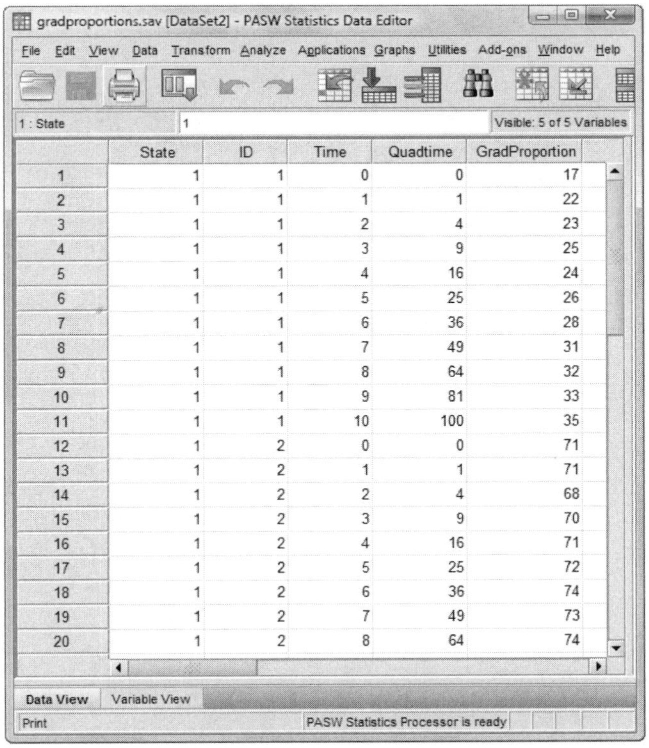

	State	ID	Time	Quadtime	GradProportion
1	1	1	0	0	17
2	1	1	1	1	22
3	1	1	2	4	23
4	1	1	3	9	25
5	1	1	4	16	24
6	1	1	5	25	26
7	1	1	6	36	28
8	1	1	7	49	31
9	1	1	8	64	32
10	1	1	9	81	33
11	1	1	10	100	35
12	1	2	0	0	71
13	1	2	1	1	71
14	1	2	2	4	68
15	1	2	3	9	70
16	1	2	4	16	71
17	1	2	5	25	72
18	1	2	6	36	74
19	1	2	7	49	73
20	1	2	8	64	74

FIGURE 6.4 Level 1 data structure for graduation proportions.

Varying intervals between measurement occasions can also be accommodated (e.g., 0, 1, 3, 7, ...). It is also possible to change the centering point to other time points in the sequence (e.g., the last time point), depending on the goals of the research. Selecting the last time point, for example, would result in a factor that describes the institutions' graduation rates at the end of the time series (e.g., $a_{it} = 10, 9, \ldots, 0$).

The choice of the appropriate modeling approach and coding of time should be based on the ease with which model parameter estimates can be interpreted, always keeping in mind the substantive questions of the research study (Raykov & Marcoulides, 2008). In this example, it is convenient to code the time variable in the following manner (0, .1, .2, .3, .4, .5, .6, .7, .8, .9, 1.0). We will call this variable *time1*, to differentiate it from the yearly time variable in the data set. This will allow us to capture the change in graduation growth over the entire period under study (i.e., the change in graduation proportion as *time1* changes from 0 to 1). We can create a similar quadratic component (*quadtime1*) by computing *time1**time1* and saving it in the database.

Defining Model 1 With SPSS Menu Commands

Note: SPSS settings will default to those used for the Null Model.

1. Go to the SPSS toolbar and select ANALYZE, MIXED MODELS, LINEAR.

This command enables access to the *Linear Mixed Models: Specify Subjects and Repeated* dialog box.

2. Within the *Linear Mixed Models: Specify Subjects and Repeated* dialog box, the variables *rid* and *stateid* are in the *Subjects* box with *time* in the *Repeated* box.

The Repeated Covariance Type displays the prior model's setting of *AR(1)*.

Click the CONTINUE button to display the *Linear Mixed Models* dialog box.

3. In the *Linear Mixed Models* dialog box, the variable *gradproportion* is displayed as the *Dependent Variable*.

Click to select the variables *time1* and *quadtime1* variables from the left column listing, then click the right-arrow button to move them into the *Covariate(s)* box.

Click the FIXED button to access the *Linear Mixed Models: Fixed Effects* dialog box.

4a. Within the *Linear Mixed Models: Fixed Effects* dialog box, locate the *Factorial* setting and click on the pull-down menu to select *Main Effects*.

b. The predictor variables *time1* and *quadtime1* appear in the *Factors and Covariates* box. Click to select *time1* and *quadtime1*, then click the ADD button to move the variables into the *Model* box.

c. Confirm *Include Intercept* is selected.

Click the CONTINUE button to return to the *Linear Mixed Models* dialog box. In the *Linear Mixed Models* dialog box, click the RANDOM button to access the *Linear Mixed Models: Random Effects* dialog box.

5. The *Linear Mixed Models: Random Effects* displays the *Random Effect 2 of 2* screen.

   a. Change the covariance type by clicking on the pull-down menu and selecting *Diagonal*.

   b. Confirm the *Include Intercept* is selected.

   c. Change the factorial setting by clicking on the pull-down menu and select *Main Effects*.

   d. In the *Factors and Covariates* listing, select *time1*, then click the ADD button to move the variable into the *Model* box.

   e. Confirm variables *rid* and *stateid* are in the *Combinations* box.

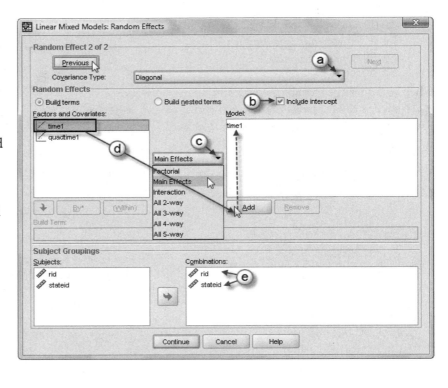

Click the PREVIOUS button to access the *Random Effect 1 of 1* screen.

6. The *Random Effect 1 of 1* screen displays settings from the prior model.

   a. Change the covariance type by clicking on the pull-down menu and selecting *Diagonal*.

   b. Confirm the *Include Intercept* option.

   c. Confirm the factorial setting is *Main Effects*.

   d. In the *Factors and Covariates* listing, select *time1* then click the ADD button to move the variable into the *Model* box.

   e. Confirm the variable *stateid* is in the *Combinations* box.

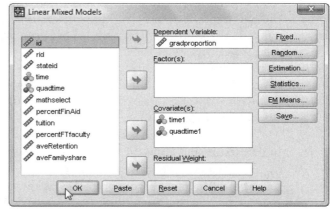

Click the CONTINUE button to return to the *Linear Mixed Models* dialog box.

7. The random effects, estimation, and statistics elements in the model remain the same settings as those used for Model 1, so skip over these buttons and click OK to run the model.

Interpreting the Output From Model 1

The fixed effect estimates are presented in Table 6.3. Readers should keep in mind that we are actually testing a population of universities and states, so statistical testing is not really needed since we are not making inferences from a sample to a population. For purposes of demonstration, however, we will interpret them as if we were making these types of inferences. Table 6.4 suggests that the linear component is necessary in describing graduation growth over time ($\gamma = 0.029$, $p < .01$). The table suggests that state graduation rates grew about 3% over the decade. The quadratic component, however, is not required ($\gamma = 0.011$, $p > .10$) to model growth over time. Because the quadratic component is not contributing to modeling the growth, we can drop it from future models.

TABLE 6.3   Estimates of Fixed Effects[a]

Parameter	Estimate	Std. Error	df	t	Sig.
Intercept	.412928	.009854	50.195	41.906	.000
time1	.028714	.009400	331.227	3.055	.002
quadtime1	.011033	.007989	1681.966	1.381	.167

[a] Dependent Variable: gradproportion.

TABLE 6.4   Estimates of Covariance Parameters[a]

Parameter		Estimate	Std. Error	Wald Z	Sig.
Repeated Measures	AR1 diagonal	.002733	7.245140E-5	37.726	.000
	AR1 rho	.287285	.017861	16.084	.000
Intercept + time1 [subject = stateid]	Var: Intercept	.002944	.000918	3.206	.001
	Var: time1	.000364	.000273	1.331	.183
Intercept + time1 [subject = rid * stateid]	Var: Intercept	.016175	.000989	16.357	.000
	Var: time1	.005441	.000552	9.856	.000

[a] Dependent Variable: gradproportion.

Next, it is important to consider the nature of the deviations of the individual growth trajectories from the mean growth trajectory. The estimates of the initial status and slope residual variances are presented in Table 6.4. Once again, the Wald Z statistic is provided as a test of homogeneity; that is, there is no true variation in individual growth parameters (0). Since the variance cannot be below 0, the Wald Z test should be conducted as a one-tailed test. For initial status, at the state level the Wald Z is 3.21, one-tailed $p < .01$. This leads to rejecting the null hypothesis that there is no variation among states' initial status graduation proportions. At the institutional level, the Wald Z was 16.36, one-tailed $p < .01$, also suggesting we should reject the null hypothesis of no significant variation in institutions' initial graduation proportions. At Level 1, the average correlation (ρ) between any two consecutive repeated measures across the time series was about 0.29.

Regarding growth rates at the state level, we would likely conclude the growth rate does vary (Wald $Z = 1.33$, one-tailed $p = .0915$), keeping in mind that in this study we actually have a population of states instead of a small ($n = 50$) random sample. The growth rates at the institutional level do appear to vary (Wald $Z = 9.86$, one-tailed $p < .01$).

The random-coefficients growth model also provides an estimate of the correlation between initial status and growth. For a linear growth model, it is the correlation between π_{0ij} and π_{1ij}. We reiterate the importance of giving some attention to its definition and scaling, because this affects the meaning one attaches to the coefficients (for other discussions, see Hox, 2002; Raykov & Marcoulides, 2008; and Singer & Willett, 2003). In this case, the correlation was -0.59 (not tabled), which suggests institutions that had lower initial graduation rates gained at a somewhat greater rate and vice versa. As we noted, defining the intercept as the end status (i.e., proportion graduating at the end of the trend) will result in a different correlation between the intercept and growth rate.

Model 2: Adding Time-Varying Covariates

We can next add two time-varying covariates to the model. These are variables that are measured through the 11-year period. In this case we will use the percentage of students within the institution receiving financial aid and the average tuition level at the institution. We will standardize each variable ($M = 0$, $SD = 1$):

$$y_{tij} = \pi_{0ij} + \pi_{1ij}a_{tij} + \pi_{2ij}X_{1tij} + \pi_{3ij}X_{2tij} + \varepsilon_{tij}, \qquad (6.14)$$

where π_{0ij} is the intercept for institutions, π_{1ij} is the linear growth rate, X_{1tij} is percentage of students receiving financial aid (standardized), X_{2tij} is the institutional tuition level (standardized), and ε_{tij} is the variability in predicting institutional graduation rates. The coefficients π_{2ij} and π_{3ij} are the regression coefficients for the two time-varying covariates.

Defining Model 2 With SPSS Menu Commands

Note: SPSS settings will default to those used for Model 1.

1. Go to the SPSS toolbar and select ANALYZE, MIXED MODELS, LINEAR.

This command enables access to the *Linear Mixed Models: Specify Subjects and Repeated* dialog box.

2. Within the *Linear Mixed Models: Specify Subjects and Repeated* dialog box, the variables *rid* and *stateid* are in the *Subjects* box with *time* in the *Repeated* box.

The *Repeated Covariance Type* displays the prior model's setting of *AR(1)*.

Click the CONTINUE button to display the *Linear Mixed Models* dialog box.

3a. In the *Linear Mixed Models* dialog box, click to select the variables *time1* and *quadtime1*, then click the left-arrow button to remove them from the *Covariate(s)* box.

b. Click to select the following variables, then click the right-arrow button to transfer them into the *Covariates* box. Although the variables could be transferred in the order they appear, to facilitate reading of the output tables the recommended sequence for entering the variables into the *Covariates* box is *percentFinAid, tuition,* and *time1.*

Click the FIXED button to access the *Linear Mixed Models: Fixed Effects* dialog box.

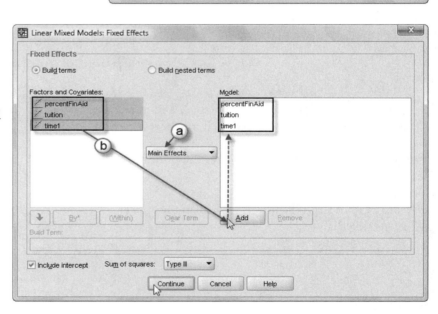

4. The *Linear Mixed Models: Fixed Effects* displays the default settings used for Model 2.

   a. Confirm the factorial setting is *Main Effects.*

   b. Click to select the variables *percentFinAid, tuition,* and *time1* from the *Factors and Covariates* box. Then click the ADD button to move the variables into the *Model* box.

Click the CONTINUE button to return to the *Linear Mixed Models* dialog box.

5. The random effects, estimation, and statistics settings remain the same, so skip over these buttons and click OK to run the model.

TABLE 6.5   Estimates of Fixed Effects[a]

Parameter	Estimate	Std. Error	df	t	Sig.
Intercept	.469222	.011242	98.626	41.737	.000
percentFinAid	.001577	.000886	5693.474	1.779	.075
tuition	.049447	.005335	5044.319	9.269	.000
time1	.016363	.005343	59.168	3.063	.003

[a] Dependent Variable: gradproportion.

TABLE 6.6   Estimates of Covariance Parameters[a]

Parameter		Estimate	Std. Error	Wald Z	Sig.
Repeated Measures	AR1 diagonal	.002681	.000070	38.123	.000
	AR1 rho	.275517	.017901	15.391	.000
Intercept + time1 [subject = stateid]	Var: Intercept	.002648	.000842	3.143	.002
	Var: time1	.000307	.000216	1.419	.156
Intercept + time1 [subject = rid * stateid]	Var: Intercept	.015394	.000946	16.276	.000
	Var: time1	.005435	.000539	10.076	.000

[a] Dependent Variable: gradproportion.

Interpreting the Output From Model 2

The fixed effect estimates are provided in Table 6.5. After adding the within-institution, time-varying covariates, the new state graduation intercept was 0.469 (or about 47%). Average tuition level was positively associated with graduation levels; that is, a 1 *SD* increase in institutional tuition would result in about a 5% (0.049) increase in initial graduation levels. Similarly, percentages of students receiving financial aid were associated with higher graduation rates ($p < .10$). After adjusting for the covariates, state graduation rates appeared to grow a little over 1.6% (0.016) over the decade.

Again, the variance components table (Table 6.6) suggests that intercepts vary across institutions and states. Linear growth rates varied across institutions (Wald $Z = 10.076$, one-tailed $p < .01$). There is some evidence suggesting they also varied across states (Wald $Z = 1.42$, one-tailed $p = .078$).

Model 3: Explaining Differences in Growth Trajectories Between Institutions

Because there was significant variation in each parameter present among individual institutions, both the intercept and growth parameters can be allowed to vary across institutions. The variation in each may likely be partially explained by between-institutional characteristics as in

Equation 6.3. In this example, we consider two predictors that may account for systematic variation in the intercept and slope parameters between institutions.

The first is selectivity in student admissions (i.e., percentages of students with 75 percentile or above SAT or ACT math scores), which we standardized ($M = 0$, $SD = 1$). The other variable is percentage of full-time faculty, which was also standardized. The two Level 2 submodels are now defined as

$$\pi_{0ij} = \beta_{00j} + \beta_{01j}(selectivity)_{ij} + \beta_{02j}(fulltime)_{ij} + r_{0ij},\tag{6.15}$$

$$\pi_{1ij} = \beta_{10j} + \beta_{11j}(selectivity)_{ij} + \beta_{12j}(fulltime)_{ij} + r_{1ij}.\tag{6.16}$$

The covariance matrix of random effects can be defined as diagonal or unstructured.

At Level 3 (between states), we will add two other predictors. The first is the percentage share that families have to pay for higher education in the state (which has also been standardized). The second variable is the average percentage of freshman retained in the state (also standardized). We consider this to be one measure of the quality of the state's public higher education system:

$$\beta_{00j} = \gamma_{000} + \lambda_{001}(Zavefamilyshare)_j + \lambda_{002}(Zaveretention)_j + u_{00j}.\tag{6.17}$$

For the moment, we will consider the growth rate to vary also across states but will not try to explain that variation:

$$\beta_{10j} = \gamma_{100} + u_{10j}.\tag{6.18}$$

Defining Model 3 With SPSS Menu Commands

Note: SPSS settings will default to those used for Model 2.

1. Go to the SPSS toolbar and select ANALYZE, MIXED MODELS, LINEAR.

This command enables access to the *Linear Mixed Models: Specify Subjects and Repeated* dialog box.

2. Within the *Linear Mixed Models: Specify Subjects and Repeated* dialog box, the variables *rid* and *stateid* are in the *Subjects* box with *time* in the *Repeated* box.

The *Repeated Covariance Type* displays the prior model's setting of *AR(1)*.

Click the CONTINUE button to display the *Linear Mixed Models* dialog box.

3. In the *Linear Mixed Models* dialog box, the variable *gradproportion* is displayed as the *Dependent Variable*.
   a. Click to select the variables *percentFinAid*, *tuition*, and *time1*, then click the left-arrow button to remove them from the *Covariate(s)* box.
   b. Click to select the variables from the left column listing and click the right-arrow button to enter them in the following sequence: *aveFamilyshare*, *aveRetention*, *mathselect*, *percentFTfaculty*, *percentFinAid*, *tuition*, and *time1*.

Click the FIXED button to access the *Linear Mixed Models: FIXED Effects* dialog box.

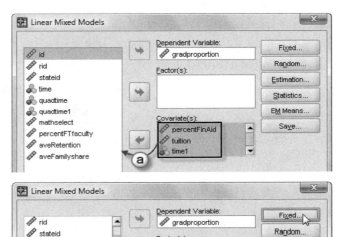

4a. Within the *Linear Mixed Models: Fixed Effects* box confirm the factorial setting is *Main Effects*.

b. Click to select all the variables from the *Factors and Covariates* box, then click the ADD button to move the variables into the *Model* box.

c. Confirm *Include Intercept* is seltected.

The next steps will be to create two interactions: *time1*mathselect* and *time1*percentFTfaculty*.

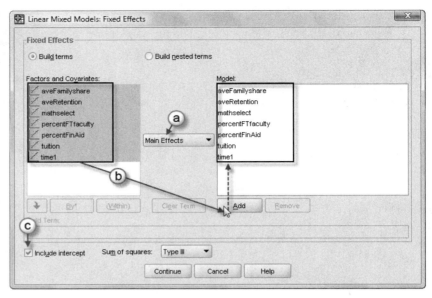

Creating Cross-Level Interactions in Model 3

time1*mathselect

5a. Click to select the *Build nested terms* option.

b. Click to select the variable *time1* from the *Factors and Covariates* column.

c. Click the down-arrow button to move *time1* into the *Build Term* box.

d. Click the BY* button to add the computational symbol (*) to the *Build Term* box.

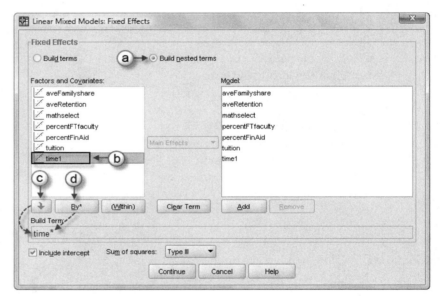

e. Click to select the variable *mathselect* from the *Factors and Covariates* column.
f. Click the down-arrow button to move *mathselect* into the *Build Term* box.
g. Click the ADD button to move the term *time1*mathselect* into the *Model* box.

time1*percentFTfaculty

6a. Click to select the variable *time1* from the *Factors and Covariates* column.
b. Click the down-arrow button to move *time1* into the *Build Term* box.
c. Click the BY* button to add the computational symbol (*) to the *Build Term* box.

d. Click to select the variable *percentFTfaculty* from the *Factors and Covariates* column.

e. Click the down-arrow button to move *percentFTfaculty* into the *Build Term* box.

f. Click the ADD button to move the term *time1*percentFTfaculty* into the *Model* box.

Click the CONTINUE button to return to the *Linear Mixed Models* dialog box.

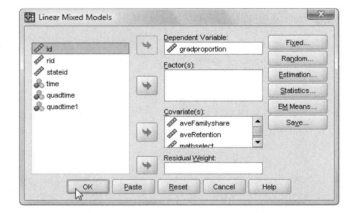

7. The random effects, estimation, and statistics settings remain the same, so skip over these buttons and click OK to run the model.

Interpreting the Output From Model 3

As the table of fixed effects indicates (Table 6.7), after adjusting for the institutional variables, the true initial status graduation proportion for states is 0.475 (or about 47.5%). At Level 3, the coefficients suggest that average family share (γ = .020, p < .01) and average Year 1 retention rates (γ = 0.046, p < .01) were both significant in explaining initial graduation levels. At Level 2, selectivity (γ = 0.094, p < .01) and percentage of full-time faculty remain significant predictors (γ = 0.037, p < .01) of initial status graduation levels. Within institutions, percentage receiving financial aid (γ = .002, p < .05) and tuition level (γ = .043, p < .01) were also significant predictors of graduation levels.

For the growth rate model (time1), the average gain over time for states was 0.019 (or about 2%). The cross-level interaction of percentage of full-time faculty was positively related to within-institution growth rates (γ = 0.019, p < .01). This implies that a 1 *SD* increase in percentage of full-time faculty would be related to a 1.9% increase in graduation growth rate over time compared with institutions at the grand mean of full-time faculty, holding the time1 slope constant. Student selectivity, however, was not related to graduation growth rates (γ = 0.006, p > .10).

TABLE 6.7 Estimates of Fixed Effects[a]

Parameter	Estimate	Std. Error	df	t	Sig.
Intercept	.475064	.008305	166.118	57.204	.000
aveFamilyshare	.020235	.005515	47.667	3.669	.001
aveRetention	.045511	.005498	44.386	8.277	.000
mathselect	.094038	.005187	706.719	18.129	.000
percentFTfaculty	.036756	.004082	651.637	9.005	.000
percentFinAid	.001884	.000893	5654.256	2.110	.035
tuition	.042925	.005201	4999.898	8.253	.000
time1	.019415	.005169	66.645	3.756	.000
mathselect * time1	.006351	.004827	678.626	1.316	.189
percentFTfaculty * time1	.019258	.003753	536.271	5.131	.000

[a] Dependent Variable: gradproportion.

TABLE 6.8 Estimates of Covariance Parameters[a]

Parameter		Estimate	Std. Error	Wald Z	Sig.
Repeated Measures	AR1 diagonal	.002815	8.266911E-5	34.057	.000
	AR1 rho	.311606	.019154	16.269	.000
Intercept + time1	Var: Intercept	.000754	.000319	2.362	.018
[subject = stateid]	Var: time1	.000307	.000192	1.602	.109
Intercept + time1	Var: Intercept	.007183	.000480	14.951	.000
[subject = rid * stateid]	Var: time1	.003833	.000480	7.984	.000

[a] Dependent Variable: gradproportion.

The variance components table (Table 6.8) suggests initial graduation rates still varied across states (Wald Z = 2.36, one-tailed p < .01) and institutions (Wald Z = 14.95, one-tailed p < .01) after inclusion of the Level 2 and Level 3 predictors. After addition of the institutional-level predictors, growth rates still varied across institutions (Wald Z = 7.98, one-tailed p < .01). Growth may also still vary across states (Wald Z = 1.60, one-tailed p = .055). Because Wald Z coefficients are likely to be too conservative in small data sets (Hox, 2002), we can try developing a model to examine growth rates across states using the same two Level 3 predictors.

Model 4: Adding a Model to Examine Growth Rates at Level 3

The new model for the state-level growth rate is as follows:

$$\beta_{10j} = \gamma_{100} + \gamma_{101}(Zavefamilyshare)_j + \gamma_{102}(Zaveretention)_j + u_{10j}. \tag{6.19}$$

Defining Model 4 With SPSS Menu Commands

Note: SPSS settings will default to those used for Model 3.

1. Go to the SPSS toolbar and select ANALYZE, MIXED MODELS, LINEAR.

This command enables access to the *Linear Mixed Models: Specify Subjects and Repeated* dialog box.

2. Within the *Linear Mixed Models: Specify Subjects and Repeated* dialog box, the variables *rid* and *stateid* are in the *Subjects* box with *time* in the *Repeated* box.

The *Repeated Covariance Type* displays the prior model's setting of *AR(1)*.

Click the CONTINUE button to display the *Linear Mixed Models* dialog box.

3. In the *Linear Mixed Models* dialog box, the variable *gradproportion* is displayed as the *Dependent Variable*.

The variables in the *Covariate(s)* box are *aveFamilyshare, aveRetention, mathselect, percentFTfaculty, percentFinAid, tuition,* and *time1*.

Click the FIXED button to access the *Linear Mixed Models: Fixed Effects* dialog box.

4a. Within the *Linear Mixed Models: Fixed Effects* box confirm the factorial setting is *Main Effects* and *Build nested terms* is the selected option.

b. Entering variables in sequential order helps facilitate reading of the output tables. So we recommend removing the two interactions to change the order of their occurrence. Click to select *time1*mathselect*, *time1percentFTfaculty*, then click the REMOVE button.

Creating Cross-Level Interactions in Model 4

We will create four cross-level interactions:

time1*aveFamilyshare,
time1*aveRetention,
time1*mathselect,
time1*percentFTfaculty

5a. Click to select the variable *time1* from the *Factors and Covariates* column.

b. Click the down-arrow button to move *time1* into the *Build Term* box.

c. Click the BY* button to add the computational symbol (*) to the *Build Term* box.

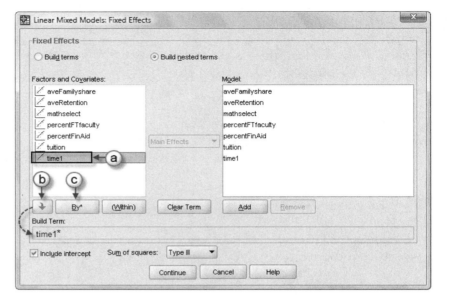

d. Click to select the variable *aveFamilyshare* from the *Factors and Covariates* column.

e. Click the down-arrow button to move *aveFamilyshare* into the *Build Term* box.

f. Click the ADD button to move the term *time1*aveFamilyshare* into the *Model* box.

g. Repeat Steps 5a through f to create three more interactions and add them to the *Model:* *time1*aveRetention,* *time1*mathselect,* *time1*percentFTfaculty.*

The four interactions and model variables are displayed in the inserted *Model* illustration.

Click the CONTINUE button to return to the *Linear Mixed Models* dialog box.

6. The random effects, estimation, and statistics settings remain the same, so skip over these buttons and click OK to run the model.

Interpreting the Output From Model 4

Our primary interest is the growth rate portion of the model in Table 6.9. The table indicates that the average state growth rate was again about 0.020. Average family share did not affect growth in state graduation rates over time ($\gamma = -.002$, $p > .10$). In contrast, however, average retention of Year 1 students was significantly related to increases in graduation growth rates ($\gamma = 0.011$, $p < .05$). This suggests a 1 *SD* increase in Year 1 student retention rates would result in about a 1% increase in graduation growth rates over time, compared with states at the grand mean in student retention rates, holding the time1 slope constant. The other fixed effects remained consistent with the previous model.

The variance components table (Table 6.10) suggests there is still Level 3 and Level 2 variance in initial status graduation levels to be explained. After adding the state-level variables to explain growth rates, there is not sufficient variability left to be explained (Wald $Z = 1.263$, one-tailed $p = .1035$). There is, however, sufficient variability in growth rates still across institutions (Wald $Z = 7.985$, one-tailed $p < .01$). We could include other predictors at the institutional level to model this variability if we desired.

TABLE 6.9 Estimates of Fixed Effects[a]

Parameter	Estimate	Std. Error	df	t	Sig.
Intercept	.474826	.008319	166.959	57.074	.000
aveFamilyshare	.020425	.005572	49.395	3.666	.001
aveRetention	.043603	.005558	46.191	7.846	.000
Mathselect	.094338	.005190	707.405	18.178	.000
percentFTfaculty	.036590	.004084	653.623	8.960	.000
percentFinAid	.001906	.000893	5655.894	2.136	.033
Tuition	.042679	.005214	5100.035	8.186	.000
time1	.019992	.004980	60.234	4.015	.000
aveFamilyshare * time1	−.001596	.004290	39.421	−.372	.712
aveRetention * time1	.010973	.004261	40.280	2.575	.014
mathselect * time1	.005200	.004828	671.231	1.077	.282
percentFTfaculty * time1	.019891	.003751	514.186	5.303	.000

[a] Dependent Variable: gradproportion.

TABLE 6.10   Estimates of Covariance Parameters[a]

Parameter		Estimate	Std. Error	Wald Z	Sig.
Repeated Measures	AR1 diagonal	.002814	.000083	34.100	.000
	AR1 rho	.311276	.019136	16.266	.000
Intercept + time1 [subject = stateid]	Var: Intercept	.000757	.000320	2.368	.018
	Var: time1	.000228	.000180	1.263	.207
Intercept + time1 [subject = rid * stateid]	Var: Intercept	.007187	.000481	14.954	.000
	Var: time1	.003831	.000480	7.985	.000

[a] Dependent Variable: gradproportion.

We can also determine how much variance in the random coefficients was accounted for by the predictors, keeping in mind our previous cautions about variance reduction in multilevel models. The proportion of variance explained is the ratio of the difference between the total parameter variance estimated from the unconditional model and the residual parameter variance from the fitted model relative to the total parameter variance. For intercepts, this amount of variance accounted for is reduced from .004104 in Table 6.1 to .002814 in Table 6.10 (.004104 – .002814 = .00129/.004104), or about 31.4% of the variance accounted for within institutions. At Level 2, the variance component is reduced from .016397 in Table 6.1 to .007187 (or R^2 of 0.562), or about 56.4% of the variance accounted for at Level 2. At the state level (Level 3), the variance is reduced from .003255 to .000757 (or R^2 of 0.767), or about 76.7% of the variance at that level.

Other Types of Random-Coefficients Growth Models

Other types of growth trajectories can also be formulated in SPSS Mixed. For example, if a policy were implemented at some point in the series of graduation measurements, one could develop a piecewise growth model—that is, where the growth trajectories are split into separate linear components, each with its own model. This type of modeling would be useful in comparing growth rates during two different periods, such as several measurements taken before and the time after a policy is introduced (e.g., see Heck & Takahashi, 2006, for one illustration). It is also possible to investigate parallel growth processes (e.g., growth in students' reading and math achievement) in one simultaneous model. This can be accomplished by stacking the measures of reading and math in one "achievement" column and then referring to either reading or math by using a categorical indicator (e.g., 1 = reading, 0 = math).

Summary

Longitudinal analysis represents a rapidly growing application of multilevel modeling techniques. Because they provide stronger ways for dealing with causal relationships between variables than cross-sectional analyses, they should continue to draw the increased attention of researchers. In this chapter, we introduced a basic multilevel model considering change at several levels of a data hierarchy. The approach is very flexible for fitting a number of research purposes and designs (e.g., experimental, time series, nonexperimental).

CHAPTER 7

Multivariate Multilevel Models

In the last chapter, we introduced a three-level modeling framework for examining change in individuals and groups over time. Another variation on the basic three-level modeling framework is a multivariate multilevel model; that is, a model that has more than one dependent variable (defined at Level 1), with individuals at Level 2, and groups at Level 3. The multivariate multilevel model, in particular, follows directly from the traditional single-level multivariate analysis of variance (MANOVA) model. One of the advantages of this type of model formulation is that it encourages the development of more complex models, such as models with multiple outcomes. One possible model of this type would be a parallel growth model, where we might examine student growth in reading and math simultaneously within and between schools, rather than examining each growth process separately. A second formulation is where several survey items (or subtests) could be used to define one or more constructs. This type of latent variable formulation allows measurement error to be incorporated into the analysis. Another advantage of this type of modeling approach in SPSS Mixed is that missing data can be included in the analysis, which is a limitation of MANOVA (Hox, 2002).

Multilevel Latent-Outcome Model

There are a number of different ways to set up multilevel models with multivariate outcomes. In this chapter we describe two ways to formulate a simple multilevel model with a multivariate outcome (e.g., see Raudenbush & Bryk, 2002, or Hox, 2002, for further examples of more complex multivariate multilevel models). One common use of a multilevel multivariate model is when the researcher wishes to combine a number of observed variables (e.g., survey items) to measure an underlying construct (e.g., job satisfaction, motivation). In this type of formulation, the Level 1 model can be used to define a measurement model that consists of multiple measures of an outcome Y nested within individuals, similar to the multiple occasions of an outcome used to define growth trajectories (Leyland, 2004; Raudenbush & Bryk, 2002). The key to fitting this type of multilevel model is to use multiple rows in the data matrix to define the separate indicators of the factor. The multilevel model with multivariate outcomes can therefore be constructed much like the growth models presented in the last two chapters.

An obvious advantage of the multivariate approach is that we can incorporate the correlations between outcomes into the analysis, as well as information about the measurement quality of the items (or subtests) being used to define the multivariate outcome. The multivariate formulation is often preferable compared with running a series of univariate models, because the former type of model provides simultaneous estimation of the outcomes. This is considered a more efficient technique, since it has the advantage of cutting down on Type I error rates (i.e., falsely rejecting the null hypothesis). This is similar to using one ANOVA to test the difference in means for four groups, rather than running six separate t-tests on pairs of means. Moreover, as suggested, the multivariate formulation allows the analyst to account for possible correlations between various measures of the outcomes in estimating the model.

One disadvantage of multivariate models, however, is that they are more complicated to specify and often more difficult to interpret (Hox, 2002). Another disadvantage of the latent-variable approach for multilevel regression models is that the Level 1 measurement models must be relatively simple (Hox, 2002). As Hox (2002) notes, the approach implies the items that define a latent variable should be measured on a similar measurement scale and have consistent error variances. Variables can be rescaled as needed prior to the analyses, however, to achieve more similar error variances. When there are several latent factors under consideration in a model, multilevel structural equation modeling (MSEM) may be an approach that is easier to implement. This requires specialized software that is not readily available in SPSS, however.

Research Questions

In this first example, we will build a three-level model to examine variability in student achievement within and between schools. At the individual level (Level 1), we will define a latent achievement construct comprised of reading, math, and language tests measured on a consistent measurement scale. At Level 2, we can define various between-student variables. At Level 3, we can investigate school-level variables that might explain differences in achievement between schools.

This example study examines three typical multilevel research questions. The first research question concerns whether a key organizational process, in this case the school's academic focus (academic press), affects achievement levels between schools, after relevant background and organizational context indicators are controlled. For this example, we include student socioeconomic status (SES) within schools (defined as a continuous variable, with mean = 0 and $SD = 1$) and student SES composition (i.e., aggregate student SES) at the school level as the controls. The second research question concerns whether the slope describing the effect of students' academic background on achievement levels varies across schools. Students' academic background consists of counselor ratings of the academic strength of students' previous course work (coded from 0 *weak* to 6 *strong*). This research question involves determining whether the size of a within-group slope varies randomly across schools. If so, the third research question focuses on whether the school's academic press moderates (increases or diminishes) the effect of students' previous academic course work on their achievement outcomes, after controlling for student SES composition.

The Data

The data consist of a random sample of 3,379 individuals in 395 schools. There are 10,137 individual achievement records at Level 1, since individuals have information on 3 subtests comprising the achievement construct ($3,379 \times 3 = 10,137$). The larger data set, however, has a considerable amount of missing data on individual subtests comprising the achievement variable and on one of the school-level predictors. As we noted in Chapter 1, missing data can introduce considerable bias into an analysis. In this example, the missing school data resulted in 39 schools, or 10% ($39/395 = 0.099$), being dropped from the analysis. In this chapter, we provide some discussion of how analysts can deal with missing data when using SPSS Mixed. The missing data on the variables is summarized in Table 7.1.

We present our analyses with the listwise data, which consists of 8,151 individual-level records on achievement. The number of individual records reflects that each individual has up to three data lines to represent the three subtest measures of achievement. As noted in Table 7.1, there are 8,817 records for achievement. This excludes individuals with missing data on all three achievement tests, as SPSS will retain individuals with partial data in the analyses when the data are in vertical format (assuming other data are not missing). The data on achievement lost,

TABLE 7.1 Descriptive Statistics

	N	Minimum	Maximum	Mean	Std. Deviation
achieve	8817	25.29	99.98	57.9626	10.07109
gmses_mean	10137	–1.04	1.52	–.0006	.35944
gmacadpress	9237	–2.51	1.22	.0001	.92226
gmses	10137	–2.33	1.52	–.0003	.65575
gmacademic	10137	–3.67	3.39	–.0021	1.19011
Valid N (listwise)	8151				

however, is nearly 13% (1,320/10,137 = .130). Because there is also missing data on a school-level variable (*gmacadpress*), this reduces the complete data to 8,151 records at Level 1 (representing nearly a 20% loss in achievement data at Level 1).

Listwise deletion of cases is only appropriate where data are missing completely at random (MCR). This typically only occurs when a random sample is drawn from a larger population. In most cases, with real data this will not occur. A more reasonable assumption is the data are missing at random (MAR), which implies the probability of missing data on the outcome may be related to missing data on a covariate (e.g., students in a data set who have more absences from school might also be more likely to have missing test data), but missing data on the covariate should not be related to subjects' standing on the outcome (Raykov & Marcoulides, 2008). In other words, for students at the same attendance level, the missing test scores should be neither systematically higher nor lower than average. Table 7.1 also suggests data were not missing on some of the other variables in the data set; yet a considerable amount of that "complete" data will be lost as well during listwise deletion. The amount of missing data is a concern, therefore, as it may potentially influence our results.

As part of our analysis, we contrast the results of our listwise analyses against an analysis where we imputed plausible values for the missing data and then estimated a full data set (i.e., 10,137 individual records in 395 schools). Common solutions for missing data provided in SPSS, such as pairwise deletion or mean substitution, will lead to biased results. Multiple imputation (MI) is one recommended approach for dealing with missing data, provided the data are at least MAR (see Peugh & Enders, 2004, or Raykov & Marcoulides, 2008, for further discussion of missing data strategies). Multiple imputation of missing values is available in SPSS with an add-on module.

The listwise data used in the example are summarized in Table 7.2. The variables, which have been grand-mean centered, include individual student SES (*gmses*), a measure of students' relative academic focus (*gmacademic*), an aggregated school social composition mean (*gmses_mean*), and a measure of the school's academic press, or relative focus on providing a strong schoolwide academic environment (*gmacadpress*) for student learning to take place.

In Table 7.3 we contrast the listwise data set with the full data set where we imputed plausible values (generating 200 replications, not shown here). In general, the imputed descriptive data match the listwise data fairly closely. This provides some supportive evidence that the listwise

TABLE 7.2 Descriptive Statistics

	N	Minimum	Maximum	Mean	Std. Deviation
achieve	8151	25.29	99.98	58.1389	9.99354
gmses	8151	–2.05	1.52	.0238	.64656
gmacademic	8151	–3.67	3.33	.0035	1.16726
gmses_mean	8151	–.83	1.52	.0137	.36268
gmacadpress	8151	–2.51	1.22	.0054	.92129
Valid N (listwise)	8151				

TABLE 7.3   Descriptive Statistics

	N	Minimum	Maximum	Mean	Std. Deviation
achieve	10137	25.29	99.98	57.8404	9.56701
gmses	10137	−2.33	1.52	−.0003	.65575
gmacademic	10137	−3.67	3.39	−.0021	1.19011
gmses_mean	10137	−1.04	1.52	−.0003	.35963
gmacadpress	10137	−2.51	1.23	−.0152	.88888
Valid N (listwise)	10137				

FIGURE 7.1   Data matrix for latent variable analysis.

data may be either missing completely at random or at random in this data set (Raykov & Marcoulides, 2008).

To set up and run a three-level multivariate model in SPSS Mixed, we will organize the subtests defining the achievement construct vertically (see Chapter 2). Closer inspection of the data in Figure 7.1 suggests there are three achievement observations per individual and that individuals' ID and school code must be repeated in the data set for each time interval. The grouping variables (*id, schcode*) are used to identify each predictor as belonging to a particular level of the data hierarchy. The variable *Index* is used to identify the vertical achievement measures. It is coded 1 for the reading subtest, 2 for the math subtest, and 3 for the language subtest. Other predictors (e.g., academic program) are repeated on each of the three lines comprising each student's data, since they will be defined at levels above Level 1. We can also see that the achievement subtests are nested within individual identification (ID) numbers, and student IDs are nested within schools.

Defining a Latent Variable for a Multilevel Analysis

As we have noted, for the multivariate multilevel formulation, the different indicators (e.g., survey items, test scores) used to define one or more constructs are the first-level units. This level can be referred to as the measurement model, which in this case consists of the three subtests (i.e., reading, math, language) defining achievement. Following Raudenbush and Bryk's (2002) notation, the Level 1 model represents variation among the items (or other measures) defining the construct (or constructs) within each individual. The general Level 1 model may be written as

$$Y_{ijk} = \sum_p \pi_{pjk} a_{pijk} + \varepsilon_{ijk}, \tag{7.1}$$

where Y_{ijk} is the observed score on indicator i for student j in school k, and π_{pjk} is the latent true score for individual j in school k on construct p. Note that a_{pijk} takes on the value of 1 if the indicator i measures construct p and 0 otherwise for constructs $p = 1, \ldots, n$. A set of dummy-coded variables can therefore be used to refer to multiple constructs at Level 1. For example, the constructs can be "stacked" vertically and dummy variables used to refer to the different constructs (e.g., see Raudenbush, Rowan, & Kang, 1991). The error term ε_{ijk} represents the error for individual j in organization k for indicator i. As Equation 7.1 indicates, in order to incorporate the multiple measures of the constructs, as well as more than one construct in the model at Level 1, we must exclude the usual intercept term at this level.

The function of the Level 1 model is to aggregate the separate indicators into one or more latent variables. It therefore exists only to produce an estimate of the Level 1 variance due to individual items comprising each construct (Hox, 2002). In our specific case, the Level 1 model can be interpreted as an estimate of the variation due to test inconsistency in measuring the achievement construct. The error variance in the composite score is given by the total variability of items (or tests) divided by the number of indicators comprising the construct. The error variability present in measuring the construct can be used to construct an internal consistency estimate at the pupil or school level (see Hox, 2002, or Raudenbush & Bryk, 2002, for further discussion). We caution that when defining constructs in this vertical manner, it is best if the items or subtests are measured on the same scale (e.g., Likert-type scales, scaled scores) and have similar variances. Keep in mind, however, that ordinal data may not meet the assumptions of continuous normal data.

The Level 2 model describes the distribution of true scores π_p across students within schools, including any predictors that are proposed to explain this variation. The general model can be written as

$$\pi_{pjk} = \beta_{p0k} + r_{pjk}, \tag{7.2}$$

where β_{p0k} is the true score mean of construct p in organization k, and r_{pjk} is the Level 2 random coefficient for individual j in school k on construct p.

At Level 3, we represent the school-level model. The intercept model with no predictors would be

$$\beta_{p0k} = \gamma_{p00} + u_{p0k}, \tag{7.3}$$

where γ_{p00} is the Level 3 intercept for construct p, and u_{p0k} is the Level 3 random effect capturing variation in school means for construct p. The dimensionality of the covariance matrices of random effects at Levels 2 and 3 depends on the number of random effects at each level.

Null Model: No Predictors

For the null model, we can examine the variability in the achievement variable that exists at each level. Because there is only one construct in the example, within individuals (Level 1), we can simply define the achievement variable with its three component measures ($i = 1, 2, 3$):

$$Y_{ijk} = \pi_{jk} + \varepsilon_{ijk}, \tag{7.4}$$

where Y_{ijk} is a subtest measure i comprising achievement for individual j in school k, π_{jk} in this case is the true value of achievement for that student, and ε_{ijk} is the measurement error associated within individual jk's responses on the ith measure of achievement. The errors are assumed to be normally distributed with a mean of 0 and some variance. We note in passing that we could also use the Repeated dialog box and the Index variable to represent the variability associated with the achievement construct within individuals. In this formulation, we could also examine the

TABLE 7.4   Model Dimension[a]

		Number of Levels	Covariance Structure	Number of Parameters	Subject Variables
Fixed Effects	Intercept	1		1	
Random Effects	Intercept	1	Identity	1	Schcode
	Intercept	1	Identity	1	schcode * Rid
Residual				1	
Total		3		4	

[a] Dependent Variable: achieve.

variability associated with each observed indicator (i.e., in this case, each subtest) by defining a diagonal covariance matrix within individuals.

The Level 2 (between individuals) model is defined as

$$\pi_{jk} = \beta_{0k} + r_{jk}.$$ (7.5)

Between schools, the model is defined as

$$\beta_{0k} = \gamma_{00} + u_{0k}.$$ (7.6)

The intercept at Level 3 is the grand mean of the subtests defining achievement. Substituting into Equation 7.1, we arrive at the single-variable, intercept-only model, which includes the fixed effect intercept and three variance components, one for each level of the model:

$$Y_{ijk} = \gamma_{00} + u_{0k} + r_{jk} + \varepsilon_{ijk}.$$ (7.7)

We can confirm this specification by examining the model dimensions for the null model in Table 7.4. The fixed effect intercept is defined along with the random effects at Level 3 (u_{0k}) and Level 2 (r_{jk}), and the Level 1 residual (ε_{ijk}).

Defining the Null Model (No Predictors) With SPSS Menu Commands

Launch the SPSS application program and select the data file *ch7multivarMLM1.sav*.

1. Go to the SPSS toolbar and select ANALYZE, MIXED MODELS, LINEAR.

This command will open the *Linear Mixed Models: Specify Subjects and Repeated* dialog box.

2. Within the *Linear Mixed Models: Specify Subjects and Repeated* dialog box, click to select the *schcode* and *Rid* (rank of student id) variables from the left column, then click the right-arrow button to transfer the variables into the *Subjects* dialog box.

Click the CONTINUE button to display the *Linear Mixed Models* dialog box.

3. In the *Linear Mixed Models* dialog
box, click to select the *achieve* variable
from the left column, then click the
right-arrow button to move it into the
Dependent Variable box.

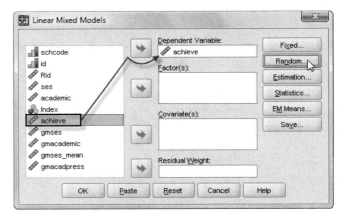

Since the model does not contain any fixed
effects, skip over the FIXED button and click
the RANDOM button to access the *Linear
Mixed Models: Random Effects* dialog box.

4. The *Linear Mixed
   Models: Random Effects*
   displays the *Random
   Effect 1 of 1* screen.
   a. First change the
      covariance type
      by clicking on the
      pull-down menu
      and selecting *Scaled
      Identity*.
   b. Click to select
      Include intercept to
      define the random
      intercept at Level 3.
   c. In the *Subject
      Groupings* box, click
      to select *schcode*,
      then click the right-
      arrow button to
      transfer it into the
      Combinations box.
   d. At the top-right section of the window, click the NEXT button to access the *Random Effect
      2 of 2* screen.

Note: The NEXT button may not work when creating multilevel models with random intercepts. This is
a problem acknowledged by SPSS for assorted software versions including 18.0 and is resolved by adding
then removing a covariate from the model, which is described in Steps e through h and Step 6.

Workaround to Activate the Random Effects "Next" Button

e. Click the CONTINUE button to return to the *Linear Mixed Models* dialog box.

f. Click to select any variable from the left-column listing. For this example, *ses* is selected, then click the right-arrow button to move the variable into the *Covariate(s)* box.

Now click the RANDOM button to return to the *Random Effect 1 of 1* screen.

g. Click to select *ses* from the *Factors and Covariates* box, then click the ADD button to move the variable into the *Model* box.

h. Now click the REMOVE button to withdraw *ses* from the *Model* box. This action will then activate the NEXT button (i).

i. Click the NEXT button to access the *Random Effect 2 of 2* screen.

5. The *Random Effect 2 of 2* screen display is similar to the first screen and requires the following changes.

   a. Change the covariance type by clicking on the pull-down menu and selecting *Scaled Identity*.

   b. Click to select *Include intercept* to include the random intercept for Level 2.

   c. In the *Subject Groupings* box, click to select *schcode* and *Rid*, then click the right-arrow button to transfer the variable into the *Combinations* box.

Click the CONTINUE button to return to the *Linear Mixed Models* dialog box.

6. Click to select *ses*, then click the left-arrow button to remove the variable from the *Covariate(s)* box.

Then click the ESTIMATION button to access the *Linear Mixed Models: Estimation* dialog box.

7. The *Linear Mixed Models: Estimation* dialog box displays various settings.

The estimation method default is restricted maximum likelihood (REML) and will be used for this and subsequent models.

Click the CONTINUE button to return to the *Linear Mixed Models* dialog box.

8. In the *Linear Mixed Models* dialog box, click the STATISTICS button to access the *Linear Mixed Models: Statistics* dialog box.

Click and select the following three statistics: *parameter estimates*, *tests for covariance parameters*, and *covariances of random effects*.

Then click the CONTINUE button to return to the *Linear Mixed Models* dialog box.

9. Finally, in the *Linear Mixed Models* dialog box, click the OK button to run the model.

Interpreting the Output of the Null Model

In this case we will use an identity (ID) covariance matrix at Levels 2 and 3, since there is only one random effect at those levels (i.e., the achievement intercept). Table 7.5 suggests the average school mean for achievement is 58.18 (which indicates the mean of the three subtests).

TABLE 7.5 Estimates of Fixed Effects[a]

Parameter	Estimate	Std. Error	df	t	Sig.
Intercept	58.180714	.251485	305.101	231.348	.000

[a] Dependent Variable: achieve.

The variance components associated with each level are summarized in Table 7.6. The output suggests that approximately 33% [33.00/(33.0 + 11.52 + 55.87)] of the variability in achievement lies within individuals' differing performance on the three subtests, 56% of the variability (55.87/100.39) lies between individuals, and about 11% (11.52/100.39) of the variability lies between schools.

TABLE 7.6 Estimates of Covariance Parameters[a]

Parameter		Estimate	Std. Error	Wald Z	Sig.
Residual		33.001058	.633165	52.121	.000
Intercept [subject = schcode]	Variance	11.520495	1.664309	6.922	.000
Intercept [subject = schcode * Rid]	Variance	55.869381	1.948537	28.672	.000

[a] Dependent Variable: achieve.

Model 1: Building a Three-Level Model

For the first model, we will add the individual background variables and a school control. At Level 2, we propose that students with higher individual SES and taking more academically oriented course work will have higher achievement levels. We will again grand-mean center the variables in the model (by using variables we created earlier; see Chapter 2). Note that we do not have an intercept for each measure at Level 1; therefore, the Level 2 outcome is π_{jk}, which is the achievement estimate for individual j in school k. The between-individual (Level 2) model for achievement level is

$$\pi_{jk} = \beta_{0k} + \beta_{1k}(gmses)_{jk} + \beta_{2k}(gmacademic)_{jk} + r_{jk}. \tag{7.8}$$

At the school level (Level 3), we will add aggregate SES composition as a control variable proposed to affect school achievement levels:

$$\beta_{0k} = \gamma_{00} + \gamma_{01}(gmSES\_mean)_k + u_{0k}. \tag{7.9}$$

We will assume that only the achievement intercepts vary between schools in this first model:

$$\beta_{1k} = \gamma_{10},$$

$$\beta_{2k} = \gamma_{20}. \tag{7.10}$$

Defining Model 1 With SPSS Menu Commands

Note: SPSS settings will default to those used for the Null Model.

1. Go to the SPSS toolbar and select ANALYZE, MIXED MODELS, LINEAR.

This command enables access to the *Linear Mixed Models: Specify Subjects and Repeated* dialog box.

2. The variables *schcode* and *Rid* (rank of student id) appear in the *Subjects* box within the *Linear Mixed Models: Specify Subjects and Repeated* dialog box. We will not use the *Repeated Covariance Type* option at present, since we will just assume one residual variance component at Level 1 for the three subtests defining achievement. We can model the error variance for each subtest separately if we wish, however, by opening the *Repeated* dialog box and placing *Index* in the box.

Click the CONTINUE button to display the *Linear Mixed Models* dialog box.

3. The *achieve* variable is shown as the *Dependent Variable*.

Click to select the following variables, then click the right-arrow button to transfer them into the *Covariates* box.

The variables could be transferred in the order they appear in the left column, however, to facilitate reading of the output tables, the recommended sequence for entering the variables into the *Covariates* box is *gmes_mean, gmes, gmacademic*.

Note: Variables may also be rearranged by first adding them as a group into the *Covariate(s)* box. Then by clicking to select a variable, holding down the left button of your mouse, the variable may be dragged into a different location.

Click the FIXED button to access the *Linear Mixed Models: Fixed Effects* dialog box.

4a. Within the *Linear Mixed Models: Fixed Effects* box click the pull-down menu to select *Main Effects* as the factorial setting.

b. Click to select the variables from the *Factors and Covariates* box, then click the ADD button to place them in the *Model* box: *gmses_mean, gmses, gmacademic*.

c. Confirm *Include Intercept* is selected.

Finally, click the CONTINUE button to return to the *Linear Mixed Models* dialog box.

5. The estimation, and statistics elements in the model remain the same as those used for the Null Model, so skip over these buttons and click OK to run the model.

Interpreting the Output of Model 1 (Explaining Student Achievement)

The fixed effect estimates for Model 1 are summarized in Table 7.7. After adjusting for the within-school background controls, the achievement intercept for schools is 57.97. Between individuals, both student SES ($\gamma = 3.31$, $p < .01$) and academic background ($\gamma = 2.34$, $p < .01$) affect achievement levels. Between schools, aggregate SES also affects achievement levels ($\gamma = 2.78$, $p > .01$).

The variance component output (Table 7.8) suggests that after addition of the set of predictors, there is still variance in achievement levels to be explained between schools (Wald $Z = 5.45$, $p < .01$) and individuals (Wald $Z = 27.31$, $p < .01$). Keeping in mind our previous cautions, adding the between-individual variables reduces the variance at Level 2 considerably (i.e., from $\sigma^2 = 55.87$ in Table 7.6 to $\sigma^2 = 42.98$ in Table 7.8, or a reduction of 12.89). This can be used to calculate an R^2 coefficient of 0.23 ($12.89/55.87 = .231$) for Level 2. At Level 3, the variance accounted for is 0.523 ($6.02/11.52 = .523$). Note that the residual (or subtest) variability within individuals at Level 1 remains unchanged.

TABLE 7.7   Estimates of Fixed Effects[a]

Parameter	Estimate	Std. Error	df	t	Sig.
Intercept	57.970429	.197919	291.705	292.900	.000
gmses_mean	2.775910	.583165	563.511	4.760	.000
gmses	3.314677	.266898	2480.822	12.419	.000
gmacademic	2.339894	.134532	2658.163	17.393	.000

[a] Dependent Variable: achieve.

TABLE 7.8   Estimates of Covariance Parameters[a]

Parameter		Estimate	Std. Error	Wald Z	Sig.
Residual		33.000597	.633149	52.121	.000
Intercept [subject = schcode]	Variance	5.499493	1.009772	5.446	.000
Intercept [subject = schcode * Rid]	Variance	42.983447	1.573672	27.314	.000

[a] Dependent Variable: achieve.

Model 2: Investigating a Random Slope

We may wish to see whether the effect of students' academic program on their achievement varies across schools. We can build a model for both intercepts and slopes. The model for the school intercept is summarized in Equation 7.9. We will propose that the slope describing the effect of academic course work on achievement varies across schools. This slope (β_{2k}) from Equation 7.10 can be designated as randomly varying at Level 3 (between schools) as follows:

$$\beta_{2k} = \gamma_{20} + u_{2k}, \tag{7.11}$$

where γ_{20} is the average slope effect at the school level and u_{2j} represents variation in the slope across schools.

The variance components are provided in Table 7.9 for Model 2 with the academic course–achievement slope designated as randomly varying between schools (i.e., at Level 3). We will use an unstructured (UN) matrix to capture variability in intercepts, slopes, and the covariance between the intercept and slope. We will continue to use an identity (ID) matrix at the between-student level (Level 2), which assumes that true achievement levels vary between students.

Defining Model 2 With SPSS Menu Commands

Note: SPSS settings will default to those used for Model 1.

1. Go to the SPSS toolbar and select ANALYZE, MIXED MODELS, LINEAR.

This command enables access to the *Linear Mixed Models: Specify Subjects and Repeated* dialog box.

2. The variables *schcode* and *Rid* (Rank of student id) appear in the *Subjects* box within the *Linear Mixed Models: Specify Subjects and Repeated* dialog box.

Click the CONTINUE button to display the *Linear Mixed Models* dialog box.

3a. The variable *achieve* appears in the *Dependent Variable* box with *Covariate(s)*: *gmes_mean, gmes, gmacademic.*

Click the RANDOM button to access the *Linear Mixed Models: Random Effects* dialog box.

4a. The *Linear Mixed Models: Random Effects* displays the *Random Effect 2 of 2* screen. No changes are needed, so click the PREVIOUS button to access the *Random Effect 1 of 2* screen.

b. In the *Random Effect 1 of 2* screen, click the pull-down menu to change the covariance type to *Unstructured* (previously *Scaled Identity*).

c. Change the factorial setting by clicking the pull-down menu and selecting *Main Effects*.

d. Click to select *gmacademic* from the *Factors and Covariates* listing. Then click the ADD button to move the variable into the *Model* box.

Click the CONTINUE button to return to the *Linear Mixed Models* main dialog box.

5. The estimation and statistics elements in the model remain the same as those used for Model 1, so skip over these buttons to click OK to run the model.

TABLE 7.9   Estimates of Covariance Parameters[a]

Parameter		Estimate	Std. Error	Wald Z	Sig.
Residual		33.000587	.633149	52.121	.000
Intercept + gmacademic	UN (1,1)	5.298109	1.011484	5.238	.000
[subject = schcode]	UN (2,1)	.893084	.478497	1.866	.062
	UN (2,2)	.733293	.440893	1.663	.096
Intercept [subject = schcode * Rid]	Variance	42.223666	1.597367	26.433	.000

[a] Dependent Variable: achieve.

Interpreting the Output of Model 2

The results in Table 7.9 suggest that after adding the set of variables to the model there is still significant variance in intercepts (Wald Z = 5.24, p < .01) and slopes (Wald Z = 1.66, one-tailed p = .048) between schools (Level 3). The covariance between the intercept and slope is positive (two-tailed p = .062). We will use the Wald Z two-tailed test for the covariance, since it can be positive or negative. Notice that the intercept variance components are slightly different from the previous model at Level 3 (σ^2 = 5.30) and Level 2 (σ^2 = 42.22) when the covariance matrix is specified in this way. Because the one-tailed p value for the slope (UN 2, 2) is below p = .05, we might next build a model at Level 3 to explain variation in the academic–achievement slope across schools.

Model 3: Explaining Variation in Slopes

Where there are multiple random effects (e.g., an intercept and slope), it is important to consider that group-level complications can arise because of correlations between the random effects (Raudenbush & Bryk, 2002). Variables entered in one of the between-group equations can affect estimates in another equation. Importantly, model misspecification can occur if the same variables are not included in both equations. As Raudenbush and Bryk (2002) suggest, one strategy is to enter the same group-level variables into both equations, and only if they are not significant should they be removed.

In this next analysis, the Level 1 (latent achievement variable) and Level 2 (between-individuals) models will remain the same. At Level 3, we will build an intercept and slope model simultaneously. At this level, we will add another variable describing the school's academic press (i.e., defined as the school's relative focus on an academically oriented curriculum and strong expectations for student work), with positive scores indicating stronger academic press. The Level 3 intercept model is as follows:

$$\beta_{0k} = \gamma_{00} + \gamma_{01}(gmSES\_mean)_k + \gamma_{02}(gmacadpress)_k + u_{0k}. \tag{7.12}$$

The Level 3 slope model with similar cross-level interactions to explain variation in the academic program–achievement slope is

$$\beta_{2k} = \gamma_{20} + \gamma_{21}(gmSES\_mean * gmses)_k + \gamma_{22}(gmacadpress * gmses)_k + u_{2k}. \tag{7.13}$$

Defining Model 3 (Variation in Academic Achievement Slopes) With SPSS Menu Commands

Note: SPSS settings will default to those used for Model 2.

1. Go to the SPSS toolbar and select ANALYZE, MIXED MODELS, LINEAR.

This command enables access to the *Linear Mixed Models: Specify Subjects and Repeated* dialog box.

2. The variables *schcode* and *Rid* (Rank of student id) appear in the *Subjects* box within the *Linear Mixed Models: Specify Subjects and Repeated* dialog box.

Click the CONTINUE button to display the *Linear Mixed Models* dialog box.

3. The variable *achieve* appears in the *Dependent Variable* box.
   a. Click to select and remove the variables *gmses_mean, gmses,* and *gmacademic* from the *Covariate(s)* box then clicking the left-arrow button.
   b. Click to select the variables from the left column listing and enter them in the following sequence: *gmes_mean, gmacadpress, gmes, gmacademic*.

Note: Variables may also be rearranged by first adding them to the *Covariate(s)* box. Then by clicking to select a variable and holding down the left button of your mouse, the variable may be dragged into a different location.

Click the FIXED button to access the *Linear Mixed Models: Fixed Effects* dialog box.

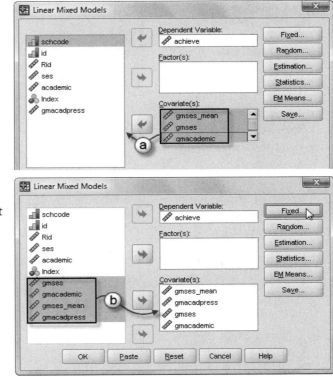

4a. Within the *Linear Mixed Models: Fixed Effects* box confirm the factorial setting is *Main Effects*.
   b. Click to select the variables from the *Factors and Covariates* box, then click the ADD button. The recommended sequence for entering the variables into the *Model* box is *gmes_mean, gmacadpress, gmses, gmacademic*.
   c. Confirm *Include Intercept* is selected.

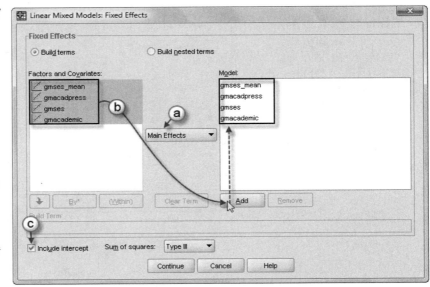

Adding Cross-Level Interactions to Model 3

gmses_mean * *gmacademic*

5a. Click to select the *Build nested terms* option.
b. Click to select the variable *gmses_mean* from the *Factors and Covariates* column.
c. Click the down-arrow button to move *gmses_mean* into the *Build Term* box.
d. Click the BY* button to add the computational symbol (*) to the *Build Term* box.

e. Click to select the variable *gmacademic* from the *Factors and Covariates* column.
f. Click the down-arrow button to move *gmacademic* into the *Build Term* box.
g. Click the ADD button to move the term *gmses_mean* *gmacademic* into the *Model* box.

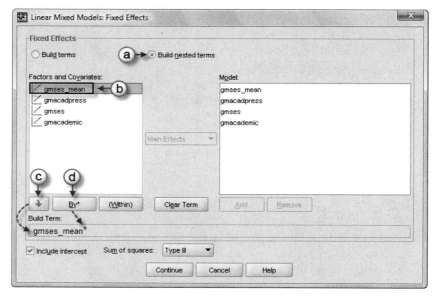

gmacadpress* gmacademic

6a. Click to select the variable *gmacadpress* from the *Factors and Covariates* column.

b. Click the down-arrow button to move *gmacadpress* into the *Build Term* box.

c. Click the BY* button to add the computational symbol (*) to the *Build Term* box.

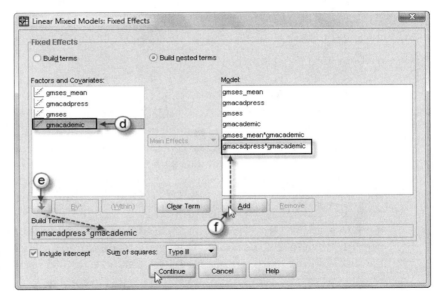

d. Click to select the variable *gmacademic* from the *Factors and Covariates* column.

e. Click the down-arrow button to move *gmacademic* into the *Build Term* box.

f. Click the ADD button to move the term *gmacadpress*gmacademic* into the *Model* box.

Click the CONTINUE button to return to the *Linear Mixed Models* dialog box.

7. The random effects, estimation, and statistics elements in the model remain the same as those used for Model 2, so skip over these buttons and click OK to run the model.

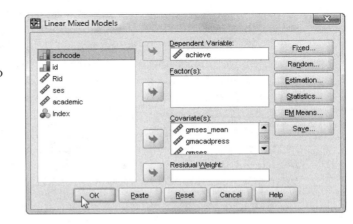

TABLE 7.10   Estimates of Fixed Effects[a]

Parameter	Estimate	Std. Error	df	t	Sig.
Intercept	58.126675	.199814	299.198	290.904	.000
gmses_mean	2.699573	.616576	559.790	4.378	.000
gmacadpress	.395357	.226730	296.657	1.744	.082
gmses	3.229015	.266886	2479.851	12.099	.000
gmacademic	2.409872	.145814	132.691	16.527	.000
gmses_mean * gmacademic	−1.401768	.411068	121.759	−3.410	.001
gmacadpress * gmacademic	.237067	.167169	154.032	1.418	.158

[a] Dependent Variable: achieve.

TABLE 7.11   Estimates of Covariance Parameters[a]

Parameter		Estimate	Std. Error	Wald Z	Sig.
Residual		33.000585	.633149	52.121	.000
Intercept + gmacademic	UN (1,1)	5.290505	1.002957	5.275	.000
[subject = schcode]	UN (2,1)	.684196	.452209	1.513	.130
	UN (2,2)	.386032	.406441	.950	.342
Intercept [subject = schcode * Rid]	Variance	42.332690	1.602110	26.423	.000

[a] Dependent Variable: achieve.

Interpreting the Output of Model 3

The fixed effects table is shown in Table 7.10. At the school level, aggregate SES affects achievement ($\gamma = 2.70$, $p < .01$). There is some evidence that academic press also affects the achievement outcome ($\gamma = 0.40$, $p < .10$). Between students, student SES and academic program remain significant predictors of achievement outcomes.

Regarding explaining variation in the academic program–achievement slope, Table 7.10 suggests school social composition (gmSES_mean) moderates the within-school relationship between academic background and achievement ($\gamma = -1.40$, $p < .01$). This suggests the effect of student academic background on their achievement is moderated by the level of SES composition in the school. To examine this relationship in more detail, a 1 *SD* decrease in school SES composition below the grand mean, for example, would result in a 1.40 point increase in the effect of academic background on achievement. In these lower SES schools, the combined effect of students' academic background on achievement would be more influential [2.70 − (−1.40) = 4.10], compared with students in schools at the grand mean for student composition. In other words, for students in lower SES school settings, their prior academic background has a greater effect on their current achievement level than for their peers in schools at the grand mean for SES composition. Conversely, for students in schools 1 *SD* above the grand mean for SES composition, being in a stronger academic program confers less additional advantage than for students in schools at the grand mean of SES composition [2.70 + (−1.40) = 1.30]. Table 7.10 also suggests that academic press does not moderate the academic–achievement slope ($p > .10$).

The variance component model (Table 7.11) suggests there is still significant variability in intercepts to be explained (Wald $Z = 5.28$, $p < .01$) after adding the school predictors to the model, but not in slopes (Wald $Z = 0.95$, one tailed $p > .171$). We could continue to add predictors to the school model to explain this variability in intercepts.

Comparing Model Estimates

In Table 7.12 we provide a comparison of our listwise model estimates with model estimates produced through using an MI software program to generate a complete data set (Peugh &

TABLE 7.12 Comparison of Listwise and Multiple Imputation (MI) Model Estimates

Variables	SPSS Listwise (N = 8,151)		SPSS MI (N = 10,137)	
	Estimate	SE	Estimate	SE
Intercept Model	58.13*	0.20	57.96*	0.16
Between Schools				
SES_mean	2.70*	0.62	2.76*	0.51
Academic press	0.40	0.23	0.38*	0.19
Within Schools				
SES	3.23*	0.27	3.24*	0.22
Academic–Achievement Slope Model	2.41*	0.15	2.44*	0.12
Between Schools				
SES_mean	–1.40*	0.41	–1.19*	0.36
Academic press	0.24	0.17	0.18	0.15

* $p < .05$.

Enders, 2004; Raykov & Marcoulides, 2008). In this example, the table indicates the listwise estimates and the multiple imputation estimates are very close, suggesting that the data on school academic press and achievement were most likely MCR. This is likely because there is a considerable amount of data available to estimate the population parameters, even with the roughly 20% missing data for achievement and school academic press. In this case (which is probably not typical), the estimates with listwise deletion appear to be "good enough" to represent the data. The one difference is academic press, which is not significant in the listwise model (i.e., $p = .08$), but is significant in the MI model ($p < .05$), likely due to more accurate estimation of the standard error. We recommend that users use multiple imputation software when considerable data are missing. Of course, what is "considerable" will depend on each unique data set. Solutions can then be compared.

Multivariate Multilevel Model for Correlated Outcomes

We can also use the multivariate multilevel formulation to define separate outcome models that take into consideration the correlation between the multiple outcome measures. This formulation is similar to the previous model, with the major difference being there is no single "achievement" construct; but, rather, we focus on building models to explain variation in each of the three correlated outcomes. The goal is to build a model where the fixed effects are used to control for differences in the means between individual responses and the random effects can be used to model the different variances for the outcomes, as well as the covariances (or correlations) between the outcome measures (Leyland, 2004). One benefit of this specific type of model is in testing the equality of the size of effect of a specific predictor on each of the outcomes.

The Data

The data used are similar to the data used in the last example, using three subtests (reading, math, and language) to define a latent achievement factor. In this case, there are 2,715 students (Level 1 $N = 8,145$ observations) nested in 353 schools. We will investigate the effect of gender (coded 1 = female, 0 = male) and *academicpress* (i.e., the same school variable indicating the relative focus on academic outcomes) on the set of correlated subtests.

Research Questions

In this example, the primary research question concerns whether gender affects students' achievement on each test. In this instance, we wish to control for the likely correlation between student performance on each test. We then can ask whether the size of the gender effect is the same across all three tests. In answering this latter question, we are interested in investigating hypotheses about the effect of gender on each of the student subtests comprising the multivariate outcome. More specifically, we wish to determine whether the effect of gender is the same across the correlated subtest outcomes or whether it may be related to some subtests but not others. In each case, the hypothesis proposed is that the strength of the effect of the predictor on the three outcomes is the same. For example, for gender, the null hypothesis would be that the three unstandardized betas would be the same:

$$H_0 = \beta_{\text{Read}} = \beta_{\text{Math}} = \beta_{\text{Languge}}.$$

We will also pose a question about whether the effect of the school's academic press is the same across the three subtests.

Formulating the Basic Model

To examine this type of model in SPSS, we will need to make some changes to the basic three-level model formulation we previously presented. We briefly describe some of these changes before actually building the model using the SPSS Menu commands. At the group level (Level 3), we define schools (using *schcode*). In contrast to the previous model, however, we use the repeated measures option to define the within-school model; that is, students nested within schools. This has the effect of combining Levels 1 and 2. More specifically, we use the REPEATED dialog box to define the covariance structure within schools and the nesting of students within schools in much the same way as the RANDOM command is used (Leyland, 2004). We will use the variable *Index1* to open up the REPEATED dialog box for the Menu commands. We must designate students nested in schools (*schcode*Rid*) on the REPEATED command line (if we refer to the syntax statements), as opposed to using a second RANDOM command as we did for the last example. In contrast to our previous formulation, we also do not specify a randomly varying intercept in the RANDOM dialog box (or syntax subcommand). Instead, the Index1 (coded 1= read, 2 = math, 3 = language) variable is used to provide an estimate of each specific subtest's intercept. Specifying the fixed effects portion of the model as having no intercept (NOINT) ensures that separate estimates are obtained for each of the three subtests. By declaring *Index1* as the random effect, we can fit a random intercept model for each subtest between schools.

As in the previous latent variable formulation and the growth model formulation in the last chapter, the individual reading, math, and language subtests are stacked in a single variable column (Y_{ijk}). The single-equation models, with a student-level predictor added within schools concerning the three subtests (using R for reading, M for math, and L for language) for individual j in school k can be written as

$$Y_{Rjk} = \beta_{R0k} + \beta_{R1k} X_{1jk} + r_{Rjk} + u_{R0k},$$

$$Y_{Mjk} = \beta_{M0k} + \beta_{M1k} X_{1jk} + r_{Mjk} + u_{M0k}, \tag{7.14}$$

$$Y_{Ljk} = \beta_{L0k} + \beta_{L1k} X_{1jk} + r_{Ljk} + u_{L0k},$$

where X_{1jk} is female (coded 1 versus male coded 0), r represents within-school residuals for each equation, and u represents the school-level residuals. Notice in this formulation, in contrast to the previous set of models we developed (e.g., see Equations 7.7 to 7.10), there is no modeling of the residual variance (ε_{ijk}) at the lowest level (i.e., Level 1) of the model (Leyland, 2004). Within-school predictors (X_p) are added as interactions in this model (e.g., *Index1*female*). We will select an unstructured variance and correlation matrix (UNR) to examine the variances and correlations between tests at the student level.

At the school level, we can add school-level predictors (W_p) as interactions (e.g., *gmacadpress*Index1*) for explaining outcomes on each subtest:

$$\beta_{R0k} = \gamma_{R00} + \gamma_{R01}W_{1k} + u_{R0k}$$

$$\beta_{M0k} = \gamma_{M00} + \gamma_{M01}W_{1k} + u_{M0k}$$

$$\beta_{L0k} = \gamma_{L00} + \gamma_{L01}W_{1k} + u_{L0k}, \tag{7.15}$$

where γ's represent structural coefficients for the school-level intercepts and slopes, W_{1k} represents the school's academic press (*gmacadpress*), and u represents random errors associated explaining school achievement for each subtest. For this example, we will consider the slope coefficients describing the relationship of gender and each subtest (β_{1k}) in Equation 7.14 to be fixed across schools ($\beta_{1k} = \gamma_{10}$). We will define an unstructured covariance matrix with correlations (UNR) also between schools.

We note that it is possible to test specific hypotheses about the equality of effects using the /TEST command in SPSS Mixed. We will illustrate a couple of such tests that might be conducted. Interested readers can find further information about using tests of contrasts in the SPSS user's manual. We can also display means for combinations of main effects and interactions, and provide tests of main effects using the EM MEANS button within the SPSS menu commands.

Null Model (No Predictors)
Defining the Null Model (No Predictors) With SPSS Menu Commands

Launch the SPSS program application and select the data file *ch7multivarMLM2.sav*.

1. Go to the SPSS toolbar and select ANALYZE, MIXED MODELS, LINEAR.

This command enables access to the *Linear Mixed Models: Specify Subjects and Repeated* dialog box.

2a. Within the *Linear Mixed Models: Specify Subjects and Repeated* dialog box, click to select the *schcode* and *Rid* variables from the left column, then click the right-arrow button to transfer the variables into the *Subjects* dialog box. This will be necessary to ensure proper nesting of individuals within schools in the *Repeated* command line of the syntax commands.

b. Click to select the *Index1* variable from the left column, then click the right-arrow button to transfer the variable into the *Repeated* box.

c. Change the *Repeated Covariance Type* by clicking the pull-down menu to select *Unstructured: Correlation Metric* (UNR).

Click the CONTINUE button to display the *Linear Mixed Models* dialog box.

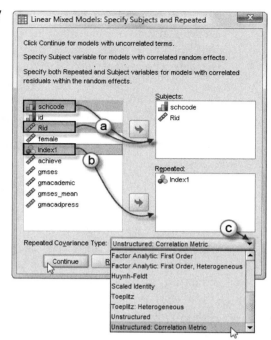

3a. In the *Linear Mixed Models* dialog box, click to select the *achieve* variable from the left column, then click the right-arrow button to move it into the *Dependent Variable* box.

b. Click to select *Index1*, then click the right-arrow button to move the variable into the *Factor(s)* box.

Click the FIXED button to access the *Linear Mixed Models: Fixed Effects* dialog box.

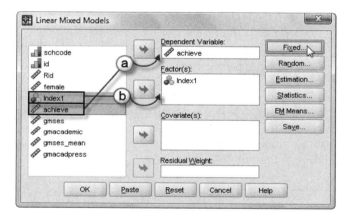

4a. Within the *Linear Mixed Models: Fixed Effects* dialog box, locate the *Factorial* setting and click on the pull-down menu to select *Main Effects*.

b. Click to select *Index1* from the *Factors and Covariates* box, then click the ADD button to move the variable into the *Model* box.

c. Click the *Include Intercept* box to remove the check mark so this option is deselected.

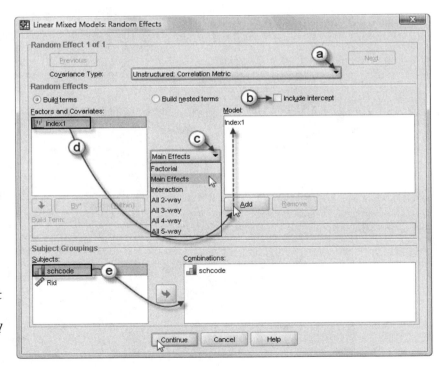

Click the CONTINUE button to return to the *Linear Mixed Models* dialog box. In the *Linear Mixed Models* dialog box, click the RANDOM button to access the *Linear Mixed Models: Random Effects* dialog box.

5. The *Linear Mixed Models: Random Effects* displays the *Random Effect 1 of 1* screen.

a. Change the covariance type by clicking on the pull-down menu and selecting *Unstructured: Correlation Metric* (UNR).

b. Leave the *Include Intercept* box unchecked so this option is deselected. This will eliminate the random intercept at the school level.

c. Change the *Factorial* setting by clicking on the pull-down Menu to select *Main Effects*.

d. Click to select *Index1* from the *Factors and Covariate(s)* box, then click the ADD button to move the variable into the *Model* box. This will ensure that a separate random intercept is estimated for each test at the school level.

e. In the *Subject Groupings* box, click to select *schcode*, then click the right-arrow button to transfer the variable into the *Combinations* box.

Click the CONTINUE button to return to the *Linear Mixed Models* dialog box.

6. In the *Linear Mixed Models* dialog box, click on the ESTIMATION button to access the *Linear Mixed Models: Estimation* dialog box.

Click to select the *Maximum Likelihood* (ML) method.

Click the CONTINUE button to return to the *Linear Mixed Models* dialog box.

7. In the *Linear Mixed Models* dialog box, click the STATISTICS button to access the *Linear Mixed Models: Statistics* dialog box.

Click and select the following three statistics: *parameter estimates*, *tests for covariance parameters*, and *covariances of random effects*.

Then click the CONTINUE button to return to the *Linear Mixed Models* dialog box.

8. We recommend viewing your syntax commands before running the null model to first check if the model has been properly specified.

Click the PASTE button on the *Linear Mixed Models* dialog box, which will open a new window that displays the null model's syntax.

Discussion of syntax occurs in the next section: "Examining the Syntax Commands."

Note: Executing the *Paste* command will generate the syntax but also close the *Linear Mixed Models* dialog box. You will then need to repeat several steps in order to reaccess the *Linear Mixed Models* dialog box where you may then be able to run the model:

a. Go to the SPSS toolbar to select ANALYZE, MIXED MODELS, LINEAR. This command enables access to the *Linear Mixed Models: Specify Subjects and Repeated* dialog box.

b. Within the *Linear Mixed Models: Specify Subjects and Repeated* dialog box click the CONTINUE button to open the *Linear Mixed Models* dialog box.

Now continue onto the final step (9).

9. Click the OK button to run the model.

Examining the Syntax Commands

We suggest examining the syntax statements to see whether the model has been set up properly using the Repeated Covariance Type menu option. The /FIXED command specifies *Index1* as the single predictor and no intercept (NOINT) in the fixed effects portion of the model. The /REPEATED command line shows the variable *Index1* has been defined to represent the subtests and that the proper nesting of students within schools was accomplished correctly (*schcode*Rid*). Next notice that the /RANDOM command includes *Index1* as a random effect, which allows the intercepts for the each test to vary across schools, and the school level (schcode) has been properly defined.

```
MIXED
 achieve BY Index1
 /CRITERIA = CIN(95) MXITER(100) MXSTEP(5) SCORING(1)
 SINGULAR(0.000000000001) HCONVERGE(0, ABSOLUTE) LCONVERGE(0, ABSOLUTE)
 PCONVERGE(0.000001, ABSOLUTE)
 /FIXED = Index1|NOINT SSTYPE(3)
 /METHOD = ML
 /PRINT = G SOLUTION TESTCOV
 /RANDOM Index1|SUBJECT(schcode) COVTYPE(UNR)
 /REPEATED = Index1|SUBJECT(schcode*Rid) COVTYPE(UNR).
```

Interpreting the Output of the Null Model

We present the fixed effects for a simple no predictors model first (Table 7.13). The means (corrected for correlations between outcomes) are as follows: reading ($M = 57.42$), math ($M = 59.24$), and language ($M = 57.82$).

We can compare the means calculated by running COMPARE MEANS for each subtest (i.e., using achievement as the dependent variable and Index 1 as the independent variable). Readers will notice they are slightly different when uncorrected for correlations between subtests. In Table 7.14, the grand mean (total) is 58.14 ($SD = 9.99$). Notice that the slightly different N's for each test reflect that there are a few missing data cases (i.e., 3) in reading and math. In the repeated measures (i.e., vertical) format, SPSS can handle situations where partial information

TABLE 7.13   Estimates of Fixed Effects[a]

Parameter	Estimate	Std. Error	df	t	Sig.
[Index1=1 Read]	57.420866	.258324	292.630	222.282	.000
[Index1=2 Math]	59.238354	.283376	305.744	209.045	.000
[Index1=3 Language]	57.816277	.275262	307.163	210.041	.000

[a] Dependent Variable: achieve.

TABLE 7.14   Mean Comparison

Achieve

Index1	Mean	N	Std. Deviation
1 Read	57.3826	2714	9.96458
2 Math	59.2117	2714	9.75239
3 Language	57.8124	2717	10.17472
Total	58.1355	8145	9.99479

TABLE 7.15   Estimates of Fixed Effects[a,b]

Contrast	Estimate	Std. Error	df	Test Value	t	Sig.
L1	−1.817489	.178245	291.209	0	−10.197	.000
L2	−.395412	.190470	288.024	0	−2.076	.039
L3	1.422077	.174792	300.792	0	8.136	.000

[a] Contrasts of Index1.
[b] Dependent Variable: achieve.

on outcomes is missing. Readers will also note that the grand mean for N = 8,145 observations is 58.14, which is close to the grand mean for achievement (58.18) in Table 7.5, with a listwise N of 8,151 observations.

We can also set up and conduct tests of contrasts for the effects in the model using the (/TEST) command (see Appendix A). We might, for example, envision a situation where we would like to test the difference between the means of a set of multiple responses (e.g., items or subtests). To illustrate how the tests might work, in Table 7.15 we set up the first contrast (L_1) to test the significance of the difference between the reading and math means (57.420866 − 59.238354 = −1.817488). The second contrast (L_2) is set up to test the difference between the reading and language means (57.420866 − 57.816277 = −0.395411). The third contrast is set up to test the difference between the math and language means (59.238354 − 57.816277 = 1.422077).

We can set up a similar type of test using the EEMEANS dialog box in SPSS Mixed. We provide procedures for conducting this test using the SPSS menu commands in the next section. Following are pairwise comparisons of the means for each subtest. In this table, the multiple comparisons have not been adjusted for the number of tests conducted (i.e., since the least significant difference approach was used to compare means). For example, in Table 7.16, the comparison between the reading (1) and language (3) means is significant (p = .039).

If we wish to adjust for the number of pairwise tests conducted, we can use the Bonferroni adjustment. This adjustment can be noted in Table 7.17, where the comparison between the math (1) and language (3) means is now not significant (p = .116).

TABLE 7.16   Pairwise Comparisons[b]

(I) Index1	(J) Index1	Mean Difference (I−J)	Std. Error	df	Sig.[a]
1	2	−1.817*	.178	291.209	.000
	3	−.395*	.190	288.024	.039
2	1	1.817*	.178	291.209	.000
	3	1.422*	.175	300.792	.000
3	1	.395*	.190	288.024	.039
	2	−1.422*	.175	300.792	.000

Note: Based on estimated marginal means.
* The mean difference is significant at the .05 level.
[a] Adjustment for multiple comparisons: Least Significant Difference (equivalent to no adjustments).
[b] Dependent Variable: achieve.

TABLE 7.17   Pairwise Comparisons[b]

(I) Index1	(J) Index1	Mean Difference (I–J)	Std. Error	df	Sig.[a]
1	2	–1.817*	.178	291.209	.000
	3	–.395	.190	288.024	.116
2	1	1.817*	.178	291.209	.000
	3	1.422*	.175	300.792	.000
3	1	.395	.190	288.024	.116
	2	–1.422*	.175	300.792	.000

Note: Based on estimated marginal means.
* The mean difference is significant at the .05 level.
[a] Adjustment for multiple comparisons: Bonferroni.
[b] Dependent Variable: achieve.

Testing for Contrasts Using EM Means With SPSS Menu Commands

Note: SPSS settings will default to those used for the Null Model.

1. Go to the SPSS toolbar and select ANALYZE, MIXED MODELS, LINEAR.

This command enables access to the *Linear Mixed Models: Specify Subjects and Repeated* dialog box.

2. The variables *schcode* and *Rid* (Rank of student id) appear in the *Subjects* box within the *Linear Mixed Models: Specify Subjects and Repeated* dialog box.

Index1 appears in the *Repeated* box and the designated covariance type is *Unstructured Correlation Metric*.

Click the CONTINUE button to display the *Linear Mixed Models* dialog box.

3. The variable *achieve* appears in the *Dependent Variable* box.
   a. Click to select *Index1*, then click the left-arrow button to remove the variable from the *Factor(s)* box.
   b. Click to select *female* and *Index1* from the left column listing, then click the right-arrow button to move the two variables into the *Factor(s)* box.

Note: An alternative method to Steps a and b is to add *female* into the *Covariate(s)* box, then drag it above *Index1*.

   c. Click to select *gmacadpress* then click the right arrow button to move the variable into the *Covariate(s)* box.

Click the FIXED button to access the *Linear Mixed Models: Fixed Effects* dialog box.

4a. Within the *Linear Mixed Models: Fixed Effects* dialog box confirm *Main Effects* is the selected factorial setting.

b. Click to select *Index1* from the *Factors and Covariates* box, then click the ADD button to move the variable into the *Model* box.

c. Confirm the *Include Intercept* box is deselected.

Click the CONTINUE button to return to the *Linear Mixed Models* dialog box.

5. Click the EM MEANS button to access the *Linear Mixed Models: EM Means* dialog box.

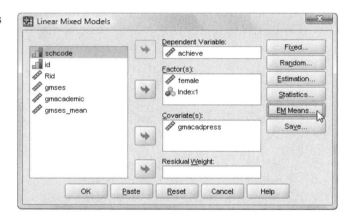

Selecting the LSD Confidence Interval Adjustment

6a. Click to select the *Overall* and *Index1* factors, then click the right-arrow button to move the two variables into the *Display Means for* box.

b. Click to select the *Compare main effects* option, which will also activate the *Confidence Interval Adjustment* submenu (c).

c. The *Confidence Interval Adjustment*s uses *LSD (none)* as the default setting so no further adjustment is needed.

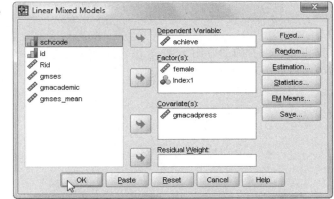

Click the CONTINUE button to return to the *Linear Mixed Models* dialog box.

7. The fixed and random effects, estimation, and statistics remain the same as those used for the Null Model, so click OK to run the model.

Selecting the Bonferroni Confidence Interval Adjustment

Note: SPSS settings will default to those used for the prior model with the LSD Confidence Level Adjustment.

8. Go to the SPSS toolbar and select ANALYZE, MIXED MODELS, LINEAR.

This command enables access to the *Linear Mixed Models: Specify Subjects and Repeated* dialog box.

9. The variables *schcode* and *Rid* (Rank of student id) appear in the *Subjects* box within the *Linear Mixed Models: Specify Subjects and Repeated* dialog box.

Index1 appears in the *Repeated* box and the designated covariance type is *Unstructured Correlation Metric*.

Click the CONTINUE button to display the *Linear Mixed Models* dialog box.

10. Within the *Linear Mixed Models* dialog box, click the EM MEANS button.

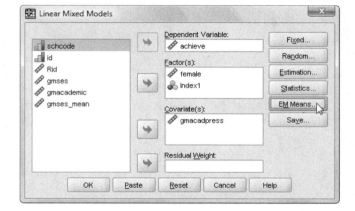

11a. Change the prior model's setting of *LSD (none)* by first clicking to select the *Compare main effects* option.

  b. Click the pull-down menu and select *Bonferroni*.

Then click the CONTINUE button to return to the *Linear Mixed Models* dialog box.

12. The fixed and random effects, estimation and statistics settings remain the same, so click OK to run the model.

Model 1: Building a Complete Model (Predictors and Cross-Level Interactions)
Defining Model 1 With SPSS Menu Commands

Note: SPSS settings will default to those used for the prior model constructed for Testing for Contrasts Using EM Means.

1. Go to the SPSS toolbar and select ANALYZE, MIXED MODELS, LINEAR.

This command enables access to the *Linear Mixed Models: Specify Subjects and Repeated* dialog box.

2. Within the *Linear Mixed Models: Specify Subjects and Repeated* dialog box, the variables *schcode* and *Rid* are in the *Subjects* box with *Index1* in the *Repeated* box.

The *Repeated Covariance Type* displays the prior model's setting of *Unstructured: Correlation Metric*.

Click the CONTINUE button to display the *Linear Mixed Models* dialog box.

3. In the *Linear Mixed Models* dialog box, the default setting from the prior model shows *achieve* (*Dependent Variable*), *female* and *Index1* (*Factors*), and *gmacadpress* (*Covariate*).

Click the FIXED button to access the *Linear Mixed Models: Fixed Effects* dialog box.

4. The *Linear Mixed Models: Fixed Effects* displays the *Random Effect 1 of 1* screen with default settings used for Model 1.

Adding Cross-Level Interactions to Model 1

*female*index1*

5a. Click to select the *Build nested terms* option.
 b. Click to select the variable *female* from the *Factors and Covariates* column.
 c. Click the down-arrow button to move *female* into the *Build Term* box.
 d. Click the BY* button to add the computational symbol (*) to the *Build Term* box.

e. Click to select the variable *Index1* from the *Factors and Covariates* column.

f. Click the down-arrow button to move *Index1* into the *Build Term* box.

g. Click the ADD button to move the term *female*Index1* into the *Model* box.

gmacadpress*index1

h. Repeat Step 5a through g to create the second interaction *gmacadpress*Index1* and add it to the *Model* box.

Click the CONTINUE button to return to the *Linear Mixed Models* dialog box. Before running the model, click the EM MEANS button, as settings used for the prior model will be removed first.

6. Within the *Linear Mixed Models: EM Means* box, click to select *(OVERALL)* and *Index1*, then click the left-arrow button to remove them from the *Display Means for* box.

Click the CONTINUE button to return to the *Linear Mixed Models* dialog box.

7. The random effects, estimation, and statistics settings remain the same as the prior model, so skip over these buttons and click OK to run the model.

Interpreting the Output of Model 1

The second model summarized in Table 7.18 presents the adjusted means (i.e., adjusted for gender), which are as follows: reading (M = 58.32), math (M = 58.47), and language (M = 56.11). Because we entered female as a categorical variable in this model (instead of a covariate), we see in Table 7.18 that there are estimates for female = 0 (i.e., male), but not for female = 1 (i.e., female). This is because when a categorical variable is used, SPSS Mixed declares the last category (i.e., female = 1) as the reference group. The output, therefore. will show estimates for the k − 1 categories comprising the variable. If one wishes to change the reference group, it is necessary to recode the variable. The output suggests that males score significantly lower than females (γ = −1.96, p < .01) in reading (*Index1* = 1, female = 0), but significantly higher than females in math (γ = 1.50, p < .01) and language (γ = 3.48, p < .01). Turning to the school portion of the model, we can observe that the school's academic press is positively related to students' achievement on each of the subtests (with γ coefficients ranging from 1.15 to 1.68 and p < .01).

For comparative purposes, we also provide the output for the same model if we defined female as a covariate instead of a categorical indicator. Table 7.19 reveals two noteworthy differences. First, the intercepts will be different. If we take the intercept from Table 7.18 for reading (58.318054) and subtract the coefficient for gender (1.962610), we get a coefficient of 56.355444,

TABLE 7.18 Estimates of Fixed Effects[b]

Parameter	Estimate	Std. Error	df	t	Sig.
[Index1=1]	58.318054	.304837	593.121	191.309	.000
[Index1=2]	58.465684	.318894	554.625	183.339	.000
[Index1=3]	56.109129	.321586	599.538	174.476	.000
[Index1=1] * [female=0]	−1.962610	.374561	2718.068	−5.240	.000
[Index1=2] * [female=0]	1.504663	.362285	2695.731	4.153	.000
[Index1=3] * [female=0]	3.476712	.377858	2709.759	9.201	.000
[Index1=1] * [female=1]	0[a]	0			
[Index1=2] * [female=1]	0[a]	0			
[Index1=3] * [female=1]	0[a]	0			
[Index1=1] * gmacadpress	1.589438	.267223	290.782	5.948	.000
[Index1=2] * gmacadpress	1.683026	.289915	304.594	5.805	.000
[Index1=3] * gmacadpress	1.148035	.288140	316.460	3.984	.000

[a] This parameter is set to zero because it is redundant.
[b] Dependent Variable: achieve.

TABLE 7.19 Estimates of Fixed Effects[a]

Parameter	Estimate	Std. Error	df	t	Sig.
[Index1=1]	56.355444	.314464	654.467	179.211	.000
[Index1=2]	59.970346	.327505	607.509	183.113	.000
[Index1=3]	59.585841	.330894	658.841	180.075	.000
[Index1=1] * female	1.962610	.374561	2718.068	5.240	.000
[Index1=2] * female	−1.504663	.362285	2695.731	−4.153	.000
[Index1=3] * female	−3.476712	.377858	2709.759	−9.201	.000
[Index1=1] * gmacadpress	1.589438	.267223	290.782	5.948	.000
[Index1=2] * gmacadpress	1.683026	.289915	304.594	5.805	.000
[Index1=3] * gmacadpress	1.148035	.288140	316.460	3.984	.000

[a] Dependent Variable: achieve.

which is the intercept for reading in Table 7.19. Second, the direction of the coefficients regarding gender is different, reflecting that when female (coded 1) is defined as a covariate, the reference group will now be males (coded 0). The coefficients in the model will now refer to females instead of males (as in Table 7.18).

Defining Gender and Academic Press as Covariates Using SPSS Menu Commands

1. To generate results shown in Tables 7.19 to 7.21, go to the SPSS toolbar and select ANALYZE, MIXED MODELS, LINEAR.

This command enables access to the *Linear Mixed Models: Specify Subjects and Repeated* dialog box.

2. Within the *Linear Mixed Models: Specify Subjects and Repeated* dialog box, the variables *schcode* and *Rid* in the *Subjects* box with *Index1* in the *Repeated* box.

The *Repeated Covariance Type* displays the prior model's setting of *Unstructured: Correlation Metric*.

Click the CONTINUE button to display the *Linear Mixed Models* dialog box.

3. In the *Linear Mixed Models* dialog box, the default setting from the prior model shows *achieve* (*Dependent Variable*), *female* and *Index1* (*Factors*), and *gmacadpress* (*Covariate*).
   a. Click to select *female*, then click the left-arrow button to remove the variable from the *Factor(s)* box.
   b. Click to select *gmacadpress*, then click the left-arrow button to remove the variable from the *Covariate(s)* box.
   c. Click to select *female* and *gmacadpress*, then click the right-arrow button to move the variables into the *Covariate(s)* box.

Note: An alternative method to Steps a and b is to remove *female* from the *Factor(s)* box, then add it into the *Covariate(s)* box, which places it below *gmacadpress*. Then drag the *female* variable above *gmacadpress*.

Click the FIXED button to access the *Linear Mixed Models: Fixed Effects* dialog box.

4 The cross-level interactions described in Model 1 need to be replicated and entered in the recommended sequence shown in the right-hand side of the screenshot.

   a. Click to select *gmacadpress*Index1*, then click the REMOVE button.

   b. Next create these two interactions and add each one into the *Model* box: *female*index1*, *gmacadpress*index1*.

(Refer to "Adding Cross-Level Interactions to Model 1" for instructions.)

Upon completion, click the CONTINUE button to return to the *Linear Mixed Models* dialog box.

5. The random effects, estimation, and statistics settings remain the same as the prior model, so skip over these buttons and click OK to run the model.

Testing the Hypotheses

We can examine whether the effect of gender and academic press are the same across the three subtests. The Type III (sum of squares) tests of the fixed effects (Table 7.20) provide this information. The significant *F*-ratios for female and academic press suggest the impact of each predictor is not the same across the subtests. We would, therefore, reject the null hypothesis for each variable.

Covariance Components

Finally, we turn our attention to the covariance components table (Table 7.21). Since we defined an unstructured covariance matrix (UNR), we will view variances in the diagonals (UN 1,1; UN 2,2; UN 3,3) and correlations in the off-diagonals of the matrix. The correlations represent the strength of relationship between the outcomes. For the repeated measures part, which we used to define the within-school variances, we see there is significant variance left to be explained for

TABLE 7.20 Type III Tests of Fixed Effects[a]

Source	Numerator *df*	Denominator *df*	F	Sig.
Index1	3	694.778	13222.772	.000
Index1 * female	3	2706.937	104.006	.000
Index1 * gmacadpress	3	297.284	14.136	.000

[a] Dependent Variable: achieve.

TABLE 7.21 Estimates of Covariance Parameters[a]

Parameter		Estimate	Std. Error	Wald Z	Sig.
Repeated Measures	Var(1)	88.602879	2.556595	34.657	.000
	Var(2)	80.254618	2.326169	34.501	.000
	Var(3)	88.498492	2.548169	34.730	.000
	Corr(2,1)	.666363	.011334	58.795	.000
	Corr(3,1)	.638314	.012051	52.969	.000
	Corr(3,2)	.690926	.010648	64.890	.000
Index1 [subject = schcode]	Var(1)	8.164823	1.581812	5.162	.000
	Var(2)	12.414012	1.883099	6.592	.000
	Var(3)	11.159258	1.797262	6.209	.000
	Corr(2,1)	.895673	.038246	23.419	.000
	Corr(3,1)	.863742	.045446	19.006	.000
	Corr(3,2)	.876464	.034085	25.714	.000

[a] Dependent Variable: achieve.

each subtest. At the individual level, the correlations between the subtests are all moderate and significant (ranging from 0.64 to 0.69 and $p < .01$). Between schools, there is also significant variation in intercepts left to be explained ($p < .01$). The correlations between subtests are also significant at the school level ($p < .01$) and are considerably stronger than the individual-level correlations (with coefficients ranging from 0.86 to 0.90).

Summary

In this chapter we presented two examples using a multilevel multivariate outcome. The composite (or latent construct) formulation is appropriate when one wishes to incorporate multiple measurements in defining constructs. Our first example provided a case where we estimated a construct with a simple error structure within individuals. Since the multilevel (i.e., vertical formulation) does not assume that all outcome data must be available for each individual, it provides another way for incorporating missing data into the analysis (Hox, 2002). We next showed how the repeated measures format at Level 1 can be used to define a multivariate type of model. We also demonstrated how it is possible to test the equality of regression coefficients across outcome measures in this type of modeling formulation.

This type of model can be extended and generalized to situations where the analyst wishes to examine more than one multivariate outcome, as in investigating parallel growth processes. For example, one might wish to examine growth in reading and math simultaneously. One way to develop this type of model is to stack the reading and math repeated measures in one achievement outcome. If each variable has three repeated observations, the *Index* variable will have six lines. A dummy variable can then be defined to specify each outcome. Linear and quadratic time-related variables can be added as needed to define each trajectory. Predictors can then be added within and between groups.

CHAPTER 8

Cross-Classified Multilevel Models

I n the models we have previously presented, the data structures have been purely hierarchical; that is, each individual was in only one Level 2 setting (e.g., a classroom) and only one Level 3 setting (e.g., a school). In this chapter we present situations where the nesting of subjects within groups is more complicated. Cross-classified data structures represent a special type of multilevel model. In school settings, for example, researchers are often interested in monitoring student progress longitudinally. This has proven difficult, however, since students move regularly (and irregularly) between classrooms and schools. Students may belong to more than one unit (e.g., classrooms) over time at a particular level of the data hierarchy. We might also be interested in studying how students transition from elementary schools to middle schools. In this latter case, within a particular state, students from several hundred elementary schools might transition to a hundred or so middle schools. Each student in the study, therefore, would be cross-classified by an elementary and middle school. Cross-classified hierarchical models extend the analytic tools available for studying student progress (Hill & Goldstein, 1998). Goldstein (1987), Hox (2002), and Raudenbush and Bryk (2002) provide general overviews of cross-classified models.

Students Cross-Classified in High Schools and Universities

Consider the contribution of students' high school and college settings to their undergraduate educational attainment. Students from any particular public high school may attend a number of different college campuses within a state's higher education system. In this first example, we examine whether student background and features of their high school and college entry point influence their college attainment. We will use students' cumulative grade point average (GPA; in the data set, the cumulative GPA variable is CUM_GPR) at the time they earned their highest undergraduate degree (associate or bachelor's) as the outcome.

Research Questions

Our first research question might ask simply: Do features of students' high school and college entry campuses affect their educational attainment, after controlling for student background? Second, we ask: Does the slope describing the effect of individual socioeconomic status (SES) on student college attainment vary randomly across either or both Level 2 units? Third, if it does vary randomly across units, are there high school and college variables that explain this variation?

The Data

In this subset of a larger data set, we randomly selected 1,767 students within 30 public high schools who entered college at 10 different campuses within a state's higher education system. This type of data is considered a two-level cross-classified data set, since we have students at Level 1 cross-classified in high schools and colleges at Level 2.

TABLE 8.1 SchlCode * Campus Cross-Tabulation

Count

		Campus										Total
		1	**2**	**3**	**4**	**5**	**6**	**7**	**8**	**9**	**10**	
SchlCode	1	2	1	41	9	0	1	1	0	0	3	58
	2	1	1	20	47	0	1	7	0	0	0	77
	3	1	0	16	41	0	0	1	0	0	0	59
	4	2	2	47	43	0	0	4	0	0	0	98
	5	1	1	40	25	0	0	5	0	0	0	72
	6	1	3	17	54	0	0	5	0	2	2	84
	7	2	0	26	25	1	29	2	0	0	1	86
	8	4	2	18	3	0	11	3	0	0	0	41
	9	3	6	27	15	1	68	7	0	0	2	129
	10	5	4	79	24	0	29	9	0	2	2	154
	11	0	0	14	7	0	3	2	0	0	1	27
	12	0	1	9	5	1	1	0	0	0	0	17
	13	1	3	17	8	0	13	1	0	0	2	45
	14	1	0	4	3	0	0	0	0	0	1	9
	15	1	4	35	16	0	58	6	0	0	1	121
	16	2	1	11	9	0	12	0	0	0	1	36
	17	0	2	33	13	0	26	3	0	0	1	78
	18	1	1	37	24	0	3	4	0	7	2	79
	19	2	1	8	2	0	3	1	0	4	0	21
	20	0	2	15	16	0	1	2	0	8	1	45
	21	1	0	17	7	0	1	2	0	3	0	31
	22	72	6	0	0	0	0	3	1	0	0	82
	23	23	3	1	0	0	0	0	1	0	0	28
	24	12	1	1	1	0	0	0	0	0	0	15
	25	9	0	2	0	0	0	0	0	0	0	11
	26	53	0	3	3	1	0	0	0	0	1	61
	27	5	2	0	0	0	0	0	0	0	0	7
	28	10	0	1	0	0	0	0	0	0	0	11
	29	107	8	0	0	0	0	2	0	0	1	118
	30	3	3	6	7	0	2	28	16	0	2	67
Total		325	58	545	407	4	262	98	18	26	24	1767

Using Raudenbush and Bryk's (2002) cross-classified terminology, in our example data matrix summarized in Table 8.1, at Level 2 we will consider high schools as the *row* data set (i.e., the larger number of Level 2 units) and colleges as the *column* data set. In the data matrix, therefore, each student at Level 1 is cross-classified by a row (high school) and column (college). The data set is considered cross-classified at Level 2 because students attend different high schools and different colleges. Readers will notice that the data in Table 8.1 are not balanced in either rows or columns. For example, in High School 1, 58 students entered the higher education system, primarily enrolling at College Campus 3. Moreover, there were five college campus cells that had small numbers of students (one to three students) and two campuses that did not receive any students from this particular high school. In this type of data configuration, the sample sizes vary considerably, and there are many cells with missing data. Typically, in a cross-classified model, the goal is to generalize from the sample to a population of high schools and college campuses. So the high school and college effects are treated as randomly varying.

The structure of the data allows us to examine the variance components in student attainment that exist *between high schools*, *between colleges*, and *within high school × college* cells. Within each high school–college cell, or the cross-classification, is a unique set of students. For example, 41 students attended High School 1 and College Campus 3. The within-cell model describes the variation among these students on an outcome of interest.

At Level 2, variation in outcomes between cells of students can be attributed to high school effects, college effects, or perhaps a school-by-college interaction. At this level, we can also develop a model to examine high school and college features on students' college attainment. In this case, we will use the mean percentage of low SES students as a high school composition variable that may influence student attainment, and a dummy variable for institutional type (i.e., 2-year or 4-year institution) as a possible college predictor of cumulative GPA. Of course, in this example the data set is a little small ($N = 10$ colleges), but it will suffice for purposes of our demonstration. We are limited, however, in the number of predictors we could use because of the small size of the college data set.

Descriptive Statistics

The descriptive statistics at student level and for the cross-classified Level 2 units are summarized in Tables 8.2, 8.3, and 8.4.

As a first model, we might examine the variance components in students' cumulative GPA that lie between high schools, between colleges, and within cells (i.e., high school × college cells). Following Goldstein (1994) and Hox (2002), at Level 1, this unconditional (no predictors) model can be defined as follows:

$$Y_{i(jk)} = \beta_{0(jk)} + \varepsilon_{i(jk)}, \tag{8.1}$$

where $Y_{i(jk)}$ is the cumulative GPA of student i within the cross-classification of high school j and college k; $\beta_{0(jk)}$ is the intercept (overall mean GPA) of students in cell jk, that is, students

TABLE 8.2   Descriptive Statistics

	N	Minimum	Maximum	Mean	Std. Deviation
female	1767	0	1	.51	.500
lowses	1767	0	1	.17	.375
CUM_GPR	1767	.00	4.00	2.9030	.63265
Valid *N* (listwise)	1767				

TABLE 8.3   Descriptive Statistics

	N	Minimum	Maximum	Mean	Std. Deviation
lowses_mean	30	.02	.46	.1752	.11480
Valid *N* (listwise)	30				

TABLE 8.4   Descriptive Statistics

	N	Minimum	Maximum	Mean	Std. Deviation
fouryear	10	0	1	.30	.483
Valid *N* (listwise)	10				

who attended high school j and college k; and $\varepsilon_{i(jk)}$ is the random student effect, that is, the deviation of student ijk's GPA from the cell mean. The residual is assumed to be normally distributed with the mean equal to zero and some variance (σ^2). The Level 1 residual can be further modeled to reflect more complex Level 1 variation if desired (Hill & Goldstein, 1998). The subscripts (jk) suggest that we assume the intercept varies independently across both high schools and colleges that are conceptually at the same level (Hox, 2002).

The Level 2, or "between cells," model is as follows:

$$\beta_{0(jk)} = \gamma_{00} + u_{0j} + \upsilon_{0k}, \tag{8.2}$$

where γ_{00} is the grand mean GPA for all students; u_{0j} is the residual error term for high school j, that is, the contribution of high school j averaged over all colleges; and υ_{0k} is the residual term for college k, that is, the contribution of college k averaged over all high schools. After substitution, we arrive at the intercept-only model,

$$Y_{i(jk)} = \gamma_{00} + u_{0j} + \upsilon_{0k} + \varepsilon_{i(jk)}, \tag{8.3}$$

where the outcome $Y_{i(jk)}$ is modeled with an overall intercept γ_{00}, an error term each for high schools and colleges, and the individual residual error term for student i in the cross-classification of high school j and college k. The single-equation model in Equation 8.3 implies three variance components (u_{0j}, υ_{0k}, $\varepsilon_{i(jk)}$) and one fixed effect (γ_{00}).

Defining Models in SPSS

SPSS is easy to use for investigating a variety of cross-classified models. Compared to models we have defined previously with nested hierarchical structures, it is relatively easy to define cross-classified structures. For a two-level cross-classified model, a random effect across high schools is referred to by using the "random" statements separately (i.e., RANDOM = high school identification code) and a random effect across colleges is referred to in a similar manner (RANDOM = college identification code). This is because the cross-classified part of the model is "independent" (i.e., students can go to different high schools and colleges). The definition of this type of cross-classified data structure is in contrast to the typical structure for a two-level nested model [(RANDOM = college code) and (RANDOM = college code*high school code)], where the statements would indicate students are nested in high schools and colleges. This latter data set would only consider students who went to the same high school and college campus.

First, we can consider the GPA intercept and the decomposition of variance across the various cells in the analysis (Table 8.5). The intercept for GPA for campuses was 2.72 ($SE = 0.129$).

Table 8.6 suggests most variance in student cumulative GPA is due to differences within individuals. As we might expect college campus attended contributes more to the total variance in GPA than high school campus.

Since within Level 2, the high school and colleges are considered to be independent, we can simply add the estimated variances in the no predictors model to obtain the total variance. We will estimate three intraunit variance components. The first is the intrarow correlation (i.e., high school), which represents the correlation between outcomes of any two students who attend

TABLE 8.5 Grand Mean[a]

Mean	Std. Error	95% Confidence Interval	
		Lower Bound	Upper Bound
2.717	.129	2.429	3.004

[a] Dependent Variable: CUM_GPR.

TABLE 8.6 Estimates of Covariance Parameters[a]

Parameter		Estimate	Std. Error	Wald Z	Sig.
Residual		.330751	.011307	29.252	.000
Intercept [subject = nschcode]	Variance	.036449	.014617	2.494	.013
Intercept [subject = campus]	Variance	.141920	.072572	1.956	.051

[a] Dependent Variable: CUM_GPR.

the same high school but attend different colleges. The intraunit correlation for high schools (*nschcode*) is therefore defined as

$$\rho_{HS} = \sigma^2_{HS} \Big/ \left(\sigma^2_{Student} + \sigma^2_{HS} + \sigma^2_{College} \right). \tag{8.4}$$

In this case, it can be calculated as .036449/(.330751 + .036449 + .141920) = .036449/.50912 = .072. This suggests that 7.2% of the total variance in students' cumulative GPA lies between the high schools they attended.

The intraunit correlation for colleges is the correspondence between outcomes of any two students who attend the same college but who attend different high schools:

$$\rho_{College} = \sigma^2_{College} \Big/ \left(\sigma^2_{Student} + \sigma^2_{HS} + \sigma^2_{College} \right). \tag{8.5}$$

This is estimated as .141920/(.330751 + .036449 + .141920) = .141920/.50912 = .279. This suggests 27.9% of the variation in students' cumulative GPAs lies between the colleges they attend. The remaining variation represents differences in GPA among students not accounted for by their high schools and colleges (roughly 65% of the variation).

Third, we can examine the correlation between outcomes of students who attended the same high school and college. This intracell component can be summarized as

$$\rho_{HS\text{-}College} = \sigma^2_{HS} + \sigma^2_{College} \Big/ \left(\sigma^2_{Student} + \sigma^2_{HS} + \sigma^2_{College} \right). \tag{8.6}$$

In this case, it is estimated as .036449 + .141920/(.330751 + .036449 + .141920) = .178369/.50912 = .350. Taken together, the correspondence in outcomes between two students who attend the same high school and college is 0.35. In other words, about 35% of the variance in cumulative GPA can be attributed to attending the same high school and college campus.

Model 1: Adding a Set of Level 1 and Level 2 Predictors

Next, we can add a set of student (Level 1) predictors to the model. In this case, we will add *female* (coded 1) and *lowSES* (code 1 = participation in federal free/reduced lunch program during high school, 0 = else). We grand-mean centered both variables and saved them in the data set. The Level 1 model is now

$$Y_{i(jk)} = \beta_{0(jk)} + \beta_{1(jk)} (gmfemale)_{i(jk)} + \beta_{2(jk)} (gmlowSES)_{i(jk)} + \varepsilon_{i(jk)}, \tag{8.7}$$

where $\beta_{0(jk)}$ is the intercept, $\beta_{1(jk)}$ and $\beta_{2(jk)}$ are structural coefficients, and $\varepsilon_{i(jk)}$ represents the Level 1 residual (mean = 0, σ^2). The regression slopes for the individual-level variables can be allowed to vary across high schools and/or colleges (as we have shown in past examples).

At Level 2, we might add high school and college predictors that explain students' grade point average. In this case, *gmlowSES_m* is an aggregate measure of socioeconomic composition for the high school and *gmfouryear* describes whether students were enrolled in a 2-year (community college) or 4-year postsecondary institution. The Level 2 intercept model is now

$$\beta_{0(jk)} = \gamma_{00} + \gamma_{01}(gmlowSES\_mean)_j + \gamma_{02}(gmfouryear)_k + u_{0j} + \upsilon_{0k}. \tag{8.8}$$

Defining Model 1 With SPSS Menu Commands

Launch the SPSS program application and select the *ch8crossclass1.sav* data file.

1. Go to the SPSS toolbar and select ANALYZE, MIXED MODELS, LINEAR.

This command enables access to the *Linear Mixed Models: Specify Subjects and Repeated* dialog box.

2a. Within the *Linear Mixed Models: Specify Subjects and Repeated* dialog box, click to select *nschcode* and *campus* variables from the left column, then click the arrow button to transfer the variables into the *Subjects* dialog box.

Click the CONTINUE button to display the *Linear Mixed Models* dialog box.

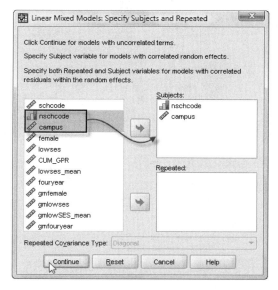

3a. In the *Linear Mixed Models* dialog box, click to select the *CUM_GPR* variable from the left column listing, then click the right-arrow button to move it into the *Dependent Variable* box.

b. Entering variables in sequential order helps facilitate reading of the output tables. Select the following variables and click on the right-arrow button to enter them into the *Covariate(s)* box in the following sequence: *gmfouryear, gmlowSES_mean, gmflowses,* and *gmfemale.*

Click the FIXED button to access the *Linear Mixed Models: Fixed Effects* dialog box.

4a. Within the *Linear Mixed Models: Fixed Effects* dialog box, locate the *Factorial* setting and click on the pull-down menu to select *Main Effects*.

b. Click to select the predictor variables *gmfouryear, gmlowSES_ mean, gmflowses,* and *gmfemale,* then click the ADD button to move the variables into the *Model* box.

c. Confirm *Include Intercept* is selected.

Click the CONTINUE button to return to the *Linear Mixed Models* dialog box. In the *Linear Mixed Models* dialog box, click the RANDOM button to access the *Linear Mixed Models: Random Effects* dialog box.

5. The *Linear Mixed Models: Random Effects* displays the *Random Effect 1 of 1* screen.

   a. Change the covariance type by clicking on the pull-down menu and selecting *Scaled Identity.*

   b. Click to select the *Include Intercept* option.

   c. In the *Factors and Covariates* listing, select *nschcode*, then click the ADD button to move the variable into the *Model* box.

   d. At the top-right section of the window, click the NEXT button to access the *Random Effect 2 of 2* screen.

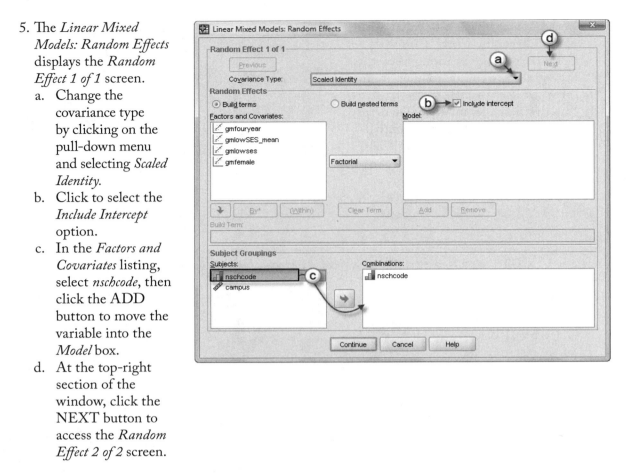

Note: The NEXT button may not work when creating multilevel models with random intercepts. This is a problem acknowledged by SPSS for assorted software versions including 18.0 and is resolved by adding then removing a covariate from the model which is described in Steps e and f and Step 6.

Workaround to Activate the Random Effects "Next" Button

e. Click to select a variable (*gmfemale* or other) from the *Factors and Covariates* box. Then click the ADD button to transfer the variable into the *Model* box, which activates the NEXT button (f).

f. Click NEXT to access the *Random Effect 2 of 2* screen.

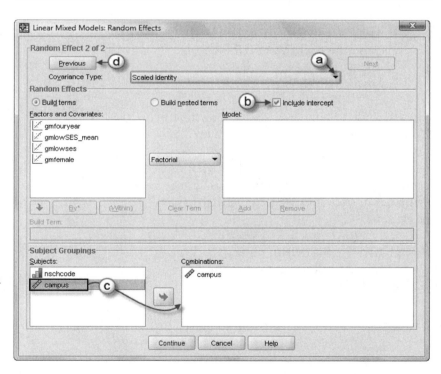

6. The *Random Effect 2 of 2* screen display is similar to the prior screen and requires the following changes.

a. Change the covariance type by clicking on the pull-down menu and selecting *Scaled Identity*.

b. Select *Include Intercept*.

c. In the *Subject Groupings* box, click to select *campus*, then click the right-arrow button to transfer the variable into the *Combinations* box.

d. Click the PREVIOUS button to return to the Level 1 screen.

7. Click to select the *gmfemale* variable, which was used as a workaround to activate the NEXT button. Then click the REMOVE button to remove *gmfemale* from the model.

Click the CONTINUE button to return to the *Linear Mixed Models* dialog box.

8. In the *Linear Mixed Models* dialog box, click on the ESTIMATION button to access the *Linear Mixed Models: Estimation* dialog box.

The estimation method choices are maximum likelihood (ML) or restricted maximum likelihood (REML). In this chapter, we will use restricted maximum likelihood (REML) to estimate the models since it produces better estimates in situations where sample size may be an issue.

Since REML is the default setting, click the CONTINUE button to return to the *Linear Mixed Models* dialog box.

9. In the *Linear Mixed Models* dialog box, click the STATISTICS button to access the *Linear Mixed Models: Statistics* dialog box.

Click and select the following three statistics: *parameter estimates*, *tests for covariance parameters*, and *covariances of random effects*.

Then click the CONTINUE button to return to the *Linear Mixed Models* dialog box.

10. Finally, in the *Linear Mixed Models* dialog box, click the OK button to run the model.

Interpreting the Output From Model 1

From the following fixed effects table (Table 8.7), we can see that of the Level 1 effects, females had significantly higher cumulative GPAs ($\gamma = 0.332$, $p < .01$); however, individual SES status did not affect cumulative GPA. At Level 2, aggregate high school social composition was significantly and negatively related to cumulative GPA ($\gamma = -1.220$, $p < .01$). Institutional type, however, was not related to cumulative GPA ($\gamma = 0.138$, $p = .655$).

TABLE 8.7 Estimates of Fixed Effects[a]

Parameter	Estimate	Std. Error	df	t	Sig.
Intercept	2.682485	.141610	9.070	18.943	.000
gmfouryear	.138241	.297549	7.933	.465	.655
gmlowSES_mean	−1.220484	.371416	32.478	−3.286	.002
gmflowses	.017483	.037044	1728.687	.472	.637
gmfemale	.331798	.027869	1735.674	11.905	.000

[a] Dependent Variable: CUM_GPR.

TABLE 8.8   Estimates of Covariance Parameters[a]

Parameter		Estimate	Std. Error	Wald Z	Sig.
Residual		.305205	.010417	29.300	.000
Intercept [subject = nschcode]	Variance	.030921	.011881	2.602	.009
Intercept [subject = campus]	Variance	.177112	.092989	1.905	.057

[a] Dependent Variable: CUM_GPR.

The variance component table (Table 8.8) suggests there was still significant variance in intercepts across high schools ($p < .01$) left to explain after the set of predictors was entered into the model. There is also still variance across colleges (Wald $Z = 1.905$, one-tailed $p = .0285$).

Model 2: Investigating a Random Slope

Level 2 high school or college variables can also be used to explain variation in Level 1 slopes. The Level 2 model can be expanded to include the random effect of gender on cumulative college GPA across high schools (u_{1j}) and colleges (v_{1k}). We first allow the female–GPA slope to vary randomly across both the high school and college they attend as follows:

$$\beta_{1(jk)} = \gamma_{10} + u_{1j} + v_{1k}, \tag{8.9}$$

where γ_{10} is the intercept, u_{1j} is the residual high school effect, and v_{1k} is the residual college effect. In this model, however, we do not attempt to explain this variation.

Defining Model 2 With SPSS Menu Commands

Note: SPSS settings will default to those used for Model 1.

1. Go to the SPSS toolbar and select ANALYZE, MIXED MODELS, LINEAR.

This command enables access to the *Linear Mixed Models: Specify Subjects and Repeated* dialog box.

2. Within the *Linear Mixed Models: Specify Subjects and Repeated* dialog box, the variables *nschcode* and *campus* are in the *Subjects* box.

Click the CONTINUE button to display the *Linear Mixed Models* dialog box.

3. In the *Linear Mixed Models* dialog box, the variable *CUM_GPR* is displayed as the *Dependent Variable*.

The *Covariate(s)* variables include *gmfouryear*, *gmlowSES_mean*, *gmlowses*, and *gmfemale*.

The fixed effects remain the same as the prior model, so click the RANDOM button to access the *Linear Mixed Models: Random Effects* dialog box.

4. The *Linear Mixed Models: Random Effects* displays the *Random Effect 1 of 2* screen with the default settings used for Model 1.

a. Change the covariance type by clicking on the pull-down menu and selecting *Diagonal.*

b. Confirm *Include Intercept* is selected.

c. Click the pull-down menu to change the factorial setting to *Main Effects.*

d. In the *Factors and Covariates* listing, select *gmfemale*, then click the ADD button to move the variable into the *Model* box.

e. Confirm the variable *nschcode* is in the *Combinations* box.

f. Click the NEXT button to access the *Random Effect 2 of 2* screen.

5. The *Linear Mixed Models: Random Effects* displays the *Random Effect 2 of 2* screen.

a. Change the covariance type by clicking on the pull-down menu and selecting *Diagonal.*

b. Confirm *Include Intercept* is selected.

c. Confirm the factorial setting is *Main Effects.*

d. In the *Factors and Covariates* listing, select *gmfemale,* then click the ADD button to move the variable into the *Model* box.

e. Confirm the variable *campus* is in the *Combinations* box.

f. Click the CONTINUE button to return to the *Linear Mixed Models* dialog box.

6. The estimation and statistics elements in the model remain the same settings as those used for Model 1, so click OK to run the model.

TABLE 8.9   Estimates of Covariance Parameters[a]

Parameter		Estimate	Std. Error	Wald Z	Sig.
Residual		.292921	.010149	28.863	.000
Intercept + gmfemale	Var: Intercept	.035683	.013054	2.734	.006
[subject = nschcode]	Var: gmfemale	.040300	.019642	2.052	.040
Intercept + gmfemale	Var: Intercept	.194063	.101705	1.908	.056
[subject = campus]	Var: gmfemale	.038094	.032979	1.155	.248

[a] Dependent Variable: CUM_GPR.

Interpreting the Output From Model 2

The variance components table (Table 8.9) suggests that the random slope (Var:*gmfemale*) varied across high schools (Wald $Z = 2.052$, one-tailed $p = .02$). However, the female–cumulative GPA slope did not vary across campuses (Wald $Z = 1.16$, one-tailed $p = .124$). One explanation for the observed lack of variation across colleges may be the small sample size.

Model 3: Explaining Variation Between Variables

Since the Level 1 slope varies across high school cells, for demonstration purposes, we will propose that a Level 2 variable explains variation in the relationship between female and cumulative GPA. We will propose that the social composition of students' high schools moderates (enhances or diminishes) the relationship between gender and cumulative GPA. The proposed cross-level interaction would look like this:

$$\beta_{1(jk)} = \gamma_{10} + \gamma_{11}(gmlowSES\_mean * gmfemale)_j + u_{1j}. \tag{8.10}$$

Equation 8.10 assumes that the random slope varies across high schools (u_{1j}) but not colleges (i.e., υ_{1k} from Equation 8.9 has been removed from the equation). This cross-level interaction can be interpreted as the effect of gender on attainment when the effect of high school social composition is controlled. For this model, in the intercept equation (see Equation 8.8) we will remove the *gmfouryear* variable explaining cumulative GPA, since it was not significant in the previous model.

Defining Model 3 With SPSS Menu Commands

Note: SPSS settings will default to those used for Model 2.

1. Go to the SPSS toolbar and select ANALYZE, MIXED MODELS, LINEAR.

This command enables access to the *Linear Mixed Models: Specify Subjects and Repeated* dialog box.

2. Within the *Linear Mixed Models: Specify Subjects and Repeated* dialog box, the variables *nschcode* and *campus* appear in the *Subjects* box.

Click the CONTINUE button to display the *Linear Mixed Models* dialog box.

3. In the *Linear Mixed Models* dialog box, the variable *CUM_GPR* is displayed as the *Dependent Variable.*

Click to select *gmfouryear* from the *Covariate(s)* box, then click the left-arrow button to remove the variable. This will leave three variables in *Covariate(s): gmlowSES_mean, gmflowses,* and *gmfemale.*

Click the FIXED button to access the *Linear Mixed Models: Fixed Effects* dialog box.

4. The *Linear Mixed Models: Fixed Effects* screen displays the default settings used for Model 1.

Creating a Cross-Level Interaction

gmlowSES_mean*gmfemale

a. Click to select the *Build nested terms* option.
b. Click to select the variable *gmlowSES_mean* from the *Factors and Covariates* column.
c. Click the down-arrow button to move *gmlowSES_mean* into the *Build Term* box.
d. Click the BY* button to add the computational symbol (*) to the *Build Term* box.
e. Confirm *Include intercept* is selected.

f. Click to select the variable *gmfemale* from the *Factors and Covariates* column.

g. Click the down arrow button to move *gmfemale* into the *Build Term* box.

h. Click the ADD button to move the term *gmlowSES_ mean*mathselect* into the *Model* box.

Click the CONTINUE button to return to the *Linear Mixed Models* dialog box. Then click the RANDOM button to access the *Random Effect 2 of 2* screen.

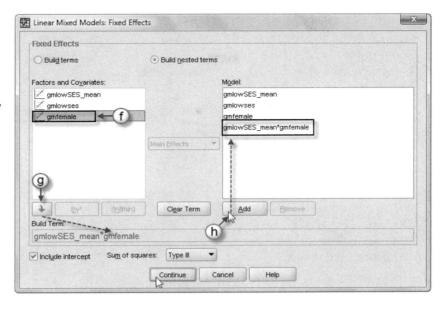

5a. In the *Random Effect 2 of 2* screen, change the covariance type by clicking on the pull-down menu and selecting *Scaled Identity*.

b. Confirm *Include intercept* is selected.

c. Confirm *Main Effects* is selected.

d. Confirm *gmlowSES_ mean*, *gmflowses*, and *gmfemale* are displayed.

e. Click to select *gmfemale*, then click the REMOVE button to withdraw the variable from the *Model*.

f. Confirm *campus* is in the *Combinations* box.

g. Click the NEXT button to access the *Random Effect 1 of 2* screen.

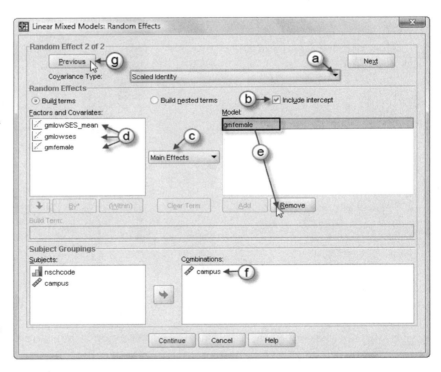

6a. In the *Random Effect 1 of 2* screen the *Diagonal* covariance type setting remains unchanged.

b. Confirm *Include intercept* is selected.

c. Confirm *gmfemale* is displayed in the *Model* box.

d. Confirm *nschcode* is in the *Combinations* box.

Click the CONTINUE button to return to the *Linear Mixed Models* dialog box.

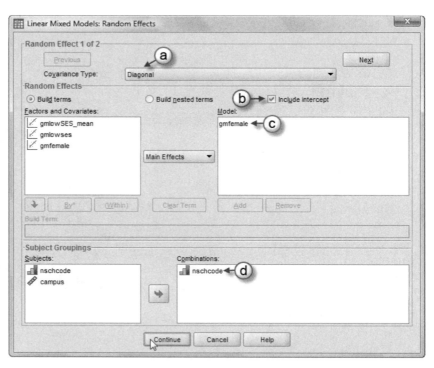

7. The estimation and statistics settings remain the same as Model 2, so click OK to run the model.

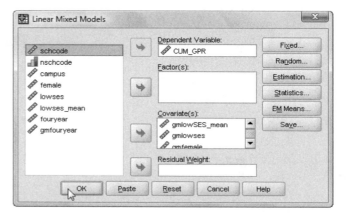

Interpreting the Output From Model 3

The fixed effects table (Table 8.10) suggests the intercept model remains about the same as before. Regarding the model to explain random slopes, the positive Level 1 female–cumulative GPA slope was moderated by high school social composition ($\gamma = -1.400$, $p < .01$). This finding is consistent with factor*covariate interactions, suggesting that slopes differ across levels of the factor. In this case, we can interpret the result as the impact of gender on cumulative GPA

TABLE 8.10   Estimates of Fixed Effects[a]

Parameter	Estimate	Std. Error	df	t	Sig.
Intercept	2.677494	.139997	10.201	19.125	.000
gmlowSES_mean	−1.200817	.383515	32.258	−3.131	.004
gmflowses	.014473	.036696	1718.681	.394	.693
gmfemale	.275125	.042353	25.535	6.496	.000
gmlowSES_mean * gmfemale	−1.400143	.428123	26.800	−3.270	.003

[a] Dependent Variable: CUM_GPR.

TABLE 8.11 Estimates of Covariance Parameters[a]

Parameter		Estimate	Std. Error	Wald *Z*	Sig.
Residual		.297447	.010251	29.017	.000
Intercept + gmfemale	Var: Intercept	.034095	.012805	2.663	.008
[subject = nschcode]	Var: gmfemale	.020457	.012779	1.601	.109
Intercept [subject = campus]	Variance	.171680	.085602	2.006	.045

[a] Dependent Variable: CUM_GPR.

when the social composition in students' high school is held constant; that is, indicating that the female–cumulative GPA slope (0.28, $p < .05$) also depends on high school composition (–1.40, $p < .05$). Combining the coefficients suggests the female coefficient is –1.12 (–1.40 + .28 = –1.12), when social composition is controlled. Therefore, when high school social composition is held constant (i.e., at the grand mean of 0), the advantage in cumulative GPA for females reported in the table (i.e., 0.28) actually disappears. Of course, this type of social composition variable is likely a proxy for more complex relationships in students' academic preparation for doing post-secondary work that might exist across high school settings within the state.

The variance component table (Table 8.11) suggests that there is still intercept variance (average GPA) to be explained between high schools (Wald $Z = 2.663$, one-tailed $p < .01$) and colleges (Wald $Z = 2.006$, one-tailed $p < .05$). After adding the random slope, there is still significant variance to be explained in the gender–GPA slopes across high schools (Wald $Z = 1.601$, one-tailed $p = .0495$).

Developing a Cross-Classified Teacher Effectiveness Model

Our second example considers the effects of teacher effectiveness on students' outcomes in math. It is similar to our example in Chapter 4, except this time we examine the effects of successive teachers' effectiveness on students' current math scores. Multilevel models hold promise for examining the contributions of successive teachers and schools to student learning because they make better use of the available information than more simplified analyses (Thum, 2003). More specifically, over time students are clustered in classrooms with teachers of differing skills and effectiveness, and in schools with differing community expectations, teacher skills, and academic processes. School factors can moderate learning conditions within classrooms (e.g., prolonged grouping assignments, differential access to curriculum, inconsistent academic experiences for students within a particular grade level). Students, therefore, share similarities with peers within these hierarchical social groupings. The sum of these varied learning contexts enhances or diminishes students' academic outcomes in direct and indirect ways.

The Data Structure and Model

In this example, we use a subset of student data ($N = 4,136$) cross-classified by two successive classrooms at Level 2 (i.e., identified by 324 Year 1 teachers and 259 Year 2 teachers). At Level 3, the students attend 81 elementary schools. The data structure is different from the three-level model in Chapter 4 (i.e., students nested within classrooms within schools) because at the classroom level the data are "cross-classified"—that is, any two students in the cohort can have different combinations of Year 1 and Year 2 teachers (i.e., both teachers in common, one teacher in common, no teachers in common).

The cross-classification of students by their previous and current teachers facilitates the accuracy of estimating the effects of successive teachers on student outcomes within the same model. One limitation to keep in mind about cross-classified models in examining the effects of successive teachers, however, is that the model assumes the effects of previous teachers do not diminish (i.e., since each classroom contributes independently) in explaining the current

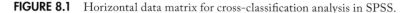

FIGURE 8.1   Horizontal data matrix for cross-classification analysis in SPSS.

achievement level (McCaffrey, Lockwood, Koretz, & Hamilton, 2003). The data structure in this example is similar to that in Figure 8.1.

Figure 8.1 indicates Student 1 and Student 2 have the same first-year teacher and second-year teacher. Students 3 and 4 have the same first-year teacher as the previous two students but different second-year teachers. Students 5 and 6 have different first-year and second-year teachers from each other, but Student 5 has the same second-year teacher as Student 4. All six of the students (with different configurations of first and second teachers) attend the same school (1). Student 7 begins a different school (2) and combination of teachers. Because we are focusing on two measurement occasions, this approach is similar to a type of gain score achievement model or a model that uses previous achievement as a control variable.

We reiterate that for cross-classified models, each RANDOM command identifies a separate cell or level. Their order does not matter. With cross-classified data structures, we need to use the unique Teacher 1 and Teacher 2 identifiers at Level 2 and not recode (i.e., rank) them within each school $(1, \ldots, n_k)$. The use of unique teacher identifiers generally will result in longer computing time needed for estimating cross-classified models compared with similar nested multilevel models. For this example, we reduced the student part of the data set substantially (i.e., from over 9,000 students to 4,136 students) and also reduced the number of Year 1 and Year 2 teachers and schools in order to decrease the time it takes to run the model from well over 1 hour to the present 4 to 5 minutes (on the final models). We note that the cost of reducing the data for demonstrating the approach, however, is a model that is a bit more challenging to fit optimally in terms of the our substantive goals (e.g., the variability in intercepts and slopes across units is reduced).

Research Questions

In this cross-classified example, we can address a number of different types of research questions. For example, we might first consider: How much variance in students' math achievement is due to their previous and current classroom settings? In examining this question, we can consider whether the intercepts describing levels of Year 2 student achievement vary across classrooms and schools. A second question we might investigate is the following: Does the effectiveness of successive teachers have a measurable effect on students' Year 2 achievement levels? Subsequently, we could also investigate whether teacher effectiveness varies across classrooms and/or schools. Third, we might ask: Does a particular variable (or set) explain possible variation in teacher effectiveness?

Model 1: Intercept-Only Model

We will begin with an intercept-only model. This model represents the average achievement score across all individuals and occasions. It provides a preliminary estimate of the repeated measures variance, the classroom-level variance, and the school-level variance. Within individuals (Level 1), the model is the following:

$$Y_{i(j1j2)k} = \pi_{0(j1j2)k} + \varepsilon_{i(j1j2)k} , \qquad (8.11)$$

where $Y_{i(j1j2)k}$ is the math outcome for individual i cross-classified in classrooms j_1 and j_2 in school k, $\pi_{0(j1j2)k}$ is the intercept, and $\varepsilon_{i(j1j2)k}$ is the residual term for individual-level model.

At Level 2, the intercept model is

$$\pi_{0(j1j2)k} = \beta_{00k} + u_{j1k} + u_{j2k}, \qquad (8.12)$$

where β_{00k} is the intercept, u_{j1k} and u_{j2k} are residuals associated with Classroom 1 and Classroom 2 in school k.

At level 3, the basic model is

$$\beta_{00k} = \gamma_{000} + \upsilon_{00k}. \qquad (8.13)$$

Through substitution, the basic random-intercept model can be specified as follows:

$$Y_{i(j1j2)k} = \gamma_{000} + \upsilon_{00k} + u_{j1k} + u_{j2k} + \varepsilon_{i(j1j2)k} , \qquad (8.14)$$

where γ_{000} is the grand mean of achievement for schools; and v, u, and ε represent residuals (i.e., normally and independently distributed in the population with an expected mean equal to zero and some variance) associated with schools, classrooms, and students, respectively. Equation 8.14 implies five parameters that must be estimated (four variance components and one fixed effect). We can confirm the five estimated effects from the print out from Model 1 (Table 8.12).

TABLE 8.12   Model Dimension[a]

		Number of Levels	Covariance Structure	Number of Parameters	Subject Variables
Fixed Effects	Intercept	1		1	
Random Effects	Intercept	1	Identity	1	schcode
	Intercept	1	Identity	1	teach2id
	Intercept	1	Identity	1	teach1id
Residual				1	
Total		4		5	

[a] Dependent Variable: math2.

Defining Model 1 With SPSS Menu Commands

Select the *ch8crossclass2.sav* data file.

1. Go to the SPSS toolbar and select ANALYZE, MIXED MODELS, LINEAR.

This command enables access to the *Linear Mixed Models: Specify Subjects and Repeated* dialog box.

2. Within the *Linear Mixed Models: Specify Subjects and Repeated* dialog box, click to select *schcode, teach1id*, and *teach2id* variables from the left column, then click the arrow button to transfer the variables into the *Subjects* dialog box.

Click the CONTINUE button to display the *Linear Mixed Models* dialog box.

3. In the *Linear Mixed Models* dialog box, click to select the *math2* variable from the left column listing, then click the right arrow button to move it into the *Dependent Variable* box.

Click the RANDOM button to access the *Linear Mixed Models: Random Effects* dialog box.

4. The *Linear Mixed Models: Random Effects* displays the *Random Effect 1 of 1* screen.

   a. Change the covariance type by clicking on the pull-down menu and selecting *Scaled Identity*.

   b. Select *Include Intercept*.

   c. In the *Factors and Covariates* listing, select *schcode*, then click the ADD button to move the variable into the *Model* box.

   d. At the top-right section of the window, click the NEXT button to access the *Random Effect 2 of 2* screen.

Note: The NEXT button may not work when creating multilevel models with random intercepts. This is a problem acknowledged by SPSS for assorted software versions including 18.0 and is resolved by adding then removing a covariate from the model, which is described in Steps e through i and Step 5.

Workaround to Activate the Random Effects "Next" Button

e. Click the CONTINUE button to return to the *Linear Mixed Models* dialog box.

f. Click to select a variable (*lowses* or other), then click the ADD button to transfer the variable into the *Covariate(s)* box.

Click the RANDOM button to return to the *Random Effect 1 of 1* screen.

g. Click to select the variable *lowses* from the *Factors and Covariates* box. Then click the ADD button to transfer the variable into the *Model* box, which activates the NEXT button (i).

h. Click the REMOVE button to remove *lowses* from the model.

i. Click NEXT to access the *Random Effect 2 of 2* screen.

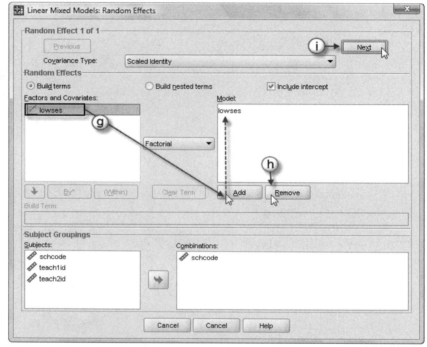

5. The *Random Effect 2 of 2* screen display is similar to the first screen and requires the following changes.

   a. Change the covariance type by clicking on the pull-down menu and selecting *Scaled Identity*.

   b. Select *Include Intercept*.

   c. In the *Subject Groupings* box, click to select *teach2id*, then click the right-arrow button to transfer the variable into the *Combinations* box.

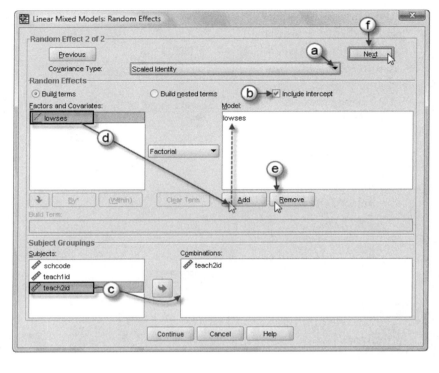

Workaround to Activate the Random Effects "Next" Button

   d. Click to select the variable *lowses* from the *Factors and Covariates* box. Then click the ADD button to transfer the variable into the *Model* box, which activates the NEXT button (f).

   e. Click the REMOVE button to remove *lowses* from the model.

   f. Click NEXT to access the *Random Effect 3 of 3* screen.

6. The *Random Effect 3 of 3* screen display is similar to the prior screens and requires the following changes.

a. Change the covariance type by clicking on the pull-down menu and selecting *Scaled Identity*.

b. Select *Include Intercept*.

c. In the *Factors and Covariates* listing, select *teach1id*, then click the ADD button to move the variable into the *Model* box.

Click the CONTINUE button to return to the *Linear Mixed Models* dialog box.

7. In the *Linear Mixed Models* dialog box, click to select *lowses*, then click the left-arrow button to remove the variable.

8. In the *Linear Mixed Models* dialog box, click on the ESTIMATION button to access the *Linear Mixed Models: Estimation* dialog box.

The estimation method choices are maximum likelihood (ML) or restricted maximum likelihood (REML).

We will continue to use restricted maximum likelihood (REML) to estimate the models, so click the CONTINUE button to return to the *Linear Mixed Models* dialog box.

9. In the *Linear Mixed Models* dialog box, click the STATISTICS button to access the *Linear Mixed Models: Statistics* dialog box.

Click and select the following three statistics: *parameter estimates*, *tests for covariance parameters*, and *covariances of random effects*.

Then click the CONTINUE button to return to the *Linear Mixed Models* dialog box.

10. Finally, in the *Linear Mixed Models* dialog box, click the OK button to run the model.

Model 2: Defining the Cross-Classified Model With Previous Achievement

For Model 2, we will add a covariate for previous achievement with a fixed (i.e., the same) coefficient for all persons; that is, we will first treat the effect as fixed across classrooms and schools. In defining the Level 1 model, we now account for previous achievement at Level 1. The Level 1 model is now

$$Y_{i(j1j2)k} = \pi_{0(j1j2)k} + \pi_{1(j1j2)k}(zmath1)_{i(j1j2)k} + \varepsilon_{i(j1j2)k}, \tag{8.15}$$

where, in addition to the parameters previously described, $\pi_{1(j1j2)k}$ represents effect of beginning math achievement on Year 2 achievement. Entering previous achievement as a covariate is similar to creating a gain score model, since there are only two achievement measurements in the model (see McCaffrey et al., 2003, for further discussion of teacher effectiveness models).

At the classroom level, we will consider beginning math achievement as fixed across classrooms:

$$\pi_{1(j1j2)k} = \beta_{10k}. \tag{8.16}$$

At Level 3 (school level), the equation with a fixed slope for previous achievement is the following:

$$\beta_{10k} = \gamma_{100}. \tag{8.17}$$

From Equation 8.14, after substitution, the basic random-intercept model can be specified as follows:

$$Y_{i(j1j2)k} = \gamma_{000} + \gamma_{100} + v_{00k} + u_{j1k} + u_{j2k} + \varepsilon_{i(j1j2)k}, \tag{8.18}$$

where γ_{000} is the grand mean of achievement for schools adjusted for initial scores; γ_{100} is the grand mean for previous achievement for schools; and v, u, and ε represent residuals (i.e., normally and independently distributed in the population with expected mean values equal to zero and some variance) associated with schools, classrooms, and students, respectively.

Defining Model 2 With SPSS Menu Commands

Note: SPSS settings will default to those used for Model 1.

1. Go to the SPSS toolbar and select ANALYZE, MIXED MODELS, LINEAR.

This command enables access to the *Linear Mixed Models: Specify Subjects and Repeated* dialog box.

2. Within the *Linear Mixed Models: Specify Subjects and Repeated* dialog box, the variables *schcode*, *teach1id*, and *teach2id* appear in the *Subjects* box.

Click the CONTINUE button to display the *Linear Mixed Models* dialog box.

3. In the *Linear Mixed Models* dialog box, the variable *math2* is displayed as the *Dependent Variable. Zmath1* appears in the *Covariate(s)* box.

Click the FIXED button to access the *Linear Mixed Models: Fixed Effects* dialog box.

4a. Within the *Linear Mixed Models: Fixed Effects* dialog box, locate the *Factorial* setting and click on the pull-down menu to select *Main Effects*.

b. Click to select *Zmath1*, then click the ADD button to move the variable into the *Model* box.

c. Confirm *Include Intercept* is selected.

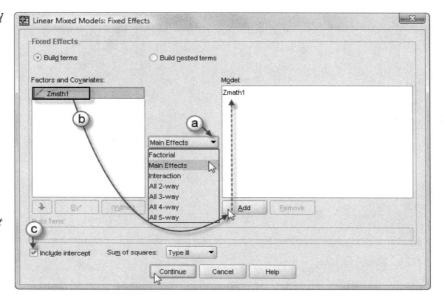

Click the CONTINUE button to return to the *Linear Mixed Models* dialog box. In the *Linear Mixed Models* dialog box.

5. The random effects, estimation, and statistics settings remain the same from Model 1, so click OK to run the model.

Interpreting the Output From Models 1 and 2

Model 1 (no predictors). Before we begin our analyses, we can examine the distribution of math achievement in the data file with 4,136 students. The fixed effect part of the model (Table 8.13) includes only the Level 3 intercept (or grand mean) for Year 2 math. The grand mean is 654.13 (SE = 2.05).

The variance components table (Table 8.14) suggests most of the variance is due to differences in individuals (Residual = 1482.26), with about 14.7% of the total variation due to schools (i.e., 266.73/1810.79 = 0.147), and trivial amounts of variance (about 2%) due to Teacher 2 and Teacher 1 in this subset of the data. As a comparison, in the full data set, the initial estimates for Classroom 1 variance was 4%, and for Classroom 2 variance it was 7%.

Model 2. In Model 2, we add the standardized (M = 0, SD = 1) previous achievement variable, which changes the intercept (which now represents achievement at Time 2 adjusted for beginning achievement) to 653.48. Previous math achievement affects subsequent achievement (γ_{100} = 28.62, p < .01). This coefficient suggests a 1 SD increase in *Zmath1* would produce a 28.62 point increase in the Math 2 score (Table 8.15).

If we compare the variance components of Model 1 (Table 8.14) and Model 2 (Table 8.16), we see that entering previous achievement variable into the model decreases the Level 1 variance

TABLE 8.13 Estimates of Fixed Effects[a]

Parameter	Estimate	Std. Error	df	t	Sig.
Intercept	654.130803	2.047298	77.947	319.509	.000

[a] Dependent Variable: math2.

TABLE 8.14 Estimates of Covariance Parameters[a]

Parameter		Estimate	Std. Error	Wald Z	Sig.
Residual		1482.261049	34.592037	42.850	.000
Intercept [subject = schcode]	Variance	266.734212	52.720395	5.059	.000
Intercept [subject = teach2id]	Variance	35.184299	15.157967	2.321	.020
Intercept [subject = teach1id]	Variance	26.622300	12.914820	2.061	.039

[a] Dependent Variable: math2.

TABLE 8.15 Estimates of Fixed Effects[a]

Parameter	Estimate	Std. Error	df	t	Sig.
Intercept	653.481781	1.313344	82.082	497.571	.000
Zmath1	28.620261	.472731	4066.184	60.542	.000

[a] Dependent Variable: math2.

TABLE 8.16 Estimates of Covariance Parameters[a]

Parameter		Estimate	Std. Error	Wald Z	Sig.
Residual		767.059705	17.907210	42.835	.000
Intercept [subject = schcode]	Variance	83.982953	20.878635	4.022	.000
Intercept [subject = teach2id]	Variance	38.201680	9.855199	3.876	.000
Intercept [subject = teach1id]	Variance	54.160377	11.229458	4.823	.000

[a] Dependent Variable: math2.

considerably (i.e., from 1482.26 to 767.06). This represents a reduction in variance (or R^2) of about 48.3% (715.2/1482.26 = 0.483). Notice also, however, that the size of the Classroom 1 variance (σ^2_{class1} = 54.16) and Classroom 2 variance (σ^2_{class2} = 38.20) components are somewhat larger than in Model 1.

As Hox (2002) notes, this often occurs in multilevel analyses, but makes it unclear which variance components to use in establishing a baseline model. As we noted in Chapter 1, this result can occur because the amount of variance explained is not a simple concept in multilevel modeling (Snijders & Bosker, 1994). As Hox explains, the sampling process in multilevel designs creates some between-group variability in all Level 1 variables even if there are in fact no real group differences in the population. The variability at successive levels (e.g., Level 2 or Level 3) may be much greater than the model assumes in calculating initial variance components, such that the intercept-only model (Model 1) can overestimate the variance at Level 1 and may underestimate the variance at Level 2 (Hox, 2002).

Model 2, with the previous achievement variable added, estimates the variance accounted for in the dependent variable and, conditional on this effect, the variance components estimated for Level 2 may be a bit more accurately estimated. Hox (2002) suggests using the classroom variance components from Model 2 as the baseline from which to make comparisons in variance reduction. We note in passing that after accounting for previous achievement in our example, the variance in remaining math achievement at the classroom level is about 6% for Class 1 and 4% for Class 2.

Model 3: Adding Teacher Effectiveness and a Student Background Control

We can next add the teacher effectiveness variables to the model. Individual teachers were evaluated from 0 to 10 in terms of their classroom effectiveness in facilitating student learning (after adjustment for student composition) based on their previous student cohort. The effectiveness scores were then transferred into the current student cohort. We display the variation in effectiveness scores in the following tables. Table 8.17 and Table 8.18 suggest that teacher effectiveness was distributed similarly across both sets of classrooms in this sample data set.

In Model 2, at Level 1 we will add a control for student SES:

$$Y_{i(j1j2)k} = \pi_{0(j1j2)k} + \pi_{1(j1j2)k}(zmath1)_{i(j1j2)k} + \pi_{2(j1j2)k}(lowses)_{i(j1j2)k} + \varepsilon_{i(j1j2)k}. \tag{8.19}$$

At Level 2, the model to explain intercepts can now be defined as

$$\pi_{0(j1j2)k} = \beta_{00k} + \beta_{01k}(teacheff1)_{(j1j2)k} + \beta_{02k}(teacheff2)_{(j1j2)k} + u_{j1k} + u_{j2k}. \tag{8.20}$$

TABLE 8.17 Descriptive Statistics

	N	Minimum	Maximum	Mean	Std. Deviation
effmath1	324	0	10	5.15	2.959
Valid N (listwise)	324				

TABLE 8.18 Descriptive Statistics

	N	Minimum	Maximum	Mean	Std. Deviation
Effmath2	259	0	10	5.01	2.293
Valid N (listwise)	259				

In this model, we will first assume that teacher effects do not vary randomly across schools:

$$\beta_{01k} = \gamma_{010},\qquad(8.21)$$

$$\beta_{02k} = \gamma_{020}.\qquad(8.22)$$

We might also consider any number of classroom controls at this level (e.g., aggregated socioeconomic status of students in the classroom, aggregated academic background of students, information about teachers' experience and other background characteristics). Because the teacher effectiveness scores were previously adjusted for student composition, we note that it is generally redundant to add similar background controls (e.g., SES) at both the student and classroom levels or to add similar controls (e.g., SES) for both classrooms, since it would not be expected that there would be much difference in the classroom demographics within schools (or over time). This could change if schools grouped students within classrooms in some particular manner (e.g., by previous math ability).

Defining Model 3 With SPSS Menu Commands

Note: SPSS settings will default to those used for Model 2.

1. Go to the SPSS toolbar and select ANALYZE, MIXED MODELS, LINEAR.

This command enables access to the *Linear Mixed Models: Specify Subjects and Repeated* dialog box.

2. Within the *Linear Mixed Models: Specify Subjects and Repeated* dialog box, the variables *schcode, teach1id,* and *teach2id* appear in the *Subjects* box.

Click the CONTINUE button to display the *Linear Mixed Models* dialog box.

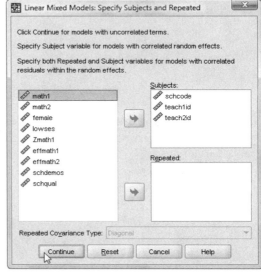

3. In the *Linear Mixed Models* dialog box, the variable *math2* is displayed as the *Dependent Variable.*
   a. Click to select *Zmath1*, then click the left-arrow button to remove the variable from the *Covariate(s)* box.
   b. Select the following variables and click on the right-arrow button to enter them into the *Covariate(s)* box in the following sequence: *effmath2, effmath1, Zmath1,* and *lowses.*

Note: An alternative method to Steps a and b is to add the variables into the *Covariates* box while retaining *Zmath1.* Then the variables may be arranged into the recommended sequence by selecting and dragging them. (Click to select a variable, hold down the left button on the mouse, then drag the variable into position.)

Click the FIXED button to access the *Linear Mixed Models: Fixed Effects* dialog box.

4a. Confirm that *Main Effects* is the selected factorial setting.

b. Click to select the variables *effmath2, effmath1, Zmath1,* and *lowses*, then click the ADD button to move the variable into the *Model* box.

c. Confirm *Include Intercept* is selected.

Click the CONTINUE button to return to the *Linear Mixed Models* dialog box.

5. The random effects, estimation, and statistics settings remain the same from Model 2, so click OK to run the model.

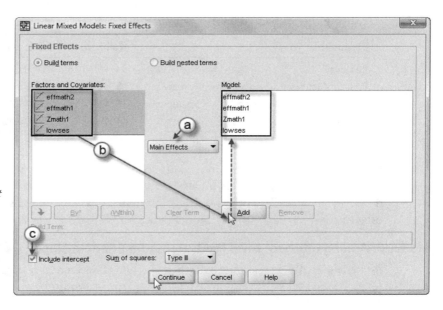

Interpreting the Output From Model 3

The fixed effect estimates (Table 8.19) suggest that in this subset of the data, the effectiveness of the first teacher ($\gamma = 1.09$, $p < .01$) contributed slightly more to ending math outcomes than the effectiveness of the second teacher ($\gamma = 0.73$, $p = .01$). Both effects, however, would be considered relatively small.

The variance components table (Table 8.20) suggests that after adding the teacher effects for Classroom 1 and Classroom 2 to the model, there is still variance in Year 2 achievement levels

TABLE 8.19 Estimates of Fixed Effects[a]

Parameter	Estimate	Std. Error	df	t	Sig.
Intercept	646.388745	2.260741	361.609	285.919	.000
effmath2	.733034	.283044	175.141	2.590	.010
effmath1	1.092727	.225024	225.841	4.856	.000
Zmath1	28.425596	.487430	4077.812	58.317	.000
lowses	−4.498367	.973893	4090.252	−4.619	.000

[a] Dependent Variable: math2.

TABLE 8.20   Estimates of Covariance Parameters[a]

Parameter		Estimate	Std. Error	Wald Z	Sig.
Residual		764.150388	17.822695	42.875	.000
Intercept [subject = schcode]	Variance	73.805762	18.826947	3.920	.000
Intercept [subject = teach2id]	Variance	35.450749	9.492972	3.734	.000
Intercept [subject = teach1id]	Variance	44.595334	10.065043	4.431	.000

[a] Dependent Variable: math2.

to be explained at the classroom and school levels. Adding the Level 2 effectiveness variables reduces the variance for each classroom, especially in the first classroom (from about 54.16 to 44.60 or R^2 = .177). The school-level variance is also reduced slightly from adding the teacher effectiveness variables to the model (from 83.98 to 73.81, or R^2 = .121).

Model 4: Adding a School-Level Predictor and a Random Slope

Next, we might investigate whether teacher effectiveness varies across schools. At the school level, the model with random effectiveness slopes would be the following:

$$\beta_{01k} = \gamma_{010} + \upsilon_{01k}, \tag{8.23}$$

$$\beta_{02k} = \gamma_{020} + \upsilon_{02k}, \tag{8.24}$$

where γ_{010} and γ_{020} is the average teacher effectiveness means for Classroom 1 and Classroom 2, respectively, and we will use υ_{01k} and υ_{02k} as the respective school residuals for the slope effects. At Level 3, we will define a diagonal covariance matrix for the intercept and slope (i.e., because we determined that the unstructured covariance matrix did not converge in this model).

Defining Model 4 With SPSS Menu Commands

Note: SPSS settings will default to those used for Model 3.

1. Go to the SPSS toolbar and select ANALYZE, MIXED MODELS, LINEAR.

This command enables access to the *Linear Mixed Models: Specify Subjects and Repeated* dialog box.

2. Within the *Linear Mixed Models: Specify Subjects and Repeated* dialog box, the variables *schcode*, *teach1id* and *teach2id* appear in the *Subjects* box.

Click the CONTINUE button to display the *Linear Mixed Models* dialog box.

3. In the *Linear Mixed Models* dialog box, the variable *math2* is displayed as the *Dependent Variable.*

The *Covariate(s)* are *effmath2*, *effmath1*, *Zmath1*, and *lowses*.

Click the RANDOM button to access the *Linear Mixed Models: Random Effects* dialog box.

4. The *Linear Mixed Models: Random Effects* displays the *Random Effect 3 of 3* screen.

a. Click the PREVIOUS button to access the *Random Effect 2 of 3* screen.
b. In the Random Effect 2 of 3 screen, click the PREVIOUS button to access the 1 of 3 screen.
c. Within the Random Effect 1 of 3 screen, click the pull-down menu to change the covariance type to Diagonal to enable model convergence.
d. Confirm Include intercept is selected.
e. Confirm Main Effects is selected.
f. Click to select effmath2 and effmath1, then click the ADD button to place the variables into the Model box.
g. Confirm sc*hcode* appears in the *Combinations* box.

Click the CONTINUE button to return to the *Linear Mixed Models* dialog box.

5. The fixed effects, estimation, and statistics settings remain the same, so click OK to run the model.

TABLE 8.21 Estimates of Covariance Parameters[a]

Parameter		Estimate	Std. Error	Wald Z	Sig.
Residual		764.310509	17.833967	42.857	.000
Intercept + effmath2 + effmath1 [subject = schcode]	Var: Intercept	46.837809	21.192822	2.210	.027
	Var: effmath2	.787756	.493189	1.597	.110
	Var: effmath1	.343200	.426s871	.804	.421
Intercept [subject = teach2id]	Variance	29.796380	9.257425	3.219	.001
Intercept [subject = teach1id]	Variance	41.052804	10.449243	3.929	.000

[a] Dependent Variable: math2.

Interpreting the Output From Model 4

We first examine whether effectiveness varies across schools. We provide the variance components table first (Table 8.21). The table suggests the effectiveness of Teacher 1 did not seem to vary across schools (one-tailed p = .205). It may be, however, that the effectiveness of Teacher 2 does vary across schools (one-tailed p = 0.055). Given these results, we can reformulate the Level 2 model by removing the random effect for Teacher 1 effectiveness (υ_{01k}) in Equation 8.23.

Model 5: Examining Level 3 Differences Between Institutions

We will then add a school-level variable that may explain differences in math achievement between schools. In this example, we will use quality of the school's educational processes (e.g., the school's leadership, academic expectations, climate) as a possible predictor of differences in school math outcomes. At Level 3, the intercept model is the following:

$$\beta_{00k} = \gamma_{000} + \gamma_{001}(schqual)_k + \upsilon_{00k}, \tag{8.25}$$

where γ_{000} is the adjusted school-level mean, γ_{001} is the coefficient representing the impact of the school-level predictor (school quality) on math outcomes, and υ_{00k} is the school-level residual. We could, of course, add other relevant school predictors to the model (e.g., school size, staff stability, student composition).

Defining Model 5 With SPSS Menu Commands

Note: SPSS settings will default to those used for Model 4.

1. Go to the SPSS toolbar and select ANALYZE, MIXED MODELS, LINEAR.

This command enables access to the *Linear Mixed Models: Specify Subjects and Repeated* dialog box.

2. Within the *Linear Mixed Models: Specify Subjects and Repeated* dialog box, the variables *schcode*, *teach1id*, and *teach2id* appear in the *Subjects* box.

Click the CONTINUE button to display the *Linear Mixed Models* dialog box.

3. In the *Linear Mixed Models* dialog box, the variable *math2* is displayed as the *Dependent Variable*.

   a. Click to select *effmath2*, *effmath1*, *Zmath1*, and *lowses*, then click the left-arrow button to remove the variable from the *Covariate(s)* box.

   b. Select the following variables and click on the right-arrow button to enter them into the *Covariate(s)* box in the following sequence: *schqual*, *effmath1*, *Zmath1*, *lowses* and *effmath2*.

Note: An alternative method to Steps a and b is to retain the variables in the *Covariates* box then add *schqual*. The variables may then be arranged into the recommended sequence by selecting and dragging them.

Click the FIXED button to access the *Linear Mixed Models: Fixed Effects* dialog box.

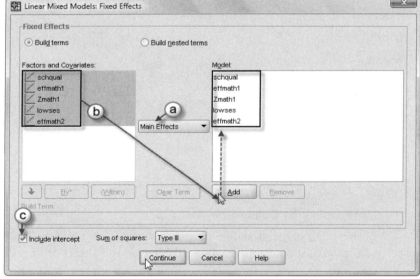

4a. The *Linear Mixed Models: Fixed Effect* dialog box displays the prior model's settings. Confirm that *Main Effects* is the selected factorial setting.

   b. Click to select the five variables (*schqual*, *effmath1*, *Zmath1*, *lowses*, and *effmath2*), then click the ADD button to move the variables into the *Model* box.

   c. Confirm *Include intercept* is selected.

Click the CONTINUE button to return to the *Linear Mixed Models* dialog box. Then click the RANDOM button to access the *Linear Mixed Models: Random Effects* dialog box.

5. The *Linear Mixed Models: Random Effects* displays the *Random Effect 1 of 3* screen.
   a. Confirm the covariance type is *Diagonal*.
   b. Confirm that *Include intercept* is selected.
   c. Confirm that *Main Effects* is selected.
   d. Click to select *effmath1* from the *Models* box. Then click the REMOVE button.
   e. Confirm *schcode* is in the *Combinations* box.

Click the CONTINUE button to return to the *Linear Mixed Models* dialog box.

6. The estimation and statistics settings remain the same, so click OK to run the model.

Interpreting the Output From Model 5

Table 8.22 suggests school quality affects student ending math achievement ($\gamma = 2.28$, $p < .10$). The variance component table (Table 8.23) provides evidence that Teacher 2 effectiveness varies across schools, remembering that we have a relatively small subset of 81 schools (Wald $Z = 1.765$, one-tailed $p = .039$)

TABLE 8.22 Estimates of Fixed Effects[a]

Parameter	Estimate	Std. Error	df	t	Sig.
Intercept	646.028734	2.195178	306.310	294.294	.000
schqual	2.277832	1.302958	89.300	1.748	.084
effmath1	1.108827	.225115	224.520	4.926	.000
zmath1	28.386359	.487718	4075.644	58.202	.000
lowses	−4.426424	.974381	4087.879	−4.543	.000
effmath2	.734971	.309181	120.918	2.377	.019

[a] Dependent Variable: math2.

TABLE 8.23 Estimates of Covariance Parameters[a]

Parameter		Estimate	Std. Error	Wald Z	Sig.
Residual		763.939534	17.817696	42.875	.000
Intercept + effmath2	Var: Intercept	49.915615	19.583604	2.549	.011
[subject = schcode]	Var: effmath2	.910653	.515885	1.765	.078
Intercept [subject = teach2id]	Variance	29.650163	9.230599	3.212	.001
Intercept [subject = teach1id]	Variance	44.841153	10.111467	4.435	.000

[a] Dependent Variable: math2.

Model 6: Adding a Level 3 Cross-Level Interaction

Finally, we will add a school-level variable that might moderate the relationship between Teacher 2 effectiveness and Year 2 math achievement. In this case, we will use quality of the school's educational processes (e.g., the school's leadership, academic expectations, climate). The Level 3 model is

$$\beta_{02k} = \gamma_{020} + \gamma_{021}(schqual * effmath2)_k + \upsilon_{02k}.$$

(8.26)

Defining Model 6 With SPSS Menu Commands

Note: SPSS settings will default to those used for Model 5.

1. Go to the SPSS toolbar and select ANALYZE, MIXED MODELS, LINEAR.

This command enables access to *the Linear Mixed Models: Specify Subjects and Repeated* dialog box.

2. Within the *Linear Mixed Models: Specify Subjects and Repeated* dialog box, the variables *schcode*, *teach1id*, and *teach2id* appear in the *Subjects* box.

Click the CONTINUE button to display the *Linear Mixed Models* dialog box.

3. In the *Linear Mixed Models* dialog box, the variable *math2* is displayed as the *Dependent Variable*.

The *Covariate(s)* are: *schqual*, *effmath1*, *Zmath1*, *lowses*, and *effmath2*.

Click the FIXED button to access the *Linear Mixed Models: Fixed Effects* dialog box.

4. The *Linear Mixed Models: Fixed Effects* screen displays the default settings.

Creating a Cross-Level Interaction

*effmath2*schqual*

a. Click to select the *Build nested terms* option.
b. Click to select the variable *effmath2* from the *Factors and Covariates* column.
c. Click the down-arrow button to move *effmath2* into the *Build Term* box.
d. Click the BY* button to add the computational symbol (*) to the *Build Term* box.
e. Confirm *Include intercept* is selected.

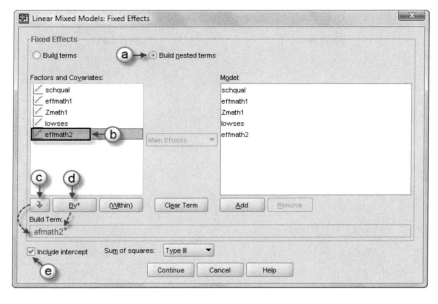

f. Click to select the variable *schqual* from the *Factors and Covariates* column.
g. Click the down-arrow button to move *schqual* into the *Build Term* box.
h. Click the ADD button to move the term *effmath2*schqual* into the *Model* box.

Click the CONTINUE button to return to the *Linear Mixed Models* dialog box.

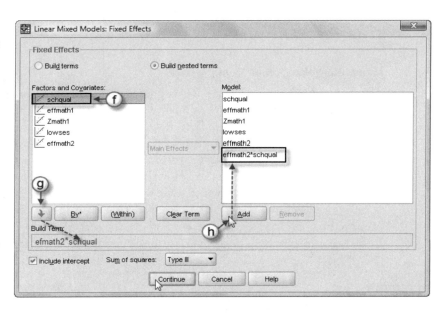

5. The random effects, estimation, and statistics settings remain the same as Model 5, so click OK to run the model.

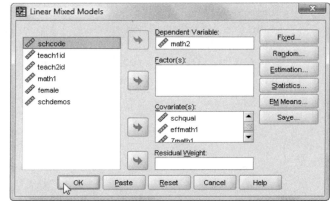

TABLE 8.24   Estimates of Fixed Effects[a]

Parameter	Estimate	Std. Error	df	t	Sig.
Intercept	645.717737	2.201058	307.461	293.367	.000
Schqual	4.220897	1.905401	183.148	2.215	.028
effmath1	1.109505	.224907	224.367	4.933	.000
zmath1	28.377708	.487710	4074.882	58.186	.000
Lowses	−4.433383	.974294	4087.802	−4.550	.000
effmath2	.814333	.314345	120.484	2.591	.011
schqual * effmath2	−.458133	.329750	90.252	−1.389	.168

[a] Dependent Variable: math2.

TABLE 8.25   Estimates of Covariance Parameters[a]

Parameter		Estimate	Std. Error	Wald Z	Sig.
Residual		763.955838	17.818701	42.874	.000
Intercept + effmath2	Var: Intercept	48.876472	19.509176	2.505	.012
[subject = schcode]	Var: effmath2	.924923	.524133	1.765	.078
Intercept [subject = teach2id]	Variance	29.528076	9.217844	3.203	.001
Intercept [subject = teach1id]	Variance	44.687765	10.099072	4.425	.000

[a] Dependent Variable: math2.

Interpreting the Output From Model 6

The fixed effects table (Table 8.24) suggests that the quality of the school's key educational processes did not moderate the relationship between Teacher 2 effectiveness and achievement levels in math ($\gamma = -0.46$, $p > .10$). The effects of the other variables on Year 2 achievement remain about the same as the previous model. Given that the cross-level interaction was not significant, for parsimony we should remove it from the final model.

The variance component table (Table 8.25) suggests that at Level 3, after adding the cross-level interaction there may still be some slope variance left to explain at the school level (Wald $Z =$ 1.765, one-tailed $p = 0.039$). There is also still significant intercept variance in ending achievement to be explained across schools and classrooms. We could continue to add predictors to the model that might explain this variation in school and classroom intercepts.

Summary

SPSS Mixed proves very flexible in handling a variety of multilevel cross-classified data sets. They extend the types of data structures and problems that can be investigated with multilevel modeling. Cross-classified models also open up additional opportunities to investigate individuals' growth over time within their organizational settings. It is important to keep in mind, however, their complexity and size will add to the challenge of trying to estimate these types of partly hierarchical data structures.

CHAPTER 9

Concluding Thoughts

In our 2009 book, *An Introduction to Multilevel Modeling Techniques* (2nd ed.), we sought to expand the application of multilevel modeling techniques to a new range of research questions. In that book we argued that most of the new variants of the simple multilevel model could, in fact, be subsumed under a general modeling framework of latent variables and simultaneous equations. The modeling we present in that book uses two popular multilevel statistical programs: HLM and Mplus. Although we are very satisfied with those excellent programs, their cost and the learning curve associated with their use present barriers to many colleagues who wanted to use the book in their graduate research courses. Unfortunately, relatively few social science computing labs make these programs available for student and classroom use. The problem makes it challenging to take full advantage of these software programs in introducing multilevel modeling techniques to students.

Our own initial solution to this problem was to generate sets of handouts we could use with our students that made use of the familiar SPSS modeling framework to introduce multilevel modeling. As we began to refine some of these materials, we realized there might be wider interest in having a set of hands-on activities that would illustrate major concepts in multilevel and longitudinal models. In this resulting workbook, we have tried to provide an applied introduction to multilevel modeling along with instruction for managing multilevel data, specifying a range of multilevel models and interpreting output generated through the SPSS Mixed procedure. After "driving it around the block" a few times, we feel that it has definite utility for investigating a variety of multilevel and longitudinal models with continuous outcomes. We also noted a few cautions along the way. In compiling the workbook, we triangulated many of our results with other software and sometimes found small differences in individual parameters but, overall, a high level of substantive convergence. Our goal has been to widen exposure to and understanding of some general multilevel modeling principles and applications. The workbook was designed as a complement to our more in-depth treatment of the statistical and conceptual issues surrounding multilevel modeling provided in our introductory multilevel book.

With an eye toward the how-to aspect of setting up a study to investigate a research problem, in the first chapter of the workbook we introduced a number of key conceptual and methodological issues. Several elements have to be brought together including knowledge of previous research, the definition and development of the specific research problem, the goals of the research, the consideration of various appropriate methods of investigation (including their advantages and shortcomings) in light of the structure of the available data, and the means of communication with potential users of the study's results. Our presentation there was designed to set the stage for the subsequent development of several different multilevel models that are the focus of the following chapters. We devoted Chapter 2 to discussing a number of conceptual and practical issues associated with the management of multilevel data. We believe readers will find the material useful in setting up their own data analyses, since each study seems to bring its own unique challenges in preparing the data for the intended analyses. Our objective there was to highlight the different ways that hierarchical data can be structured, while offering a general introduction to essential data management procedures available within SPSS.

Each of the remaining chapters dealt with a particular type of multilevel model (cross-sectional, growth, cross-classified) to cover a broad number of research possibilities. Although the traditional two- or three-level multilevel cross-sectional model has become a more common feature in social science research over the past decade, the other formulations that we introduced here are rapidly growing in their popularity and use. It is our hope that making these modeling capabilities available through SPSS will make them more accessible to a wider audience, even though we only scratched the surface regarding the use of these techniques with longitudinal and cross-classified data structures and more complex research designs (e.g., time series, regression discontinuity). We hinted at some of these possibilities (e.g., parallel growth processes, piecewise growth models that examine changes before and after an intervention is introduced) that can be specified in SPSS Mixed, albeit with a bit more difficulty in setting up the data set.

As the reader can tell from the treatment we provide in this workbook, multilevel models can get quite complex. It is one thing to dump a set of variables into a single-level ordinary least squares (OLS) regression model but quite another to adopt a recklessly exploratory approach in a multilevel framework. Although exploratory analysis is an important and necessary feature of empirical research, the models we covered in this workbook demand a more disciplined approach to model conceptualization and specification. With multiple levels of analysis and the possibility for numerous cross-level interactions, choices about fixed or random slopes and intercepts, centering, weighting, and to estimation algorithms, as well as the interpretation of the results from these models can quickly become bogged down and rendered useless or, worse, misleading.

In our book and this workbook we began with the principle that quantitative analysis represents the translation of abstract theories into concrete models and that conceptual frameworks are essential guides to empirical investigation. The statistical model is therefore designed to represent a set of proposed theoretical relationships that are thought to exist in a population from which we have a sample of data. With this as a guiding principle, the researcher makes conscious decisions about the analysis that define research questions, design, data structures, and methods of analysis. The potential complexity of the multilevel model thus demands the careful attention of the analyst.

As we pointed out in Chapter 1, this does not ignore the importance of exploratory work. We recognize its place and suggest only that such work be conducted with careful thought about the possible relationships one might expect to see. The myriad combinations of model specification rule out the multilevel model as an effective "data-mining" tool. In fact, the models are very data demanding and will perform poorly without adequate data at each level of interest. But with an ample framework for organizing the analysis, adequate data, and careful thought to sensible model specification, the multilevel framework opens up dramatic new possibilities for exploratory work.

This workbook is written at a time when multilevel statistical models are better able to capture the complex contextual or environmental factors that condition the behaviors and attitudes of lower level units operating within those contexts or environments. Coincidently, we also find ourselves at a moment where large-scale hierarchical data are more readily available than they were even 10 years ago. Although it would seem to be an incredibly exciting time for social science researchers (and indeed it is), we still find ourselves in want of data to drive empirical models suggested by our conceptual frameworks. Perhaps satisfaction on this front will be ever elusive; that is, as our modeling ability and statistical knowledge expand, so will our need for data to drive ever more demanding models.

One issue we call attention to through the activities we provided in this workbook is that multilevel models are quite demanding of data, and the analyst should be very aware of the limitations that exist as model specification becomes more complicated. As an example, our initial data sets (e.g., 100 to 200 individuals in 25 or 30 units) that we selected were fine for illustrating fixed effects; however, the moment we wished to illustrate random slopes, we needed much larger data sets to identify significant differences across groups. They often required 20 to 30 individuals within groups and 200 or more groups to be able to detect variability in the slopes. This gave us pause to consider that many published multilevel studies may report nonsignificant results due primarily to making Type II errors (i.e., failure to reject the null hypothesis) related to not having adequate data to detect the effects to begin with; that is, the available data are not up to the task of sufficiently supporting the complexity of the desired analyses. This suggests the failure may not always be the proposed conceptual model but, rather, the shortcomings of the data and, perhaps, their measurement qualities. Hence, we emphasize that just because a model can be complex does not mean it should be complex. Parsimony is one indicator of a good empirical application of theory.

Another issue we touch upon concerns the sampling scheme for the data used in multilevel studies. Researchers have for some time now been concerned about so-called design effects resulting from complex sampling schemes; that is, where a combination of multistage cluster sampling and disproportionate stratified sampling is used. The multilevel model actually capitalizes on such sample designs, incorporating the nesting of data that result from multistage clustering. Although the multilevel model incorporates this important sample design feature, it does not address the disproportionate stratified sampling that generally occurs with such sampling. This aspect of the design is usually dealt with through the application of sampling weights during the model specification stage. Weighting is pretty routine and straightforward in single-level analyses but becomes more challenging in the multilevel framework. Although some programs such as HLM can now accommodate weights at multiple levels of analysis (e.g., student level weights and school level weights), SPSS uses a global weight and, therefore, forces the researcher to choose between weights that may exist across levels.

The efficacy of various weighting schemes used in different software programs is an issue that needs further research. Applying or not applying sample weights can change model estimates of standard errors considerably. Failure to take sample design into account by applying the appropriate weights can bias estimates of standard errors downward. Because standard errors are used in determining hypothesis tests about individual parameters, downward-biased estimates can lead to more findings of significance than should be the case. For the time being, we recommend that sample weights be used when available, and that the analyst choose the weight at the lowest level of analysis (i.e., students in our earlier example). This will improve the accuracy of individual-level estimates. Level 2 estimates should then be approached with some caution since, depending on the sampling scheme, some types of units may be overrepresented. Where weights cannot be used or do not exist, one might choose to include variables that are known to be related to the sample design in an effort to control for some of the effect (Stapleton & Thomas, 2008). For example, if institutions at Level 2 are stratified by type (i.e., public–private), the analyst could include a public–private indicator at Level 2 to minimize the stratification effect in the absence of a weight.

A third issue we ask readers to consider is missing data. Missing data can present serious challenges for the researcher and should be dealt with as forthrightly as possible. Rarely are data missing completely at random (MCAR). If one were to go with the SPSS defaults regarding missing data, any case with even one piece of missing data would be eliminated from the analysis (i.e., where data are not vertically organized). We emphasize researchers need to be aware of this and, where possible, seek viable solutions for data sets that contain considerable amounts of missing data. We favor situations where the software will actually estimate model parameters in the presence of the missing data (e.g., where variables are arranged vertically in SPSS) since, in truth, there is no way of completely compensating for the fact that data have been irreversibly lost (Raykov & Marcoulides, 2008). We can try to obtain further information about the patterns of missing data and use this information to help devise a manner for dealing with the missing data. We do not recommend regression-based missing data substitution, which is an option within SPSS. For SPSS Mixed, we instead encourage the analyst to employ multiple imputation strategies, which produce multiple imputed data sets by repeatedly drawing values for each missing datum from a distribution (Raykov & Marcoulides, 2008). Unfortunately, this procedure is not available in the SPSS Base or Advanced program, so it must be purchased separately. At a minimum, we encourage the analyst to become very familiar with the data being used, to identify where data are missing, and to develop a strategy for testing the effects of missing data on the results generated by the model.

Finally, as should be very clear from the models we have developed throughout the workbook, there is a logical process underlying the development of the models and a series of steps involved for moving from the partitioning of variance between levels to the specification of models that may have random intercepts and slopes. We strongly encourage readers to devise their own naming system to keep track of the various models used in any given analysis. Without a clear history of model specification, it is sometimes very difficult to understand how one arrived at a final model. At the risk of twisting an old saw, it is often the journey that is more telling than the final destination.

Multilevel modeling provides us with another powerful means for investigating the types of processes referred to by our theories in more refined ways. Although the models presented in this workbook were simplified for purposes of demonstrating the techniques, we hope that our step-by-step guide serves as a foundation for the more thorough models that can be formulated and tested. We encourage the reader searching for more detail to consult the many other excellent resources available and referenced throughout this workbook.

References

Bryk, A. S., & Raudenbush, S. W. (1992). *Hierarchical linear models: Applications and data analysis methods.* Newbury Park, CA: Sage.

Bloom, H. S., Hill, C. J., Black, A. R., & Lipsey, M. W. (2008). Performance trajectories and performance gaps as achievement effect-size benchmarks for educational interventions. *Journal of Research on Educational Effectiveness, 1*(4), 289–328.

Curtin, T. R., Ingels, S. J., Wu, S., & Heuer, R. (2002). *National educational longitudinal study of 1988: Base-year to fourth follow-up data file user's manual (NCES 2002-323).* Washington, D.C.: U.S. Department of Education, National Center for Education Statistics.

Duncan, T. E., Duncan, S. C., & Strycker, L. A. (2006). *An introduction to latent variable growth curve modeling: Concepts, issues and applications* (2nd ed.). Mahwah, NJ: Lawrence Erlbaum Associates.

Goldstein, H. (1987). Multilevel covariance component models. *Biometrika, 74*(2), 430–431.

Goldstein, H. (1995). *Multilevel statistical models.* New York: Halsted.

Goldstein, H. (2003). *Multilevel statistical models* (3rd ed.). New York: Oxford University Press [Distributor].

Hamilton, L. C. (1992). *Regression with graphics: A second course in applied statistics.* Belmont, CA: Duxbury Press.

Heck, R. H., & Takahashi, R. (2006). Examining the impact of proposition 48 on graduation rates in Division 1A football and program recruiting behavior. *Educational Policy*, 20(4), 587–614.

Heck, R. H., & Thomas, S. L. (2000). *An introduction to multilevel modeling techniques.* Mahwah, NJ: Lawrence Erlbaum.

Heck, R. H., & Thomas, S. L. (2009). *An introduction to multilevel modeling techniques* (2nd ed.). New York: Psychology Press.

Hill, P. W., & Goldstein, H. (1998). Multilevel modeling of educational data with cross-classification and missing identification for units. *Journal of Educational and Behavioral Statistics, 23*(2), 117–128.

Hofmann, D. A., & Gavin, M. B. (1998). Centering decisions in hierarchical linear models: Theoretical and methodological implications for organizational science. *Journal of Management, 24*(5), 623–641.

Hox, J. (2002). *Multilevel analysis: Techniques and applications.* Mahwah, NJ: Lawrence Erlbaum Associates.

Kreft, I., & de Leeuw, J. (1998). *Introducing multilevel modeling.* Thousand Oaks, CA: Sage.

Kreft, I., de Leeuw, J., & Aiken, L. S. (1995). The effect of different forms of centering in hierarchical linear models. *Multivariate Behavioral Research, 30*(1), 1–22.

Lam, W. (2008). *The impact of environmental and institutional factors on state higher educational performance: A longitudinal study across 50 states (1997–2006)* (Unpublished dissertation). University of Hawai'i at Manoā, Honolulu.

Lee, V. E., & Bryk, A. S. (1989). A multilevel model of the social distribution of high school achievement. *Sociology of Education, 62*(3), 172–192.

Leyland, A. H. (2004). *A review of multilevel modelling in SPSS.* Retrieved from http://stat.gamma.rug.nl/reviewspss.pdf

Loh, W. (1987). Some modifications of Levene's test of variance homogeneity. *Journal of Statistical Computation and Simulation, 28*(3), 213–226.

Longford, N. T. (1993). *Random coefficients models.* Oxford: Clarendon Press.

Marcoulides, G. A., & Hershberger, S. L. (1997). *Multivariate statistical methods: A first course.* Mahwah, NJ: Lawrence Erlbaum.

McCaffrey, D. F., Lockwood, J. R., Koretz, D. M., & Hamilton, L. S. (2003). *Evaluating value-added models for teacher accountabillity.* Santa Monica, CA: Rand.

Mehta, P. D., & Neale, M. C. (2005). People are variables too: Multilevel structural equation modeling. *Psychological Methods, 10*(3), 259–284.

Morris, C. N. (1995). Hierarchical models for educational data: An overview. *Journal of Educational and Behavioral Statistics, 20*(2), 190–200.

Muthén, B. O., & Satorra, A. (1995). Complex sample data in structural equation modeling. In P. V. Marsden (Ed.), *Sociological methodology 1995* (pp. 267–316). Boston: Blackwell.

Muthén, L. K., & Muthén, B. O. (1998–2006). *Mplus user's guide* (4th ed.). Los Angeles: Author.

Neter, J., Kutner, M. H., Nachtsheim, C., & Wasserman, W. (1996). *Applied linear regression models* (3rd ed.). Chicago, IL: Irwin.

Paccagnella, O. (2006). Centering or not centering in multilevel models? The role of the group mean and the assessment of group effects. *Evaluation Review, 30*(1), 66–85.

Pedhazur, E. J., & Schmelkin, L. P. (1991). *Measurement, design, and analysis: An integrated approach.* Hillsdale, NJ: Lawrence Erlbaum Associates.

Peugh, J. L., & Enders, C. K. (2004). Missing data in educational research: A review of reporting practices and suggestions for improvement. *Review of Educational Research, 74*(4), 525–556.

Plewis, I. (1989). Comment on "centering" predictors in multilevel analysis. *Multilevel Modeling newsletter, 1*(3), 6, 11.

Preacher, K. J. (2003). *A primer on interaction effects in multiple linear regression.* Retrieved from http://people.ku.edu/~preacher/interact/interactions.htm

Rabe-Hesketh, S., & Skrondal, A. (2008). *Multilevel and longitudinal modeling using Stata* (2nd ed.). College Station, TX: Stata Press.

Raudenbush, S. W. (1988). Educational applications of hierarchical linear models: A review. *Journal of Educational Statistics, 13*(2), 85–116.

Raudenbush, S. W., & Bryk, A. S. (2002). *Hierarchical linear models: Applications and data analysis methods* (2nd ed.). Thousand Oaks, CA: Sage.

Raudenbush, S. W., Bryk, A. S., Cheong, Y., & Congdon, R. T., Jr. (2004). *HLM 6: Hierarchical linear and nonlinear modeling.* Lincolnwood, IL: Scientific Software International.

Raudenbush, S. W., Rowan, B., & Kang, S. J. (1991). A multilevel multivariate model for school climate and estimation via the EM algorithm and application to U.S. high school data. *Journal of Educational Statistics, 1*(14), 295–330.

Raykov, T., & Marcoulides, G. A. (2008). *An introduction to applied multivariate analysis* (2nd ed.). New York: Routledge.

Robinson, W. S. (1950). Ecological correlations and the behavior of individuals. *Sociological Review, 15*, 351–357.

Sable, J., & Noel, A. (2008). *Documentation to the common core of data state nonfiscal survey of public elementary/secondary education: School year 2006-07 (NCES 2009-300).* Washington, DC: National Center for Education Statistics, Institute of Education Sciences, U.S. Department of Education.

Scherbaum, C. A., & Ferreter, J. M. (2009). Estimating statistical power and required sample sizes for organizational research using multilevel modeling. *Organizational Research Methods, 12*(2), 347–367.

Singer, J. D., & Willett, J. B. (2003). *Applied longitudinal data analysis: Modeling change and event occurrence.* New York: Oxford University Press.

Snijders, T. A. B. (2005). Power and sample size in multilevel linear models. In B. S. Everitt & D. C. Howell (Eds.), *Encyclopedia of statistics in behavioral sciences* (Vol. 3, pp. 1570–1573). New York: Wiley.

Snijders, T. A. B., & Bosker, R. J. (1994). Modeled variance in two-level models. *Sociological Methods & Research, 22*(3), 342–363.

Snijders, T. A. B., & Bosker, R. J. (1999). *Multilevel analysis: An introduction to basic and advanced multilevel modeling.* Thousand Oaks, CA: Sage.

SPSS. (1990). *SPSS/PC+ Advanced Statistics 4.0.* Chicago: Author.

SPSS. (2002). *Linear mixed effects modeling in SPSS: An introduction to the MIXED procedure* (Technical report LMEMWP-1002). Chicago: Author.

Stapleton, L., & Thomas, S. L. (2008). The use of national datasets for teaching and research: Sources and issues. In A. A. O'Connell & D. B. McCoach (Eds.), *Multilevel modeling of educational data* (pp. 11–58). Charlotte, NC: Information Age Publishing.

Tabachnick, B. G. (2008, March). *Multivariate statistics: An introduction and some applications.* Workshop presented to the American Psychology-Law Society, Jacksonville, FL.

Thomas, S. L., & Heck, R. H. (2001). Analysis of large-scale secondary data in higher education research: Potential perils associated with complex sampling designs. *Research in Higher Education, 42*(5), 517–540.

Thum, Y. M. (2003). Measuring progress toward a goal: Estimating teacher productivity using a multivariate multilevel model for value-added analyses. *Sociological Methods & Research, 32*(2), 153–207.

Verbeke, G., & Lesaffre, E. (1997). The effect of misspecifying the random-effects distribution in linear mixed models for longitudinal data. *Computational Statistics and Data Analysis, 23*(4), 541–556.

Willett, J. B. (1989). Some results on the reliability for the longitudinal measurement of change: Implications for the design of studies of individual growth. *Educational and Psychological Measurement, 49*(3), 587–602.

Appendix A: Syntax Statements

Please note that syntax statements obtained through the "Paste" feature in SPSS Mixed menu commands will insert an additional command line: /CRITERIA. While the /CRITERIA command provides information concerning default values it is not required to run a model and has been omitted.

Chapter 3: Defining a Basic Two-Level Multilevel Regression Model

The Null Model: No Predictors

```
MIXED math
 /FIXED=| SSTYPE(3)
 /METHOD=REML
 /PRINT=G SOLUTION TESTCOV
 /RANDOM=INTERCEPT | SUBJECT(schcode) COVTYPE(VC).
```

Model 1: Level 1 Random Intercept Model

```
MIXED math WITH ses
 /FIXED=ses | SSTYPE(3)
 /METHOD=REML
 /PRINT=G SOLUTION TESTCOV
 /RANDOM=INTERCEPT | SUBJECT(schcode) COVTYPE(VC).
```

Model 2: Level 1 Random Intercept Model

```
MIXED math BY public WITH ses_mean per4yrc ses
 /FIXED=public ses_mean per4yrc ses | SSTYPE(3)
 /METHOD=REML
 /PRINT=G SOLUTION TESTCOV
 /RANDOM=INTERCEPT | SUBJECT(schcode) COVTYPE(VC).
```

Model 2b: Treat "Public" Variable as a Covariate

```
MIXED math WITH public ses_mean per4yrc ses
 /FIXED=public ses_mean per4yrc ses | SSTYPE(3)
 /METHOD=REML
 /PRINT=G SOLUTION TESTCOV
 /RANDOM=INTERCEPT | SUBJECT(schcode) COVTYPE(VC).
```

Model 3: Random Slope and Intercept Model

```
MIXED math WITH public ses_mean per4yrc ses
 /FIXED=public ses_mean per4yrc ses | SSTYPE(3)
 /METHOD=REML
 /PRINT=G SOLUTION TESTCOV
 /RANDOM=INTERCEPT ses | SUBJECT(schcode) COVTYPE(VC).
```

Model 3b: Table 3.19 (Cross-Level Interaction ses_mean*ses)

```
MIXED math WITH ses_mean ses
 /FIXED=ses_mean ses ses*ses_mean | SSTYPE(3)
 /METHOD=REML
 /PRINT=G SOLUTION TESTCOV
 /RANDOM=INTERCEPT | SUBJECT(schcode) COVTYPE(ID).
```

Model 4: More Complex Random Slope and Intercept Models

```
MIXED math WITH public ses_mean per4yrc ses
 /FIXED=public ses_mean per4yrc ses ses_mean*ses per4yrc*ses public*ses |
SSTYPE(3)
 /METHOD=REML
 /PRINT=G SOLUTION TESTCOV
 /RANDOM=INTERCEPT ses | SUBJECT(schcode) COVTYPE(VC).
```

Model 4b: Table 3.20—Removed Nonsignificant Interactions (ses_men*ses, per4yrc*ses)

```
MIXED math WITH public ses_mean per4yrc ses
 /FIXED=public ses_mean per4yrc ses public*ses | SSTYPE(3)
 /METHOD=REML
 /PRINT=G SOLUTION TESTCOV
 /RANDOM=INTERCEPT ses | SUBJECT(schcode) COVTYPE(VC).
```

Chapter 4: Three-Level Univariate Regression Models

The Null Model: No Predictors

```
MIXED math
 /FIXED=| SSTYPE(3)
 /METHOD=ML
 /PRINT=G SOLUTION TESTCOV
 /RANDOM=INTERCEPT | SUBJECT(schcode) COVTYPE(ID)
 /RANDOM=INTERCEPT | SUBJECT(schcode*Rteachid) COVTYPE(ID).
```

Model 1: Predictors at Each Level

```
MIXED math WITH gmlowses gmteacheffect gmclasslowses_mean gmschlowSES_mean
gmaggtcheffect
 /FIXED=gmschlowSES_mean gmaggtcheffect gmteacheffect gmclasslowses_mean
gmlowses | SSTYPE(3)
 /METHOD=ML
 /PRINT=G SOLUTION TESTCOV
 /RANDOM=INTERCEPT | SUBJECT(schcode) COVTYPE(ID)
 /RANDOM=INTERCEPT | SUBJECT(schcode*Rteachid) COVTYPE(ID).
```

Model 2: Group-Mean Centered Variables

```
MIXED math WITH gmschlowSES_mean gmaggtcheffect groupteacheffect
groupclasslowses_mean grouplowses
```

```
/FIXED=gmschlowSES_mean gmaggtcheffect groupteacheffect groupclasslowses_
mean grouplowses |
 SSTYPE(3)
 /METHOD=ML
 /PRINT=G SOLUTION TESTCOV
 /RANDOM=INTERCEPT | SUBJECT(schcode) COVTYPE(ID)
 /RANDOM=INTERCEPT | SUBJECT(schcode*Rteachid) COVTYPE(ID).
```

Model 3: Slope Varies Randomly Across Classroom and Schools

```
MIXED math WITH gmlowses gmteacheffect gmclasslowses_mean gmschlowSES_mean
gmaggtcheffect
 /FIXED=gmschlowSES_mean gmaggtcheffect gmteacheffect gmclasslowses_mean
gmlowses | SSTYPE(3)
 /METHOD=ML
 /PRINT=G SOLUTION TESTCOV
 /RANDOM=INTERCEPT gmteacheffect | SUBJECT(schcode) COVTYPE(UN)
 /RANDOM=INTERCEPT | SUBJECT(schcode*Rteachid) COVTYPE(ID)
```

Model 4: Level 2 Interactions

```
MIXED math WITH gmlowses gmteacheffect gmclasslowses_mean gmschlowSES_mean
gmaggtcheffect
 /FIXED=gmschlowSES_mean gmaggtcheffect gmteacheffect gmclasslowses_mean
gmclasslowses_mean*gmteacheffect gmlowses | SSTYPE(3)
 /METHOD=ML
 /PRINT=G SOLUTION TESTCOV
 /RANDOM=INTERCEPT gmteacheffect | SUBJECT(schcode) COVTYPE(UN)
 /RANDOM=INTERCEPT | SUBJECT(schcode*Rteachid) COVTYPE(ID).
```

Chapter 5: Examining Individual Change With Repeated Measures Data

Figures 5.1 and 5.2 (Select Cases)

```
USE ALL.
COMPUTE filter_$=(id < 18).
VARIABLE LABEL filter_$ 'id < 18 (FILTER)'.
VALUE LABELS filter_$ 0 'Not Selected' 1 'Selected'.
FORMAT filter_$ (f1.0).
FILTER BY filter_$.
```

Graphing the Figures

```
EXECUTE.
GRAPH
 /SCATTERPLOT(BIVAR)=time WITH test BY id
 /MISSING=LISTWISE.
```

Conducting Repeated Measures ANOVA

```
GLM test1 test2 test3
 /WSFACTOR=time 3 Polynomial
 /MEASURE=Test
```

```
/METHOD=SSTYPE(3)
/PLOT=PROFILE(time)
/EMMEANS=TABLES(OVERALL)
/EMMEANS=TABLES(time)
/CRITERIA=ALPHA(.05)
/WSDESIGN=time.
```

Adding Between-Subjects Predictors

```
GLM test1 test2 test3 BY effective WITH ses
/WSFACTOR=time 3 Polynomial
/MEASURE=Test
/METHOD=SSTYPE(3)
/PLOT=PROFILE(time time*effective)
/EMMEANS=TABLES(OVERALL) WITH(ses=MEAN)
/EMMEANS=TABLES(time) WITH(ses=MEAN)
/EMMEANS=TABLES(effective*time) WITH(ses=MEAN)
/PRINT=PARAMETER
/CRITERIA=ALPHA(.05)
/WSDESIGN=time
/DESIGN=ses effective.
```

Model 1: Does the Slope Vary Randomly Across Individuals?

```
MIXED test WITH time quadtime
/ /FIXED=time quadtime | SSTYPE(3)
/METHOD=REML
/PRINT=G SOLUTION TESTCOV
/RANDOM=INTERCEPT time | SUBJECT(id) COVTYPE(UN).
```

Investigating Other Level 1 Covariance Structures Using SPSS Menu Commands

Diagonal Covariance Matrix

```
MIXED test WITH time quadtime
/FIXED=time quadtime | SSTYPE(3)
/METHOD=REML
/PRINT=G SOLUTION TESTCOV
/RANDOM=INTERCEPT time | SUBJECT(id) COVTYPE(UN)
/REPEATED=time | SUBJECT(id) COVTYPE(DIAG).
```

Unstructured Covariance Matrix

```
MIXED test WITH time quadtime
/FIXED=time quadtime | SSTYPE(3)
/METHOD=REML
/PRINT=G SOLUTION TESTCOV
/RANDOM=INTERCEPT time | SUBJECT(id) COVTYPE(UN)
/REPEATED=time | SUBJECT(id) COVTYPE(UN).
```

Autoregressive Covariance Matrix

```
MIXED test WITH time quadtime
/FIXED=time quadtime | SSTYPE(3)
```

```
 /METHOD=REML
 /PRINT=G SOLUTION TESTCOV
 /RANDOM=INTERCEPT time | SUBJECT(id) COVTYPE(DIAG)
 /REPEATED=time | SUBJECT(id) COVTYPE(AR1).
```

Model 2: Adding the Between-Subjects Predictors

```
MIXED test WITH ses effective time quadtime
 /FIXED=ses effective time time*ses time*effective quadtime | SSTYPE(3)
 /METHOD=REML
 /PRINT=G SOLUTION TESTCOV
 /RANDOM=INTERCEPT time | SUBJECT(id) COVTYPE(UN)
 /REPEATED=time | SUBJECT(id) COVTYPE(DIAG).
```

Graphing the Growth Rate Trajectories

```
GRAPH
 /LINE(MULTIPLE)=MEAN(test) BY time BY effective.
```

Chapter 6: Methods for Examining Organizational-Level Change

The Null Model: No Predictors

```
MIXED gradproportion
 /FIXED=| SSTYPE(3)
 /METHOD=REML
 /PRINT=G SOLUTION TESTCOV
 /RANDOM=INTERCEPT | SUBJECT(stateid) COVTYPE(ID)
 /RANDOM=INTERCEPT | SUBJECT(rid*stateid) COVTYPE(ID)
 /REPEATED=time | SUBJECT(rid*stateid) COVTYPE(AR1).
```

Model 1: Adding Growth Rates

```
MIXED gradproportion WITH time1 quadtime1
 /FIXED=time1 quadtime1 | SSTYPE(3)
 /METHOD=REML
 /PRINT=G SOLUTION TESTCOV
 /RANDOM=INTERCEPT time1 | SUBJECT(stateid) COVTYPE(DIAG)
 /RANDOM=INTERCEPT time1 | SUBJECT(rid*stateid) COVTYPE(DIAG)
 /REPEATED=time | SUBJECT(rid*stateid) COVTYPE(AR1).
```

Model 2: Adding Time-Varying Covariates

```
MIXED gradproportion WITH percentFinAid tuition time1
 /FIXED=percentFinAid tuition time1 | SSTYPE(3)
 /METHOD=REML
 /PRINT=G SOLUTION TESTCOV
 /RANDOM=INTERCEPT time1 | SUBJECT(stateid) COVTYPE(DIAG)
 /RANDOM=INTERCEPT time1 | SUBJECT(rid*stateid) COVTYPE(DIAG)
 /REPEATED=time | SUBJECT(rid*stateid) COVTYPE(AR1).
```

Model 3: Differences in Growth Trajectories Between Institutions

```
MIXED gradproportion WITH aveFamilyshare aveRetention mathselect
percentFTfaculty percentFinAid
 tuition time1
 /FIXED=aveFamilyshare aveRetention mathselect percentFTfaculty percentFinAid
tuition time1
 time1*mathselect time1*percentFTfaculty | SSTYPE(3)
 /METHOD=REML
 /PRINT=G SOLUTION TESTCOV
 /RANDOM=INTERCEPT time1 | SUBJECT(stateid) COVTYPE(DIAG)
 /RANDOM=INTERCEPT time1 | SUBJECT(rid*stateid) COVTYPE(DIAG)
 /REPEATED=time | SUBJECT(rid*stateid) COVTYPE(AR1).
```

Model 4: Adding a Model to Examine Growth Rates at Level 3

```
MIXED gradproportion WITH aveFamilyshare aveRetention mathselect
percentFTfaculty percentFinAid
 tuition time1
 /FIXED=aveFamilyshare aveRetention mathselect percentFTfaculty percentFinAid
tuition time1
 time1*aveFamilyshare time1*aveRetention time1*mathselect
time1*percentFTfaculty | SSTYPE(3)
 /METHOD=REML
 /PRINT=G SOLUTION TESTCOV
 /RANDOM=INTERCEPT time1 | SUBJECT(stateid) COVTYPE(DIAG)
 /RANDOM=INTERCEPT time1 | SUBJECT(rid*stateid) COVTYPE(DIAG)
 /REPEATED=time | SUBJECT(rid*stateid) COVTYPE(AR1).
```

Chapter 7: Multivariate Multilevel Models

The Null Model: No Predictors

```
MIXED achieve
 /FIXED=| SSTYPE(3)
 /METHOD=REML
 /PRINT=G SOLUTION TESTCOV
 /RANDOM=INTERCEPT | SUBJECT(schcode) COVTYPE(ID)
 /RANDOM=INTERCEPT | SUBJECT(schcode*Rid) COVTYPE(ID).
```

Model 1: Building a Three-Level Model

```
MIXED achieve WITH gmses_mean gmses gmacademic
 /FIXED=gmses_mean gmses gmacademic | SSTYPE(3)
 /METHOD=REML
 /PRINT=G SOLUTION TESTCOV
 /RANDOM=INTERCEPT | SUBJECT(schcode) COVTYPE(ID)
 /RANDOM=INTERCEPT | SUBJECT(schcode*Rid) COVTYPE(ID).
```

Model 2: Investigating a Random Slope

```
MIXED achieve WITH gmses_mean gmses gmacademic
 /FIXED=gmses_mean gmses gmacademic | SSTYPE(3)
 /METHOD=REML
 /PRINT=G SOLUTION TESTCOV
 /RANDOM=INTERCEPT gmacademic | SUBJECT(schcode) COVTYPE(UN)
 /RANDOM=INTERCEPT | SUBJECT(schcode*Rid) COVTYPE(ID).
```

Model 3: Explaining Variation in Slopes

```
MIXED achieve WITH gmses_mean gmacadpress gmses gmacademic
 /FIXED=gmses_mean gmacadpress gmses gmacademic gmses_mean*gmacademic
gmacadpress*gmacademic |
 SSTYPE(3)
 /METHOD=REML
 /PRINT=G SOLUTION TESTCOV
 /RANDOM=INTERCEPT gmacademic | SUBJECT(schcode) COVTYPE(UN)
 /RANDOM=INTERCEPT | SUBJECT(schcode*Rid) COVTYPE(ID).
```

Multivariate Multilevel Model for Correlated Outcomes

The Null Model: No Predictors

```
MIXED achieve BY Index1
 /FIXED=Index1 | NOINT SSTYPE(3)
 /METHOD=ML
 /PRINT=G SOLUTION TESTCOV
 /RANDOM=Index1 | SUBJECT(schcode) COVTYPE(UNR)
 /REPEATED=Index1 | SUBJECT(schcode*Rid) COVTYPE(UNR).
```

Testing for Contrasts Using EM Means With SPSS Menu Commands

LSD Confidence Interval Adjustment

```
MIXED achieve BY female Index1 WITH gmacadpress
 /FIXED=Index1 | NOINT SSTYPE(3)
 /METHOD=ML
 /PRINT=G SOLUTION TESTCOV
 /RANDOM=Index1 | SUBJECT(schcode) COVTYPE(UNR)
 /REPEATED=Index1 | SUBJECT(schcode*Rid) COVTYPE(UNR)
 /EMMEANS=TABLES(OVERALL)
 /EMMEANS=TABLES(Index1) COMPARE ADJ(LSD).
```

Bonferroni Confidence Interval Adjustment

```
MIXED achieve BY female Index1 WITH gmacadpress
 /FIXED=Index1 | NOINT SSTYPE(3)
 /METHOD=ML
 /PRINT=G SOLUTION TESTCOV
 /RANDOM=Index1 | SUBJECT(schcode) COVTYPE(UNR)
 /REPEATED=Index1 | SUBJECT(schcode*Rid) COVTYPE(UNR)
 /EMMEANS=TABLES(OVERALL)
 /EMMEANS=TABLES(Index1) COMPARE ADJ(BONFERRONI).
```

Model 1: Building a Complete Model (Predictors and Cross-Level Interactions)

```
MIXED achieve BY female Index1 WITH gmacadpress
 /FIXED=Index1 female*Index1 gmacadpress*Index1 | NOINT SSTYPE(3)
 /METHOD=ML
 /PRINT=G SOLUTION TESTCOV
 /RANDOM=Index1 | SUBJECT(schcode) COVTYPE(UNR)
 /REPEATED=Index1 | SUBJECT(schcode*Rid) COVTYPE(UNR).
```

Model 1b: Defining Gender and Acadmic Press as Covariates

```
MIXED achieve BY Index1 WITH female gmacadpress
 /FIXED=Index1 female*Index1 gmacadpress*Index1 | NOINT SSTYPE(3)
 /METHOD=ML
 /PRINT=G SOLUTION TESTCOV
 /RANDOM=Index1 | SUBJECT(schcode) COVTYPE(UNR)
 /REPEATED=Index1 | SUBJECT(schcode*Rid) COVTYPE(UNR).
```

Chapter 8: Cross-Classified Multilevel Models

Model 1: Adding a Set of Level 1 and Level 2 Predictors

```
MIXED CUM_GPR WITH gmfouryear gmlowSES_mean gmlowses gmfemale
 /FIXED=gmfouryear gmlowSES_mean gmlowses gmfemale | SSTYPE(3)
 /METHOD=REML
 /PRINT=G SOLUTION TESTCOV
 /RANDOM=INTERCEPT | SUBJECT(nschcode) COVTYPE(ID)
 /RANDOM=INTERCEPT | SUBJECT(campus) COVTYPE(ID).
```

Model 2: Investigating a Random Slope

```
MIXED CUM_GPR WITH gmfouryear gmlowSES_mean gmlowses gmfemale
 /FIXED=gmfouryear gmlowSES_mean gmlowses gmfemale | SSTYPE(3)
 /METHOD=REML
 /PRINT=G SOLUTION TESTCOV
 /RANDOM=INTERCEPT gmfemale | SUBJECT(nschcode) COVTYPE(DIAG)
 /RANDOM=INTERCEPT gmfemale | SUBJECT(campus) COVTYPE(DIAG).
```

Model 3: Explaining Variation Between Variables

```
MIXED CUM_GPR WITH gmlowSES_mean gmlowses gmfemale
 /FIXED=gmlowSES_mean gmlowses gmfemale gmlowSES_mean*gmfemale | SSTYPE(3)
 /METHOD=REML
 /PRINT=G SOLUTION TESTCOV
 /RANDOM=INTERCEPT gmfemale | SUBJECT(nschcode) COVTYPE(DIAG)
 /RANDOM=INTERCEPT | SUBJECT(campus) COVTYPE(ID).
```

Model 1: Intercept-Only Model

```
MIXED math2
 /FIXED=| SSTYPE(3)
 /METHOD=REML
```

```
/PRINT=G SOLUTION TESTCOV
/RANDOM=INTERCEPT | SUBJECT(schcode) COVTYPE(ID)
/RANDOM=INTERCEPT | SUBJECT(teach2id) COVTYPE(ID)
/RANDOM=INTERCEPT | SUBJECT(teach1id) COVTYPE(ID).
```

Model 2: Cross-Classified Model With Previous Achievement

```
MIXED math2 WITH Zmath1
/FIXED=Zmath1 | SSTYPE(3)
/METHOD=REML
/PRINT=G SOLUTION TESTCOV
/RANDOM=INTERCEPT | SUBJECT(schcode) COVTYPE(ID)
/RANDOM=INTERCEPT | SUBJECT(teach2id) COVTYPE(ID)
/RANDOM=INTERCEPT | SUBJECT(teach1id) COVTYPE(ID).
```

Model 3: Adding Teacher Effectiveness and a Student Background Control

```
MIXED math2 WITH effmath2 effmath1 Zmath1 lowses
/FIXED=effmath2 effmath1 Zmath1 lowses | SSTYPE(3)
/METHOD=REML
/PRINT=G SOLUTION TESTCOV
/RANDOM=INTERCEPT | SUBJECT(schcode) COVTYPE(ID)
/RANDOM=INTERCEPT | SUBJECT(teach2id) COVTYPE(ID)
/RANDOM=INTERCEPT | SUBJECT(teach1id) COVTYPE(ID).
```

Model 4: School-Level Predictor and Random Slope

```
MIXED math2 WITH effmath2 effmath1 Zmath1 lowses
/FIXED=effmath2 effmath1 Zmath1 lowses | SSTYPE(3)
/METHOD=REML
/PRINT=G SOLUTION TESTCOV
/RANDOM=INTERCEPT effmath2 effmath1 | SUBJECT(schcode) COVTYPE(DIAG)
/RANDOM=INTERCEPT | SUBJECT(teach2id) COVTYPE(ID)
/RANDOM=INTERCEPT | SUBJECT(teach1id) COVTYPE(ID).
```

Model 5: Level 3 Differences Between Institutions

```
MIXED math2 WITH schqual effmath1 Zmath1 lowses effmath2
/FIXED=schqual effmath1 Zmath1 lowses effmath2 | SSTYPE(3)
/METHOD=REML
/PRINT=G SOLUTION TESTCOV
/RANDOM=INTERCEPT effmath2 | SUBJECT(schcode) COVTYPE(DIAG)
/RANDOM=INTERCEPT | SUBJECT(teach2id) COVTYPE(ID)
/RANDOM=INTERCEPT | SUBJECT(teach1id) COVTYPE(ID).
```

Model 6: Adding a Level-3 Cross-Level Interaction

```
MIXED math2 WITH schqual effmath1 Zmath1 lowses effmath2
/FIXED=schqual effmath1 Zmath1 lowses effmath2 effmath2*schqual | SSTYPE(3)
/METHOD=REML
/PRINT=G SOLUTION TESTCOV
/RANDOM=INTERCEPT effmath2 | SUBJECT(schcode) COVTYPE(DIAG)
/RANDOM=INTERCEPT | SUBJECT(teach2id) COVTYPE(ID)
/RANDOM=INTERCEPT | SUBJECT(teach1id) COVTYPE(ID).
```

Appendix B: Model Comparisons Across Software Applications

Chapter 1: HLM, Mplus, and SPSS Results

The HLM outcome variable is ACHIEVE.

FINAL HLM ESTIMATION OF FIXED EFFECTS (WITH ROBUST STANDARD ERRORS)

Fixed Effect	Coefficient	Standard Error	t-Ratio	Approx. df	p-Value
Model for INTRCPT1, P0					
For INTRCPT2, B00					
INTRCPT3, G000	58.241	0.190	306.421	383	0.000
Mplus	57.348	0.218	263.519	383	0.000
SPSS	57.960	0.199	290.756	304.28	0.000
ACADPRES, G001	0.445	0.216	2.058	383	0.040
Mplus	0.449	0.213	2.108	383	0.035
SPSS	0.379	0.226	1.681	298.77	0.094
SES_MEAN, G002	2.750	0.628	4.380	383	0.000
Mplus	2.793	0.620	4.503	383	0.000
SPSS	2.745	0.618	4.443	575.99	0.000
For SES, B01					
INTRCPT3, G010	3.183	0.269	11.856	2936	0.000
Mplus	2.779	0.253	10.991	2936	0.000
SPSS	3.229	0.267	12.110	2479.30	0.000
Model for ACADEMIC, B02					
INTRCPT3, G020	2.476	0.145	17.081	383	0.000
Mplus	2.539	0.152	16.660	383	0.000
SPSS	2.439	0.145	16.869	131.22	0.000
ACADPRES, G021	0.179	0.157	1.145	383	0.253
Mplus	0.072	0.145	0.496	383	0.620
SPSS	0.245	0.165	1.487	150.44	0.139
SES_MEAN, G022	−1.363	0.361	−3.771	383	0.000
Mplus	−1.190	0.328	−3.630	383	0.000
SPSS	−1.372	0.406	−3.376	121.36	0.001

FINAL ESTIMATION OF LEVEL 1 AND LEVEL 2 VARIANCE COMPONENTS

Random Effect	Standard Deviation	Variance Component
INTRCPT1, R0	6.49123	42.136
SPSS	(na)	42.313
Level 1, E	5.80643	33.715
Mplus (within schools)	(na)	32.542
SPSS	(na)	33.016

FINAL ESTIMATION OF LEVEL 3 VARIANCE COMPONENTS

Random Effect	Standard Deviation	Variance Component
INTRCPT1/INTRCPT2, U00	2.16909	4.705
Mplus (Between)	(na)	4.397
SPSS		5.245
INTRCPT1/ACADEMIC, U02	0.76827	0.590
Mplus Slope (Between)	(na)	0.661
SPSS		0.296

Chapter 1: Mplus and SPSS Results (Two-Level Model With Interaction Term)

MODEL RESULTS

	Estimate	SE	Est./*SE*	Two-Tailed *p*-Value
Within Level				
MATH ON				
FEMALE	6.642	0.944	7.036	0.000
(SPSS)	6.623	0.877	7.549	0.000
Residual Variances				
MATH	1234.087	42.756	28.864	0.000
SPSS	1234.088	21.784	56.652(Wald)	0.000
Between Level				
MATH ON				
CSES	12.563	1.050	11.967	0.000
SPSS	12.565	1.178	10.666	0.000
ESS	3.239	1.430	2.264	0.024
SPSS	3.232	1.318	2.452	0.016
INTERACT	0.511	1.237	0.413	0.679
SPSS	0.510	1.264	0.404	0.687
Intercepts				
MATH	657.751	1.328	495.137	0.000
SPSS	657.773	1.324	496.838	0.000
Residual Variances				
MATH	141.699	24.665	5.745	0.000
SPSS	141.715	22.580	6.276(Wald)	0.000

Chapter 8: HLM and SPSS Results (Cross-Classified Model)

Fixed Effect	Coefficient	Standard Error	*t*-Ratio	*p*-Value
Grand mean	2.646736	0.151444	17.477	0.000
SPSS	2.641013	0.168416	15.681	0.002
LOWSES_M, G02	−1.205519	0.363517	−3.316	0.001
SPSS	−1.220484	0.371416	−3.286	0.002
FOURYEAR, B01	0.134616	0.266145	0.506	0.613
SPSS	0.138241	0.297549	0.465	0.655
Level 1 Variables				
FEMALE	0.331589	0.027851	11.906	0.000
SPSS	0.331798	0.027869	11.905	0.000
LOWSES	0.017498	0.037020	0.473	0.636
SPSS	0.017483	0.037044	0.472	0.637

FINAL ESTIMATION OF ROW AND LEVEL 1 VARIANCE COMPONENTS

Random Effect	Standard Deviation	Variance Component	*df*	Chi-Square	*p*-Value
INTRCPT1, b00	0.17016	0.02895	27	127.119	0.000
SPSS	na	0.03092		2.602(Wald)	0.004
Level 1, e	0.55220	0.30492			
SPSS	na	0.30521		29.300(Wald)	0.000

FINAL ESTIMATION OF COLUMN-LEVEL VARIANCE COMPONENTS

Random Effect	Standard Deviation	Variance Component	*df*	Chi-Square	*p*-Value
INTRCPT1, c00	0.37432	0.14011	7	766.382	0.000
SPSS	na	0.17711		1.905(Wald)	0.029

Author Index

Subject Index